BOOM AN

BOOM AND BUST

The Politics and Legacy
of Gordon Brown

SIMON LEE

ONEWORLD
OXFORD

A Oneworld Book

First published by Oneworld Publications in hardback as *Best for Britain?* 2007
First published in this revised trade paperback edition, 2009

Copyright © Simon Lee 2007, 2009

ISBN 978–1–85168–664–3

Typeset by Jayvee, Trivandrum, India
Cover design by designedbydavid.co.uk
Printed and bound in Great Britain
by Cox & Wyman, CPI Group

Oneworld Publications
185 Banbury Road
Oxford OX2 7AR
England
www.oneworld-publications.com

In memory of my mother, Joan Ethel Lee,
with love and thanks

Contents

PART II: Gordon Brown's Domestic Policy Agenda

PART III: Gordon Brown's Foreign Policy Agenda

Preface

As I wrote the concluding chapters of this book, the United Kingdom embarked upon a critically important period of economic and political change, described by Gordon Brown as 'a time when one chapter ended and another began'.[1] Years of 'non-inflationary consistently expansionary' economic performance, depicted by Mervyn King, the Governor of the Bank of England, as the 'nice' decade, and by his Deputy, Sir John Gieve, as 'the Great Stability', came to an abrupt end.[2] Following two three-monthly quarters of contraction by 0.6 per cent and then 1.5 per cent, its worst performance since 1980, the United Kingdom economy officially entered a recession for the first time since 1991. The housing market collapsed. During 2008, average property prices fell by 16.6 per cent, and gross mortgage lending declined by forty-nine per cent from its 2007 level, the worst performance since 1974.[3] By the end of December 2008, unemployment had risen in a year by 369,000 to nearly two million, and was widely forecast to rise to three million or above during 2009. This reflected the very weak performance of major manufacturing industries. For example, car production had declined by 58.7 per cent in a year, necessitating a major government rescue package.[4] The City of London experienced its first run on a domestic bank for 129 years. The Brown Government bailed out, recapitalised and nationalised major British banks in a series of interventions more reminiscent of Old Labour than New Labour.

Government borrowing soared to its highest levels since 1946. Even in the Treasury's highly optimistic forecasts, the United Kingdom's national debt would mushroom from £526.8 billion or 36.3 per cent of GDP in 2007–2008 to £1,020 billion or 57.1 per cent of GDP in 2011–2012, a figure fully £352 billion or 18.5 per cent of GDP beyond that forecast in Brown's final Budget report.[5] With total United Kingdom personal debt at £1,457 billion at the end of 2008, and unfunded public sector pension schemes totalling £650 billion, the United Kingdom's total debt rose to over double its annual national income.[6] The Bank of England cut interest rates to 0.5 per cent, their lowest level in its 315-year history. Inflation at more than three per cent above the Government's official two per cent target in September 2008 was replaced at the end of January 2009 by the very real fear of deflation. Fiscal prudence and economic stability had fled. Market volatility and uncertainty had become endemic. The 'nice' decade had been supplanted by a new nasty era of public and private austerity. Ed Balls, Gordon Brown's closest economic adviser for more than a decade, warned that the recession was 'the worst we have seen, I think, probably for more than 100 years'.[7] Boom had become bust.

For British politics too, the transition from economic boom to bust threatened to be marked by a parallel political busting of the boom years of New Labour's three consecutive General Election victories. Gordon Brown and the Labour Party's prospects of winning an unprecedented fourth term of office were diminishing rapidly. During 2008, opinion polls showed net public satisfaction (the percentage satisfied minus the percentage dissatis-fied) with the government ranging between –twenty-three per cent and –fifty-nine per cent. Public satisfaction with Gordon Brown as Prime Minister ranged between –nine per cent and –fifty-one per cent.[8] Throughout 2008, net economic optimism (the percentage expecting improvement minus the percentage expecting the economy to worsen) ranged between –thirty-five per cent and –sixty-four per cent.[9] On unem-ployment, taxation, education and health care, the Brown Government's policies were diminishing in popularity. By February 2009, opinion polls were showing a consistent lead for David Cameron's Conservative Party of between ten and twenty per cent. The Brown Government was heading for a heavy General Election defeat.

Eighteen months earlier, when Gordon Brown had succeeded Tony Blair as leader of the Labour Party and Prime Minister, the political and eco-nomic scenario had been very different. Three days before he became Prime Minister, Brown confidently set out his future plans for his government. He promised to form 'a new government with new priorities to meet the new challenges ahead'. He claimed to have 'listened and learned from the British people'.[10] Confronted by what Brown claimed were the new challenges of climate change, global competition and tackling extremism, but with which in reality the Blair Government had actually grappled for a decade, Brown stated that 'the Labour Party must renew ourselves as the party of change'.

This was because the Labour Party's mission had 'always been to be the party of progressive change', and had become a governing party because it had 'championed the need for economic and social change'. Brown confidently asserted, 'I am a conviction politician'. Because of his own personal moral sentiments of 'duty, honesty, hard work, family and respect for others', he would lead the construction of 'a new progressive consensus'. This would embrace a national mission 'to be world class in education'; to make the National Health Service (in England) his 'immediate priority'; and nothing less than 'a new constitutional settlement for Britain', based upon the principles of:

> Government giving more power to Parliament; both government and Parliament giving more power to the people; Parliament voting on all major issues of our time including peace and war; civil liberties safeguarded and enhanced; devolution within a Union of nations: England, Scotland, Wales and Northern Ireland – a Union that I believe in and will defend; local government strengthened with new powers – local communities empowered to hold those who make decisions to account; and with community ownership of assets – greater power for more people to control their lives.[11]

Brown's message to the electorate and his own party was clear. The Blair era was over. He would end the period of drift and unpopularity for New Labour, by re-energising his inherited third term government with a fourth state-led modernisation programme, previously implemented by the first way of Clement Attlee, the second way of Margaret Thatcher and the third way of Tony Blair.

Gordon Brown made a promising start as Prime Minister. On 27 June 2007, when he entered Number Ten Downing Street as Prime Minister, Brown's economic legacy as Chancellor appeared untarnished and golden. He had delivered the United Kingdom economy from the 'boom-bust instability of the past'.[12] In his final Budget statement, he had boasted of 'the longest period of economic stability and sustained growth in our country's history', an expansion without precedent in the United Kingdom's postwar history.[13] The Brown Boom was entrenched. Brown's British model of political economy appeared unassailable. His 'light touch system' of financial regulation was 'fair, proportionate, predictable and increasingly risk-based'. Brown predicted 'an era that history will record as the beginning of a new golden age for the City of London'. Britain could become 'one of the great success stories in the new global economy'.[14]

Events also seemed to favour Brown. In the days before he became Prime Minister, heavy rain caused flooding across England. In the days after he entered Number Ten Downing Street, terrorist attacks were launched on London and Glasgow. In both instances, Brown co-ordinated his government's response with the sure touch of a confident statesman. Growing public confidence in the Brown Government was reflected in twin by-election victories on 19 July 2007, which contrasted with the humiliating by-election defeats in Wales and Scotland that had marked the final months of Blair's premiership. A 'Brown Bounce' surge of popularity for the Labour Party was registered in successive opinion polls, reversing a negative poll trend under Blair since David Cameron's election as Conservative Party leader in December 2005. By the time of the 2007 Labour Party annual conference, the Brown Government's opinion poll lead over the Conservatives was averaging between ten and thirteen per cent. Rumours of a snap General Election were rife among the media. Brown did nothing to quash them. An historic fourth General Election victory seemed assured. To secure a fresh popular mandate to perpetuate the Brown Boom, all the Prime Minister had to do was call an election.

But then Brown dithered. On 7 October 2007, he confirmed he would not be calling a General Election. Attempting to seize the moral and political high ground, he claimed that he thought he would win an election, but had taken 'a bigger view of the situation'. Brown's 'first instinct' was that he wanted more time to set out his vision for the future of the United Kingdom and had not yet had the chance to set out his vision for health, housing, education or the future of the economy.[15] Few believed the Prime Minister. Indeed, no other candidate for the leadership of his political party or the office of Prime Minister of the United Kingdom succeeded his predecessor with such a carefully planned political agenda or such a major political and economic legacy.

None of his predecessors as Chancellor of the Exchequer had enjoyed such unprecedented power over the conduct of domestic economic and social policy as Brown enjoyed during his decade at the Treasury. No previous occupant of the Treasury exercised such power that he at times appeared to challenge or defy the authority of the incumbent Prime Minister. Nor had any previous candidate for the leadership of his party and state entered a leadership contest with the political advantage of a track record of ten years of economic growth and financial stability. Paradoxically, despite his ubiquitous presence as Chancellor of the Exchequer, most people, including many members of his own political party and most voters, remained in the dark as to what Gordon Brown's leadership would mean for both the Labour Party's ideology and policy, and the very future of the United Kingdom.

The greatest inspiration for this book is my genuine fear that the greatest legacy of the transition from boom to bust during the tenure of the Brown Government is to have helped engineer a return to a political scenario akin to that of the late 1970s. This has once more made possible the election of a Conservative Government, this time led by David Cameron, but committed to introducing a new era of British state-led modernisation inspired by Margaret Thatcher's ideas and policies of the 1980s. Thanks to their policies and statecraft, the Blair and Brown Governments' principal legacy is a United Kingdom that is once more 'over-governed, over-spent, over-taxed, over-borrowed and over-manned'.[16]

Brown's greatest legacy is to have left England governed in the public realm of the state by a colonial British administration, overmanned by an unelected, ineffectual and unaccountable quangocracy. Nationalisation has been of policy design and resource allocation, resulting in the denial of English citizenship and identity, and the English tradition of individual liberty. New Labour and Brown's legacy in the private realm of the market is to have left it too long overmanned by ineffectual regulators and unaccountable traders and bankers. The latter were entrusted to regulate themselves by Brown's risk-based, tripartite approach, and his own moral sense that open markets would provide the freedom for the expression of the essential human moral sentiments of duty, responsibility, sympathy and fairness. In practice, Brown's moral compass and risk-based approach to financial regulation simply gave traders and bankers the freedom to demonstrate greed and other immoral sentiments, as they relentlessly embraced risk in the pursuit of personal reward. The result has been nationalisation of failing banks, on a scale that Old Labour rarely contemplated let alone practised, at a huge cost to present and future generations of taxpayers. This time, solving the banking problem is the key to British recovery.

In writing this book, it is my contention that, rather than a further rolling forward of the frontiers of market liberalisation, deregulation and privatisation, the onset of the credit crunch has demonstrated the need for a different political economy. The great conceit of Brown's British model of political economy, that markets can be made to work better and in the public interest, because market actors can be orchestrated in the same manner as institutions in the public sector, has been proven to be wrong. The relationship between the state and market must be redrawn to instil greater public purpose. Brown has long known this, and in the evolution of his personal political philosophy has sought a reconciliation of Labour Party social democracy with the New Deal liberalism of the Democratic Party of the 1930s and 1960s. He has tried to reinvent both British domestic policy and the institutions of global governance. Ironically, with the onset of the credit crunch and worldwide recession, and the election of Barack Obama in November 2008, economic and political developments have provided a rich opportunity for such a project. However, successive opinion polls have suggested that, despite his best attempts to reinvent himself as the leader of a new era of co-ordinated global governance, Gordon Brown may have suffered too much collateral damage politically to win another term of office.

It is equally my thesis that Gordon Brown's top-down, centralised approach to government, with its nationalisation of policy design and resource allocation, has been implemented to the detriment of democratic accountability and citizenship in England. The Blair and Brown Governments' constitutional reforms have led to a democratic deficit in participation, accountability and legitimacy for most people in England. The populations of the other constituent nations of the United Kingdom have seen their opportunities for democratic citizenship extended by the creation of elected institutions at Holyrood, Cardiff and Stormont. With the exception of the citizens of Greater London, who now vote for their assembly and mayor, the people of England have been denied similar democratic empowerment. Power has instead been devolved to unelected quangos and publicly unaccountable transnational corporations. The consequence has been parallel deficits in both policy and resources for England. Brown has also deliberately confused England with Britain and Englishness with Britishness. The possibility of reflecting and embracing the contemporary reality of a multi-ethnic and multi-cultural England in a collective, inclusive and democratic English identity – an English Way – rooted in the English civic tradition of liberty, has been ruled out by

Brown's own British nationalism. As Prime Minister, Brown has governed England as a colony of the British state.

This book has been designed to enable the reader to understand how Gordon Brown's political ideas and policy agenda for British state-led modernisation – his British Way – should, to a large degree, be held responsible for the transition from boom to bust. It would not have been possible for me to write the book without the support of the Department of Politics and International Studies at Hull University. Whatever insight I am able to offer into Brown's thinking and policies is largely the result of my having spent the past decade teaching undergraduates about the politics of New Labour. This has given me the chance to study in detail the speeches and policy documents that have emanated from Gordon Brown, The Treasury, and the Prime Minister's Office.

For this opportunity, I must thank our Head of Department, Justin Morris. I also wish to express my gratitude to my other colleagues for their respective encouragement for and interest in this project. In particular, I wish to thank my friends Richard Woodward, Colin Tyler, Claire Hairsine, and William and Neena Lawton for their continuing support and humour, and Helen McGarry for sharing eighteen months of her life with me. I also owe a considerable personal debt to Mike Harpley at Oneworld for commissioning this book, and having the patience to await the overdue manuscript. However, my greatest inspiration remains the love and family support I have enjoyed from my sister Chris Clarke, my brother-in-law Roy Clarke, my niece Joanna and my nephew Adam, my uncle Alan Cudmore, and above all, my father, Norman Arthur Lee. He taught me the value of learning and first ignited my interest in politics. Finally, this book is dedicated to the memory of my mother, Joan Ethel Lee, who helped give me the higher education for which she and my father had the aptitude, but never the opportunity to enjoy.

Introduction

ELECTORAL ASSET OR LIABILITY?

As he stood outside Number Ten Downing Street to make his first statement as Prime Minister, Gordon Brown appeared the ideal candidate to revive the political and electoral fortunes of a third term Labour Government which had been performing ineffectively during the final year of Tony Blair's premiership, and destined not to win an historic fourth consecutive General Election. Brown promised 'a new government with new priorities'. As Prime Minister, he would be 'strong in purpose, steadfast in will, resolute in action in the service of what matters to the British people – meeting the concerns and aspirations of our whole country'.[1] Brown reassured his party and the electorate:

> I have listened and I have learnt from the British people – and as Prime Minister I will continue to listen and learn from the British people – I have heard the need for change. Change in our NHS, change in our schools, change with affordable housing, change to build trust in government, change to protect and extend the British way of life. This change cannot be met by the old politics.[2]

Brown's commitment to renewal and change immediately raised a number of problems, because unlike Barack Obama's bold plans for economic recovery and 'a new era of responsibility', he was not starting with a blank canvas.[3] First, the British people had just lived through a decade of constant change under New Labour. With Tony Blair, Brown had been one of the principal architects of that change. Second, Brown had been a cornerstone of 'the old politics'. In promising to 'reach out beyond narrow party interest', and to build 'a government that uses all the talents',[4] Brown neglected the fact that he had built his political career as a brilliant exponent of the narrow party interests of the Labour Party. During a decade at the Treasury, his statecraft had been driven by a government that used few talents, namely his, and those of his economic adviser, Ed Balls, and a close inner circle of political confidants. Even before he became Prime Minister, Gordon Brown had a major political and economic legacy.

When his political and economic legacy was compared with the track record of his principal rivals both for the leadership of the Labour Party and the office of Prime Minister, Gordon Brown's credentials for leadership appeared unassailable. As his eleventh and final Budget report had reminded the British people, 'Over the past 10 years, the Government's macroeconomic framework has delivered more stability in terms of GDP growth and inflation rates than in any decade since the war'.[5] Indeed, the United Kingdom's economic expansion was 'not only without precedent in the post-war history of the UK, but is [was] also the longest on post-war record for any G7 economy and the longest expansion of any OECD country'.[6] The Brown Boom, as the longest expansion 'since records began in the year seventeen hundred and one',[7] stood in stark contrast to David Cameron's notoriety as economic adviser to Norman Lamont at the time of 'Black Wednesday'. It was the United Kingdom's departure from the Exchange Rate Mechanism on 16 September 1992 that actually ushered in the 60 consecutive three-monthly quarters of economic prosperity during Brown's tenure as Chancellor. Brown's central role in helping to secure an unprecedented three consecutive Labour Party General Election victories compared very favourably to Cameron's dismal failure as chief policy co-ordinator for the Conservative Party during its 2005 General Election campaign.

Paradoxically, despite Brown's rich political and economic legacy, the opinion polls displayed a worrying trend for Gordon Brown and the Labour Party. Voters only grudgingly acknowledged Brown's economic legacy. In a YouGov poll, conducted to coincide with Brown's delivery of the 2007 Budget, the number of respondents (forty per cent) identifying Brown as an asset for the Labour Party only exceeded those regarding him as a liability by two per cent. While forty-four per cent acknowledged that he was doing a good job as Chancellor of the Exchequer, thirty-six per cent stated that he was not. Only ten per cent rated his performance over the past ten years as 'excellent', compared to twenty-seven per cent who thought it 'good'. No fewer than nineteen per cent thought Brown's record 'poor', with twenty-nine per cent rating his performance as merely 'fair'. Most worryingly for Brown, more people (thirty-five per cent) preferred Tony Blair than Brown (twenty-five per cent) as Prime Minister. Most worryingly for the Labour Party, thirty-nine per cent indicated their intention to vote Conservative, compared to only thirty-one per cent support for Labour.[8] This reflected a broader trend in five other polls conducted between 19 January and 8 March 2007, which saw an average 38.5 per cent vote for the Conservative Party, and only 31.6 per cent for Labour.[9]

These polls confirmed a longer term trend in British public opinion. Gordon Brown's political stock with the general public had been waning for some time. At the time of the 2005 Budget, fifty-two per cent thought Gordon Brown as Chancellor was doing a better job than Tony Blair (seventeen per cent) as Prime Minister. In 2006, thirty-seven per cent thought Brown was doing the better job, compared to a twenty-two per cent endorsement of Blair. However, in March 2007, only thirty per cent thought Brown was better, compared to twenty-four per cent for Blair.[10] During the Brown Boom, Gordon Brown had been a diminishing electoral asset for the Labour Party. With the onset of the Brown Bust, Brown as Prime Minister was in danger of becoming an electoral liability. For example, an Ipsos MORI poll conducted in mid-February 2009 identified that sixty-four per cent of respondents were dissatisfied with the way he was doing his job, and only twenty-six per cent were satisfied.[11] In a similar vein, a Guardian/ICM poll conducted in the same period found that sixty-three per cent of voters thought the Labour Party would do better with another leader, with only twenty-eight per cent of voters identifying Brown as the leader most likely to attract support to Labour on polling day. Most damagingly of all for Brown, while forty-five per cent of Labour voters regarded Brown as the best leader, forty-nine per cent thought the Labour Party would be better off with a different leader.[12] Following the transition from boom to bust, the prospects of a fourth consecutive General Election victory for the Labour Party were diminishing rapidly.

A 'PSYCHOLOGICALLY FLAWED' POLITICIAN?

Like Margaret Thatcher, Gordon Brown is a politician who tends to divide people and opinion, especially in relation to his personality and character.

As Prime Minister, Brown has compared himself with Emily Brontë's Heathcliff, albeit 'an older Heathcliff, a wiser Heathcliff', and, most bizarrely, the Renaissance Venetian painter, Titian.[13] The latter had admitted that it had taken him until the age of ninety to begin finally to learn how to paint. Brown bemused an audience at the 2009 World Economic Forum in Davos by comparing Titian's protracted learning process to his own in dealing with 'the first financial crisis of the global age'.[14] His political opponents tended not to be so flattering. Most memorably, following the resignation of Peter Hain, the Work and Pensions Secretary, and a series of embarrassing losses of confidential personal data, Vince Cable, the Liberal Democrat MP and Treasury spokesman, delivered the most telling of political put-downs at Prime Minister's Question Time: 'The House has noticed the Prime Minister's remarkable transformation in the past few weeks from Stalin to Mr Bean creating chaos out of order, rather than order out of chaos'.[15]

This was far from the first occasion on which Gordon Brown's character had been called into question. As the odds of his succeeding Tony Blair as Labour Party leader shortened with every passing week, questions were raised about his suitability to succeed Blair as Prime Minister of the United Kingdom of Great Britain and Northern Ireland. Former colleagues very publicly questioned his credentials to succeed Tony Blair. For example, Charles Clarke, his former Cabinet colleague, accused Brown of being a control freak, who 'thinks he has to control everything', and is 'totally, totally uncollegiate'.[16] Lord Turnbull, the former Permanent Secretary to the Treasury, endorsed this judgement, claiming that Brown had not allowed Cabinet colleagues 'any serious discussion about priorities. His view is that it is just not worth it and "they will get what I decide"'. Indeed, he further suggested that 'you cannot help [but] admire the sheer Stalinist ruthlessness of it all'.[17] Between them Clarke and Turnbull had identified a serious list of possible character flaws in this prospective Prime Minister-in-waiting, accusing him of being variously a perfectionist, who is not a risk-taker; a politician who lacks courage; delusional over Blair's having to anoint him as his chosen successor; and having 'a Macavity quality. He is not there when there is dirty work to be done'.[18]

Brown's character had also come under scrutiny when a political insider with 'an extremely good claim to know the mind of the Prime Minister' informed the *Observer* journalist Andrew Rawnsley, 'You know

Gordon, he feels so vulnerable and so insecure. He has these psychological flaws'.[19] It was widely assumed that these non-attributable remarks had been made by Alistair Campbell, the Prime Minister's Chief Press Secretary. However, such had been the sensitivity between the rival Blair and Brown camps over the Prime Minister and Chancellor's working relationship, and such had been the enduring furore surrounding such poisonous character assassination, that when Lance Price, a former Downing Street spin doctor, suggested that the source of the remarks had been the Prime Minister and not Campbell, Tony Blair chose to confirm at Prime Minister's Question Time that he had never used these words.[20]

Since becoming Prime Minister, much of the debate surrounding Brown's suitability for the leadership of both the Labour Party and the United Kingdom has emanated from the uncertainty that has surrounded his ideas and policies for dealing with the credit crunch and deepening recession. Brown has called for 'a global new deal', i.e. 'a grand bargain where each continent accepts its responsibilities and its obligations to act to deal with what is a global problem that can only be solved with a global solution'.[21] He has also asserted his belief that 'markets need not just money-men but morals, that being fair matters far more than being laissez-faire and that banks must always serve the public, not just serve themselves'.[22] However, while his Chancellor not only admitted that 'There are a lot of lessons to be learnt', but also joined Ed Balls, Brown's former chief economic adviser at the Treasury, in conceding that 'In retrospect, it is clear we were nowhere near tough enough' when regulating London's financial markets, Brown himself refused repeatedly to apologise for the recession, and to accept that the problems of the British economy were in large part the fault of the model he had engineered during his decade at the Treasury.[23]

While Gordon Brown's personal and political biography has been extensively and expertly documented, less attention has been paid to his political philosophy and policy record.[24] And yet, it is not possible to establish the degree to which Brown should be held personally responsible for the United Kingdom economy's transition from boom to bust, or to comprehend his government's response to the collapse of major British banks, without first understanding the particular evolution of Brown's political philosophy, and his domestic and foreign policy agenda. This book offers the reader a detailed analysis of Gordon Brown's record both as Chancellor and as Prime Minister in order that his political and economic legacy can be established.

This book is divided into three parts. Part One explores the evolution of Gordon Brown's political philosophy through a political odyssey that has seen Brown travel full circle from being a withering critic of capitalism, to becoming the most powerful advocate of the interests of the City of London's financial markets, and then reverting to being a fierce opponent of the excesses of liberalised financial markets. This odyssey is divided into four phases. The first two phases, from Brown's formative years at university, through his first decade as an MP at Westminster, saw his advocacy of British industrial modernisation through supply-side and parliamentary socialism, a vision rooted firmly in the values and traditions of the Labour Party. The second two phases have seen Brown distance himself from the Labour Party's history of ideas, and abandon socialism in favour of liberalism. Brown has undertaken a messianic conversion to the liberalism of Adam Smith, and set out the parameters of a New British Enlightenment, based upon a sympathetic liberalism that articulates a moral defence of the virtues of the market, entrepreneurship and competition. Brown has also returned to the American liberalism of the 1930s New Deal and 1960s Great Society programme first taught to him by his father. Like Margaret Thatcher and Tony Blair, Gordon Brown is shown to have based his future modernisation programme for Britain upon an ideology of liberalism, implemented through an approach to government that entails the further rolling forward of the frontiers of centralised state control.

Part Two of the book is devoted to a detailed explanation and analysis of Gordon Brown's domestic policy agenda for the economy, public services, and citizenship and identity. Brown devised the British model of political economy, in partnership with his economic adviser Ed Balls, during a decade at the Treasury. While it delivered the Brown Boom, an unprecedented period of sustained monetary stability and economic growth, the British model left a catastrophic legacy of debt and imprudence which resulted in the nationalisation of the major British banks, at huge cost to the taxpayer, and the worst recession since the 1930s. Brown's agenda for the public services nationalised policy design and the allocation of resources for public spending bodies in England. It delivered both a seemingly permanent revolution of reforms and a significant increase in funding for public services, but with mounting evidence of growing disillusionment with the resulting 'postcode lottery' in the availability of services. Brown's British Way has sought to defend the British Union and Britishness as a focal point for national identity. However, the British Way has been based upon examples of Englishness and English history, conflated or misconstrued as examples of Britishness and British history.

Part Three of the book analyses Gordon Brown's foreign policy agenda of a New Atlanticism and Pro-European Realism, before evaluating the Brown Government's response to the credit crunch and Gordon Brown's political and economic legacy. Although many expected Brown to distance the Labour Government from the 'war on terror' in Iraq and Afghanistan, Brown is as much, if not more, of an advocate of the 'special relationship' with the United States as either Tony Blair or Margaret Thatcher. Indeed, in seeking a 'global new deal' with the Obama Administration, and to persuade the United States' Congress to 'seize the moment' by supporting his quest for a global plan for prosperity and recovery,[25] Brown's foreign policy legacy has deepened, rather than challenged, the tenets of the neo-liberal 'Washington Consensus' that has dominated the theory and practice of global governance for the past quarter-century.

Brown's passionate Atlanticism is contrasted with the open Euroscepticism of his pro-European realism. The roots of Brown's opposition to the participation of sterling in the European Monetary Union are traced to his defence of the British model of political economy, his broader advocacy of an Anglo-American model of capitalism, and a 'Global Europe' vision for Europe that largely accords with Margaret Thatcher's Bruges speech to the College of Europe, and which seeks supranational convergence towards his British model. However, the tenure of the Brown Government is then explored to show how each of the core elements of Brown's British model of political economy, and the assumptions underlying them, have been undermined by the transition from the Brown Boom to the Brown Bust. While Brown cannot be held entirely responsible for the onset of the credit crunch, he did preside over an unsustainable boom driven by consumption, financial services and property prices, fuelled by imprudent levels of private debt. He did choose to ignore repeated warnings from the International Monetary Fund (IMF), the Bank of England and other agencies, of the attendant dangers arising from that debt and imprudence. He also did nothing to challenge the orthodoxy of neo-liberal globalisation, being enthralled by the political economy of a risk-based approach to

financial regulation. This framework has been shown to have been fundamentally flawed. To this extent, Brown must be held responsible for the
transition from boom to bust.

Gordon Brown's political legacy is to have promised a new kind of politics and a new style of politics, but in practice to have continued the same
top-down, centralised, command-and-control approach to government
that characterised his tenure as Chancellor. In terms of his economic legacy,
the demise of Brown's British model of political economy, in the transition
from boom to bust, has ushered in a new era of austerity for both the private
and public sectors. Brown's principal historical legacy will be to have helped
to make the Conservative Party once more capable of winning a General
Election on the basis of a quintessentially Thatcherite agenda. In so doing,
Brown may have hastened the very break-up of the United Kingdom that
his British Way was intended to prevent.

PART I

Gordon Brown's Political Philosophy

Chapter 1

From Supply-Side Socialism to Supply-Side Liberalism

WINNING THE BATTLE OF IDEAS

During his life, Gordon Brown has undertaken a lengthy personal ideological journey. Part One is dedicated to mapping that journey. Brown's elevation to the role of Labour Party leader and Prime Minister of the United Kingdom of Great Britain and Northern Ireland has come almost forty years since he went up to Edinburgh University as the university's youngest-ever undergraduate and twenty years after Neil Kinnock appointed him to his Shadow Cabinet.

During long political careers, it is not especially surprising if a politician's ideas evolve . However, what is truly remarkable (and will be surprising to the uninitiated) in Brown's political philosophy is the extent to which he has abandoned the ideas of the mainstream Scottish Labour Party and its socialist heritage. Brown has instead embraced the liberalism and moral political economy of Adam Smith and the Scottish Enlightenment, whose moral sense, and sentiments, have moved him to closer to the values he first learned from his parents.

I begin by identifying the importance of his parents' values as the personal inspiration for Brown's political career, followed by an exploration of the first phase of Brown's political philosophy, to emphasise its origins in the mainstream Labour Party tradition of parliamentary socialism. I shall then consider the key aspect of the second phase, a commitment to supply-side socialism and the Labour Party's ambition to implement a techno-cratic, state-led industrial modernisation programme as its alternative to Thatcherism. Following the Labour Party's fourth consecutive General Election defeat in April 1992 and Tony Blair's election as Labour Party leader in July 1994, Brown's political philosophy entered a third phase of supply-side liberalism. Following the Labour Party's election victory in May 1997, Brown's philosophy entered its fourth and current phase, during which he has abandoned the socialist tradition within the party. As an alter-native, Brown has embraced the moral sentiments of Adam Smith. These third and fourth phases are analysed in Chapter Two.

WINNING THE BATTLE OF IDEAS: SETTING THE AGENDA FOR MODERNISATION

Winning the battle of ideas has been particularly important to recent British Prime Ministers. They have identified this battle as one of two prerequisites for the implementation of their respective modernisation agendas. (The other was the learning of vital lessons from the perceived failures of previ-ous governments and designing policies to avoid their repetition.) For Margaret Thatcher, being able to implement the policies she deemed best for Britain depended on 'winning not just power but the battle of ideas'.[1] Her closest ideological ally, Sir Keith Joseph, argued that by the mid-1970s the Conservative Party, like British politics in general, had become 'stranded on the middle ground' that had arisen from 'the left-wing ratchet' of Keynesian social democracy.[2] The Tories had therefore been 'inhibited from fighting a vigorous battle of ideas', when they should have been frankly analysing 'the developments of the whole post-war settlement, as it grinds into a dead end'.[3] When the first Thatcher Government was elected, in May 1979, Sir Keith Joseph proclaimed to the House of Commons:

> The new government bring with them a different analysis and a differ-ent set of policies. The analysis takes into account the lessons that we have learnt from the past during periods of Conservative Governments and, certainly, Labour Governments. A fresh set of policies will arise out of that analysis.[4]

Tony Blair followed a similar path. In his 1994 Labour Party leadership election statement, *Change and National Renewal*, Blair stated that the Labour
Party 'must do more than just defeat the Conservatives on grounds of competence, integrity and fitness to govern. We must change the tide of ideas'.[5]
As leader, in April 1995 Blair told the special Labour Party conference on the
new party constitution that Britain needed 'new energy, ideas and vision – a
government free of dogma, not hidebound by ideology but driven by
ideas'.[6] New Labour would learn the lessons of Labour's landslide election
victory in 1945: 'the need for a clear sense of national purpose [and] the
need to win the battle of ideas'.[7] Its task would be 'nothing less than national
renewal', necessitating 'economic renewal, social renewal and political
renewal'.[8] The 1997 Labour Party General Election manifesto asserted that
its aim was 'to put behind us the bitter political struggles of left and right
that have torn our country apart for too many decades'. New Labour would
be the 'party of ideas and ideals but not of outdated ideology. What counts
is what works. The objectives are radical. The means will be modern'.[9]

Once he became Prime Minister, Tony Blair followed the precedent set
by Margaret Thatcher; definitive statements of the ideology underpinning
his modernisation programme were not published until well after he had
entered 10 Downing Street. (The 1979 Conservative Party manifesto made
no mention of privatisation, the signature policy of Thatcherism[10] and
'Thatcherism' itself was not coined until after she had become Prime
Minister and even then was a product of her opponents.[11]) Neither Blair nor
his closest academic ally, Anthony Giddens, published definitive statements
of the 'Third Way' renewal of politics until the year after his election.[12] Bill
Clinton had used the term 'Third Way' before but not until six years into his
presidency.[13] Like Thatcher, Blair attempted only to give retrospective ideological coherence to his government's modernisation programme.

Gordon Brown is different. Not since Margaret Thatcher has British
politics witnessed a Prime Minister whose speeches are so frequently and so
richly punctuated with quotations. Thatcher's speeches of the late 1970s
were littered with references to the work of philosophers and economists,
with a relatively narrow focus on conservative thinkers and the liberal political economy of Adam Smith, Friedrich Hayek and Milton Friedman.[14] In
comparison, two features stand out in Brown's speeches. The first is the
sheer eclecticism of the sources from which his politics come. In a collection
of fourteen selected speeches, the 'further reading' (based on the sources

cited), listed 122 authors, ranging from major Enlightenment philosophers (Adam Smith, David Hume, Francis Hutcheson and Adam Ferguson), senior religious figures (Pope John Paul II, the Archbishop of Canterbury and the Chief Rabbi), major literary figures (notably John Milton, François Voltaire, James Joyce and George Orwell), American Presidents (Abraham Lincoln, Robert Kennedy and George W. Bush) to an international rock musician (Bono Vox) and an Eskimo poet. The second is the conspicuous absence of references to major Labour Party politicians or political thinkers. Only fifteen sources in the edited collection had a direct link with the Labour Party and were outnumbered more than two-to-one by references to liberal and conservative philosophers or politicians.[15] This, in itself, is an important indication of the evolution of Brown's political philosophy.

Long before he had the opportunity to contest and win the Labour Party leadership or contest a General Election as Prime Minister, Brown drew up a detailed blueprint of his modernisation agenda. He was determined to win the battle of ideas by specifying his philosophy beforehand rather than retrospectively. In so doing, he not only demonstrated how far his political thinking had moved from its radical socialist origins but also how much it had returned to the values and lessons his parents taught him during his childhood.

Brown has said that he sees winning the battle of ideas not only as key to domestic modernisation but also to Britain's foreign policy goals. He has argued that the Cold War was disputed and won not only with military and intelligence weaponry but also through 'a cultural Cold War – a Cold War of ideas and values', fought 'not just through governments but through foundations, trusts, civil society and civic organisations'.[16] That cultural Cold War must now be renewed: Brown identified as crucial to defeating international terrorism the isolation of 'murderous extremists' through the mobilisation of 'the essential decency and moderation of all our communities ... to win the battle of ideas and minds'.[17] The existence of the Internet means that this battle must now be fought in the interests of the moderate majority at the global level.[18]

RESOLVING THE PROGRESSIVE DILEMMA

Gordon Brown is intent on fighting the battle of ideas and wants to launch a new phase of British national renewal. The thesis underpinning his 'British

Way' is that 'as the tasks of government change, the way we govern must change, not just new policies but new politics too. A new politics founded on responsibilities as well as rights'.[19] Given that Brown worked closely with Tony Blair from their election to Westminster in the June 1983 General Election, it is important to establish whether, and to what extent, the tenets of Brown's political philosophy are different from Blair's. Of particular concern to Labour Party members and voters is the question of whether Brown will return the Labour Party to any of the traditional core values that New Labour is held to have abandoned. It is also important to establish whether Brown's philosophy will be capable of resolving the progressive dilemma between liberalism and social democracy which has blighted the Left's electoral prospects in British politics since the end of the First World War.

When Tony Blair was first elected, he appeared genuinely committed to a fundamental ideological realignment of British politics.[20] This realignment would have seen first, the Labour Party and the Liberal Democrats working increasingly closely and second, a referendum on the voting system, in an attempt to resolve the 'progressive dilemma' of British politics. This dilemma, as depicted by David Marquand, had prevented the Labour Party from constructing a successful progressive coalition on the Left of British politics similar to that which had been led by the Liberal Party before 1914. The electoral consequence from 1918 was the distribution of the majority of votes on the Left at successive General Elections but a predominance of Conservative governments.[21]

Throughout the twentieth century, the largest share and, in most cases, the majority of voters at British General Elections tended to cast their votes for social democratic parties of the Centre-Left. However, because those votes were divided between the Labour Party, the Liberal Party and various other parties of the Left (notably the Social Democratic Party during the early 1980s) and because of the vagaries of the first-past-the-post electoral system, the Conservative Party was able to hold power for sixty-eight of the century's years, more than twice as long as its social democratic opponents. Blair's Third Way promised to resolve the progressive dilemma, by drawing 'vitality from uniting the two great streams of left-of-centre thought – democratic socialism and liberalism – whose divorce this century did so much to weaken progressive politics across the West'.[22]

This ambition was given concrete form by the participation of Liberal Democrats in a Cabinet committee and the appointment in December 1997 of the Liberal Democrat peer and leading social democratic thinker, Lord Jenkins, as head of an independent commission into the future of the voting system.[23] The General Election manifesto had stated 'We are committed to a referendum on the voting system for the House of Commons'.[24] However, by the time the Jenkins Commission had reported, in October 1998, the *realpolitik* of New Labour's 179-seat majority at Westminster (delivered by the existing first-past-the-post voting system) had won the day. The quest for ideological realignment was quickly abandoned and the commitment to introduce a more proportionate and fairer voting system left to wither on the vine.[25]

Within a few months of the election of the first Blair Government, prominent social democratic commentators exhibited their disillusionment with the Third Way. They argued that Blair lacked a public philosophy and the Third Way marked the death of Labour re-distributionism and signified the establishment of a neo-liberal consensus in British politics.[26] Bryan Gould, a prominent member of Neil Kinnock's Shadow Cabinet, argued that 'New Labour is not Labour renewed. It is Labour rejected, Labour renounced. New Labour is a negative. New Labour is and is meant to be, Not Labour'.[27] For his part (having left the Labour Party to join the Social Democratic Party but returned following Blair's election as leader), the former Labour MP, David Marquand, contended that Tony Blair's defining characteristic – and 'what makes New Labour new' – was the acceptance of 'the foundational assumption of the Thatcher counter-revolution in political economy', namely 'free choice in the marketplace [and] the entrepreneurial ideal of the early nineteenth century'.[28]

Blair failed to resolve the progressive dilemma in British politics: the question naturally arises as to whether Gordon Brown can do any better. He has frequently reminded the Labour Party that:

> ... when we make a compelling case and trust the progressive instincts of the British people we can build a shared sense of national purpose, we can build a progressive consensus that inspires the country, a consensus that prosperity and justice for all can advance together.[29]

However, when Brown's political rhetoric and statecraft as Chancellor of the Exchequer are taken into account, in terms of the location of Brown's political philosophy in relation to the history of ideas in progressive politics in general and the Labour Party's traditions in particular, they appear to point in opposing directions. On the one hand (as I shall set out in greater detail in Chapter Four), Brown's actions as Chancellor place him firmly in the Fabian tradition of technocratic modernisers, who have no qualms about basing their politics on, in the words of W. H. Greenleaf, 'wise and authoritative direction from above'.[30] In their quest for national efficiency (and mirroring Brown's quest for a shared sense of national purpose), since the era of Sidney and Beatrice Webb, Fabian modernisers have placed their faith in socialism becoming, as Sidney Webb said, 'more and more the business of elaborately trained experts'.[31] From his decision to give responsibility for setting interest rates to the unelected Monetary Policy Committee (consisting of economists and financial experts) to his increasing proclivity for commissioning studies on important matters of public policy from individual technical experts beyond the scrutiny of democratic institutions, Brown has governed in the Fabian technocratic tradition.[32]

On the other hand, Gordon Brown's political rhetoric, at least during the two earliest phases of the evolution of his political philosophy, places him sturdily in the tradition of English ethical socialism and the thinking of, among others, R. H. Tawney, George Orwell and T. H. Marshall. In *English Ethical Socialism*, Dennis and Halsey define this tradition by its positive commitment to fraternity, liberty and equality, harnessed to 'a sense of the enormous contribution that a society's past makes to its present morality and institutions and that its present choices and failures to choose will be profound in their consequences'.[33] Above all, ethical socialism embraces 'a shared belief in the power of moral character to perfect a person and ennoble a nation' and, in short, advances 'a theory of personality and society which places moral motivation as the mainspring of individual conduct and social organisation'.[34] In this tradition, R. H. Tawney argued, during the inter-war period, that Britain's problems were attributable to the absence of the spiritual and ethical foundation necessary for economic and social affairs.[35] Tawney's socialism was 'above all personal, moral and religious'.[36]

These characteristics shaped Gordon Brown's socialism in the formative years of his political development. During his childhood, the Brown family's politics were, like Tawney's, personal, moral and religious. As Brown told the 2006 Labour Party conference, his father was a minister of the Presbyterian Church of Scotland but 'his motivation was not theological zeal but compassion' and he was 'more of a social Christian than a fundamentalist'.[37] What he particularly learned from his father was the importance of public service as a person's duty to others and the importance of community and of civic associations as the basis of community. As a consequence, Brown's religion 'is built on a far greater sense of people's importance and potential'.[38]

The specific values taught by his parents were 'duty, responsibility and respect for others', allied to a belief in 'honesty and hard work and that the things that matter had to be worked for'. Every individual had the opportunity to leave their mark on the world, for good or ill, and therefore everyone had a duty to use whatever talents they possessed 'to help people least able to help themselves'. However, while some people possessed a talent, their ability would remain 'lost and forever unfilled' unless they had supportive people to champion them. Consequently, Brown joined the Labour Party 'out of faith – faith in people, that they should have the opportunity to realise their potential'. For this reason, 'at all times the Labour Party must stand for more than a programme: we must have a soul'.[39]

Moral sense and the ethical dimension of politics have been central to Brown's philosophy all his adult life. His parents 'were more than an influence, they were – and still are – my inspiration. The reason I am in politics'. They taught him that 'each of us should live by a moral compass' and by 'a simple faith with a fundamental optimism'.[40] Like the English ethical socialists, Brown believes in the power of character, inspired by fundamental moral sentiments, to perfect a person and ennoble a nation and defines the 'British Way' in terms of the moral character and particular qualities of the British people.[41] Brown has used speeches on Britishness to argue that a society's past contributes to its present morality and institutions and that the choices it makes – and any failures to choose – will have profound consequences.[42] In 2006, Brown reminded the Labour Party conference of his belief that the values of opportunity and responsibility 'are even more relevant to the future of our country as we face profound change [from] the momentous challenges of terrorism and security, global economic competition ... the threat to our planet from climate change'.[43] However, the moral sense and moral sentiments of the Scottish Enlightenment thinkers, which will shape the policies of the Brown Government are far removed from the tradition of ideas that shaped Brown's political philosophy during its earliest phase.

PHASE ONE: BROWN'S ETHICAL AND PARLIAMENTARY SOCIALISM

The importance of politics as a moral duty was evident from the beginning of Gordon Brown's political career: and he was politicised at a very early age. As he recounted to his biographer, the journalist Paul Routledge: 'I grew up and became politically aware in the early Sixties when the Tory government was failing and the idea of change – even for a twelve-year-old – was an important thing'.[44] In November 1972, when standing (successfully) for the post of Rector of Edinburgh University at the age of twenty-one, Brown's manifesto stated 'I am an idealist, a radical and a reformer ... Society's problems today are not technical but social and moral. I believe the university must play a leading role in setting social and moral standards in a civilised society'.[45] Similarly, when Brown attended a vital meeting of the Scottish Labour Party executive in November 1981, he identified the importance of drawing up a party manifesto that would 'start a moral crusade backed by the vast majority of party members'.[46]

The importance of ideas in the development of Brown's moral crusade was vividly illustrated towards the end of his tenure as Rector when Brown helped assemble and edit a collection of essays, *The Red Paper on Scotland*. This collection demonstrates the extent to which, during the 1970s, his politics were firmly in the mainstream of the Scottish Labour Party. It was published against the backdrop of the peak of the Wilson Government's travails with the consequences of Britain's relative economic decline, the genesis of Thatcherism as a critique of post-war social democratic modernisation and the resurgence of Scottish nationalism following the discovery of North Sea Oil. The *Red Papers* series was intended as the Left's ideological counterweight of *The Black Papers on Education*, an important symbol of the emergence of the New Right in British politics.[47]

In his introduction to *The Red Papers*, entitled 'The Socialist Challenge', Brown developed the thesis that a combination of the Royal Commission on the Constitution (the Kilbrandon Report), the issue of North Sea Oil and Britain's wider economic crisis had fostered 'a barren, myopic, almost suffering consensus which has tended to ignore Scotland's real problems – our unstable economy and unacceptable level of unemployment, chronic inequalities of wealth and power and inadequate social services'. The key question confronting Scotland was 'who shall exercise power and control the lives of our people?' and what sort of social structure could 'guarantee to people the maximum control and self-management over the decisions which affect their lives, allowing the planned co-ordination of the use and distribution of resources, in a co-operative community of equals?'[48] Brown's answer was that Scotland's social conditions and political predicament demanded 'a new commitment to socialist ideals', including 'a new social vision for Scotland'[49] that was humane, democratic and revolutionary.

At this time, Brown's politics were couched in impeccably socialist terms and expressed in a commitment to community democracy, a planned economy and the empowerment of workers. His political economy identified capitalism as the cause of Scotland's economic and social problems, rejecting the alternative explanations of national suppression and London mismanagement, although, he claimed, 'we have had our share of both'. First, Brown asserted, the root cause of Scotland's problems was 'the uneven and uncontrolled development of capitalism and the failure of successive governments to challenge and transform it'. Second, Brown claimed, capitalism had for centuries 'sacrificed social aspirations to private ambitions' and thereby stultified the 'real resources of Scotland', which lay in 'the collective energies and potential of our people' rather than North Sea Oil or the 'ingenuity of native entrepreneurs' which was to be championed by Margaret Thatcher and Sir Keith Joseph.[50]

Brown identified 'the long standing paradox of Scottish politics ... the surging forward of working-class industrial and political pressure (and in particular the loyal support given to Labour) and its containment through the accumulative failures of successive Labour Governments'. In the 1920s, socialism had been 'a qualitative concept, an urgently-felt moral imperative, about social control' but that heritage had been lost. The rise of modern Scottish nationalism should be understood as 'less an assertion of Scotland's permanence as a nation than a response to Scotland's uneven development'.[51] Intriguingly, he did not dismiss the nationalist cause out of hand. On the contrary, he merely suggested that, because of the urgency of Scotland's problems, Scottish socialists could not support 'a strategy for independence which postpones the question of meeting urgent social and economic needs until the day after independence'.[52] By implication, a Scottish nationalism which accorded priority to those social and economic needs would be worthy of support. At the same time, Brown argued that Scottish socialists could not give 'unconditional support to maintaining the integrity of the United Kingdom – and all that entails – without any guarantee of radical social change'. This was because the question was 'not one of structures nor of territorial influence but of democracy', of how working people in Scotland could increase their control over 'the decisions which shape their lives and the wealth they alone produce'.[53]

To redress the 'gross inequality' he identified in Scotland, Brown advocated 'policies for mobilising social and economic as well as educational resources in an overall strategy for ending inequality'. What would be required was nothing less than 'a massive and irreversible shift of power to working people, a framework of free universal welfare services controlled by the people who use them'[54]. Moreover, socialism would have to be won 'at the point of production – the production of needs, ideas and particularly of goods and services'. Existing economic strategies had failed to generate 'a new economic base for sustained economic growth', not least because of the clear industrial divide between 'the giants of finance and industry on an international scale (including British multinationals, second only to the Americans) and the small firms on the national market'.[55]

As a socialist alternative, Brown argued for a planned economy to cure 'a vicious circle of low productivity, bad labour relations, low investment and poor entrepreneurship'. He rejected 'the familiar tried formulas of wider incentives, tax reliefs, assured labour markets, growth areas and native entrepreneurs' because such 'public intervention will only be as effective as the efficiency of the private sector permits'.[56] In short, the private control of industry had become 'a hindrance to the further unfolding of the social forces of production'. Whether through investment in state-owned industries or through the application of intermediate technology, what was needed was 'the erosion of the power of the market – and of the multinationals who now manipulate the market – to determine the social priorities that are the forging ground for socialist progress'.[57]

To empower the workers, Brown rejected as inadequate proposals for worker shareholdings, favouring the co-ordination of workers' activity in different industries and unions. This could be achieved through the revival of the Institute of Workers' Control, which had been proposed at the time of the occupation of Upper Clyde Shipbuilders during the Heath Government. In relation to the wider question of the relationship between socialism and nationalism, Brown argued that Scottish identity had been forged on the anvil of successful British capitalism. Responding to the

Scottish National Party's (SNP) agenda, Brown asserted that they had, mistakenly, presumed 'the familiar priorities of wealth and power over people' and assumed 'the subservience of Scottish workers to private international controls'.[58] In short, the SNP had merely brought the professional and commercial classes back into politics.

For Brown, in the mid-1970s, the way forward for the Labour movement in Scotland lay in the creation of 'a socialist society, a coherent strategy with rhythm and modality to each reform to cancel the logic of capitalism', achieved through 'social reorganisation – a phased extension of public control under workers' self-management and the prioritising of social needs set by the communities themselves'.[59] Claiming that devolution had become 'all things to all people', including 'the insertion of a sixth tier of government which threatens to make us the most over-governed country in Europe',[60] Brown concluded his socialist challenge by focusing on the opportunity presented by events 'to force the pace towards socialism in Britain as a whole'. This could be accomplished by convincing people of the need for social control, as had been understood by 'Scotland's socialist pioneers, Hardie, Smillie, Maxton, Maclean, Gallacher, Wheatley and others'.[61]

Gordon Brown's list of Scotland's socialist pioneers was significant, demonstrating his commitment to a gradual, parliamentary socialism, rather than to a more radical form of political organisation. The most significant of these Scottish pioneers to Brown's political philosophy was James Maxton, Independent Labour Party MP for the Glaswegian constituency of Bridgeton from the 1922 General Election until his death in July 1946. Maxton's philosophical influence was reflected in the prominence of his work in Brown's PhD thesis.[62] For example, during the late 1920s, Maxton had campaigned for the Independent Labour Party's manifesto, *Socialism in Our Time*, which had called for 'a new approach to politics' and contended that 'on the issues of Socialism and the abolition of poverty there is no room for compromise'.[63]

James Maxton also developed the notion of 'the third alternative ... neither a long period of misery under capitalism, nor a great economic and social collapse'. He claimed the third alternative 'aims at securing political power by the ordinary political machine, aims at developing industrial power by strengthening of the trades unions and at increasing economic power by strengthening the co-operative movement'.[64] (Maxton's development of this concept may explain why Brown never felt comfortable with and refused to use the term 'Third Way' when Chancellor of the Exchequer.)

Shortly before Maxton's death, as Brown recorded in his biography, Winston Churchill described him as 'The greatest gentleman in the House of Commons'. After he died, the *Daily Mail* asserted that he had given Westminster 'a moral authority'.[65] Brown has sought to impart this quality of moral authority to his politics and, following in the footsteps of James Maxton, to his parliamentary career.

PHASE TWO: SUPPLY-SIDE SOCIALISM

Having unsuccessfully contested the Edinburgh South constituency in the May 1979 General Election (which he lost by only 2460 votes, reducing the Conservative majority by nearly one thousand votes), Brown was elected to Westminster in the June 1983 General Election as MP for the Fife constituency of Dunfermline East. Brown was elected with 18515 votes (no less than 51.5 per cent of the votes cast) and a majority of 11301.

Brown made his maiden speech on 27 July 1983, choosing a debate on social security.[66] The choice of his personal, political and historical reference point is deeply instructive: the 1942 Beveridge Report, written by a card-carrying member of the Liberal Party, with not a reference to any ideas of the Labour Party. (Twenty-four years later, he was to choose the 1944 White Paper on Employment and the goal of full employment identified by John Maynard Keynes, another Liberal Party member, as his reference point when setting out the Blair Government's economic policy objectives.) In this maiden speech, he sought to defend the welfare state as a correction to the wrongs wrought by Victorian values, citing Winston Churchill, not Ramsay McDonald, Clement Attlee, Harold Wilson, James Callaghan or any other previous Labour Party leader. He began his speech by highlighting the impact of de-industrialisation on the people of Dunfermline East and the assault on social justice inflicted by 'mass unemployment and its inevitable consequence, mass poverty'. Using normally unpublished statistics from the Government's Manpower Services Commission, Brown identified 'a new arithmetic of depression and despair' that had arisen from the Thatcher Government's desire to cut welfare benefits for the unemployed.[67]

In Scotland, welfare dependency had increased. In 1979, 405,000 were on supplementary benefit; by July 1983, 750,000 received means-tested benefits. Paradoxically, even with benefits as low as £26 per week, the government argued that they were a disincentive to employment, although a study from the influential think-tank, the Institute for Fiscal Studies, indicated that only one claimant in 40 was receiving more income than they would have received from employment. Brown asserted that to seek to cut unemployment benefit was not a necessary act of economic policy, as Nigel Lawson implied, but 'an act of vindictiveness to the poorest in our community'. Brown's conclusion was that the Government was 'proposing and enshrining a new definition of the national minimum, a new poverty line and a new safety net'.[68] This would not only contradict the tenets of the 1942 Beveridge Report but also be 'devoid of all logic, bereft of all morality and vindictive even beyond monetarism'.[69]

Gordon Brown thus began his parliamentary career by demonstrating his commitment to social justice. He underlined that commitment by co-editing (with Robin Cook) a study of poverty and deprivation in Scotland. Brown's introduction highlighted the new poverty in Scotland, where more than one million people existed on or below the Government's official poverty line. He attributed Scotland's high level of deep-seated poverty to the industrial and occupational structure of the Scottish economy and, in particular, the highly uneven and uncontrolled character of Scotland's economic development.[70] Brown claimed the welfare state was now endangered by 'a new Tory social ideology which is doing to the legacy of Beveridge what "monetarist" dogma has done to the heritage of Keynes'. He noted that the New Right's proposals for the welfare state would mean market forces would determine the shape and price of social services. This meant the Friedman–Hayek analysis underpinning this agenda was 'as much at odds with the facts of life in a complex society and the climate of social values as is Mrs Thatcher's incantation of Victorian bliss'.[71]

As an alternative, Brown advocated the Left should re-assess its social strategy to address changing circumstances, if not the ideological challenge posed by the Thatcherite New Right. The Left should argue the case for equality and identify badly-needed new principles for social security. In this, he drew on the thinking of R. H. Tawney and identified five initiatives that would 'narrow the space between valley and peak ... by radically reforming the existing tax, social security and welfare systems'. The initiatives were: an end to mass unemployment, a legal minimum wage, a more generous definition of the minimum 'safety net', raising the levels of public expenditure on the areas and groups most in need and the redistribution of income and wealth, by re-establishing the principles that 'those who cannot afford to pay tax should not have to pay it' and 'taxation should rise progressively with income'.[72]

Brown extended these ideas beyond Westminster, using the very public platform of the Labour Party's annual conference. He castigated the second Thatcher Government for an approach to the welfare state that was about 'the redistribution of poverty among the poor when it should be about the redistribution of wealth from rich to poor'. He was equally contemptuous of those who had left the Labour Party in 1981, claiming that 'the Social Democrats cannot fight the new Right because they *are* the new Right'. He also asserted that there was more talent 'stagnating at the Labour Exchange than speculating on the Stock Exchange'.[73] Given Brown's later role at the Treasury as the champion of the interests of the City of London, the length of his ideological odyssey from his early parliamentary socialist roots becomes apparent.

From his first election to Westminster until the Labour Party's fourth consecutive General Election defeat (in April 1992), Gordon Brown's political philosophy remained firmly within the traditions, aims and values of the Labour Party and indeed, those of the broader labour movement. He was a consistent and skilled advocate of state-led industrial modernisation. His analysis of the United Kingdom's relative decline was clear and consistent with that of the party leader, Neil Kinnock. In his manifesto for state-led industrial modernisation of 'machines and methods', Kinnock defined democratic socialism as 'the politics of production' and identified essential measures to plan investment in and expansion of the manufacturing industry.[74] This was the period of development of Brown and the Labour Party's supply-side socialism.

To differentiate it from the Thatcher Government's medium-term financial strategy, the Labour Party promised a medium-term industrial strategy and 'a science-based, high-tech future'[75] in which the Party's commitment to supply-side socialism would reflect the fact that 'The Conservatives are the party for the City. We are the party for industry'.[76] Demonstrating a growing commitment to macro-economic stability and fiscal prudence, the Labour Party would pursue 'a policy of sustained and balanced growth' but would be prepared to follow the French and Germans in harnessing 'private resources for publicly-led investment'.[77] Above all, the Party would be committed to the modernisation of Britain, providing the stable conditions and the strategic policies to help industry succeed. For the economy, modernisation would mean 'a modern industrial policy, based on partnership between government and industry, where government encourages long-term investment in skills and technologies'.[78] To finance and deliver its industrial modernisation programme and to correct the short-termism and failure of the City of London's financial markets to invest sufficiently in manufacturing industry, the Labour Party committed itself to a National Investment Bank, a National Recovery Programme, an Investment Decade for Britain and the establishment of a British Technology Enterprise and English Regional Development Agencies.[79]

In 1989, Brown published *Where There is Greed*, a withering critique of Thatcherism that reflected his commitment to supply-side socialism. In it, he accused Margaret Thatcher of betraying Britain's future by failing to make the public investments necessary for industrial modernisation. For him, the 1980s had been 'a decade not of achievement but of missed opportunity', during which the free market had failed, creating 'under-funded and over-extended' public services and 'an industrial desert'.[80] This failure had arisen because of Thatcher's doctrinaire prejudice and short-term vision, in which her blind conviction that the British decline could be attributed to the over-reaching state had obstructed the 'greater role for organised and supportive interventions by the state [in] education and training, in innovation and in technology support and in enhanced long-term investment'. Unaided, the market would fail to 'educate and train our workforce, plan and fulfil national research goals or restore or even compensate for our battered infrastructure'.[81]

Brown's alternative was to re-cast the state as catalyst and co-ordinator and introduce a new supply-side socialism, whose principal themes would be 'investment in skills and science, with teamwork, collective effort and the involvement of the workforce'.[82] This would deliver 'the necessary remedial action: supply-side measures to stimulate investment in the regions, in education and research and to ensure proper balance in the economy'.[83] Based on a classically technocratic and rational approach to national self-interest, Brown's series of co-ordinated supply-side interventions would attend to the under-investment in Britain's infrastructure, not least her 'overcrowded, underfinanced, under-planned, under-maintained and sometimes dangerous transport system'.[84]

This was Kinnock's 'politics of production' writ large. Brown's state-led modernisation agenda firmly attached him to the Labour Party tradition of Harold Wilson's white heat of technology, with its Ministry of Technology and the Callaghan Government's National Enterprise Board. More broadly, he had set out a classic developmental state model, whose focus on the development of national productive powers through public investment was solidly in the tradition of the nineteenth-century German political economist, Friedrich List.[85] In his great work, *The National System of Political Economy*, List set out, for industrialising economies seeking to catch up with their more advanced competitors, the definitive alternative to Adam Smith's liberal economics.[86] Rather than following Smith's example of believing that 'politics and political power cannot be taken into consideration in political economy', List argued that political power should be used to increase both internal prosperity and foreign commerce by nurturing the nation's productive powers.[87] Brown's supply-side socialism set out an agenda to harness political power for the purpose of state-led industrial modernisation.

Supply-side socialism underpinned the Labour Party's 1992 General Election campaign and manifesto. Only three months before the election, the Labour Party launched *Made in Britain*, a statement of the economic and industrial policy priorities of a potential Labour government.[88] At its launch, John Smith, the Shadow Chancellor, emphasised two important facets of Labour's strategy: first, that it would clearly divide Labour and the Tories on industrial policy and second, that Labour's industrial policies would be prudent, costing no more than around £1.1 billion, because 'the first responsibility of government is to create a stable economic framework so that business can plan and invest for the future'.[89] Despite the Labour Party's very public commitment to macro-economic stability and fiscal prudence and the fact that the backdrop of the General Election was the worst domestic recession since the 1930s, supply-side socialism still sent the Labour Party to its fourth consecutive General Election defeat. It won only 271 seats (albeit a net gain of forty-two seats over the 1987 General Election) and took a 34.4 per cent share of the vote (up by only 3.6 per cent from Labour's poor performance in 1987).

In his role as Shadow Chief Secretary to the Treasury, Gordon Brown had attempted either to remove costly proposals from the Labour Party's

Policy Review documents or to preface spending commitments with the qualification that they would be implemented only when economic circumstances allowed.[90] However, even such prudential supply-side socialism was insufficient to persuade enough of the electorate to vote for Labour, especially in the more affluent marginal constituencies of the English Midlands and Home Counties. John Major's Conservative Party piled up a record total of 14.09 million votes, against the Labour Party's 11.56 million. Despite the domestic recession, a month before the election, a MORI opinion poll revealed the Conservative Party to have an eleven per cent lead over Labour on the question of economic competence. Forty-seven per cent of respondents thought John Major best equipped to manage the economy, compared to only 31 per cent support for Neil Kinnock.

Supply-side socialism had failed politically. If the Labour Party were ever to govern Britain again, a major review was needed: one that would not only be confined to policy and strategy but would also embrace the ideas and political philosophy of the Labour Party.

PHASE THREE: FROM SUPPLY-SIDE SOCIALISM TO SUPPLY-SIDE LIBERALISM

The need for fundamental change and a wholesale reinvention of the Left was well-understood by the group of politicians who, after John Smith's death, became the principal architects of New Labour's modernisation under Tony Blair. In his leadership election statement, Blair asserted that the Labour Party: 'must do more than just defeat the Conservatives on grounds of competence, integrity and fitness to govern. We must change the tide of ideas'.[91]

Gordon Brown had understood this need long before. Following the Labour Party's General Election defeat, he was one of a number of Shadow Cabinet members who studied the Democratic Party's campaign strategy and platform for the November 1992 American Presidential election. Brown learnt three, very specific, lessons from Labour's defeats and Clinton's victory. The first was that, for the Labour Party, 'the most important thing is that we lay down the principles that guide our future policy': winning the battle of ideas, rather than detailing policy, must become the party's over-riding priority.[92] Brown felt Clinton had won because he had:

... found an echo throughout America for his central idea that government had responsibilities to the whole community to deal with the huge problems of unemployment, the weaknesses of the American manufacturing sector and training in skills and, of course, for the argument that there were entrenched economic interests, privileged elites in American society, that were denying people opportunity.[93]

Brown's focus was still on supply-side issues but his second great lesson from Clinton's victory opened an alternative ideological framework for his modernisation agenda. This lesson concerned the central importance of globalisation in economic policy. Brown contended that 'we're living in an increasingly global economy. There's global sourcing of companies, a global capital market, 24-hour speculative activity'. Allied to the other great challenge, that of how the microelectronics revolution was affecting industry and services and completely changing the working of the economy, the third lesson the Labour Party would have to learn was that 'increasingly, the most important thing about national economic strength is the level of skill in the economy. Government has a responsibility to ensure that training, education and investment are maintained at a satisfactory level'.[94]

This was a supply-side socialist politician, who at a Party conference less than a decade before had lambasted financial speculators and supported Kinnock's politics of production as an alternative to the Conservatives' politics of the City. Brown now proposed a wholesale redefinition of the political economy of the Labour Party and its long-standing assumptions about the respective roles of the state and market. Globalisation, and the need to maintain Britain's international competitiveness, provided Gordon Brown with ideological grounds on which he could justify major changes in the Labour Party's economic and social policy priorities.

From this point, Brown's political philosophy would increasingly embrace a neo-liberal perspective on globalisation, with its advocacy of market liberalisation and deregulation and its unshakeable faith in entrepreneurial initiative as the prime agency of innovation and social change (exercised through competition and risk-taking in open markets). As I shall show in Chapter Three, in economic policy terms, this transition in Brown's thinking was given additional momentum and consolidated by two events: first, the Treasury and Bank of England's political and economic humiliation on 'Black Wednesday', when sterling's humiliating departure from the European Exchange Rate Mechanism followed the defeat of the

Government's monetary policy by financial speculators and second, Brown's appointment of Ed Balls as his personal economic adviser. Balls's liberal political economy, and particularly his critique of some of the central assumptions of macro-economic policy, helped propel Brown away from supply-side socialism and towards supply-side liberalism.

THE POLITICS OF POTENTIAL

Brown's political economics might have been in flux but he still sought to define a new politics that would sustain his conviction that 'prosperity requires a just society. Individuals must be given the opportunity to realise their potential to the full'.[95] Brown followed Neil Kinnock's, and the Labour Party Policy Review's, vision of socialism for the 1990s, based on a rejection of the failed 'old ideologies – command economy at one extreme, crude free market economics at the other', in favour of the individual's freedom to develop their potential.[96]

In this vein, Brown wrote a Fabian pamphlet: *Fair is efficient: a socialist agenda for fairness*, in which he sought to put the case for a new economics that would demonstrate how 'attacking poverty and a lack of opportunity at their source is the route both to a fairer society and a more prosperous economy'.[97] To achieve this, progressive taxation, the welfare state and good public services would have to be at the heart of the Labour Party's fairness agenda. The philosophical basis underpinning the new economics was that socialism's objective:

> ... had always been that every individual should have the opportunity to realise his or her potential to the full, to enable people to bridge the gap between what they are now and what they have it in themselves to become.[98]

Moreover, the Labour Party's vision of fairness had 'always meant more than an aspiration to provide opportunities for all. It also embodies an analysis of society which shows how we can achieve this'.[99]

Brown contended that socialism's unique contribution had been to understand that:

> ... the strength of society – the community working together – is essential not only to tackle the entrenched interests and accumulations of

power that hold ordinary people back but also positively to intervene to promote the realisation of potential. In other words, the power of all of us is essential to promote the potential of each of us.[100]

Even though Brown's political economy was now pointing firmly in the direction of supply-side liberalism, he continued to set out his political agenda within the English ethical socialist tradition. He recalled that R. H. Tawney had acknowledged 'the importance of both spreading individual opportunities to all and of the community in making personal freedom meaningful'.[101] Tawney's *Equality* stated that a society would only be free:

... in so far and only in so far, as within the limits set by nature, knowledge and resources, its institutions are such as to enable all its members to grow to their full stature, to do their duty as they see it.[102]

Brown also reminded his readers of Aneurin Bevan's mantra that 'democratic socialism is a child of modern society'.[103] Therefore, Brown's new economic egalitarianism would be concerned with modernisation and would ensure the availability of the helping hand of government at critical moments in people's lives.[104]

At this time of reflection for the Labour Party, Brown contributed significantly to a collection of essays, *Reinventing the Left*, edited by the future Blair loyalist, David Miliband. The theme of the collection was the identification of a politics of autonomy, to provide the basis for a radical new identity for the Left, countering the anti-politics of the New Right's neo-liberalism. For Miliband, the four underlying themes of this reinvention of the Left were the extension of personal autonomy in an increasingly interdependent world, an integration of public action and market decisions to secure social interests, a politics defined by relations of power beyond the labour process as well as within it and the need to surmount traditional modes of political organisation both within and beyond the nation state.[105]

Brown's contribution to the reinvention of the Left was to elaborate upon his concept of the politics of potential. Brown advocated a new popular socialism, based on four foundations of a new redistribution of power, through an enabling state, a new constitutional settlement embracing devolved power wherever possible, the reconstruction of the idea of community as a prerequisite for re-inventing government and a new economic egalitarianism.[106] These tenets were derived from three ethical principles identified by the writers of the 1918 Labour Party constitution but which

Brown held to be as true as ever: first, that 'individual potential is far greater than can be realised in a wholly capitalist society', second, that 'individuals are not just self-centred' and third, that 'not only individuals thrive best in a community and that the potential of the individual is enhanced by membership of a community but also that a strong community is essential for the advancement of individual potential'.[107]

Brown contended that in the nineteenth century, controlling the means to life had meant controlling the means of production, distribution and exchange but this ignored the environmental impact of production and consumption. Now, in the interests of enhancing individual freedom, controlling the means to life meant 'controlling the environment of which the economy is a part and that requires collective action'.[108] Subsequently, under New Labour, for Brown it was to mean controlling the process of resource generation and allocation through centralised and prescriptive control of the domestic policy process in England. Treasury power was to be exercised in a manner that denied the notion of a politics of autonomy. Furthermore, in his attempted redefinition of the notion of community, Brown argued that people are interdependent and both emerge from society and are part of it. However, rather than being spontaneous, community, 'the idea that people see themselves as mutually dependent [must] be constructed and not just assumed'.[109]

Brown contended that 'in recognition of our interdependence people must accept their responsibilities as individuals and as citizens and community action should never be a substitute for the assumption of personal responsibility'. This broader notion of community should be separated from the narrower notion of the centralised state, to protect individual rights and to enable the community to explore how its affairs might be organised 'in a decentralised way, more sensitively and flexibly'. Brown argued that 'hierarchical and centralised bureaucracies designed in the 1940s and 1950s simply do not do the job in a rapidly changing, information-rich, knowledge-intensive society'.[110] In practice, Brown and Balls's development of the British model of political economy, based on the principle of 'constrained discretion', has witnessed a new form of centralisation of political power, in which communities' autonomy has been restricted to administering central policies under the guise of 'new localism' (see Chapter Four).

The potentially dangerous implications for accountability in Brown's agenda were immediately identified by one of his fellow essayists in

Reinventing the Left. Anne Phillips did not dissent from Brown's multiplication of the possible avenues along which citizens might participate in decisions but she did query whether such a process could be based upon 'a community that does not – and may never – exist' and whether Brown's lack of precision in his definition of community might extend into 'a lack of precision over democratic accountability and control'. This, in turn, could scupper any radical transfer of power from the centre to communities.[111] Phillips' comments were prescient. This is precisely what happened in England following the election of the Blair Government: unprecedented personal autonomy was extended to the individual as consumer but the political autonomy of the individual as citizen was severely constrained. Because England has been by-passed by the process of political devolution implemented in the other constituent nations of the United Kingdom, enhanced democratic accountability has been denied to its communities. As an alternative to a genuine politics of autonomy, in the reform of their public services these communities have instead been offered 'earned autonomy' by the Prime Ministers and 'constrained discretion' by the Chancellor of the Exchequer (see Chapter Four).

THE TRIUMPH OF THE TECHNOCRATIC OVER THE ETHICAL

In defining a new politics of potential, Gordon Brown revisited the theme of the importance of developing the potential of people, first learnt from his parents. He also began to revisit ethical socialism and the moral dimension of his political philosophy. This process continued when, after the Labour leader, John Smith's, sudden death, Brown co-edited the volume of tributes to his life and work with the journalist James Naughtie. In his essay on Smith's socialism, Brown highlighted three features also readily identifiable in his own thinking: first, the importance of there being a purpose in politics; second, the importance of recognising the relationship between economic prosperity and social justice and third, and most significantly, the importance of the relationship between Christianity and socialism. Brown underscored how Smith had depicted R. H. Tawney as an uncompromising ethical socialist and himself drawn attention to the importance of 'applying our moral principles in a way which results in practical benefits to our fellow citizens'.[112]

This theme was developed further in Brown's introduction to an anthology of socialism he co-authored with the Labour MP, Tony Wright. In it, Brown provided the clearest statement yet of his concept of socialism. Having identified the values of equality, community and democracy, Brown and Wright asserted that:

> Perhaps the most distinctive feature of British socialism historically has been its insistence on the moral basis of politics. A century ago this kind of ethical socialism may have looked like an aberration in terms of general socialist doctrines but it has been triumphantly vindicated.

In short, socialism had always been 'a matter of moral choice [and] more of an ethic of society than an economic doctrine'.[113] Brown and Wright contended that while 'there should be no doubt that socialism is primarily an ethical doctrine', at the same time its moralism 'should be severely practical'. British socialism had always combined the ethical with the practical by sustaining 'a dual focus on efficiency and equality'.[114]

This meant that an unregulated economy would be 'incapable of delivering either a decent economy or a decent society' and therefore 'capitalism had to be socialised in the public interest'.[115] In its preoccupation with public ownership, Wright and Brown contended that British socialism had provided 'a classic inversion of ends and means, historically understandable but morally and intellectually deficient'. However, following the Labour Party's modernisation of its archaic 1918 constitution, it was now understood that the public interest need not necessarily conflict with the continued existence of markets. On the contrary, rather than seeking to abolish markets, the key task for the state would now be 'to set standards in a way that ensures that markets work in the public interest'.[116]

While the public interest would remain constant, the role of the state would be redefined in a dynamic way, such that government would become 'partner, catalyst, enabler, financier or simply regulator, rather than owner, employer or manager only; just as government may be local and international as well as national'. The modern state would engage in active partnerships in pursuit of public interest objectives, for 'public and private, state and market, capital and labour, national and international: these are the components of a modern partnership economy'.[117] Rather than a choice between capitalism and socialism as forms of ownership, the contemporary choice would be between 'responsibility and irresponsibility, social market and unsocial market, a stakeholder economy and footloose capitalism'.[118] Furthermore, the socialist version of community should be 'an argument about power and its control, enabling people to participate in the decision processes that affect their lives'. The notion of social responsibility arising from the stakeholder economy would go 'far beyond traditional notions of devolution and de-centralisation [and] an encouragement to participation and involvement [to] redistribute power from State to individual'.[119]

Brown and Wright's choice of 'stakeholder economy', with its implications for a radical redistribution of political and economic power, was significant. On 7 January 1996, Tony Blair had made a major speech in Singapore, which focussed on the concepts of trust and the stakeholder economy. Blair had defined trust as 'the recognition of a mutual purpose for which we work together and in which we all benefit' and the stakeholder economy as one 'in which opportunity is available to all, advancement is through merit and from which no group or class is set apart or excluded'. For Blair, trust and stakeholding not only provided the economic justification of social cohesion but also the key to achieving competitiveness in an increasingly competitive global economy.[120]

For the Labour Party, the implications of pursuing such an agenda would have been profound. It would have meant not only a commitment to tackle long-term and structural unemployment but also a wholesale reform of the welfare state. For Will Hutton, writing in the *Observer*, the speech had 'lapses into a language of platitudinous generality'. Despite this, it was hailed as having initiated 'a political exchange of fundamental importance'[121] within and between Britain's two major political parties and to signify a genuine departure in British politics, which might inspire 'a reformist political programme in five chief areas: the workplace, the welfare state, the firm and the City, the constitution and economic policy more generally'.[122]

In the event, the radicalism of stakeholding and its major ramifications for Labour Party policy were sufficient for it to disappear from both Brown and Blair's thinking. During the six months between the Singapore speech and the publication of the Labour Party's major policy statement, *New Labour, new life for Britain*, the concept of stakeholding was hollowed out.[123] Its radical constitutional, financial and corporate governance reforms, which would have upset both British businesses and the City of London, were either diluted or removed.[124]

The Labour Party focussed instead on learning the three key lessons of the Attlee Government's General Election victory of 1945: first, 'the need for a clear sense of national purpose'; second, the need to win the battle of ideas' and, third, 'the need to mobilise all people of progressive mind around a party always outward-looking, seeking new supporters and members'.[125] These themes, and the language used to describe them, were redolent of the previous two decades of Brown's political philosophy but the actual words were spoken by Tony Blair. The Labour Party now focussed relentlessly on 'nothing less than national renewal', which would require 'economic renewal, social renewal and political renewal'.[126] From this time, until the 1997 General Election, Tony Blair made the definitive statements of New Labour's political philosophy, because he, not Brown, had succeeded John Smith as the Labour Party's leader.

Tony Blair located his political philosophy firmly within the ethical socialist tradition, describing it as 'the only one that has stood the test of time'.[127] He acknowledged his personal debt to the Scottish moral philosopher, John MacMurray, and his view that life had 'a moral purpose that encompassed the notion of duty'.[128] For Blair, socialism was:

> ... never about nationalisation or the power of the state; not just about economics or politics even. It is a moral purpose to life; a set of values; a belief in society, in co-operation, in achieving together what we are unable to achieve alone.[129]

Paradoxically, while Blair's philosophical focus was on ethical socialism, Gordon Brown's role, as Shadow Chancellor of the Exchequer, was the overseeing of the Labour Party's policy agenda for domestic economic and social modernisation. His desire to micro-manage and centrally prescribe policy development and resource allocation increasingly placed him within the top-down, technocratic Fabian tradition of Labour modernisers. More importantly, as Brown focussed increasingly on globalisation, macroeconomic stability, fiscal prudence and the long-standing supply-side weaknesses of the British economy, the philosophical basis for his political economy became more attuned to supply-side liberalism than supply-side socialism.

Brown's movement towards supply-side liberalism was accelerated by the events that followed John Smith's death. On 31st May 1994, Brown had dinner with Tony Blair at *Granita*, a restaurant in Islington. During the meal, Brown agreed to lay aside his own ambitions to lead the Labour Party, in favour of Blair's candidature. The price extracted by Brown was to secure an unprecedented control over the design and delivery of domestic economic and social policy. In the aftermath of the dinner, a draft memorandum (later leaked to *The Guardian*) was drawn up, purportedly by Peter Mandelson. Originally, the memorandum read:

> In his Wales and Luton speeches, Gordon has spelled out the fairness agenda – social justice, employment opportunities and skills – which he believes should be the centerpiece of Labour's programme and Tony is in full agreement with this and that the party's economic and social policies should be further developed on this basis.[130]

On the leaked copy of the memorandum, Gordon Brown had crossed out 'is in full agreement with' and instead written 'has guaranteed this will be pursued'.[131] By so altering the wording, Brown skilfully ensured that he, rather than Blair, the potential future Prime Minister and First Lord of the Treasury, would be the prime mover of New Labour's domestic modernisation agenda.

CONCLUSION

The Labour Party's economic and social policy agenda for the 1997 General Election was shaped by Gordon Brown's growing fixation on globalisation and its implications for Britain's domestic policy choices. The political rhetoric of the Party's key policy documents and 1997 General Election manifesto remained technocratic and pragmatic. The promise was of a partnership between government, shareholders, managers and workers, who would put behind them 'the old battles: public versus private, state versus market'.[132] New Labour was 'a party of ideas and ideals but not of outdated ideology ... what counts is what works'.[133] In practice, Brown was proposing to tackle Britain's long-standing supply-side weaknesses by harnessing the energy of the market, dynamic entrepreneurs and successful companies. Competition would be used as 'a spur to innovation, investment and improved productivity – the vital organs of a dynamic economy'.[134] Consumers would be provided with better information, to enable them to exercise greater individual choice. Ironically, the last time such faith had been shown in the dynamic properties of open markets, competition and individual enterprise was in January 1988. Then, at the height of Thatcherism, the Department of Trade and Industry published, *DTI – The Department for Enterprise*, the definitive statement from Whitehall of the Thatcher Government's determination to 'champion all the people who make it happen, rather than just individual sectors, industries or companies'.[135]

The supply-side liberalism of Gordon Brown's nascent 'British model' of political economy was now to gamble that it could deliver modernisation by harnessing and manipulating the actions and investment of private market agents, such as corporations, entrepreneurs and consumers, in the same way that supply-side socialism had previously orchestrated nationalised industries, trades unions and public corporations.

Chapter 2

The New British Enlightenment

INTRODUCTION

During the decade that Gordon Brown served as Chancellor of the Exchequer, his political philosophy evolved significantly. The purpose of this chapter is to chart and explore that philosophical journey, which has left an important political legacy, both for the United Kingdom and for Brown personally, as Prime Minister.

The evolution of Brown's thinking is best understood by dividing its development during his decade at the Treasury into two periods. In the first, from May 1997 until April 1999, Brown laid down and refined the tenets of his supply-side liberalism. With the notable exception of one lecture, in November 1997, in which he set out the principles of his 'British Way' of politics,[1] Brown focussed relentlessly on the development of the British model of political economy (which I shall explore at greater length in Chapter Three). Key economic policy reforms were implemented, notably granting to the Bank of England's Monetary Policy Committee its operational independence over the setting of interest rates, the announcement of the decision that the pound would not be joining the Euro for the lifetime of the Parliament and the completion of the year-long Comprehensive Spending Review and new fiscal policy framework.

During this consolidation of supply-side liberalism, Brown concentrated on showing how fiscal prudence, macro-economic stability and supply-side liberalism would provide the British economy with a policy

environment in which to meet the challenges of globalisation. The culmi-
nation of this particular phase was the delivery of two speeches in the spring
of 1999. In the second, Brown announced to the Institute for Fiscal Studies
that the Treasury's new mission would be no less than the modernisation of
the British economy. Fifty years of 'sterile and self-defeating conflicts
between state and market, managements and workforce, public and private
sectors' would be brought to a decisive end by the pursuit of 'a new national
purpose based on an end to short-termism and an understanding of the
need to take a long-term view of government, industry and the financial
community.'[2] Brown's renewed engagement in the battle of ideas was not to
be limited to economic modernisation. On the contrary, as his first speech,
given five weeks before to the Smith Institute had indicated, Brown's quest
for a new national purpose would take him beyond the parameters of economic modernisation, to the much broader themes of national identity,
constitutional reform and key aspects of global governance.[3]

The development of this fourth phase in Brown's political philosophy
was made possible because he, unlike his Labour predecessors as
Chancellor, was not preoccupied with devaluation or balance-of-payments
crises. Moreover, the combination of the decisions to give operational independence to the Bank of England's Monetary Policy Committee and to conduct fiscal policy through a series of biennial Spending Reviews driven by
the Treasury gave Brown the licence to roam across government departments and explore policy issues previously beyond the remit of the
Chancellor. Exploiting this freedom, Brown embarked on a series of lectures and keynote speeches in which he sought to set out his vision of 'the
new Britain and a new and inclusive vision of Britishness for the twentieth
century'. Brown envisaged a re-discovery of British values, during a transition 'from an over-centralised and uniform state – the old Britain of subjects – to a pluralist and decentralised democracy – the new Britain of
citizens'.[4] This vision would encompass 'a new understanding to the rights
and responsibilities of the citizen and to the reach and role of government',
involving 'a credible and radical view of citizenship as responsible citizenship and a new view of the state as an enabling state'.[5]

In the event, and following from the earlier phases of ethical socialism,
parliamentary and supply-side socialism and supply-side liberalism, this
phase of Brown's political philosophy has seen him embrace a sympathetic
liberalism and moral political economy. These ideas have underpinned the

development of his 'British Way', in domestic policy and his vision for 'Global Europe' and an Atlanticist New Global Deal for poverty and development, in foreign policy. There are a number of remarkable aspects of this phase. As Prime Minister, Brown's 'British Way' is the fourth post-war modernisation programme to be based on liberalism; in developing this sympathetic liberalism, Brown has largely abandoned the socialist tradition of ideas within the Labour Party's history of thought in favour of the philosophy of the Scottish Enlightenment in general and the moral sentiments of Adam Smith in particular; he has returned to the personal, moral and religious philosophical origins of his childhood by drawing extensively on the insights of the Chief Rabbi, Jonathan Sacks and the increasing influence of Enlightenment thinking has drawn him into ideological territory long occupied by the British and Conservative New Right.

In articulating the tenets of his new British Enlightenment, this former, passionate, socialist critic of capitalism has aligned his moral compass to some of the most vigorous defenders of free-market capitalism. This threatens to leave British politics stranded on the ideological common ground first identified by Sir Keith Joseph more than thirty years ago.

THE LIBERAL CENTURY

Seldon and Ball called their 1994 collection of essays *The Conservative Century*. The Conservative Party was electorally dominant in the twentieth century, holding office for more than twice as long as its political opponents were in government.[6] However, in ideological terms, the century would more accurately be described as 'The Liberal Century'. In its first half, the Asquith Government succeeded in laying the foundations for the welfare state and the redistributive taxation system needed to finance it. It legislated for two of the most vital constitutional changes in the United Kingdom's modern political history (the 1911 Parliament Act and the 1914 Government of Ireland Act) and placed the trades unions within a stable legal framework for the first time.[7]

During the latter half of the century, two card-carrying members of the Liberal Party inspired the social democratic 'First Way' of post-war reconstruction. For a generation of politicians – both from Left and Right – John Maynard Keynes specified a macro-economic blueprint for winning both the Second World War and the peace after it.[8] He did so by identifying the ideological and policy conditions for full employment.[9] Sir William Beveridge performed a similar task in relation to the welfare state.[10]

From the mid-1970s, 'The Liberal Century' entered a new phase. Margaret Thatcher and Sir Keith Joseph sought to modernise Britain, by harnessing conservatism and the Conservative Party to the market liberalism of Adam Smith, Milton Friedman and Friedrich Hayek.[11] Thatcher frequently referred to the importance of the moral philosophy of Adam Smith in her redefinition of conservatism and Sir Keith Joseph summarised his new philosophy for government for his senior civil servants at the Department of Industry, adding a reading list which included Adam Smith's *Theory of Moral Sentiments* and *The Wealth of Nations*.[12] When Nigel Lawson defined 'New Conservatism' in August 1980, he noted how new Conservatives had turned to new sages, such as Friedrich Hayek and Milton Friedman, precisely because these thinkers had reinterpreted 'the traditional political and economic wisdom of Hume, Burke and Adam Smith in terms of the conditions of today'.[13] Thus, the 'Second Way' of Thatcherite modernisation owed a significant philosophical debt to liberalism.

Tony Blair's 'Third Way', with its mantra that 'government should not try to run business. The days of picking winners are over' and its retention of the philosophy that 'the role of government in a modern economy is limited but critical', largely left untouched the liberalism of the political economy of its predecessors.[14] Indeed, in the extension of the role of consumer choice and private finance to the organisation and funding of public services, the 'Third Way' rolled forward the frontiers of market-led modernisation.

This raises the key question of whether the Labour Government led by Gordon Brown will embark on a 'Fourth (British) Way' modernisation project, also underpinned by liberalism. The answer is resoundingly in the affirmative, demonstrated by the fourth and latest phase in the development of Gordon Brown's political philosophy. A careful analysis of Brown's speeches and policy statements reveals that he has drawn on the liberal political philosophy of the Scottish Enlightenment, the American liberalism of the 'New Deal' and 'Great Society' Democrat programmes and an eclectic mix of liberal philosophers, whose ranks include Alexis de Tocqueville, John Stuart Mill, T. H. Green, J. A. Hobson, J. M. Keynes, William Beveridge, Jonathan Sacks, Michael Sandel and Michael Walzer.

GORDON BROWN'S MORAL SENSE: 'THE BEST HEAD AND THE BEST HEART'

The key figures who emerged from the heart of the fourth phase of the development of Gordon Brown's political philosophy might seem surprising, given Brown's political and philosophical provenance as a Labour Party politician and ethical socialist. They make more sense when we recall Brown's admission that his parents gave him a world view that was personal, moral and religious. Like Margaret Thatcher and Tony Blair before him, his modernisation programme is for the restoration of British national purpose. Like Thatcher, Brown's project is firmly rooted in the moral sense and moral sentiments of the Scottish Enlightenment, and in particular the moral philosophy and political economy of Adam Smith. For Thatcher, and her closest ideological ally, Sir Keith Joseph, the harnessing of conservatism to liberalism was a genuine Messianic conversion. Brown has simply returned to the philosophy of Adam Smith, a fellow Langtonian, a citizen of the 'Lang Toun' [long town] of Kirkcaldy, where Brown spent his childhood years.

Giving the Pope Paul VI memorial lecture in 2004, Brown advanced three propositions for the reintroduction of moral sense into British politics and political economy: first, 'that our dependence on each other should awaken our conscience to the needs not just of neighbours but of strangers'; second, 'more than that, our moral sense should impel us to act out of duty and not just self interest'; and third, 'that the claims of justice are not at odds with the liberties of each individual but a modern expression of them that ensures the dignity of all – and there is such a feeling as a moral universe'.[15] Brown noted how the great Enlightenment philosophers saw that 'liberty was not at odds with justice or duty but liberty and duty advanced together'. Citing Martin Luther King, Brown spoke of 'an inescapable network of mutuality, together woven into a single garment of destiny'. Brown's belief was that:

> ... even if we are strangers in many ways, dispersed by geography, diverse because of race, differentiated by wealth and income, divided by partisan beliefs and ideology, even as we are different, diverse and often divided, we are not and we cannot be moral strangers for there is a shared moral sense common to us all: call it as Lincoln did – the better angels of our nature; call it as Winstanley did – the light in man; call

it as Adam Smith did – the moral sentiment; call it benevolence, as the Victorians did; virtue, the claim of justice, doing one's duty. Or call it as Pope Paul VI did – 'The good of each and all'.[16]

Where Thatcherism focused on Smith's invisible hand of the pursuit of individual self-interest, as the key to the restoration of an entrepreneur-driven enterprise culture and the creation of a property-owning, share-owning popular capitalism, Brown focused on *The Theory of Moral Sentiments* and Smith's helping hand that matched the invisible hand of his wealth of nations. Brown sought to emphasise Smith's selflessness, in contrast to Thatcherism's self-interested individualism.[17] Brown noted how as he died, Adam Smith:

> ... was writing a new chapter for his *Theory of Moral Sentiments* entitled 'On the corruption of our Moral Sentiments' which is occasioned by 'the disposition to admire the rich and great and to despise or neglect persons of poor and mean condition'.[18]

The importance that Brown attaches to the philosophy of Adam Smith provides insight into his frequent use of the term 'prudence'. What began as a simple concern with being careful in how he spent taxpayers' money has developed into a complex concern with prudence as the expression of moral duty towards others.

In the opening sentence of the first paragraph of Part One of *The Theory of Moral Sentiments*, Adam Smith places sympathy at the heart of his exploration of moral sentiments: 'How selfish so ever man may be supposed, there are evidently some principles in his nature, which interest him, though he derives nothing from it except the pleasure of seeing it'.[19] In the political economy of Gordon Brown, from his specification of the Blair Government's central economic objectives, the moral sentiment and virtue of prudence played a more salient role.[20]

For Smith, there were at least two proper objects of prudence. The lesser of these was 'the care of the health, of the fortune or the rank and reputation of the individual, the objects on which his comfort and happiness in this life are supposed principally to depend'. The superior level of prudence embraced 'wise and judicious conduct, when directed to greater and nobler purposes than the care of the health, the fortune, the rank and reputation of the individual'.[21] While Smith regarded security as 'the first and the principal object of prudence', he regarded the superior prudence of the great general, statesman or legislator, as supposing 'the utmost perfection of all the intellectual and of all the moral virtues'.[22] Prudence is 'the best head joined to the best heart' and, when combined with other virtues, constituted the noblest, for Smith. By the same token, imprudence, combined with other vices, constituted the 'vilest of all characters'.[23]

SYMPATHETIC LIBERALISM: CLAIMING ADAM SMITH FOR THE LEFT

Gordon Brown understood that he could not claim to be a truly prudential politician, in possession of 'the best head joined to the best heart', unless he could reclaim Adam Smith's work from the New Right. On 25 April 2002, Brown chaired an 'Enlightenment Series' lecture at Edinburgh University. The theme was 'Can both the Left and Right claim Adam Smith?', so Brown invited the audience to consider whether Adam Smith would have felt more at home in the left-of-centre Smith Institute (named after the late John Smith MP) or the right-of-centre Adam Smith Institute. That question has been broached in *Radical and Egalitarian: An Interpretation for the Twenty-First Century*, written by a fellow Scot, Professor Iain McLean of Oxford University, in which he sought to set out the case for Adam Smith to be reclaimed by the Left as a radical and egalitarian.

Developing his thesis, McLean argued that the importance of Adam Smith's Scottishness has been understated and that his radical egalitarianism was rooted in the Scotland that he grew up in.[24] By the same token, that could also be said of Gordon Brown. McLean has identified a 'subterranean' theme of his book as 'once a Presbyterian, always a Presbyterian, even if you reject the doctrines of the Church of Scotland'. Adam Smith's tastes for frugality and egalitarianism are 'uncannily similar' to those of Gordon Brown, for 'both the eminent sons of Kirkcaldy are puritanical about ostentation in clothes or tastes. "Prudence" is the favourite word of both'.[25]

The most importance convergence between Adam Smith and Gordon Brown lies not in the realm of their respective characters but in their philosophy and political economy. For any politician, their understanding of market failure (that is, where markets fail to deliver either an efficient allocation or sufficient and affordable supply of vital public goods) will determine where and when they resort to government intervention. McLean has noted how Brown and Smith concur that 'the central question of political economy is where the boundary between the market and the state should lie, in the face of partial market failure'.[26] Indeed, he contends that 'what we might call a social-democratic reading is truest of all to the historical Adam Smith'.[27] This is superior to the New Right's libertarian conservative interpretation because that 'does not acknowledge the depth of Smith's analysis of market failure, nor of his case for redistributive taxation'.[28] For example, Smith's first maxim of taxation anticipated progressive taxation by stating: 'The subjects of every state ought to contribute towards the support of the government, as nearly as possible, in proportion to their respective abilities'.[29] The source of Smith's profound egalitarianism is his focus on the human moral sentiment of sympathy: it is 'our capacity for sympathetic insight into others that allows us to take up the role of impartial spectator towards ourselves'.[30] By reflecting on our own behaviour and how that must appear to other people, we have the capacity not only to liberate ourselves from our own faults but also to identify the condition of others and to offer them a helping hand.

At the root of Smith and Brown's philosophy is their sympathetic liberalism and belief in humans' possession of an innate moral sense. McLean's thesis is that this common philosophical platform has led them to share six main arguments. First, both oppose rent-seeking by vested interests. For Brown, this means that producer interests should not be treated as being synonymous with the public interest. Second, both reject selfishness as the sole motive of human life, reflected in Brown's exploration of the moral limits of markets. Third, both Smith and Brown understand market failure and fourth, have identified the role that the state has to play in correcting it but, fifth, recognise that the state does not have to provide public goods itself. Sixth, Brown shares Smith's four maxims of taxation, announcing that he had them at his side when preparing his 2002 Budget.[31]

The increasing influence of Adam Smith's ideas on Brown's political philosophy and the simultaneously diminishing importance of the Labour Party's tradition of ideas in general and ethical socialism in particular was demonstrated in October 2006 when Brown gave the Donald Dewar Memorial Lecture (a tribute to the former First Minister of Scotland and principal architect of Scottish devolution). Brown used this opportunity not only to chart Dewar's 'rich and complex political legacy' but also to set out his vision for politics and government in the twenty-first century. The common denominator was the central importance of the philosophy of the Scottish Enlightenment. Having made a solitary (and brief) reference to the importance of equality and the work of R. H. Tawney in Dewar's politics, Brown explored at length how the idea of liberty, understood as individual empowerment rather than a narrow selfish individualism, had come alive in the Scottish Enlightenment. Indeed, it had been at Glasgow University, where Dewar had studied, that Adam Smith had delivered the lectures which 'first laid the foundations of a modern moral philosophy and political economy'.[32]

Having located both Dewar's and his own politics firmly within the ideological tradition of the Scottish Enlightenment, Brown now set out his vision for politics in the twenty-first century. His thesis was that:

> If the challenges of the last half of the last century focused on economic instability and prosperity, unemployment and underinvestment in our public services, the major challenges ahead are now also terrorism and security, global economic competition and climate change and meeting the rising aspirations of individuals and the yearning for stronger communities.[33]

These challenges could be met through a partnership which gave equal place 'to the active, responsible citizen, the empowered community and [an] enabling, empowering government working together'. However, this would only be accomplished with the rediscovery of 'our rich culture of rights and responsibilities', by remembering that the state was the servant and not the master of the people and by forging a partnership between 'individual civic society and the institutions of government'. This would be possible for the British people, because their passion for liberty had not degenerated into self-interested individualism; what Jonathan Sacks terms 'a British libertarianism'.[34] On the contrary, that possibility had been denied precisely because of the influence of Adam Smith and the Enlightenment writers. Smith, in *The Wealth of Nations*, stated 'All for ourselves and nothing for other people, seems, in every age of the world, to have been the vile maxim of the masters of mankind'[35] and in *The Theory of Moral Sentiments* (for Brown, Smith's most important book), he showed how 'the helping hand of individuals supporting other individuals' complimented the invisible hand of *The Wealth of Nations*.[36]

In consecutive years, Brown invited both Alan Greenspan, Chairman of the United States' Federal Reserve and Mervyn King, Governor of the Bank of England, to deliver the Adam Smith Memorial Lecture in Kirkcaldy,

Smith's birthplace and Brown's home town. Ironically, Greenspan used his lecture to emphasise the legacy of Smith's 'invisible hand' and its importance for 'the relative economic stability we experience daily' rather than Brown's 'helping hand' interpretation of Smith's moral sentiments.[37]

King closed his lecture by announcing that Adam Smith was to be the new face on the Bank of England's £20 note; Smith's portrait duly appeared on the new issue of 13 March 2007.[38] This action – and its timing – was deeply symbolic. Not only was Adam Smith the first Scotsman to appear on a Bank of England note but he appeared just one week before Brown was to deliver his eleventh (and probably final) Budget statement. Even greater political symbolism lay in the fact that Smith's image replaced Edward Elgar's. Not only is Elgar widely regarded as the quintessential English composer but also his *Pomp and Circumstance March No 1* is the setting for the words of *Land of Hope and Glory*; the theme often used at sporting events, such as the Commonwealth Games, as an unofficial English national anthem. Elgar's replacement came in the year of the 150th anniversary of his birth, which prompted an Early Day Motion for his reinstatement in the House of Commons. However, Brown stood firm: two Unionist sons of Kirkcaldy triumphed over an icon of English national identity.

THE RE-MORALISATION OF BRITAIN

Adam Smith's work has become increasingly influential on Gordon Brown's agenda for both domestic economic and social reform and his approach to tackling global poverty. However, a second vital philosophical datum point for the calibration of his moral compass is the work of the Chief Rabbi, Jonathan Sacks. References to Sacks's *The Politics of Hope* and, more recently, *The Dignity of Difference* have littered Brown's speeches and Sacks's thesis of the moral dimension of politics and the market economy resonates, with increasing power, with Brown's sense of moral duty.[39] Sacks argues that the dominant concepts of a free society, the liberal and the libertarian, have shared the ideal of 'an arena in which the state guarantees the freedom of the individual to realise his or her own choices'. It has been assumed both that 'morality has no part to play in politics beyond fair procedures and the transparency and accountability of governments' and that therefore 'morality itself is a purely individual concern'.[40]

For Sacks, it is evident that social order has failed and has instead delivered social disorder. The alternative is to restore a liberal order and a civil society which rest on covenantal moral relationships arising from families, friends and citizens rather than governments. Salvation lies in a re-moralisation of society through a 'politics of hope' that will develop 'a public language of shared values rather than private claims' to enable people to identify the goods which we hold in common.[41]

This is precisely the public language of shared values in which Brown has attempted to articulate his 'British Way' (see Chapter Five). The world of self-interested individualism, in which morality is privatised and relationships defined in terms of contracts and vested interests, must be rejected and replaced with a stronger recognition by society of the importance of covenantal obligations, in which the moral component is exercised through loyalty and fidelity to one's family, friends and community and the voluntary associations which constitute the basis of civil society.[42]

In *The Dignity of Difference*, Sacks addressed a question at the heart of Brown's politics: globalisation. Sacks's thesis is that the politics and economics of globalisation possess 'an inescapably moral dimension', because both create problems and both raise issues that cannot be resolved by either one alone.[43] Sacks's proposal for the resolution of such matters is a covenant of hope based on recognition of 'the dignity of difference'.[44] The free market is acknowledged as 'the best means we have yet discovered for alleviating poverty and creating a human environment of independence, dignity and creativity'. However, Sacks held that the market 'has done more than open up extremes of poverty and wealth. It has subverted other institutions – families, communities, the bonds that link members of a society to a common fate'.[45]

In conditions of 'maximal uncertainty' and reflecting Brown's increasing emphasis on the importance of moral sense and moral sentiments, Sacks asserted that human behaviour should be guided by six simple moral principles: control, contribution, creativity, co-operation, compassion and conservation. These six are the prelude to a seventh: the 'new global covenant of human solidarity',[46] which would serve as an overdue corrective to the demoralisation of society during the past half century, which has signalled 'both a loss of moral meanings and a loss of hope'.[47]

The way forward in political economy, for example, is to make the moral case for the market economy, recognising that 'mankind was not created to serve markets. Markets were made to serve mankind'.[48] By exploring the moral dimensions of the market in a global age, it will be possible for us to identify 'the values that should guide us if we are to create a more humane world'. For Sacks, 'the ethical imperative is ubiquitous and non-negotiable. Beyond every "is" lies the claim of "ought" '.[49] This is precisely what Brown is attempting domestically in his 'British Way' for politics and internationally in his 'global New Deal' promises. By drawing on the insights of Enlightenment thinkers, Brown is seeking to expose the moral dimensions of contemporary markets and the moral sentiments that can help to create a more humane world.

Sacks's moral political economy has likewise drawn on the work of Enlightenment thinkers such as David Hume and Adam Smith. In *The Dignity of Difference*, Sacks cited Smith's famous observations in *The Wealth of Nations* about the invisible hand to highlight the fact that 'markets work on the basis of self-interest rather than altruism'.[50] Nevertheless, for Sacks 'The very act of market exchange is the supreme embodiment of the idea of the dignity of difference' because, as long as everyone has something to contribute, the division of labour and Ricardo's *Law of Comparative Advantage* will ensure that 'everyone gains through the contribution of others'. (David Ricardo was another Enlightenment thinker. His theory of comparative advantage argued that 'by specialising in producing and trading those goods for which they have greater cost advantage, nations and their populations maximise their access to wealth and welfare'.[51])

In short, the market offers 'the paradigm of the win-win scenario and the non-zero-sumness of human relationship', which in turn has 'not merely economic but moral and spiritual consequence'.[52] The best hope for avoiding conflict and war is to engage in market exchange because 'Unlike the battlefield, the market is an arena in which both sides can win'.[53]

Jonathan Sacks has provided Gordon Brown with an important moral justification for the market and his advocacy of trade liberalisation and deregulation as the key to human development (see Chapter Six). Rather than basing his political economy on questions of efficiency of allocations and individual self-interest, Sacks's work seeks to base future human exchange on the basis of a covenant and not a contract. Unlike a contract, a covenant is 'not limited to specific conditions and circumstances'; it is 'open-ended and long-lasting [and] not based on the idea of two individuals, otherwise unconnected, pursing personal advantage. It is about the

"We" that gives identity to the "I" '.[54] Gordon Brown's 'war against poverty', Global New Deal and International Finance Facility are simply Sacks's proposal of a global covenant transposed onto the global international stage.[55] For Brown: 'What is morally wrong cannot be economically right' and so we must move 'from economics to morality, from enlightened self interest that emphasises our dependence on the other to the true justice that summons us to our duty'.[56]

CIVIC SOCIETY AND THE MORAL LIMITS OF MARKETS

For Gordon Brown, the key to giving further effect to the moral sentiments of Adam Smith's 'helping hand' and Jonathan Sacks' 'politics of hope' is the restoration of civic society. Giving the Hugo Young Memorial Lecture in 2005, Brown noted how 'it was Britain and British ideas that led the way into the modern world by focusing on benevolence, improvement, the civic society and the moral sense as necessary for social progress'.[57] Brown wants to restore these qualities to British society but they can only be realised through families, voluntary associations, churches, faith groups and public service. Brown claimed that: 'we, the British people, have consistently regarded a strong civic society as fundamental to our sense of ourselves – that moral space, a public realm in which duty constrains the pursuit of self-interest'.[58]

Brown's childhood in Kirkcaldy taught him the value of the 'network of civic society'. Speaking at the National Council for Voluntary Organisations' (NCVO) conference in 2000, he described how a town with strong community and voluntary organisations at its heart could make people 'feel they belonged and, in turn, could contribute, as part of an intricate network of trust, recognition and obligation'.[59] The free and co-operative association in civic society which Brown wishes to promote is based on the Scottish Enlightenment philosophers' concept of moral sense, that is, 'a set of moral sentiments of dispositions that all human being possess in common': human sociability as 'a shared feeling of mutual sympathy'. The British way 'is not to exalt self-interested individualism but throughout the centuries to foster a uniquely rich and continuously-evolving relationship between individual community and state, a strong vibrant civil society where there is opportunity for all'.[60]

In another lecture in 2000, the Arnold Goodman Lecture, Brown argued that responsible citizenship meant 'respect for order, family and responsibility with agreement to pursue the values of civic society and a shared sense of social purpose'.[61] To the NCVO, he stated that the most important aspect of civic society is that it is not a contract, that is, 'a deal based on self-interest and sustained through the external force of law' but rather a covenant; 'an agreement that is morally based and internally sustained, through shared values, common purposes and mutual obligations'.[62] From this, in Brown's perspective, two key consequences follow:

> ... the new covenant – and the society it leads to – will be one in which we extend opportunity and demand responsibility in return [and] the outcome will be an active civic engagement, not a passive civic obedience, restoring the principles of voluntary and community action to a central social place.

Brown wants people to give 'active social expression to our shared moral impulses to sympathy, fairness, self-control and duty', to exercise the personal responsibility which he claims was ignored by 'the social engineering of the old left'.[63]

The problem with Brown's vision of civic society is that it sits very uneasily with the emphasis on competition and the pursuit of risk, profit and innovation in liberalised markets that are at the heart of the British model of political economy (see Chapter Three) – a model that has encouraged active and contractual individual entrepreneurship and consumerism. Civic society is also difficult to reconcile with (and to a significant degree contradicts) the Treasury's nationalisation of policy design and resource allocation in England (see Chapter Four), which has actively discouraged covenantal citizenship. On the one hand, Brown has sought to promote the virtues of voluntary action because of its four great practical strengths: its local character, its greater flexibility to innovate, its individual, personal approach and its capacity to strengthen citizenship. Because contemporary social problems would not lend themselves to 'a standardised, uniform, one-size-fits-all solution or to an impersonal approach', Brown claimed that the state has had to devolve power to 'those organisations that have the deepest local knowledge and the broadest capacity for innovation and the greatest experience in the one-to-one approach'.[64] On the other hand, the devolution of political power has by-passed England, where eighty-five per cent of the United Kingdom's citizens live.

The political legacy of Brown's decade at the Treasury was a postcode lottery for citizenship and civic society. For his fellow Scots, the re-establishment of the Scottish Parliament enabled Scotland's rich tapestry of voluntary associations to interact with a new forum holding devolved and autonomous political power with which civic society and the extension of active democratic citizenship worked in partnership.

His legacy to England was very different. He stated, in July 2000, that he believed a new relationship was taking shape between the individual, communities and government: 'Call it a giving age, active citizenship, call it community – it is Britain becoming Britain again'.[65] In 2005, to the *Volunteering* conference, Brown again outlined his vision of Britain as a civic society: 'Call it community, call it civic patriotism, call it the giving age or call it the new active citizenship, call it the great British society – it is Britain being Britain'.[66] However, Brown failed to explain why, in the other constituent nations of the United Kingdom, 'new active citizenship' meant the devolution of political power to democratically-elected institutions but in England, the political framework for voluntary action and civic society must be of passive citizenship, administrative devolution to unelected and locally unaccountable bodies and micro-management in accordance with the priorities of the biennial Spending Reviews and Public Service Agreements.

In Brown's political philosophy, one of the key functions of civic society is to impose limits on markets, referring to Michael Sandel's identification (in the Tanner Lecture series *What Money Can't Buy*) of the 'moral limits of markets' as 'the dimensions of life that lie beyond consent, in the moral and civic goods that markets do not honour and money cannot buy'.[67] Sandel identified what money cannot buy by distinguishing two reasons why market valuation and exchange should not be extended to certain areas of life. First, 'when people buy and sell things under conditions of severe inequality' market exchanges are not necessarily voluntary. Coercion might arise when, for example, someone living in poverty has to sell a kidney to feed their family. Second, if certain moral or civic goods are bought and sold for money, the resulting market exchange and valuation has a degrading effect on those goods and practices. Sandel illustrated this moral limit to the market using the example of prostitution which, while it may not be illegal, is inevitably morally degrading for the prostitute. Furthermore, the excessive role for markets in important aspects of public life will have a corrupting impact on citizenship as defined by the republican tradition, whose particular concept of citizenship argues that 'to be free is to share in self-rule, i.e. citizens' freedom depends on their capacity to participate in shaping the forces that govern their collective destiny'. However, to exercise that freedom, citizens must first 'possess or come to acquire certain qualities of character or civic virtues'.[68]

This aspect of Sandel's thesis on the moral limits of markets is particularly interesting for Brown's concept of citizenship. Sandel noted that citizenship may be defined in liberal terms, which emphasise 'toleration and respects for the rights of others' or in republican terms, in which it aims:

> ... to cultivate a fuller range of virtues, including a moral bond with the community whose fate is at stake, a sense of obligation for one's fellow citizens, a willingness to sacrifice individual interests for the sake of the common good and the ability to deliberate well about common purposes and ends.[69]

For Brown, who regards politics as a moral duty, the republican concept of citizenship is much closer to his own, even though the core elements of his 'British Way' and the values and virtues of the national character he has identified include the virtues of tolerance and respect for the rights of others.

From Sandel's perspective, the problem with Brown's political legacy is that, through market-driven reforms of public services, it has extended the role of markets into certain aspects of public life yet has simultaneously diminished English citizens' self-rule by denying them the political devolution that would enable them democratically to participate in shaping the forces that govern their collective destiny. In 1999, at the Smith Institute, Brown spoke of a transition from 'an over-centralised and uniform state – the old Britain of subjects – to a pluralist and decentralised democracy – the new Britain of citizens'.[70] However, that commitment has long been abandoned.

In defining the limits to markets, Brown cited *Spheres of Justice*, the work of the political philosopher Michael Walzer, in which Walzer developed the notion of 'blocked exchanges' to denote those aspects of life which money cannot buy and where market exchanges cannot represent value, for example, the sale of human beings as slaves, freedom of speech and political and civil rights.[71] Brown also noted how in his book *Equality and Efficiency*, the economist Arthur Okun saw that 'the market needs a place and the market needs to be kept in place'.[72] Okun's thesis for policy-makers was that government needs the market-place as both a support, to provide the tax revenue to finance public services and as a counterweight, to check and balance the centralised power of the state. At the same time, the market needs government to make and enforce property rights and the rule of law and to provide the human and physical infrastructure.[73]

Okun's emphasis on the role of markets as check and balance highlights a further, salient, aspect of Brown's emphasis on civic society. In all his major speeches on this topic, Brown has drawn almost exclusively on comparisons with and examples from the United States. He has cited John Dilulio, who served in the first term of George W. Bush's administration as Director of the White House's Faith-Based and Community Initiatives, President Kennedy, in his instigation of the Peace Corps, President Clinton's AmeriCorps, President George W. Bush's Freedom Corps,[74] the 'superb' www.mentoring.org website and corporate giving through 'Business Strengthening America'.[75] Brown has quoted Robert Kennedy and mentioned his own late father's belief in Martin Luther King's words that 'everybody could be great because everyone can serve'.[76] For Brown's philosophy, the apposite point about the United States is that there, individuals and civic associations operate within the democratic framework of a written constitution, in which centralised political power is heavily checked and balanced. Democratic citizenship therefore operates, as it does in Scotland, in parallel with civic society. Brown's legacy to England is to have operated as Chancellor and Prime Minister for more than a decade without similar constitutional checks and balances on his political power.

BROWN'S COMMON GROUND WITH THE NEW RIGHT

As Gordon Brown's personal political philosophy has become increasingly distant from the history of ideas of the Labour Party and ever more dependent on liberal political thinkers, so he has moved ever closer to the ideological foundations of the New Right. In particular, he has moved on to philosophical ground shared not only with Margaret Thatcher and Keith

Joseph but also with the contemporary neo-conservatives whose ideas have informed the policies of George W. Bush's administration. A conspicuous feature of Brown's speeches in recent years is his increasing use of quotations from prominent American conservative commentators, philosophers and historians.

When Brown gave the first Donald Dewar Memorial Lecture in 2006, he cited the prominent conservative commentator, David Brooks, writing in an article for the *New York Times*:

> If the big contest of the twentieth century was between planned and free market economies, the big questions of the next century will be understanding how cultures change and can be changed, how social and cultural capital can be nurtured and developed, how destructive cultural conflict can be turned to healthy cultural competition.[77]

Citing a commentator from the Right in a lecture dedicated to an eminent colleague and friend from the Left was in itself extraordinary and the choice of Brooks particularly interesting. Brooks had been on the liberal Left of American politics until 5 April 1983, when he participated in a televised debate with Milton Friedman, doyen of the New Right. As Brooks later recalled, this encounter was his road to Damascus moment in his conversion to the political ideology of the Right because 'The show was essentially me making a point and he making a two-sentence rebuttal which totally devastated my point and then me sitting there with my mouth hanging open, trying to think what to say'.[78] Brown's intellectual conversion may not have been as sudden as Brooks' but he too appears to have undertaken an equally significant philosophical odyssey.

In his quest to reintroduce morality into the British political conversation, Brown has cited the work of the American conservative philosopher, James Q. Wilson. For Brown's political philosophy, Wilson's *The Moral Sense* provides an important further and direct connection to the Scottish Enlightenment through its exploration of the sources of moral sentiments: 'human nature, family experience, gender and culture'.[79] Wilson also furnished a comprehensive analysis of the four aspects of the moral sense: 'sympathy, fairness, self-control and duty'.[80] Brown wants to bring these four qualities to British politics, both through his own example and by virtue of the policies he wishes to implement. For example, he entitled his speech to the 2005 Labour Party annual conference 'Politics as a moral duty'.

In this particular speech, Brown acknowledged his personal moral compass, set by what his parents had brought him up to believe. His lodestone was not only 'to do my best and to work hard but to treat everyone equally, to respect others, to tell the truth, to take responsibility' but also to understand that 'for every opportunity there was an obligation, for every demand a duty, for every chance given a contribution to be made'. Having identified the importance to his politics of a moral sense, Brown identified the Labour Party's moral cause: 'that every child has the best start in life, that no one is left behind ... a vision that defines us as a community and as a country inspires a new sense of mission'.[81] Moral sentiments could thus be linked directly to the continuing project of national renewal and with Brown's redefinition of Britishness.

James Q. Wilson portrayed his thinking as 'a continuation of work begun by certain eighteenth-century English and Scottish thinkers, notably Joseph Butler, Francis Hutcheson, David Hume and Adam Smith'.[82] The particular importance that Brown attached to this work was demonstrated when he spoke at the 2006 Cheltenham Literature Festival. Asked whether he had found wisdom or inspiration in any contemporary novel, Brown responded that the sole contemporary influence on his work had been Wilson's *Moral Sense*, because of its emphasis on the importance of shared communal bonds and values to modern life.[83] In the Pope Paul VI Memorial Lecture in 2004, Brown had asserted that Wilson had 'so brilliantly' described the moral sense as 'a small candle flame flickering and spluttering in the strong winds of passion and power, greed and ideology'.[84]

Given his desire to fashion a New British Enlightenment, it is perhaps not surprising that Brown should admire a political philosopher who has argued that 'we all live in a world shaped by the ambiguous legacy of the Enlightenment'.[85] However, what will surprise socialists and social democrats in general, and Labour Party politicians in particular, is that Brown aligns his personal moral compass by reference to the ideas of a man so intimately connected with the American Right. These links are reflected not only in Wilson's position as Ronald Reagan Professor of Public Policy at Pepperdine University, California but also his role as the Chairman of Academic Advisors to the free-market American Enterprise Institute. Awarding Wilson the Presidential Medal of Freedom in July 2003, George W. Bush described him as 'the most influential political scientist in America since the White House was home to Professor Woodrow Wilson'.[86]

Wilson's purpose in *The Moral Sense* was 'to help people recover the confidence with which they once spoke about virtue and morality'.[87] This means engaging in an age-old war, 'a cultural war, a war about values': a war in which Brown wishes to engage as the basis of his 'hearts and minds' security and foreign policies against international terrorism (see Chapter Eight). For Wilson, moral sense means 'an intuitive or directly felt belief about how one ought to act when one is free to act voluntarily (that is, not under duress)',[88] defining 'ought' as 'an obligation binding on all people similarly situated'.[89] In choosing 'sympathy, fairness, self-control and duty' as his four examples of moral sense, Wilson wished to challenge what he portrayed as the 'fatally flawed assumption of many Enlightenment thinkers, namely, that autonomous individuals can freely choose or will, their moral life'.[90]

As an alternative, Wilson sought to identify those aspects of moral life that are universal and refined in the crucible of parent-child and extended relationships among families and peers. This led him to the conclusion that moral sense entails 'a network of commitments that we have and that we share with others' and which includes loyalties to 'our towns and teams, our nations and people [which] transcend the costs and benefits of daily transactions'.[91] This vision accorded closely with Brown's personal experience of community and civic associations while growing up in Kirkcaldy. Wilson's thesis was that, in many of the ideologies of the nineteenth and twentieth centuries, the idea of commitment had been replaced by the idea of choice. However, Wilson concluded that the freedom people want 'is not unconstrained choice; it is rather the opportunity to express themselves, enrich themselves and govern themselves in a world that has already been organised and defined by a set of intuitively understood commitments'.

Wilson dismissed the idea of 'autonomous individuals choosing everything – their beliefs and values, their history and traditions, their social forms and family structures' as vainglorious.[92] Wilson found solace from individual autonomy over values and morality in the insights of the Enlightenment thinkers' notion of sympathy as an 'innate sensitivity to the feelings of others' and the idea that 'The natural sociability of mankind gives rise to sentiments of sympathy, fairness and reciprocity in every culture that we can imagine'.[93] Each person's 'moral sense, however weak or imperfect, helps explain social order because that sense grows out of, and reflects, the fact that we are social beings, dependent on one another'.[94] Brown has placed precisely these qualities at the heart of his definition of the values and character of Britishness (see Chapter Five).

Brown focussed on Wilson's concept of character, which Wilson defined as the 'distinctive combination of personal qualities by which someone is known (that is, a personality) and moral strength or integrity'.[95] Brown's is the Aristotelian vision of becoming virtuous by the practice of virtue, by practice rather than precept, an habitual morality. In this regard, Brown also cites the work of another American academic, Joseph Campbell, who focussed on the importance of heroes and myths for the contemporary world. In *The Power of Myth*, using the example of Martin Luther King, Campbell defined a hero as 'someone who has given their life to something bigger than themselves'.[96] For Campbell, the importance of myths is that they help put the mind in touch with the rapture of being alive, providing 'clues to the spiritual potentialities of the human life'.[97] They also offer 'life models' but these have to be 'appropriate to the time in which you are living'.[98]

For Campbell, the contemporary world has unfortunately become demythologised but nevertheless it needs 'myths that will identify the individual not with his local group but with the planet'. Campbell's model is the thirteen colonies that, through the Declaration of Independence, decided to act together in the national interest against their British colonial rulers.[99] Campbell claimed that when the United States belatedly entered the First World War, it cancelled that Declaration and 're-joined the British conquest of the planet'.[100] For Campbell, myths serve four functions: mystical, cosmological, sociological and pedagogical. While the mystical and cosmological might not be important to the politics of Gordon Brown, the sociological and pedagogical clearly are. The sociological function of myths is 'supporting and validating a certain social order' while their pedagogical function is to teach people 'how to live a human lifetime under any circumstances'.[101]

In his political philosophy, Brown is attempting to create the myth of Britishness (see Chapter Five), to support and validate the social order of modern British society. He has sought to turn Enlightenment thinkers, notably Adam Smith, into heroes and draw on Smith's moral sentiments to teach the British people how to live their lives under different circumstances. Recently, in his book *Courage: Eight Portraits*, Brown identified exemplars and icons whose personal belief and moral purpose enabled 'these people of courage' to be 'driven and sustained by higher ideas'.[102] What is particularly interesting about Brown's selection is that none of the people of courage emanated from the Labour Party or the wider Labour movement. Indeed, the only politicians included in the group are Martin Luther King, Robert Kennedy, Nelson Mandela and Aung San Suu Kyi.

David Brooks and James Q. Wilson are not the only prominent American conservative philosophers who have been praised in Brown's speeches. He has also paid fulsome tribute to Gertrude Himmelfarb and her book, *The Roads to Modernity*.[103] Brown identified with Himmelfarb's analysis because she, like him, sought to reclaim the philosophy of the Enlightenment and restore it to the British, who helped create it. An intriguing aspect of Brown's praise for Himmelfarb is that much of her academic work has drawn attention to the nineteenth-century British morality that helped inspire Margaret Thatcher's belief in Victorian values.[104] Himmelfarb is also a significant figure, ideologically, by marriage: her husband is Irving Kristol, one of the principal architects of American neo-conservatism.[105]

In *Roads to Modernity*, Himmelfarb sought to identify the three 'alternative approaches to modernity, alternative habits of mind and heart, of consciousness and sensibility' pursued by Britain, the United States and France.[106] These differences could be attributed to a variety of factors, notably:

> ... the very different political characters of the countries and the relationship of classes within these political systems; the nature and authority of the churches and their role in the state; economies at various levels of industrialism and subject to different kinds and degrees of government regulation; and all the other historical and social circumstances that were unique to each country and helped to shape its temper and character.[107]

Himmelfarb asserted that the British approach was based on moral philosophers who were sociologists, being 'concerned with man in relation to society, they looked to the social virtues for the basis of a healthy and humane society'. In contrast, the American approach was based on an attempt to furnish 'a new "science of politics" ' that would establish the new republic on a sound foundation of liberty. The French chose an alternative third approach, making 'reason the governing principle of society as well as mind, to "rationalise", as it were, the world'.[108] Himmelfarb depicted the British approach as a non-revolutionary, reformist 'sociology of virtue', characterised by a social ethic and moral sense, compared to the American 'politics of liberty' and the French 'ideology of reason'.

Himmelfarb noted how many of the Scottish moral philosophers of the Enlightenment chose to identify themselves as 'North Britons' rather than as Scots. David Hume, for example, changed the spelling of his name from the Scottish 'Home' to the Anglicised 'Hume'.[109] Other important Enlightenment thinkers were English, notably John Locke, Isaac Newton and the Earl of Shaftesbury.[110] Therefore, it would be more appropriate to describe them all as thinkers of the British rather than the Scottish Enlightenment. This aspect of Himmelfarb's thesis is the most pertinent to the development of Gordon Brown's 'British Way', since he too has sought to emphasise his British, rather than his Scottish, identity. Furthermore, Himmelfarb claimed that the distinctive feature of the political economy of the British Enlightenment was its basis in moral philosophy. Adam Smith advocated capitalism for the sake of economic, civil and religious freedom rather than for the sake of monetary gain and 'by far the most important effect of commerce: its civilising, moderating and pacifying effect on peoples and societies'.[111] This too accords with Brown's interpretation of Smith's work and his moral defence of capitalism and the virtues of the City of London.

Himmelfarb concluded that Adam Smith's moral vision of political economy currently characterises the United States.[112] This is a further source of its appeal to Gordon Brown; by basing his political philosophy on the moral sense and sentiments of Adam Smith, he is now able to justify his advocacy of trade liberalisation, his 'New Atlantic' foreign policy and his past work at the International Monetary Fund (conducted in partnership with the United States Treasury), in terms of a shared philosophical platform (see Chapter Six).

Intriguingly, in her Epilogue, Himmelfarb also noted that Margaret Thatcher, who revived the notion of Victorian values, could have gone back further, to Adam Smith and the moral philosophers, to discover the moral sense that was 'the genesis of those values and that gave then an undeniably social character'.[113] Thatcher and Sir Keith Joseph in fact did this, drawing extensively on both *The Wealth of Nations* and *The Theory of Moral Sentiments*. This serves to illustrate the philosophical and political bedfellows Gordon Brown has risked having to share with in aligning his moral compass so firmly to the philosophers who inspired the New Right. His key challenge as Prime Minister is to win the battle of ideas in British politics, by persuading people that Adam Smith's true legacy is the 'helping hand' of government, rather than the pursuit of selfish individualism more redolent of David Cameron's liberal conservatism (see Chapter Eight).

CONCLUSION

When Gordon Brown began his political career his moral compass was firmly aligned to ethical socialism and the development of a withering critique of capitalism based on a moral sense passed on by his parents. Brown is now an equally adamant advocate of the market economy and, in particular, the liberty and opportunity open markets offer for the fulfilment of individual potential. Brown's political philosophy has evolved from supply-side socialism via supply-side liberalism to its current sympathetic liberalism. The constant element throughout this political and philosophical odyssey has been Brown's moral sense and commitment to politics as a moral duty. However, rather than looking to R. H. Tawney and the English ethical socialist tradition for his political ethics, Brown has turned to the moral sentiments of Adam Smith and the thinkers of the Scottish Enlightenment.

Like his predecessors Margaret Thatcher and Tony Blair, Gordon Brown has attached great importance to winning the battle of ideas in British politics as the prerequisite for the successful implementation of his modernisation agenda. Also like his predecessors, liberalism will provide the primary ideological underpinning to his politics, maintaining a long-standing tradition in British politics. The liberalism of John Maynard Keynes and William Beveridge provided the platform on which the full employment and welfare state of the post-war First Way settlement was built. When the efficacy of that settlement was challenged in 1976 by the Callaghan Government and then largely dismantled by the 'Second Way' of Thatcherism, liberalism was once more harnessed to traditional Conservative values. When Tony Blair's 'Third Way' succeeded the eighteen years of Conservative rule, it placed its faith in the capacity of liberalism, entrepreneurial initiative and market competition to reform the United Kingdom's ailing public services.

Brown's New British Enlightenment has launched a fourth 'British Way' of modernisation, which draws on the liberalism of the moral sentiments of Adam Smith.

These moral sentiments are the political legacy of the three phases of Gordon Brown's philosophical odyssey. In Parts Two and Three, I shall explore their impact on Brown's domestic and foreign policy choices.

PART II

Gordon Brown's Domestic Policy Agenda

Chapter 3

The British Model of Political Economy

INTRODUCTION

Economic policy is the most important dimension of Gordon Brown's political legacy: his credibility as successor to Tony Blair was based on his record as the prudent 'Iron' Chancellor of the Exchequer for the whole Blair Government decade. The essence of Brown's appeal, both to the Labour Party and to the electorate as a whole, is of a political heavyweight, who has succeeded in delivering a decade of stability, prudence and prosperity.

This legacy can be contrasted with that of Brown's Labour predecessors, whose failure allowed the Labour Party to be cast as the party of devaluation. Brown, in his 'British Model' of political economy, took important lessons from the failures of the past and delivered an unprecedented decade of growth. More importantly, in the run-up to the next General Election, and with his record set against Brown's economic legacy, David Cameron has been cast as a political novice.[1] Cameron has no experience of serving as a Cabinet minister but does have the dubious record of being a special adviser to Chancellor Norman Lamont at the time of 'Black Wednesday'.

Black Wednesday (16 September 1992) was the day sterling left the European Exchange Rate Mechanism (ERM), as the City of London's financial speculators, led by George Soros, routed Lamont (then Chancellor), the Treasury and the Major Government's 'unassailable' economic policy. It was a national political humiliation, from which the Conservative Party never regained its previous reputation for economic competence.[2]

Ironically, that humiliation marked the onset of the longest period of sustained economic growth in the United Kingdom's modern history.

During his decade as Chancellor, Gordon Brown constructed an institutional and policy model that he and Ed Balls described as the 'British Model'.[3] This model received much praise, especially from abroad. Highlighting its openness and flexibility, the Executive Board of the International Monetary Fund (IMF) welcomed 'the UK economy's remarkable performance that has lasted for more than a decade', while IMF staff reported that 'during 1996–2005, the growth of real GDP [Gross Domestic Product] per capita was higher and less volatile than in any other G7 country'.[4] By July 2007, the UK economy had grown for fifty-nine consecutive quarters, including forty quarters under Brown's stewardship. The Treasury noted that this expansion 'is not only without precedent in the post-war history of the UK but is also the longest on post-war record for any G7 economy and the longest expansion of any OECD country' and it would take 'at least nine years before the UK's current expansion could be eclipsed by another G7 country'.[5] By redefining (three times) the Treasury's official definition of the United Kingdom's economic cycle, so that the previous cycle was both held to have begun in 1997–1998 and to have ended in early 2007, Brown ensured that his time at the Treasury delivered a decade of growth. This encouraged Brown to boast that Britain was experiencing its longest period of sustained growth since the start of the Industrial Revolution and 'since records began in the year seventeen hundred and one'.[6]

In this chapter, I shall outline the principles of Gordon Brown and Ed Balls's British model of political economy and evaluate the extent to which the 'Brown Boom' had delivered prudence and a sustainable prosperity by the time Brown became Prime Minister. When, in May 1999, Brown redefined the role of the Treasury as nothing less than the modernisation of the British economy, he claimed that this broke 'decisively with the short-termist, secretive and unstable record of macroeconomic policy-making of the past two decades by setting a credible framework' for monetary and fiscal policy.[7] It is undoubtedly true that Brown's economic legacy, in terms of stability, is better than that of any of his modern peacetime predecessors as Chancellor. However, I shall also demonstrate that Brown's legacy is equally one of consistent private and increasing public imprudence.

None of the longstanding supply-side weaknesses of the United Kingdom economy, such as under-investment in education, training, transport and communications infrastructure, have been redressed during the 'Brown Boom'. The 'British model' resolved the previous tensions between the interests of industrial modernisation and manufacturing on the one hand and those of the City of London on the other. This resolution was accomplished by simply abandoning the Labour Party's historic and Brown's former commitment to wholesale industrial modernisation through supply-side socialism and casting macro-economic policy decisively in the interests of the City. However, it has not insulated the United Kingdom's economy from instability. On the contrary, as the IMF has noted, by encouraging the United Kingdom economy to become even more closely linked to global financial markets, the 'British model' increased the vulnerability of the United Kingdom economy to global risks and contagion.[8] Moreover, rather than rejecting the core tenets of Thatcherism, Brown, with all the zeal of a convert, embraced and celebrated entrepreneurship and the merits of economic development through risk-taking, market liberalisation and deregulation. The passionate socialist critic of the market has been transformed into the Labour Party's most vocal champion of capitalism.

THE ROLE OF THE TREASURY

The Treasury lies at the heart of the British model of political economy and has frequently been at the centre of the narrative of British decline. It has been held to have subordinated long-term investment in the United Kingdom's industrial success to the short-term political expediency of 'stop-go' or 'boom-bust' economics, with artificially inflated periods of economic growth timed to coincide with General Election campaigns. The Treasury has been accused of possessing 'a contempt for production', of being part of a 'core institutional nexus' (with the Bank of England and the City of London) at the heart of British society which has been held to have frustrated consecutive state-led modernisation programmes.[9] Under previous Labour Governments, the Treasury oversaw sterling's departure from the Gold Standard in 1931 and damaging sterling crises and devaluations in July–August 1947, September 1949 and November 1967. The ultimate humiliation occurred in September 1976 when a Labour Chancellor of the Exchequer applied to the IMF for $3.9 billion (then the largest credit ever extended by the IMF) to finance the UK's balance of payments crisis and the repayment of short-term credit.

Although the Treasury has retained its historic role as the guardian of the public finances and the guarantor of monetary stability, the 'British model' of political economy defined a new mission for the Treasury: the modernisation of the British economy. In Brown's definition, the Treasury was to be 'not just a Ministry of Finance but also a Ministry working with other departments to deliver long-term economic and social renewal'.[10] In practice, working with other departments has meant the Treasury exercising an unprecedented degree of control over the design of policy and the allocation of resources through the Treasury-led biennial Spending Reviews, ten-yearly Comprehensive Spending Reviews and the Public Service Agreements. However, because of devolution to elected institutions in other parts of the United Kingdom, the 'British model's' political power has only been exercised in England, where no such constitutional checks and balances operate on Treasury power (other than in London).

The economic policies of the Macdonald, Attlee, Wilson and Callaghan Labour Governments were undermined by the constraints on domestic modernisation programmes generated by the global commercial interests of the City of London. Attempts to create modernising agencies to rival the Treasury, notably the Department of Economic Affairs and Ministry of Technology in the 1960s and the National Enterprise Board in the 1970s, led to conflict regarding the Treasury's domination over economic policy. This reached its zenith in the failed social revolution of the National Plan, when the Wilson Government attempted to fashion 'a state of competitive existence' between the Treasury and the newly-created Department of Economic Affairs (DEA), led by George Brown, but actually only delivered an economic strategy based on 'two diametrically opposed policies'. As early as 1971, George Brown suggested that 'Some Government, some day, will re-create a department on the lines of the DEA and limit the out-dated authority of the Treasury'.[11]

Gordon Brown deliberately did not follow George Brown's 1960s model. Rather than limiting the authority of the Treasury by creating an alternative focal point for economic modernisation, he made modernisation the remit of the Treasury. Its power was strengthened and deepened. By establishing the Treasury as the pilot agency of the state of British development, the 'British model' surmounted the creative tension that once existed between rival economic departments in Whitehall. And by ceding responsibility for monetary policy to the Bank of England's Monetary Policy Committee (MPC), the Treasury was given the space and opportunity to intervene, in a way unprecedented in peacetime, in economic and social policy (see Chapter Four). The creation of the MPC made possible the new developmental role for the Treasury. The domestic modernisation programmes of previous Labour Governments had been undermined by inflation and devaluation. Freed of these constraints, the elite of the bureaucracy at the Treasury identified and selected the sectors of the United Kingdom economy to be developed: the City of London's financial and commercial services, the property market, defence and aerospace manufacturing and science-based industries (notably pharmaceuticals and biotechnology).

In these sectors, the 'British model' sought to develop market-improving methods of state intervention and administrative guidance and to supervise competition in accordance with the principles of Brown and Balls's doctrine of 'constrained discretion'. As the price that had to be paid for maintaining economic stability, this doctrine limited the freedom of public spending bodies in England to determine their own policy choices and to allocate their resources as they saw fit. The 'British model' imposed centrally-determined policy choices and decisions about resource allocations on hospitals, schools and local authorities in England.

Because of the Blair Governments' large parliamentary majorities after May 1997 and their proclivity for policy to be designed in Whitehall by unelected committees of technical experts (most notably the Monetary Policy Committee), the Treasury has operated in a political system that has given it latitude to operate as the lead agency of British modernisation.[12] The Treasury has operated as a pilot, using a mix of powers to steer policy design and resource allocation in England, by-passing (with the exception of Greater London) the process of creating elected, devolved institutions that now operate in the other constituent territories of the United Kingdom and constrain the Treasury's power there.

DEVISING THE 'BRITISH MODEL': THE ROLE OF ED BALLS

It is important to understand Brown's economic legacy as a 'British model' of political economy, rather than the narrower notion of a 'British model' of economic policy. The model embraced a particular understanding of the appropriate relationship between and respective roles for the state and market. The 'British model' is based on the fatal conceit of being able 'not only to support but positively enhance markets'. Brown's closest economic advisers have contended that 'markets are a powerful means of advancing the public interest'.[13] Markets can be made to work better by manipulating the behaviour of the private market to act for the general public good, in the manner that previous Labour governments sought to orchestrate nationalised industries, trades unions and the other components of the architecture of the public domain. Like his predecessors as Prime Minister, Margaret Thatcher and Tony Blair, Brown cast his model in terms of a free economy accompanied by a strong state, prepared to defend the commercial interests of corporations, both at home and abroad.[14]

The British model was driven by the Treasury and devised by Brown in partnership with Ed Balls (appointed Secretary of State for Children, Schools and Families in June 2007 and formerly Economic Secretary to the Treasury). As Brown's Economic Adviser from 1994 to 1999 and Chief Economic Adviser to the Treasury from 1999 to 2004, Balls was not only Brown's closest confidant but also a major influence on Brown's thinking about economic policy. No other individual was as influential in shaping the political economy of both Gordon Brown and New Labour during the decade of the Blair Governments. It was Balls who provided Brown with an analysis of the failure of macro-economic policy under both Labour and Conservative Governments and during the era of both the post-war social democratic 'First' and Thatcherite 'Second Ways' of British modernisation. This analysis shaped the agenda for economic policy that later was to be termed (by Balls) the 'British model' of stability and prudence. The model provided Brown with an alternative economic policy to United Kingdom participation in the Euro and placed fiscal prudence at the heart of domestic economic policy.

Gordon Brown and Ed Balls first met in October 1992, at Brown's instigation.[15] Within two months, Balls had published a pamphlet, through the Fabian Society, in which he identified the agenda for national economic policy which was to shape much of Brown's subsequent economic strategy for the next decade. Balls' thesis was that Britain had suffered 'a misguided and ultimately unsustainable bout of economic self-destruction' for the second time in little more than a decade. Leaving the ERM on Black

Wednesday had torn off its 'fig leaf' and exposed 'the vacuum of ideas and institutions at the heart of British economic policy-making'.[16] Balls filled that ideological and institutional vacuum by firmly rejecting the 'European brand of monetarism' that had been implemented by the ERM. He wanted Labour to offer 'a break from the past' and in particular the 'dangerous and unworkable' economic implications of the Maastricht Treaty, specifically the 'economically and politically misconceived project' of monetary union, in its envisaged form and under the declared timetable. The central lesson from the ERM debacle was that 'Britain's European monetary commitments must be complementary to, not an excuse for the absence of, a credible national economic policy'.[17] The British model would furnish the requisite credibility.

For Balls, if the United Kingdom economy were simply to go for growth, by slashing interest rates and loosening fiscal policy, this, in the absence of institutional reform, would be 'a recipe for disaster'. Not only had individuals and institutions been discredited by the events of recent years but 'the entire theory and practice of UK economic management'.[18] An alternative economic strategy was needed, pursuing macro-economic stability, set within a European framework but drawing on a range of other important policies to stimulate 'balanced, industry-orientated growth and full employment'.

Delivering this model needed two prerequisites: first, 'a transparent, accountable and predictable monetary policy', that would permit sterling to re-enter the ERM without the need for the Government to pledge not to devalue the pound and second, 'a medium-term industrial strategy', that emphasised both the direct responsibilities of government, (that is, fiscal policy, public infrastructure and education) and its indirect role in fostering profits, investment and higher living standards for all.[19]

The first element of Balls' alternative economic strategy required 'active macro-economic management', that is, lower interest rates and higher public investment as a remedy for recession and rebuilding confidence not the 'Old-style Keynesianism' of short-term government borrowing and tax cuts which 'pursued for too long, simply leads to high and rising inflation, unwieldy fiscal deficits and finally damaging recessions'. To avoid boom-bust cycles and achieve low and stable inflation, economic growth and full employment, administration of monetary policy would have to be taken away from the Treasury because 'no one had mastered the art of boom-bust economics better than the Treasury'. Balls considered that the power of the Treasury remained absolute and that 'This degree of centralised and unaccountable executive and bureaucratic power over economic policy [was] inefficient and out of date'.[20] This was quite a statement from a man who later, as the Chancellor's Chief Economic Adviser, wielded unprecedented, unaccountable, centralised and bureaucratic power until his election to Parliament at the 2005 General Election.

Balls's remedy for macro-economic instability was 'a carefully reconstituted and statutorily-controlled central bank, empowered to pursue low and stable inflation'. The Bank would have a number of characteristics. First, the Bank's decision-making council, appointed by government, should include representatives from industry and the unions as well as the City of London. Second, the Bank should answer directly to Westminster; its Governor giving regular testimony to House of Commons committees. Third, although autonomous, it would administer a monetary policy approved by the House of Commons, which would have the power 'to override a decision by the Bank in extreme circumstances'. However, the Bank should not be responsible for supervising the City of London's financial markets. This arrangement would deliver 'a transparent, accountable and predictable monetary policy', providing, most importantly, credibility and meaning for the subsequent 'British Way' and 'British model' of political economy, that 'a Labour chancellor would be free to concentrate on the many other aspects of policy'.[21]

LEARNING THE LESSONS OF THE PAST

A central feature of the 'British model' is that claims to have learnt vital lessons from the mistakes made by previous British governments. The central conceit of the model is that, unlike its predecessors, it has managed to identify a successful formula for reconciling domestic economic, social and political modernisation with the constraints of global financial markets and the need to maintain the United Kingdom's international competitiveness. Globalisation has been used as a political weapon to justify important changes in domestic and social policies and to discipline popular expectations of what the role of the state should be. The cost of significant areas of public welfare (notably pensions) have increasingly been transferred from the state, the corporation and the general taxpayer to the individual. Like Thatcherism before it, Brown's model identified the unfettered capitalism of the City of London, the liberalised markets for property and financial services and the consumer demand driven by those sectors as the key agents of economic modernisation. When Brown first entered Parliament, the Labour Party had based its electoral strategy on becoming the 'Party of Production' in contrast to the Conservative 'Party of the City': Brown's legacy is to have based his 'British model' on the City and the services sector rather than manufacturing industry and predominantly consumer rather than producer interests.

The 'British model' learnt one important lesson learnt from past British economic mismanagement: politicians and policy-makers paid insufficient attention to economics when making key decisions. This was true of Churchill's disastrous return in April 1925 to the pre-1914 'gold standard' of global fixed exchange rates backed by gold reserves, in which the pound sterling was set at its pre-1914 level of $4.86. This decision eventually led, in 1931, to the Labour Party being labelled the 'Party of Devaluation'. It was also true of the Attlee Government's decision, in 1946, to re-enter sterling into a fixed exchange rate system with the dollar set at the pound's pre-war rate of $4.03. The Wilson Government was equally culpable in its 1964 decision to reject devaluation, only to be forced into it in November 1967, resulting in deflation, rising unemployment, fiscal retrenchment and the resignation of James Callaghan from the Chancellorship. From Balls's perspective, too little economics also led to the Major Government's decision to withdraw an over-valued pound from the ERM on 'Black Wednesday', having ushered in the longest recession since 1945.[22]

Giving the Ken Dixon Lecture, at the University of York in 2004, Balls declared the 'British model' to be 'post-monetarist', because of monetarism's mistaken foundation on the discretionary fine-tuning of the macro-economy, based in turn 'on an assumed long-term trade-off between unemployment and inflation'.[23] In Brown and Balls's opinion, Milton Friedman proved as long ago as 1968 that an expansionary monetary policy and fiscal policy could not deliver, let alone sustain, full employment.[24] The monetarist model had 'collapsed intellectually and empirically'; its failure, both in continental Europe and domestically in the pre-1993 ERM, was because of its 'inflexibility in prioritising low money supply growth as the route to low inflation and growth', just when the liberalisation of capital markets and innovation in financial products was undermining the seemingly stable relationship between the growth of the money supply and inflation. A means had to be found to deal with the problem of 'time inconsistency', that is, the temptation to make a dash for short-term growth at the expense of long-term stability.[25] The British model claimed to have resolved that matter and made 'a decisive step forward to a credible model of macro-economic policy-making in Britain' through Bank of England independence and the introduction of a Code for Fiscal Stability.[26]

EMPOWERING THE TREASURY THROUGH 'CONSTRAINED DISCRETION'

In 1997, in his first major announcement as Chancellor of the Exchequer, Gordon Brown identified the central economic objectives of the Blair Government to be 'high and stable levels of growth and employment', which would be achieved by rebuilding 'British economic strength with a modern industrial base, high levels of investment and a culture of entrepreneurship'.[27] These objectives were couched in terms of a reaffirmation of a commitment made in the May 1944 White Paper *Employment Policy*: the acceptance 'as one of their primary aims and responsibilities the maintenance of a high and stable level of employment after the war'.[28] Brown contended that a new paradigm of monetary and fiscal policy was needed to achieve these goals.[29] The policy needed to escape from 'the short-termism of the past' and the economic instability that had characterised the British economy for most of the twentieth century, basing its break-out on 'the solid rock of prudent and consistent economic management, not the shifting sands of boom and bust'.[30] Long term commitments to monetary stability, fiscal stability, higher levels of investment in people and businesses, far-reaching modernisation of the welfare state, free trade and 'constructive engagement' with Europe were needed.[31]

From the outset, Brown and Balls based their 'British model' on the principle of 'constrained discretion'; the key to policy-making 'in a modern open economy'.[32] 'Constrained discretion' meant limiting the freedom of agents and institutions, especially those spending taxpayers' money, so that they could not undertake any actions that would undermine or challenge the priorities of the Treasury's economic policy agenda. The Treasury's vital insight was that:

> ... the discretion necessary for effective economic policy – short-term flexibility to meet credible long-term goals – is possible only within an institutional framework that commands market credibility and public trust with the government constrained to deliver clearly defined long-term policy objectives and with maximum openness and transparency.[33]

For Balls, the ERM failure demonstrated that the stability and low inflation required to realise and sustain high and stable levels of growth and employment would not be achieved by adhering to destabilising 'fixed and intermediate policy rules'.[34] As an alternative, constrained discretion would limit the capacity to destabilise macro-economic policy and performance by requiring policy-makers to deliver long-term objectives through institutional arrangements. In return for this commitment, policy-makers would benefit from 'the maximum operational flexibility that is consistent with achieving that goal [of stability]'.[35] Constrained discretion would be credible through aligning policy-makers' incentives with long-term objectives: flexibility, through the devolution of operational responsibility for decision-making to front-line agents and transparency, through both the provision of clear, precise and publicly-stated objectives and the regular reporting of agents' performance against their objectives.

Constrained discretion placed particular importance on the principle of credibility in policy-making: 'the elusive elixir of modern macro-economics'.[36] The then chief Economist (and later Governor of the Bank of England), Mervyn King, noted how credibility was 'a question of whether announced intentions are believable'. This was a matter of trust but markets were naturally suspicious, given the propensity of politicians to manipulate economic policy for short-term advantage. For King, credibility was:

> ... not an all or nothing matter. Policy is neither credible nor incredible but rather a continuous variable. Therefore, because the current behaviour of economic agents would depend on their expectations about the future actions of monetary authorities, the key to credibility for the British model would be the maxim. 'Say what you do and do what you say'.[37]

The vital lesson Balls learnt from the ERM debacle was that because the globalisation of international capital markets was 'the most significant change in the world economy', it was evident that 'the power of "the markets" is always and everywhere' and would 'immediately punish any government which strays from the macro-economic straight and narrow'.[38]

From Brown and Balls's perspective, basing their British model on the principle of constrained discretion had two huge political advantages. First, it legitimised constraints on the freedom of policy-makers and other actors, including those in receipt of public expenditure, as dictated by their commitment to institutional arrangements and policy objectives prescribed by the Treasury. Second, it simultaneously legitimised a division of labour whereby Brown, Balls and other elite Treasury officials were able to design policy and determine resource allocation at the centre, while those in charge of delivering public goods and services were responsible for administering policy priorities as dictated by the demands of constrained discretion. Policy design was effectively nationalised, through the Treasury's biennial Spending Reviews and attendant Public Service Agreements and thereby became increasingly divorced from administration in the delivery of public services, with major implications for policy, performance and, above all, democratic accountability in England (see Chapter Four).

Despite Brown's assertion that 'old command and control systems of management are not the way forward',[39] constrained discretion had engineered a top-down, technocratic, highly-centralised and Treasury-driven approach to domestic economic and social modernisation that would become one of the definitive features of policy-making under New Labour.

THE 'BRITISH MODEL' OF MONETARY POLICY

The principle of constrained discretion was applied first to monetary policy. This too was an area where the British model learnt lessons from past experience. During the 1970s, the final decade of the post-war social democratic 'First Way' of British modernisation, annual inflation averaged thirteen per cent, peaking at nearly twenty-seven per cent in August 1975, during Dennis Healey's tenure as Chancellor of the Exchequer . During the 1980s, the era of the Thatcherite 'Second Way', annual inflation averaged seven per cent (compared with three per cent in Germany and five per cent in the United States), peaking in the early 1990s at more than nine per cent. This meant that between 1980 and 1997 the United Kingdom's economy suffered the second highest annual average inflation rate among the Group of Seven (G7) industrialised economies, with only France and Italy suffering greater variability.[40]

The 'British model' derived four key lessons from this experience. First, Britain had suffered from poor institutional arrangements: correct monetary policy should be a stabilising force for the economy. Second, monetary policy had been based on a fundamental misunderstanding about the relationship between inflation and unemployment: unemployment could be cut by stimulating demand, albeit with the trade-off of higher inflation. In practice, any reductions in unemployment had been temporary and inflation had accelerated. Third, because monetary policy decisions had been taken by politicians, this fostered the suspicion that decisions were based on short-term political expediency rather than the long-term interests of the economy. Fourth, because monetary policy decisions had been taken in secret, there had been a lack of transparency, with little or no explanation for the conduct of policy.[41] To rectify these parallel deficits in effectiveness and transparency, one of Gordon Brown's first major policy announcements, in May 1997, was the aforementioned transfer of responsibility for meeting the Government's monetary policy objectives to a newly established Monetary Policy Committee (MPC) of the Bank of England. The Committee would be responsible for honouring the Labour Party's manifesto commitment to match the Major Government's inflation target of 2.5 per cent or less.[42]

Constrained discretion would be achieved through three policies: first, sound long-term objectives, through a symmetrical inflation target (requiring the MPC to respond when the inflation rate was too low, as well as too high). Such symmetry would avoid any deflationary bias and would not target both inflation and the short-term exchange rate.

Second, a commitment to credible institutional arrangements, through a division of labour in economic policy: the Government would set the broader economic strategy and objectives for monetary policy and the MPC would take the monthly decisions on how to meet the Government's inflation targets. Since the MPC would be composed of the Governor and four executives of the Bank, plus four members appointed by the Chancellor and with a non-voting Treasury official in attendance, its operational independence would be very heavily constrained. Not only (given the Chancellor's influence over the appointment of Governor) would the

Treasury effectively appoint a majority of the MPC but the presence of the non-voting Treasury official would ensure that the Chancellor was fully briefed by someone not distracted by the responsibility of voting. Co-ordination of monetary and fiscal policy and the capacity to respond to sudden events would be achieved through an 'Open Letter' system. Where inflation was one per cent higher or lower than the Government's target, an open letter would be sent by the Governor of the Bank of England to the Chancellor accounting for the divergence and explaining what remedial action would be taken.[43]

Third, monetary policy would have maximum transparency, through the publication of both the minutes of the monthly meetings and of the votes of the members of the MPC.[44] However, the publication of individual voting patterns would inevitably lead to certain MPC members being cast as 'doves' or 'hawks' depending on their preparedness to adjust interest rates to meet the Government's inflation target.

On 10 December 2003, Gordon Brown confirmed that the new infla-tion target for the MPC would no longer be based on the Retail Price Index (RPIX). Instead, the MPC would be required to set monetary policy to achieve a target of two per cent inflation, measured by the annual increase in the Consumer Price Index (CPI). If inflation were to deviate by more than one per cent from this target, the MPC would be required to send an open letter of explanation to the Chancellor.[45]

This change apart, Brown's legacy to monetary policy is to have main-tained macro-economic stability. The Treasury has claimed during the decade from 1997–2007, 'the UK has enjoyed more stability in terms of GDP growth and inflation than in any decade since the war'. This is reflected in the fact that:

> ... inflation, on the RPI measure, has remained within a range of ¾ to 4¾ per cent over the past ten years, compared with a range of 1 to 11 per cent in the 1990s, 2½ to 22 per cent in the 1980s and 5 to 27 per cent in the 1970s.

The Treasury has also pointed to 'the longest period of sustained low infla-tion for the past 30 years' and (Japan excepted) lower average inflation in the United Kingdom for the past decade than any other G7 economy.[46]

However, in abandoning the RPI (X) measure of inflation, in favour of the CPI-based system, the 'British model' excluded the cost of mortgage interest payments from its calculations. This meant the official calculation of inflation excluded the major item of expenditure for the majority of households in the United Kingdom. These payments were a principal source of inflation during the housing boom of the 1980s and 1990s, when the rise in average house prices far outstripped the rise in the general cost of living. This meant that June 2007, when Gordon Brown succeeded Tony Blair as Prime Minister, according to the Office for National Statistics (ONS), while CPI annual inflation had fallen from 2.5 per cent in May 2007 to 2.4 per cent in June, RPI (X) inflation had risen from 4.3 per cent in May to 4.4 per cent in June, reflecting the 0.25 per cent rise in mortgage interest rates during May. Even if mortgage interest payments were excluded from the calculation of RPI (X) annual inflation, at 3.3 per cent in June 2007, this was still 0.9 per cent higher than the Brown Government's own calculation.[47] In effect, the Government claimed political credit for a measure of inflation that bore little relation to the true price increases affecting individuals and households in the real economy. The ONS also said that the 'British model' gave 'the MPC the flexibility to respond decisively to unexpected economic events over recent years'.[48] It also meant that during his tenure as Chancellor of the Exchequer, Gordon Brown enjoyed unprecedented power over the conduct of domestic policy.

Brown's decision to set up the MPC has had two important effects: first, unlike his post-war Labour predecessors (Sir Stafford Cripps, James Callaghan, Roy Jenkins and Denis Healey) whose respective periods at the Treasury witnessed the sacrificing of modernisation programmes on the altar of sterling crises, devaluation, public spending cuts and trades union unrest, Brown was not preoccupied with the macro-economy and the immediate responsibility for administering monetary policy. Second, having been freed of the responsibility for setting interest rates, Brown had the time and policy space to intervene in many areas of domestic policy not previously thought to be within the Treasury's compass. This nationalisation of policy design and resource allocation had been implemented through the new fiscal policy framework, the second element of the 'British model' of political economy.

THE 'BRITISH MODEL' OF FISCAL POLICY

Gordon Brown's fiscal policy inheritance when he entered the Treasury in May 1997 was the failure to control public spending during the 'First' and

'Second Ways' of British modernisation. For example, during the Wilson Governments, public spending increased from 38.1 per cent of GDP in 1964–1965 to a post-war record of 49.5 per cent of GDP in 1975–1976. Furthermore, despite the Thatcher and Major Government's rhetorical ambition to roll back the frontiers of the state, from 1978–1979 and 1996–1997 the average annual real growth in public spending had been 1.9 per cent, driven upwards by, for example, a 3.1 per cent average annual increase in health spending.[49] There had been a rise in net government debt from 31 per cent of GDP in 1988–1989 to 44 per cent of GDP in 1996–1997[50] and the tax burden, as a share of GDP, had risen slightly from 34.25 per cent to 36.25 percent.

However, although the UK's tax burden in 1997 was greater than that of either the United States or Japan, Britain remained 'a strikingly low-tax country', especially when compared with its European competitors.[51] In the run-up to the 1997 General Election, Brown's predecessor as Chancellor, Kenneth Clarke, pledged to impose on public spending an austerity policy without precedent in post-war history; limiting the planned average annual real percentage growth in public spending to just 0.4 per cent in 1996–97 and 1999–2000. This would have had severe implications for vital areas of public service, notably the health service, where spending between 1997–98 and 1999–2000 was planned to increase by an annual average of only 0.6 per cent.[52]

From this experience, the 'British model' derived two key lessons for fiscal policy. First, it should take a prudent approach, adjusting for the economic cycle and building in a margin for uncertainty. Second, policy should be open and transparent, to be achieved by setting stable fiscal rules and clearly explaining fiscal policy decisions.[53]

Speaking at the Lord Mayor's Dinner (to the City of London) in 1997, Brown declared that the first principle of constrained discretion, sound long-term objectives, would be imparted to fiscal policy by two fiscal rules. First, the so-called 'golden rule'; over the economic cycle the Government would borrow only 'to finance public investment and not to fund public consumption' and second, the 'sustainable investment rule'; the United Kingdom's net debt as proportion of GDP would be kept 'at a prudent and sensible level' over the economic cycle.[54] The 'golden rule' was later defended as 'a clear rule based on widely accepted and internationally agreed accounting principles'. It was conceded that a better measure of inter-generational equity (how the burden of taxation would be divided between current and future generations of taxpayers) would have been a 'balance sheet' approach to borrowing and spending; monitoring indicators such as net worth. However, according to Ed Balls, this approach would not have been feasible at the time because of many technical and methodological issues.[55]

The 'British model' had chosen to follow a rule which committed it, unlike its predecessors, not to borrow money to finance current expenditure (for example to spend on welfare benefits) but only to borrow for capital investment in new infrastructure and building projects. This potentially gave a dangerous hostage to fortune because, as the experience of the Major Government during the early 1990s had demonstrated, the onset of a deep recession might lead to significantly lower levels of revenue and demand significantly higher levels of spending to pay for unemployment benefit and the maintenance of effective demand in the national economy. The strength of the recovery from recession might not be sufficient to absorb the increases in taxes needed to generate compensatory budgetary surpluses to counteract the earlier borrowing. Furthermore, in the run-up to a General Election, voters might not be attracted by the merits of fiscal discipline when public services urgently needed money. The principal political advantage of the 'golden rule' was left to the Treasury to define the precise duration of the 'economic cycle'. Consequently, it might be possible for New Labour to extend or abbreviate the cycle to create the most favourable scenario for meeting the 'golden rule'.

In relation to the sustainable investment rule, Brown and Balls chose to commit the Blair Government to maintaining debt below forty per cent of GDP in each year of the economic cycle. There was no particular reason to select this specific. They could equally well have chosen thirty-eight per cent or forty-two per cent. The Maastricht convergence criteria for participation in the EMU (Economic and Monetary Union) had set a level of net debt at sixty per cent of GDP, so when New Labour took power the United Kingdom already enjoyed one of the lowest figures for net debt among industrialised economies. That low debt level was a tribute to two decades of privatisation and massive under-investment in the public services and the national infrastructure (as anyone who regularly travelled by train or used the NHS during the early 1990s could have testified). Consequently, it might have been argued that, in the face of such long-term neglect, the

'British model' should have been less conservative in its plans for increased public sector capital investment.

Gordon Brown also planned to increase the role of the Private Finance Initiative (PFI) and Public–Private Partnerships (PPPs) in total capital investment. Paradoxically, on the capital markets the Government could borrow to finance investment at a lower interest rate than the private sector. Adhering to the sustainable investment rule threatened both to brake the capacity to modernise the crumbling national infrastructure and unnecessarily to inflate the cost of modernisation, by a superfluous reliance on private sector investment which, as railway privatisation had already demonstrated, might never materialise. Furthermore, the Blair Government inherited a situation in which the Major Government's post-ERM controls of public spending and buoyant tax revenue from consecutive years of economic growth made both fiscal rules eminently achievable, even before the Blair Government committed itself to the Major Government's planned austerity policy on public spending for 1997–1998 and 1998–1999.

The efficacy of the rules-based approach may have been exaggerated by both Balls and Brown. As the Institute for Fiscal Studies (IFS) suggested, 'Both are reasonable rules of thumb but neither has particularly firm analytical or statistical foundations as defined operationally ... the direct economic importance of strictly obeying the rules as defined has been overstated'.[56] The problem with such rules was that they led Gordon Brown

> ... to stake his credibility on predictions or premises that rely on an unrealistic degree of forecasting accuracy [placing] a rhetorical weight on strictly meeting his definition of the rules that neither their theoretical nor statistical foundations can reasonably be expected to bear.[57]

For example, the Treasury predicted in the 2005 Pre-Budget Report that the golden rule would be met by a cumulative surplus of only £12.8 billion over the twelve-year economic cycle which would conclude in 2008–2009. However, as the IFS demonstrated, the Treasury's average absolute error in forecasting just one year ahead in public sector net borrowing averaged twelve billion pounds (at 2005–2006 prices) during 1977–1978 to 2004–2005.[58] Moreover, since one of the principal motivations of the golden rule was to achieve inter-generational fairness in the distribution of the costs and benefits of taxation and expenditure, there was no obvious rationale for achieving a budget surplus, as opposed to a budget balance, since a surplus would appear unduly to penalise the current generation of taxpayers. Nor was it clear why fiscal policy should not embrace a similar degree of transparency and delegation as monetary policy through the transfer of responsibility for providing official tax revenue forecasts to an independent agency.[59]

In applying the second principle of constrained discretion to fiscal policy (commitment to credible institutional arrangements), Brown and Balls considered whether to duplicate the role of the MPC in monetary policy and create an independent fiscal committee to adjudicate on questions of taxation and expenditure. However, according to Ed Balls, this option was ruled out because 'the wider political complexity of fiscal policy making – the different impacts that the different levers have on a range of different objectives of which stabilisation is only one – would have implied a politically unsustainable break with UK parliamentary tradition'.[60] However, this argument could also have been made about passing operational control over interest rates to the MPC, since monetary policy could be said to have an impact on a range of objectives other than price stability, notably the international competitiveness of manufacturing industry and the United Kingdom's balance of payments position.

To address the third principle of constrained discretion (credibility through maximum transparency), the 'British model' introduced the 'Code for Fiscal Stability'. The Code specified how the five principles of the Government's fiscal policy (transparency, stability, responsibility, fairness (including between generations) and efficiency) would relate to its formulation and implementation. The Code would require fiscal policy to adhere to clearly stated objectives and rules, have its underlying key assumptions independently audited and its issues regularly and openly reported. Although the Chancellor of the Exchequer would continue to make the key decisions in fiscal policy, in 2004, Ed Balls explained the Treasury would also publish full five-year forecasts for the public finances, twice-yearly statements of the economic and other underlying assumptions informing public finance projections, the government's estimates of the output gap and cyclically adjusted fiscal aggregates so that progress against the fiscal rules could be assessed across the economic cycle and an end of year fiscal report and long-term public finance report, which would furnish a detailed analysis of the long-term projections for public finances over the next fifty years.[61]

The final element of the rules-based British model of fiscal policy was the year-long Comprehensive Spending Review (CSR), incorporating no fewer than thirty zero-based reviews, not only of departmental spending plans but also their objectives and policies. The CSR was to be followed by three Biennial Spending Reviews, before a second CSR. This innovation in fiscal policy particularly signified the manner in which Gordon Brown took an iron grip on the conduct of domestic economic and social policy, a grasp not seen in earlier peacetime Chancellorships (see Chapter Four). Monetary policy had been insulated from manipulation for short-term political gain but fiscal policy was more politicised. The ability of the rules-based approach to deliver prudence and credibility would largely depend on the precise definition of the economic cycle over which the fiscal rules had to be met.

The credibility of the British model was undermined by Gordon Brown's politically-inspired redefinition of the economic cycle on three occasions. In July 2005, it appeared that Brown would not meet his first golden rule (not to borrow to finance current government spending over the economic cycle). He used an appearance before a Select Committee (of the House of Commons) to announce, without warning, that the Treasury had calculated that the economic cycle had started in 1997–1998, not in 1999–2000 as had previously been claimed.[62] Had Brown gone by the earlier definition of the economic cycle, he would have broken his golden rule by £5.5 billion, because of the £15.1 billion deficit on the current budget recorded in 2005–2006. Brown announced a second unanticipated redefin-ition of the economic cycle in December 2005, extending the economic cycle by three years, coming to an end in 2008–2009.[63] Once more, the rede-finition appeared to be little more than a political convenience to ensure that Brown met his golden rule. Brown completed a hat-trick of unan-nounced redefinitions of the economic cycle a year later, when in his 2006 Pre-Budget Report statement he announced that the end of the economic cycle (which the 2006 Budget had confirmed at 2008–2009), would be early 2007.[64] This neatly defined the economic cycle as coinciding precisely with the beginning and (anticipated) end of Brown's Chancellorship and thereby enabled him to claim that his economic legacy to Britain was unbroken economic growth.

Brown's politically-driven redefinitions of the economic cycle meant that the golden rule of fiscal policy was met (according to the IFS) with a margin of around £11.6 billion (0.1 per cent of GDP).[65] As the Treasury noted: 'the introduction of strict fiscal rules and clear objectives for fiscal policy have put the public finances on a more sound and sustainable footing than in previous economic cycles' and that a surplus of 0.1 per cent of GDP for the current cycle was 'in contrast to the last cycle's average deficit of 2.0 per cent of GDP and the 1977–78 to 1986–87 cycle's average deficit of 1.8 per cent of GDP'.[66] This performance appears less creditable, if we remember that, in his 2001 Budget statement, Brown confidently forecast that the budget would be in surplus to the tune of £118 billion over the economic cycle. By the time of his (pre-election) 2005 Budget, the forecast surplus had decreased, to only five billion pounds. The IFS estimated that around one quarter of this fiscal deterioration was the result of policy decisions to increasing spending but the remainder reflected unexpected weakness in tax revenues.[67]

The problem with the British model of fiscal policy is that it delivered only short-lived fiscal prudence. Brown's initial austerity policy reduced public spending to 37.7 per cent of GDP in 1999–2000, its lowest level since 1960–61. Having been in deficit by only £1.4 billion (0.2 per cent of GDP) during his first year in office, the budget produced surpluses from 1998–99 until 2000–01(artificially buoyed by the £22.5 billion raised from the auction of mobile phone licences). Brown's fiscal prudence delayed substantial new investment in the public services, especially health and education, until after the publication of the 2000 Spending Review. However, it did enable him to reduce public sector net debt, as a share of national income, from 43.6 per cent of GDP in May 1997 to 31.3 per cent by the 2001 General Election. By contrast, during the Blair Government's second term, Brown's increasing fiscal imprudence led to public sector net debt rising by 3.7 per cent to 35.0 per cent of GDP by the 2005 General Election. Further deterioration has seen net debt rise to £515.9 billion or 37.5 per cent of GDP by the end of June 2007.[68]

In 2007, the IFS judged Brown's fiscal legacy to Alistair Darling, his successor as Chancellor, to be four-fold. First, he increased public spending from 40.8 per cent of GDP in 1997–1998 to 42.0 per cent in 2007–2008, about £25.0 billion in cash terms. Second, during the same period he increased receipts by about 2.8 per cent of GDP, about £39.6 billion. Third, he reduced net borrowing by around 1.1 per cent of GDP, about £14.6 billion. Fourth, he reduced net public debt by 5.4 per cent of GDP, around £74.4 billion.[69]

This golden legacy was soon to rapidly dissipate. His third redefinition of the economic cycle, abbreviating the current economic cycle by two years, enabled Brown to engineer a small surplus on the cycle, at the expense of starting the next economic cycle with two years that witnessed major current budget deficits.[70] This meant Alistair Darling would have much greater difficulty in meeting either the Golden Rule, or the Sustainable Investment Rule. In the event, as Chapter Eight explains, Darling chose to suspend both fiscal rules in the face of rapidly deteriorating public finances.

THE TRIUMPH OF THE CITY

One of the most distinctive features of the British model of political economy was its abandonment of the Labour Party's long-standing commitment to state-led industrial modernisation. The British model increasingly chose instead to champion the interests of the City of London. Brown claimed that a 'new industrial policy' had replaced 'the old centralisation of national champions, picking winners or offering special subsidies to loss makers, with a level playing field for all'.[71] In practice, Brown's industrial policy was to continue the practice of picking winners. Indeed, he picked precisely the same winners as the Thatcher and Major Governments before him: the City of London and the financial services sector; the property market, defence manufacturing, civil aerospace; and pharmaceuticals. Each of these was supported by major policy initiatives, institutional innovation or large-scale subsidies. At the same time, the British model attempted to bridge the long-standing productivity gap between the United Kingdom economy and its major competitors through a series of interventions, driven by Brown's supply-side liberalism.

The abandonment of manufacturing was the only element of Ed Balls's December 1992, post-ERM analysis that was not incorporated into the British model. The second element of his alternative economic strategy was the adoption of a medium-term industrial strategy', as a counterweight to the Conservatives' previous medium-term financial strategy. Balls claimed that sustainable growth and full employment would not be achieved without a manufacturing and export-led recovery, brought about by a macroeconomic platform and supported by the micro-economic management of laws, regulations and taxes to foster dynamism and enterprise to ensure that 'individual actions serve the public interest'.[72] Balls thus framed one of the definitive characteristics and potential flaws of the future British model; the belief that state intervention could manipulate private market agents such as entrepreneurs and corporations (as if they were public sector agencies) to change their pattern of behaviour from short-term under-investors to long-term investors.

In his analysis, Balls took the inspiration for his 'non-monetarist alternative' from Australia, asserting that 'the Australian experience [of the 1980s] should be a model for what must happen in the UK'.[73] In the 1980s, the Australian Labour Party won five consecutive General Election victories (in 1983, 1984, 1987, 1990 and 1993) first under Bob Hawke and then, from December 1991, under Paul Keating's leadership; it did not lose office until 2 March 1996. The Labour Administration negotiated a Prices and Incomes Accord through a series of corporatist arrangements: the National Economic Summit Conference, the Tax Summit, the Economic Planning Advisory Council and the Australian Labor Advisory Council. Balls contended that the Australian example recognised 'the need to put profits and investment before higher real wages and built a public consensus around the need to do so'.[74]

For Balls, economy-wide wage restraint was a prerequisite for the success of a medium-term industrial strategy. To implement this in the United Kingdom, four steps would be necessary. First, a consensus, embracing public and private employers and the unions and endorsed by both the Confederation of British Industry and the Trades Union Congress, to deliver 'the kind of wage inflation that is needed to boost profits, investment and jobs'.[75] Second, the creation of a Council of Economic Advisors to provide independent advice to industry, the unions and the electorate about sustainable rates of pay inflation and the damage that would arise from high settlements. Third, an independent Central Bank to pay – and announce that it was paying – specific attention to the rate of inflation in average earnings when setting monetary policy. Irresponsible pay settlements would be rewarded with higher interest rates. Fourth, a return to the ERM (but only when German interest rates had fallen), to provide an external discipline on pay.[76]

In terms of the viability of this alternative strategy for state-led industrial modernisation, Balls conceded that the United Kingdom's history of statutory incomes policies was far from encouraging and that the problem of short-termism might well run too deep.[77] The desire to cast off, once and for all, the image of being the party of devaluation had not yet been accompanied by a similar desire to distance the Labour Party from the demise of the Social Contract in the 1979 'Winter of Discontent'. However, by the time Gordon Brown became Chancellor, the idea of a medium-term industrial strategy had been abandoned. There would not be a return to the corporatism of beer and sandwiches at Number 10. The British model would reduce expectations and discipline wage inflation in the public sector through an initial freeze on wages, dictated by the austerity policy of public spending during the Blair Government's first two years in office. Wage discipline would be imposed on the private sector through the threat of higher interest rates, playing on workers' increasing indebtedness and exposure to large-scale mortgage borrowing.

Gordon Brown and Ed Balls picked the City of London as the key winner to be backed. For the British model the City has provided the most tangible evidence of the benefits to innovation and entrepreneurship brought about by meeting the challenges of globalisation with a policy approach based on competition, liberalisation and deregulation of markets. In June 2006, at the Lord Mayor's Dinner, Brown proclaimed:

> The message London's success sends out to the whole British economy is that we will succeed if like London we think globally. Move forward if we are not closed but open to competition and to new ideas. Progress if we invest in and nurture the skills of the future, advance with light touch regulation, a competitive tax environment and flexibility. Grow even stronger if this is founded on a strong domestic market built on the foundation of stability.[78]

Brown (and Balls) admitted that financial and business services accounted for only twelve per cent of the national economy and 1.1 million jobs across Britain but London was celebrated as, paradoxically, the home of twenty per cent of cross-border lending, thirty per cent of world foreign exchange turnover, forty per cent of the over-the-counter derivatives market and seventy per cent of the global secondary bond market.[79] The major beneficiaries of the British model were the leading United Kingdom banks, whose 2006 net earnings totalled more than forty billion pounds.[80] Previous Labour Chancellors regarded the City as the class enemy, likely to undermine the prospects of domestic modernisation by serving as the catalyst for balance-of-payments' and devaluation crises but Brown paid homage to this global centre of casino capitalism. He asserted that 'we can demonstrate that, just as in the nineteenth century industrialisation was made for Britain, in the twenty-first century globalisation is made for Britain'.[81]

Also speaking in the City of London in 2006, Balls paid fulsome tribute to the liberalisation and deregulation of the City of London by the Thatcher Government's 'Big Bang' of late 1986. He also pointed to how much of the Treasury's work during Brown's early years as Chancellor was devoted to the creation of a new, independent and unified regulator, the Financial Services Authority, to redress the City's critical competitive weakness: a 'fragmented, overlapping, burdensome, self-regulatory system'. Although civil manufacturing (with the notable exception of aerospace and pharmaceuticals) was left to compete without significant state intervention, Balls argued that 'we cannot take London's status for granted'.[82]

Consequently, Brown established the Chancellor's High Level Group of leading City financiers to work in partnership and 'ensure the continued global success and competitiveness of UK financial services'.[83] The first meeting of the Group was attended by Lord Aldington, Chairman of Deutsche Bank; ironically, the previous Lord Aldington, a year before the 'Big Bang' celebrated by Balls, had chaired a House of Lords' Committee that had warned the Thatcher Government that there was the possibility of 'a major social and economic crisis in our nation's affairs in the foreseeable future', if national attitudes and policy in Britain towards trade and manufacturing did not change radically.[84] The 'British model' chose to ignore such warnings and abandoned the modernisation of civil manufacturing for the Labour Party to become the 'party of the City'.

THE SUPPLY-SIDE FAILURE

The 'British model' has not altogether neglected manufacturing, for the Blair Government continued the long-standing tradition of large-scale state financial assistance to the aerospace industry. Despite British Aerospace (BAe) and Rolls-Royce being highly profitable trans-national corporations, under Brown the Treasury sanctioned £980 million of repayable launch investment for the Airbus A380 'super-jumbo' aircraft. Despite this subsidy, the Treasury refused to intervene in BAe's later sale of its twenty per cent stake in the Airbus consortium, a commercial decision that has threatened the long-term future of civil aircraft manufacturing in Britain. BAe chose to concentrate on the defence sector which, during Brown's tenure, remained the manufacturing sector receiving the largest public investment. In December 2005, the Blair Government published its Defence Industrial Strategy, setting out its vision for the United Kingdom's future defence requirements and the industrial capacity that would be needed to procure the equipment needed. Other than in the realms of the City of London and the warfare state, it would be unthinkable for the 'British model' to sanction such large-scale state intervention.

The extent of the failure of the model to redress any of the long-standing supply-side weaknesses of the United Kingdom economy was demonstrated by the fact that Ed Balls contended that, for the Brown Government, 'raising skills levels is the central economic challenge of the next decade'.[85] This raised the question of what the Treasury had been doing to address these issues from 1997 to 2007. According to the IFS, business investment in the United Kingdom had been a paradox in recent years: on the one hand, corporate profitability and company balance sheets appeared 'unusually healthy' on the other, investment expenditure appeared anaemic, despite the cost of capital being low and pre-tax real rates of return on corporate capital (both net and gross of depreciation and relative to net or gross capital employed) being 'close to 40-year highs'.[86] During 2006, business investment fell by 4.7 per cent and had only grown by a paltry 3.25 per cent in 2005.[87] Leading analysts described this performance as 'disappointing'.[88] Investors continued to prefer to exploit the freedom offered by the City of London's liberalised markets to invest overseas or trade speculatively.

The 'British model' also failed to bridge the productivity gap between the United Kingdom and its leading competitors. In 2005, ONS figures showed that productivity per worker in the United Kingdom remained nine per cent below the G7 average and twenty-five per cent behind the United States. This marked a considerable improvement on 1997, when the United Kingdom had been fifteen per cent behind the G7 average and twenty-eight per cent behind the United States.[89] The productivity gap had been narrowed but not bridged. At the outset of his tenure as Chancellor, Brown promised that the Blair Government would 'identify the barriers to growth and productivity' and then 'relentlessly work to remove them'.[90] A year later, Brown laid down a challenge to 'the country's business leaders and to every shareholder, every employee, every citizen of the country' to work together 'to bridge the productivity gap'. Invoking 'a sense of national economic purpose, to agree a new long term direction for Britain', Brown portrayed the role of government as ensuring lasting stability, the role of industry as investment for the long term and the role of the financial community as a refusal 'to resort to the short-termism and stop-go attitudes which have bedevilled us since the war'.[91]

Neither finance nor industry rallied to Brown's patriotic cause: the necessary investment was not forthcoming. Brown's decision, in his inaugural July 1997 Budget, to abolish the tax credits paid to pension funds and companies, as a disincentive to the payment of dividends rather than the reinvestment of profits, returned to haunt him a decade later. An attempt to counter short-termism, at a time of pension fund surpluses and holidays, was retrospectively portrayed as a hidden, 'stealth tax' which may have caused a shortfall of up to seventy-five billion pounds in existing assets.[92]

The most damning evidence that 'British model' had not redressed supply-side weaknesses came from its failure to reverse the trend of United Kingdom current account deficits (which cover all transactions in goods, services, income and current transfers); indeed, it strengthened and deepened those deficits. The United Kingdom had experienced current account deficits every year since 1984 and a trade deficit every year since 1982 (and in all but six years since 1900). ONS figures show that in 2007, the United Kingdom recorded a deficit of £52.6 billion (–3.8 per cent of GDP), an increase from the 2006 deficit of £47.8 billion (–3.7 per cent of GDP) and the highest recorded deficit in cash terms.[93] The deficit in trade in goods was a cash record of £89.3 billion. This deficit was in no sense balanced by a record £41.8 billion surplus on the United Kingdom's trade in services. Thus, the overall deficit on trade in goods and services was £47.5 billion (–3.4 per cent of GDP), compared to £54.4 billion in 2006 (–4.3 per cent of GDP).[94]

This is the price that the national accounts have had to pay for the British model's neglect of domestic manufacturing industry, which remains the most internationally-tradable sector of the global economy. Despite its undoubted success, the City of London's earnings are nowhere near sufficient to compensate for the lost employment, output and income from the loss of more than one million manufacturing jobs during Brown's Chancellorship. Manufacturing may account now for less than twenty per cent of GDP but, as the United Kingdom's trade figures will attest, it is still the principal source of export revenue for Brown's successor.

THE RISK OF VOLATILITY AND CONTAGION: THE MYTH OF LOCKED-IN STABILITY

One of Gordon Brown's most frequent boasts was that the 'British model' had 'locked-in' stability. In practice, the model could not lock in stability, because the openness of the City of London's financial markets meant that the door was set ajar for volatility and contagion. In recent years, the United Kingdom had to borrow from abroad to finance its continuing current account deficit, with the consequence that inward investment (United Kingdom liabilities) now exceeded outward investment (United Kingdom assets). Since 1995, the level of the United Kingdom's external assets and liabilities has more than trebled. At the end of 2006, total net assets stood at £5279 billion but total net liabilities had risen to £5544.2 billion. This meant that during the year, the United Kingdom's net liabilities had risen, by £124.8 billion, from £140.4 billion at the end of 2005. This signified a deterioration from liabilities equivalent to −11.4 per cent of GDP at the end of 2005 to −20.6 per cent of GDP at the end of 2006[95] and that 'net UK overseas liabilities as a percentage of GDP were at their highest for 30 years'.[96] At the end of 2007, the United Kingdom's net liabilities had increased to £381.6 billion, including a record £220.7 billion of liabilities for United Kingdom banks.[97]

Between 1966 and 1994, under Labour and Conservative Governments, assets had tended to exceed liabilities, reaching a record £86.4 billion in 1986. However, from 1995 and throughout Brown's tenure as Chancellor, ONS statistics show the UK recorded a net liability.[98] Furthermore, in 2005, for the first time since 1990 direct investment in the United Kingdom was greater than direct investment abroad.[99] That trend continued during 2006, with direct investment abroad of £43.2 billion far exceeded by direct investment in the United Kingdom of £75.8 billion.[100] Such imbalances risked loss of confidence by and willingness among foreign investors to continue to fund the United Kingdom's deficits, with potentially destabilising consequences for the future value of sterling, especially since sterling operated outside the collective stability of the Eurozone.

The significance of the United Kingdom's current account deficit has been doubted, on the grounds that United Kingdom residents' assets are weighted towards equity-type investments, which have higher average returns than debt-type assets. Moreover, if the stocks of assets and liabilities are adjusted to their market value, United Kingdom assets continue to exceed liabilities. However, even this optimistic analysis has its doubters; Stephen Nickell, in his paper *The UK Current Account Deficit and All That*, concluded that the current position is only 'probably sustainable' and that there risks arise from 'a continuing and rapid increase in the trade deficit' that could undermine the United Kingdom's favourable adjusted net asset position. These include a 'significant fall in the long-term returns on equity relative to returns on debt'; a movement by foreign residents towards equity-type investments through major purchases of United Kingdom companies; and 'a large and permanent real appreciation of sterling' that would 'significantly reduce UK assets relative to UK liabilities'.[101]

This appears a dangerously complacent conclusion, given the rapid deterioration in the United Kingdom's trade and current account balances, the sheer scale of its assets and liabilities (around four times GDP)and the fact that the determination of whether the United Kingdom's international investment account moves further into deficit is in the hands of private corporations and investors (both British and foreign) and outside the Treasury's direct control. As the deterioration in the United Kingdom's international investment demonstrated, the 'British model' could not lock in stability any more than could the economic policies of previous United Kingdom governments, because of the freedom enjoyed by agents in liberalised financial markets to invest and disinvest for profit wherever they please, without checking with Gordon Brown's moral compass or sense of national economic purpose.

A LEGACY OF PRIVATE IMPRUDENCE, DEBT AND INEQUALITY

During Gordon Brown's time as Chancellor, economic growth was overwhelmingly consumer-led and borrowing-driven. It was not investment-led. People took advantage of the opportunities offered by liberalised and deregulated financial and property markets to borrow record amounts of money, which they set against the rising value of their assets – notably their houses and shares. This capacity to borrow was assisted by the innovations with which liberalised financial markets found new ways to finance debt. Where once home-buyers would have been limited to borrowing up to three times their current salary, it was now possible for them to borrow up to six times.

Neither did Brown's sense of moral purpose extend to prudence and thrift in the use of credit cards. Admittedly, during 2006, total spending in the United Kingdom on credit cards fell by two per cent, from £122 billion to £120 billion. However, that decline (the first fall for more than forty years), was more than offset by a fifteen per cent increase in spending on debit cards, which rose to £195 billion. Figures from the Association of

Payment Clearing Systems (APACS) showed that in December 2006, spending on plastic cards reached a record high of thirty-one billion pounds, including £19.6 billion from 472 million transactions conducted on debit cards, up 15.3 per cent from the previous year.[102] Total United Kingdom personal debt stood at £1,291 billion by the end of December 2006, an annual increase of 10.6 per cent (around £114 billion). Of this total, £1,078 billion was secured against property, an annual increase of 11.5 per cent. The remaining £213 billion was consumer credit lending to individuals (an annual increase of 6.2 per cent), of which £54.9 billion was owed on credit cards. This meant that the average United Kingdom household's debt was £53,326 including mortgages or £8,791 excluding mortgages. These debts cost an average of £3,400 a year to service. Indeed, the average United Kingdom adult now owed £27,445 (including mortgages), including £4,524 of debt held on credit cards, motor and retail finance deals, overdrafts or unsecured personal loans.[103]

An increasing number of people could not manage their debts. During the financial year 2005–2006, the Citizens Advice Bureau (CAB) received 1.4 million requests for advice on debt problems, an annual increase of eleven per cent. During January 2007 alone, the number of cases of debt problems rose to 83,000, an annual increase of fifteen per cent. The CAB has estimated that it would take its clients an average of seventy-seven years to pay back their average debt of £13,000, because that amount is nearly 17.5 times their average monthly income.[104] The 'British model' did little to curb the United Kingdom's addiction to credit and borrowing. On the contrary, it fed the habit, because it was the motive force behind the 'Brown Boom' decade of economic growth. In February 2007, Credit Action stated that the United Kingdom's personal debt has been increasing by one million pounds every 3.85 minutes.[105]

The problem for Gordon Brown in his Prime Ministership was that such high levels of debt would have consequences for the United Kingdom's economic performance in the next economic cycle. Brown did not attempt to dampen the growth of debt by setting a tax on consumer credit. In the 1980s, under the then Chancellor, Nigel Lawson, the Treasury did contemplate the introduction of a one per cent tax on outstanding consumer credit (including mortgages). Lawson concluded that the consumer- and property-led boom of the late 1980s was 'to a considerable extent a once-and-for-all occurrence: the change from a financially regulated to a financially deregulated economy'.[106] He was wrong: under Lawson's successors, notably Brown, the United Kingdom has become locked into a permanent condition of financial risk, volatility and debt-financed consumption.

In the months before Gordon Brown became Prime Minister, there was little sign of an end to the 'Brown Boom'. In January 2007, the Halifax House Price Index showed that the annual rate of house price inflation was 9.9 per cent, with the average house costing £186, 954 – an increase of 605 per cent since January 1983.[107] During 2006, such was the inflation in the housing market that the typical house increased in value by forty-five pounds per day, compared to a daily increase of £12.50 during 2005. However, during 2006, the number of first-time buyers was estimated to have fallen by seven per cent to 315,000, a decline of 37.4 per cent on their 1997 level (503,000) and the lowest total since 1980. This reflected an eleven per cent rise in the price of the average United Kingdom first-time house purchase, to £151,565, an increase of ninety-five per cent since 2001. House price inflation has meant a ninety-one per cent increase in the average mortgage, to £123,435 in 2006, For the first-time buyer in London, the average purchase price has risen to £250,819, requiring an average deposit of £53,136.

Such rampant house price inflation appeared unsustainable. The gap between the average income of the first-time buyer and that of people in their twenties has widened significantly during Brown's stewardship of the economy. In 1997, when the Blair Government first took power, the average first-time buyer's income was £16,053, only 1.1 per cent greater than the average full-time earnings of people between the ages of twenty-two and twenty-nine years (£15,839). However, by 2001, the gap in incomes had widened to more than twenty per cent and by 2006 to more than thirty-five per cent. Average houses are now unaffordable for first-time buyers in ninety-three per cent of towns in the United Kingdom, compared to only thirty-seven per cent in 2001.[108] Housing had become so expensive that thirty-three per cent of mortgages taken out during November 2006 were 'interest only' (compared to twelve per cent during June 2006) and of these twenty-six per cent did not incorporate a repayment plan for the capital borrowed.[109] Fewer and fewer young people were now able to enter the housing market and in much of the United Kingdom entrance had become beyond the range of many people, including key workers in the public services. The housing market had become an engine of increasing inequality in income and wealth, with inflation in asset values far outstripping the effects of limited redistribution arising from the tax credit reforms implemented by Brown.

Gordon Brown sought to infuse his 'British model' of political economy with the same moral purpose that he brought to public life; the commitment to duty and the service of others. However, the evidence of executive pay and remuneration to workers in the City of London suggested that their reward had been of a very different – pecuniary – form and of an order of magnitude far removed from the income of the average citizen. A survey of 1340 FTSE 100 directors found that directors' pay for the financial year 2005 rose by twenty-eight per cent, from £590 million to £753 million. Of this, no less than £678 million was paid to just 540 full-time executives (an average of £1.24 million).This compared with an increase in average earnings of 3.7 per cent and an inflation rate of 2.5 per cent. While the average pay of Tesco's 368,000 workers fell from £12,713 to £11,594, the pay of Tesco's Chief Executive rose to £5.4 million; 466 times the average remuneration of a Tesco employee.[110] There was little evidence to suggest that the explosion in executive pay in 2005, to seventy-six times that of the average worker (compared with a ratio of 10:1 in 1980), had been either performance-related or the product of labour market risk. On the contrary, research from the Work Foundation suggested that there was scant justification for paying FTSE 100 directors many times the Prime Minister's £186,000 a year salary. For Iles, in *The Risk Myth*, this 'winner-take-all' and excessive level of remuneration constituted both 'a form of market failure', because it threatened the long-term competitiveness of these companies and a major social cost, because 'inequality matters. High levels of inequality in wider society act as a brake on social mobility and high levels of inequality within organisations act as a brake on performance'.[111]

CONCLUSION

The 'British model' of political economy delivered forty consecutive quarters of economic growth during Gordon Brown's Chancellorship. This was a much better-sustained performance than those of any of his predecessors, Labour or Conservative. In acknowledging that undoubted success, we must also recognise that the 'British model' largely failed in its attempt to rally the private sector to a shared sense of national economic purpose. At the start of his tenure, Brown promised not to pursue 'a policy of "Whitehall knows best" ' but to be 'a supporter and friend of all that is best in British entrepreneurial culture'.[112] In the event, he discovered that, left to themselves to enjoy the freedom of liberalised markets, British entrepreneurs may choose the culture of short-termism and domestic under-investment that prompted Whitehall intervention in the past.

The effect of the 'British model' of political economy was to reinforce competitive advantage. Its winners were the City of London, investors in the housing market and the Treasury (which enjoyed unprecedented power over the design of policy and the allocation of resources in England). Its losers were manufacturing industry and first-time buyers on the property market. Brown's economic legacy was to reinforce rather than reverse the trend towards greater inequality in income and wealth established during the Thatcher and Major Governments. Furthermore, implementing the 'British model' was a quintessential top-down, technocratic exercise. Despite its claims to have accorded priority to economics over politics, it was a highly-politicised agenda, driven by a committee of two: Gordon Brown and his former Chief Economic Adviser and closest political confidant, Ed Balls. Vital decisions concerning macro- and micro-economic policy were entrusted to a series of unelected committees and experts appointed or approved by Brown, much of whose work was beyond the democratic scrutiny of the British people.

Despite a decade of hyperactivity in the publication of Treasury reports, there was little evidence that any of the principal long-term supply-side constraints on the performance of the United Kingdom economy had been alleviated. The long tail of under-performing companies and individuals first highlighted by the Commission on Public Policy and British Business immediately before the election of the Blair Government remained.[113] The fact that Brown's tenth and final Pre-Budget Report identified the challenge for the next decade as the creation of 'a new British framework for investment and innovation, a British strategy to make the next stage of globalisation work for the British people' was itself testament to the extent of the failure of the British model to redress significantly the long-term supply-side weaknesses of the United Kingdom economy.[114]

Initially, Gordon Brown was prudent for a purpose. During the Blair Government's first term, he demonstrated his commitment to macro-economic stability and fiscal prudence to the City of London's investors while showing both his Cabinet colleagues and the trades unions in the public sector that there would be no sudden windfall from the election of a Labour Government. Latterly, during the Blair Government's second and third terms, Brown was increasingly imprudent, for the purpose of investing in the public services. Rather than marking an end to 'boom to bust', and a permanent change in the economic performance of the United Kingdom, the Institute for Fiscal Studies (IFS) has identified how Gordon Brown's decade at the Treasury demonstrated some remarkable similarities with the pattern and performance of fiscal policy during the first twelve years of the Thatcher and Major Governments. Both Conservative and Labour Governments had delivered 'three years of impressive fiscal consolidation, eight years of drift (masked by economic overconfidence), and then a big jump in borrowing thanks to recession and newly-discovered structural weaknesses'.[115, 116]

At the end of the eleventh year of both the Thatcher/Major and Blair/Brown Governments, a structural deficit in the public finances had developed, equivalent to 2.6 per cent of national income in 1989–1990 and 2.9 per cent of national income in 2007–2008. Moreover, as the IFS has noted, the falls in public sector borrowing and indebtedness which Brown's British model of fiscal policy had delivered by 2007–2008 had occurred 'while most other industrialised countries were doing more to strengthen their public finances than the UK'. Indeed, no fewer than nineteen of twenty-four industrialised economies had done more to reduce their structural deficits than the United Kingdom since 1996. Having had the second lowest deficit in the G7 and the thirteenth highest deficit (of twenty-three) in the OECD in 1990, by the time Brown became Prime Minister the United Kingdom had the second highest structural deficit in the G7 and the fourth highest (of twenty-six) in the OECD. Similarly, in relation to the ratio of public debt to national income, in 1996 the United Kingdom had the third lowest public debt ratio in the G7 and the tenth highest among twenty-seven OECD countries. However, by 2007, the United Kingdom possessed the third highest public debt ratio in the G7 and the eleventh highest debt in the OECD.[117] As a consequence, as Chapter Eight outlines, by international standards the United Kingdom entered the recession with a structural budget deficit not only bigger than that in most other industrialised economies, but also bigger than that with which the Major Government had entered the previous recession in 1991.[118]

The price paid for New Labour's initial fiscal austerity during the Blair Government's first term was that 'public sector net investment was lower on average in Labour's first term – at 0.6% of national income – than in any other four-year period since the Second World War'.[119] However, where government revenues had risen by 2.2 per cent of national income during New Labour's first term, resulting in a current budget surplus of 2.4 per cent of GDP, during the Blair government's second term, spending increased by 3.9 per cent of GDP and tax revenues weakened, resulting in a current budget deficit of 1.6 per cent by 2004–2005.[120] The British model did deliver a marked improvement in the current budget. Over the economic cycle estimated by the Treasury to have run from 1997–1998 to 2006–2007, there was an average annual surplus of 0.14 per cent of national income, equivalent to around £2 billion in 2008–2009 terms. Consequently, Gordon Brown met his golden rule over the economic cycle that marked his tenure as Chancellor. By contrast, under the Callaghan, Thatcher and Major Governments, during the previous economic cycles estimated by the Treasury to have run from 1978 to 1986 and 1986 to 1996, 'the golden rule – had it been in place – would have been missed by £26.8 billion per year and £28.4 billion per year in today's terms, respectively'.[121]

Admittedly, in the period from 1996–1997 to 2007–2008, the Treasury could point towards an estimated increase in real national income of £12,700 per family, from which families had paid £5,600 in tax, leaving them with additional income of £7,100 after tax.[122] In overall terms, Brown's British model would ensure that forty-four per cent of every extra pound in national income generated under New Labour would be taken in tax, compared with only twenty-nine per cent during the Thatcher and Major Governments.[123] However, as I shall show in Chapter Four, the speed with which public spending has increased the resources available to public services, combined with the combination of a centrally-driven, permanent revolution of market-based reforms, meant that the 'British model's' growing fiscal imprudence yielded a disappointing dividend and legacy in terms of performance and productivity for England's public services.

Chapter 4

Reforming the Public Services: The Nationalisation of Policy Design and Resource Allocation

INTRODUCTION

In its 1997 General Election manifesto, the Labour Party made some bold commitments to services. It promised that 'education will be our number one priority and we will increase the share of national income spent on education as we decrease it on the bills of economic and social failure'.[1] In fact, the National Health Service (NHS) was the Blair Government's number one priority. New Labour wanted 'to save and modernise the NHS'.[2] It promised to do this by ending the Conservatives' internal market in health care and by increasing spending on the NHS in real terms every year. This was to be accomplished (while still adhering to the Conservatives' very low planned public spending allocations for the first two years in office), by reallocating spending 'from economic failure to investment'.[3] To bring about the necessary changes in the NHS, there was to be 'continuity as well as change or the system cannot cope. There must be pilots to ensure that change works. And there must be flexibility, not rigid prescription, if innovation is to flourish'. The fundamental purpose of reform would be 'to restore the NHS as a public service working co-operatively for patients, not a commercial business driven by competition'.[4]

New Labour delivered on its spending commitments. Up to 2007–2008, education spending, in real terms, increased annually by an average of 4.6 per cent. This compares with a paltry 1.5 per cent average annual real terms' increase from 1979 to 1997. Health spending under New Labour increased by an average annual rate of 6.1 per cent, compared with a 3.1 per cent annual increase during the Thatcher and Major Governments.[5] The planned total public expenditure for the Department of Health for 2007–2008 is £104.1 billion, an 8.1 per cent increase in real terms, following 7.8 per cent and 5.1 per cent real terms increases in the previous two years.[6]

Although money was provided for the modernisation of the public services, paradoxically, opinion polls repeatedly demonstrated a consistent level of general public dissatisfaction with the returns from that investment, in terms of the quality of service experienced. For example, in May 2007, a MORI opinion poll identified that more people (fifty-one per cent) disagreed than agreed (thirty-eight per cent) that in the long term the government's policies would improve the state of Britain's public services.[7] And despite the investment, morale among workers in the public sector remained much lower than in the private and not-for-profit sectors. No fewer than thirty-nine per cent of managers in the public sector believed morale to be low in their organisation, compared to only sixteen per cent of private sector managers and six per cent of not-for-profit managers.[8]

Even before he became Prime Minister, Gordon Brown was warned by Dr Jonathan Fielden, Chairman of the British Medical Association's Central Consultants and Specialists' Committee, that morale in the NHS was 'at an all time low' and that 'political meddling has brought it to its knees'. His allegation was that the NHS in England had seen: 'incoherent policy dividing and fragmenting. No long term strategy for sustained improvement ... The real barriers to progress are government policies – we all bear the scars on our backs from these – patients, the public and notably the profession'. Having promised to abolish the internal market in the NHS, he accused the Blair Government of leaving a legacy that had gone from 'the Bazaar to the

Bizarre: a messianic belief in the market, redirecting billions of pounds into poor-value-for-money schemes'. As incoming Prime Minister, Fielden exhorted Brown to 'Go on Gordon go for it; get your legacy in days where Tony has failed in a decade!', by valuing and giving back leadership to the medical professions and by freeing the NHS from 'political meddling'.[9]

During his tenure at the Treasury, Gordon Brown certainly engaged in extensive 'political meddling' in the public services, especially in England, where the absence of devolution had resulted in the absence of institutional and democratic checks and balances on the exercise of micro-management through centralised prescription. Brown further entrenched his control over domestic policy by sitting on eighteen of the thirty-two principal ministerial committees of the Cabinet, including all those concerned with reform of the public services. Brown, rather than Blair, chaired the Cabinet committee on Public Services and Public Expenditure, whose terms of reference were 'to review public expenditure allocations and to make recommendations – including on Public Service Agreements – to Cabinet, and to review progress in delivering the Government's programme of investment and reform to renew the public services'.[10] To understand Brown's policies for and legacies to the public services, in this chapter I will show that, where once the Labour Party nationalised industries and failing sectors of the economy, under Gordon Brown's stewardship the Treasury implemented a technocratic statecraft of constrained discretion. This enabled it to nationalise policy design and the allocation of resources for public spending bodies in England.

Through the Treasury's biennial spending reviews and the framework of the Public Service Agreements, Brown engineered a top-down framework of centralised prescription over public services reform. Because it bypassed or eliminated many of the previous checks and balances on executive power (including those exercised by the Prime Minister, his Cabinet colleagues, Westminster, local government and individual citizens), constrained discretion delivered both a seemingly permanent revolution of reforms and a significant increase in funding for public services, notably health and education. Thus, it was possible for modernisation to alienate both public sector workers and their representatives at a time of record investment. There was also increasing evidence that the political legacy of an approach based on partnerships with the private sector and a consumer-led approach to public service delivery was a growing disillusionment with the resulting postcode lottery in the availability of services. The perception was widespread that increased resources had not been matched by corresponding increases in the quality of services.

BROWN'S CONSTRAINED DISCRETION VERSUS BLAIR'S EARNED AUTONOMY

The reform of public services in England caused the most bitter of the battles over domestic policy between Gordon Brown and Tony Blair. This battle was the most visible legacy of the *Granita* accord, when Brown stood aside from the contest to succeed John Smith as Labour Party leader in return for a central role in domestic policy formulation. The battle also produced two rival but essentially similar models for modernisation, advanced by the Treasury and the Prime Minister. Tony Blair set out his model of 'earned autonomy', which was enshrined, for example, in the July 2000 publication *The NHS Plan*. This plan (made for England alone, a fact not once acknowledged in it) promised that investment and reform would be implemented through 'a new system of earned autonomy' that would 'devolve power from the centre to the local health service as modernisation takes hold'.[11] The Treasury advanced its alternative model of 'constrained discretion'. This demanded commitment, through institutional arrangements and procedural rules, to clear and sound long-term policy objectives, in return for 'the maximum operational flexibility that is consistent with achieving that goal'.[12] In other words, the freedom of schools, hospitals, local government and other providers of public services was to be limited, in return for accepting the Treasury's national standards as the political price to be paid for receiving the money for modernisation.

Both modernisation models followed the same centralised prescription for and nationalisation of policy design, standards and resource allocation for public services in England (not feasible elsewhere in Britain, because of devolution). Blair's model of 'earned autonomy for schools, hospitals, local government and other public services' had enabled 'locally-elected representatives to adopt approaches to public services reflecting their own national priorities and concerns' – but only in Scotland, Wales and Northern Ireland.[13] In England, Blair held that 'devolved delivery can only operate with national standards and accountability'. Public services' reform must be based on a clear demarcation between central government's pre-scription for an 'overall vision' – that is, policy design and specification of 'national standards' (again for England alone, a fact not once acknowl-edged) – and the delivery of that vision by subordinate layers of administra-tion 'by devolution and delegation to the front line'.[14]

Brown's Treasury model of modernisation claimed that the 'command and control systems of public service management employed in the past had serious drawbacks; in particular they lacked devolution, transparency and accountability'. Constrained discretion purported to be 'bottom-up not top-down, with national government enabling powerful regional and local institutions to work by providing the necessary flexibility and resources'.[15] However, the fact that the Treasury specified that it, rather than England's regions and localities, would provide the necessary 'flexibility and resources' was ample testament to the degree which Brown too had nation-alised policy-making and resource allocation in England. The crucial differ-ence between Blair and Brown's intended nationalisations was that New Labour's commitment to Spending Reviews and their accompanying Public Service Agreements gave Brown the means by which to institution-alise his framework for domestic economic and social policy and to ensure the subordination of Blair's.

One way in which the rivalry between Blair and Brown affected the reform of the public services was encapsulated in the row over health service funding in January 2000. During a television interview with David Frost, and against the backdrop of Lord Robert Winston's (a leading fertility expert) accusations that his Government had failed to deliver NHS reform and funding, Blair committed himself to raising health spending to the European Union average over five years. He stated 'If we run the economy properly, I am entirely confident we will get those five per cent real term rises'.[16] Not only did Blair's statement break an agreement with Brown that additional funding would be dependent on future economic growth and reform but it also committed the government to a target that was 'huge, imprecise and moving'. Andrew Rawnsley, in *Servants of the People*, reported that Brown was purportedly incandescently angry that Blair had pre-empted his Budget statement.[17]

To reassert his control over this vital aspect of the public services' agenda, in March 2001 Brown commissioned a review of the long-term trends affecting the NHS.[18] Blair responded, in August, by commissioning his own review of health strategy.[19] However, the triumph of Brown over Blair was signalled in April 2002 when the spending profile identified by the (Brown-commissioned) Wanless Report as necessary for the United Kingdom to catch up and sustain best practice in healthcare became the basis for government policy. The July 2002 Spending Review announced a growth in the United Kingdom's health spending of 7.3 per cent in real terms per annum until 2008, matching the Wanless Report's blueprint for annual average real increases of between 7.1 and 7.3 per cent during this period.[20]

THE PERMANENT REVOLUTION OF CONSTRAINED DISCRETION

The permanent revolution of modernisation and reform of the public services in England reflected the influence of the hypothesis of the reinvention of government, first put forward in the early 1990s. This reinvention sought to transform the public sector, creating 'entrepreneurial government', which, according to Osborne and Gabeler in *Reinventing government*, would 'constantly use their resources in new ways to heighten both their efficiency and their effectiveness'.[21] Among the characteristics of entrepreneurial government Osborne and Gabeler described were:

> ... the promotion of competition between service providers, the empowerment of citizens by 'pushing control out of the bureaucracy, into the community', the measurement of the performance of public agencies by 'focusing not on inputs but on *outcomes*', the redefinition of clients for services as 'customers', who would be offered 'choices – between schools, between training programs, between housing', a preference for market mechanisms over bureaucratic mechanisms and a focus 'not simply on providing public services but on *catalyzing* all sectors – public, private and voluntary – into action to solve their community's problems'.[22]

Rejecting the 'Reaganite' mantra that government was not the solution but the problem, the hypothesis of entrepreneurial government asserted that 'the central failure of government today is one of *means*, not *ends*'.[23] The focus was not on the quantity of government: Osborne and Gabeler's hypothesis was that 'we have *the wrong kind of government*' and that consequently what was needed was better government or 'to be more precise, we need better *governance*' (which they defined as the process by which society collectively solves its problems and meets its needs).[24] This needed managerial systems that separated 'policy decisions (steering) from service delivery (rowing)'.[25] The steering role would require government to 'set policy, deliver funds to operational bodies (public and private) and evaluate performance [but] seldom play an operational role themselves'.[26] However, while entrepreneurial government would allow service delivery to be contracted out to the private sector or the third sector of civic society groups and voluntary, not-for-profit associations, steering (policy design, resource allocation and governance) could not. Policy design must remain the province of government, so that decisions could be taken collectively, markets regulated, a sense of equity and altruism be maintained and unprofitable public and social services be sustained, so as not to overburden the third sector.[27]

The hypothesis of entrepreneurial government is an accurate depiction of the Treasury's approach to the governance of public services during Brown's Chancellorship. The separation of policy design and resource allocation and service delivery was institutionalised, through the control mechanisms of the two Comprehensive Spending Reviews, the intervening biennial Spending Reviews and their attendant Public Service Agreements. Under previous Labour Prime Ministers, from Attlee to Callaghan, the relationship between the Treasury and government departments was characterised by negotiation through policy networks within Whitehall. Public services were delivered through hierarchical or vertically-integrated agencies. The Treasury had been able to exercise only discretionary authority over policy and resources, because its power was 'constrained by the exercise of countervailing power by each autonomous spending department' (Thain and Wright: *The Treasury and Whitehall*).[28] Under the Thatcher and Major Governments, negotiated discretion in expenditure planning and public service delivery had been abandoned only temporarily. Privatisation led to a departure from the principles of hierarchical or vertically-integrated public service provision towards provision based on contractual relationships. The boundaries between the public and private sectors had become blurred.

During Gordon Brown's tenure as Chancellor, the previous constitutional and practical checks and balances on Treasury power were largely removed. This was a paradigm shift, from negotiated discretion to centralised prescription for the control of policy and the allocation of resources for the public services. Competition was introduced between service providers in the public services in England. Public Service Agreements, performance indicators and output measures institutionalised an emphasis on the measurement of performance and a focus on outcomes, not inputs. The clients of public services were redefined as customers. There was an almost messianic faith in markets and the capacity of the private sector to innovate and to enhance efficiency and productivity in the use of resources.[29]

THE SPENDING REVIEWS AND PUBLIC SERVICE AGREEMENTS

The principal instruments through which the Treasury nationalised the design of policy and allocation of resources for the public services were the Comprehensive Spending Reviews (1998 and 2007), the intervening biennial Spending Reviews (2000, 2002 and 2004) and their accompanying Public Service Agreements (PSAs). Although these instruments gave the Treasury a greater degree of centralised control over the budgetary and policy-making processes, they did not necessarily ensure that resources flowed consistently to the public services or indeed that the resources allocated for modernisation were spent effectively or in an equitable manner.

The first year-long Comprehensive Spending Review (CSR), which covered 1999–2000 to 2001–2002, established the Treasury's central prescription for policy and resources. It incorporated thirty-six zero-based reviews by the Treasury not only of individual departmental spending plans but also their objectives and policies. Effectively, the Treasury was reviewing the rationale of policy and even long-held assumptions about policy were open to challenge. One sixth of these reviews were conducted cross-departmentally, to ensure integration and co-ordination. However, because expenditure was planned to grow by only 2.25 per cent on average in real terms over the CSR's life, this meant a period of austerity for the public services.[30] Public spending under the Major Government had grown more quickly, at an annual real terms' average of 2.4 per cent. Indeed, at the end of the Blair Government's first term, total public spending was 2.6 per cent of national income lower than when New Labour had taken office. In 1999–2000, at 37.4 per cent of GDP, public spending was at its lowest level since 1960–1961.[31] Health spending had also declined as a share of national income, from 5.5 per cent of GDP in 1996–1997 to 5.4 per cent in 1999–2000 and education spending likewise, from 4.7 per cent of GDP to 4.4 per cent.[32]

No change in the available resources for the public services occurred until the year before the 2001 General Election. The July 2000 Spending Review announced that current public spending would increase by an annual average of 2.5 per cent. However, spending on health would increase by 6.1 per cent in real terms from 2000–2001 to 2003–2004, while education spending would increase by 5.4 per cent.[33] The July 2002 Spending Review planned to accelerate spending on these key services: in the five years to 2008, education spending in England would grow by six per cent a year in real terms and health spending in the United Kingdom by an average of 7.3 per cent.[34] The momentum was maintained by the July 2004 Spending Review, which planned expenditure growth for education in England of 4.4 per cent between 2004–2005 and 2007–2008. By 2007–2008, NHS spending was planned to increase to ninety-two billion pounds, compared to only thirty-three billion in 1996–1997.[35]

Whether this significant acceleration in investment in the public services delivered an improvement in the quantity and quality of services depended on the Government's ability to translate investment into enhanced efficiency. Through the Spending Reviews, the Treasury identified three 'building blocks' of its approach to raising the productivity of the public services: first, a focus on outcomes as the central aim of policy, as opposed to the solitary focus on inputs; second, constrained discretion for local service providers, 'increasing their operational freedoms and flexibilities, subject to appropriate minimum standards and regular performance monitoring'; third, improved governance of public services, through 'reforming institutions to reflect the importance of clear objectives, appropriate incentives and good performance information in the achievement of higher productivity'.[36] There was also a greater emphasis, notably in the preparation of the second CSR, on the catalytic role of the private and third sectors, to complement the role of the public sector.

The essential contradiction in the Treasury's approach to the reform of the public services in England was that constrained discretion could in practice operate only by decreasing the freedom and flexibility of local communities and public spending bodies to make autonomous choices about the design (as opposed to the administration and delivery) of policy.

Constrained discretion meant limited freedom. Furthermore, the Treasury's 'appropriate minimum standards' facilitated the nationalisation of policy design and resource allocation in England. The Treasury's 'regular performance monitoring' fed an audit culture, in which a fixation on meeting performance targets and indicators all too often led to a neglect of the broader picture of effective delivery of public service.

PSAs were introduced in the July 1998 report of the first CSR. As part of the 'money for modernisation' agenda, PSAs incorporated 'new objectives and measurable efficiency targets', monitored by a Cabinet Committee chaired by the Chancellor of the Exchequer.[37] From the very outset of the Blair Government's reform of the public services, Gordon Brown had thus engineered an institutional structure and approach to policy-making that allowed him to micro-manage policy design and resource allocation. When the July 2000 Spending Review was published, it announced the strengthening and deepening of performance measurement, through the introduction of Service Delivery Agreements (SDAs) and Technical Notes. SDAs explained how the government aimed to deliver its targets in the PSAs and how it itself would modernise and reform to give better value for money. The Technical Notes underpinned departmental PSAs and would specify the precise performance criteria against which PSA targets would be measured.[38] The Treasury thus possessed an extensive framework for monitoring progress in the reform and modernisation of public services.

The degree to which the creation of the biennial Spending Reviews, PSAs, SDAs and Technical Notes enhanced the Treasury's power not only over the public services but also over 'the strategic direction of the Government', soon became apparent to the rest of Whitehall and to Westminster. The Treasury Select Committee accused the Treasury of exerting 'too much influence over policy areas which are properly the business of other departments and that is not necessarily in the best interests of the Treasury or the Government as a whole'.[39] It was not thought desirable for the Treasury to set both 'the framework within which departments should operate, using the Spending Review and PSA process and to act as the sole assessor of whether or not departments are achieving their objectives'.[40] It recommended that the Treasury's power to monitor PSAs should be curtailed, by reducing the dominance of Treasury ministers on the Public Services and Public Expenditure Cabinet Committee (a recommendation the Treasury never accepted). However, it also conceded that Parliament lacked the resources to hold the Treasury to account, because 'the Treasury's role in allocating public expenditure, determining, monitoring and adapting PSAs and influencing policies which have economic effects is opaque, hidden behind a curtain of Whitehall secrecy'.[41]

This open acknowledgement that Westminster lacked the resources to hold it fully to account meant that a major constitutional check on the centralised prescription-writing of the Treasury's constrained discretion had been removed. However, it soon became apparent that the objective of micro-managing reform of the public services through performance targets had been too ambitious. The number of targets was almost halved between the July 1998 and July 2002 Spending Reviews. This trend continued in March 2004, when the Treasury published the results of its Devolved Decision Making Review.[42] This specified fewer nationally-set targets and a greater emphasis on locally-determined outcomes. This change was tantamount to an admission that the Treasury's command-and-control approach had been inflexible and denied local management the autonomy needed to develop effective local performance management. This trend continued in the 2007 CSR, when the number of PSAs was further reduced to 'less than a third of the number of PSAs' in the 2004 Spending Review.[43] In a similar vein, in October 2006, introducing the White Paper on local government, Ruth Kelly, then Secretary of State for Communities and Local Government, announced a 'new settlement between central government, local government and citizens', which promised a 'radical reduction in national targets and the introduction of a lighter touch inspection system'. In practice, this still meant around 200 performance indicators for local government in England (compared to the previous 'between 600 and 1,200 indicators'[44]). It showed how centralised and nationalised policy design, resource allocation and performance monitoring had become in England under constrained discretion, when the retention of such a large measure of centralised prescription could be presented as a radical act of devolution.

HELPING MARKETS WORK BETTER: GORDON BROWN ON PUBLIC SERVICES

In *Microeconomic Reform in Britain*, Ed Balls and his co-editors held that a central assumption underpinning the policy of constrained discretion was that 'markets are a powerful means of advancing the public interest'. The essential conceit of constrained discretion was that the Treasury had the capacity 'not only to support but positively enhance markets'.[45] Such intervention was held to be necessary because 'markets can fail to deliver socially optimal outcomes requiring intervention to make markets work in the public interest'.[46] In healthcare, the role of state was vital because of:

> The existence of multiple market failures ... [and] ... price signals don't always work; the consumer is not sovereign; there is potential abuse of monopoly power; it is hard to write and enforce contracts; it is difficult to let a hospital go bust; and we risk supplier-induced demands.[47]

The provision of healthcare by the market would 'lead to neither the most efficient nor the most equitable outcome, jeopardising the delivery of opportunity and security for all'.[48]

For Gordon Brown, there was a key test of whether the appropriate balance had been established between the market and the state in the delivery of public services:

> whether the public interest – that is, opportunity and security for all – and the equity, efficiency and diversity necessary to achieve it, are best advanced by more or less reliance on markets or through substituting a degree of public control or ownership for the market; and whether, even when there is public sector provision, there can be contestability.[49]

Brown identified the failure of the Labour Governments of the 1960s and 1970s 'to take on vested interests' and criticised post-war politicians on both sides of the political spectrum for wrongly seeing the centralised state as 'the main, and sometimes the sole, expression of community'.[50] Brown's thesis was that the relationship between the state and the market must be renegotiated, because of the way in which globalisation and technology had challenged traditional assumptions. There must be an agreement 'on where markets should have an enhanced role and where market failure has to be addressed'. The public interest must not be confused with public ownership or producer interests. Nor must the Labour Party 'adhere to failed means lest we fail to achieve enduring ends'.[51]

This was when Brown invoked his thesis of the importance of civic society and the moral limits of markets (see Chapter Two). On the one hand, by identifying that there were certain 'moral and civic goods that markets do not honour and money cannot buy', Brown sought to clarify the limits of market provision.[52] On the other, by arguing that market failure should be redressed 'not by abolishing markets but by strengthening markets and enabling them to work better', Brown also sought to show the role markets could play in the delivery of public services. Rather than replace market failure with state failure, Brown asserted that the application of the same public interest test to each could deliver 'equity, efficiency and diversity by reforming and modernising the public realm for the decades ahead, in particular through devolution, transparency and accountability'.[53]

Brown claimed that markets could be enabled to work better by the provision of 'fair and accurate information' to the consumer, fair competition among suppliers, low barriers to entry, producers who are 'not monopolists with the power to dictate prices' and mobility, through the freedom of capital, labour and consumers to go elsewhere. Competition must be embraced, rather than greeted with suspicion, because without it 'vested interests accumulate' and an entrepreneurial culture celebrated as a source of market dynamism and innovation. Where the market had delivered 'insufficient investment and a damaging short-termism', the state must intervene 'to enable markets to work better and for the long term'.[54] For example, by publicly funding health care, the state could surmount the absence of consumer sovereignty. It could overcome the 'chronically imperfect and asymmetric information', the failure of private insurance to 'cover all of the people all of the time' and the fact that essential medical and surgical specialities had, by their very nature, to be delivered locally and therefore, by definition, were 'akin to natural monopolies'.[55]

The problem with Brown's 'pro-market principles' was that while they may have been readily applicable to the liberalised and deregulated markets of the City of London and the privatised utilities, they were less easily applicable to the public services. Brown pointed out how increased investment had been matched by policies such as 'devolution with multi-year budgets for primary care and hospital trusts'; 'more payment by results'; and 'NHS foundation hospitals with greater management flexibility'. He emphasised the importance of the Private Finance Initiative (PFI) as an approach 'quite distinct from privatisation', which had seen the private sector 'rightly helping in public service delivery'.[56] The Treasury's rationale for PFI was that it enabled the public sector 'to take advantage of private sector management skills incentivised by having private finance at risk'. It also claimed it would only use PFI 'where it is appropriate and where it expects it to deliver value for money', based on 'an assessment of the lifetime costs of both providing and maintaining the underlying asset and of the running costs of delivering the required level of service'.[57]

The Treasury maintained that the PFI had been used only where it could deliver efficiency, equity and accountability and offer value for money but 'not at the expense of the terms and conditions of the staff'.[58] The problem was that a large body of evidence challenged these assertions, and the PFI, both in theory and practice. First, the PFI was seen to have undermined the public service ethos, because it fostered privatisation and turned public services into commodities that had become detached from their role of serving the public, rather than private interests.[59] Second, the PFI was driven by the Treasury's desire to keep borrowing off the public sector balance sheet, rather than to improve public services. Third, PFI projects were known to be more costly than conventionally funded public sector projects, because the private sector had to borrow at higher interest rates than government. PFI contracts also had very high start-up costs, because of the number of lawyers and consultants employed by both public and private agencies,[60] and the private sector demanded high returns from PFI projects, which further inflated their cost to the taxpayer and were not in the public interest.[61] Fourth, there was significant evidence that workforces employed by private contractors experienced worse pay and conditions than those enjoyed by public sector workers.[62] Finally, there was little evidence of the genuine transfer of risk from the public to the private sector to justify the premium cost of PFI contracts. Pollock and Price, in *Public risk for private gain?* noted that risk transfer was 'largely unevaluated for central government PFIs' and therefore there was little empirical basis for the claimed benefits.[63]

A detailed analysis (by Pollock and others) of Treasury evidence for cost and time over-run concluded that the PFI was 'A Policy Built on Sand'.[64] The Treasury claimed that eighty-eight per cent of PFI schemes had been delivered on time, whereas seventy per cent of non- PFI projects were delivered late and seventy-three per cent over budget. Treasury guidance required the estimated costs of non- PFI projects to be inflated by as much as twenty-four per cent 'to take into account the risks of cost and time over-runs'.[65] However, an evaluation of five reports on the PFI, including the Treasury report, *PFI: meeting the investment challenge,*[66] concluded that 'there is no evidence to support the Treasury's chief justification for the policy, namely, that PFI generates value for money savings by improving the efficiency of construction procurement. Government policy guidance on optimism bias is flawed and misleading'.[67]

Parliamentary scrutiny of PFI debt refinancing revealed that the Government had received only £93 million as its dividend from voluntary sharing arrangements with private PFI contractors, compared with the expected £175–200 million. By contrast, the refinancing of four early PFI projects enabled private investors to raise their rate of return from between 15.5 and 23.0 per cent (before refinancing) to between 56.0 and 71.3 per cent (after refinancing).[68] This was hardly a shining legacy for Brown's approach to public service reform.

Despite the evidence of the limits of market-based reforms of the public services, Brown further asserted that 'even when a market is inappropriate, old, centralised, command and control systems of management are not the way forward'. His alternative, for the NHS and other public services, was 'a decentralised means of delivery compatible with equity and efficiency'.[69] Brown endorsed the balance between national standards and local autonomy of Tony Blair's 'earned autonomy' model for public services, claiming that:

> ... national targets work best when they are matched by a framework of devolution, accountability and participation – empowering public services to make a difference ... Local autonomy without national standards may lead to increased inequalities between people and regions and the return of the postcode lotteries.[70]

Brown pointed out there had been 'more devolution to English regions in the last few years than in the preceding one hundred years', emphasising the freedom given to Regional Development Agencies (RDAs) to consider local needs in budgets affecting public services in the fields of economic development and planning.[71]

Like Blair, Brown never explained why constrained discretion and centrally prescribed targets must only apply to public services in England. Likewise, outlining 'the modern model for the British NHS', Brown never once acknowledged that, in practice, this market-based model only related to England.[72] The result was a postcode lottery of citizenship rights and funding for public services.

It could not be said that the postcode lotteries had returned because, under the pre-Thatcher Barnett Formula (which the reforms of Brown's

'British model' by-passed (see Chapter Three)), these lotteries in the funding of public services between and within the nations of the United Kingdom never went away. For example, Treasury statistics showed that in 2006–2007, identifiable expenditure on services per head in England was £7,121, less than ninety-seven per cent of the United Kingdom average. By contrast, in Scotland, identifiable expenditure was 117 per cent. In England, per capita spending on health was ninety-eight per cent of the United Kingdom average and for education and training ninety-seven per cent; in Scotland, the equivalent was 112 per cent and 117 per cent.[73]

With identifiable spending also significantly higher in Wales and Northern Ireland, such inequalities in funding enabled the Scottish Parliament and the National Assembly for Wales to offer free public services for which English people were charged. For example, from 1 April 2007, patients in Wales were entitled to free prescriptions; people in England were charged at least £6.85. Welsh breast cancer patients at an English hospital in Shrewsbury received the drug Herceptin for free, while English patients had to pay £47,000 for the equivalent drug.[74] The extent to which cancer patients from deprived communities in England were disadvantaged by the NHS Cancer Plan was duly highlighted by parliamentary scrutiny.[75]

A further anomaly of Brown's legacy to the public services in England was that he never explained why English devolution had to mean merely administrative decentralisation to unelected and appointed agencies (not least the RDAs and their northern consortium, the Northern Way), within tightly prescribed national standards, when devolution of policy and resources was sanctioned for the Scottish Parliament and National Assembly for Wales.[76] It was claimed that the pre-1997 model of public service delivery lacked 'devolution, transparency and accountability', which had suppressed local initiative, constrained innovation, undermined employees' morale, ignored local needs and circumstances and potentially led 'to the delivery of one-size-fits-all, poor quality services to diverse communities'.[77] Brown claimed that during his tenure, the Treasury's alternative model had seen 'decentralised public service delivery to ensure greater freedom and flexibility to local providers'.[78] However, rather than granting the freedoms enjoyed by Scottish and Welsh communities to decide autonomously how to allocate resources and design policies, the Treasury retained tight control of that process in England, through a top-down nationalisation of resource allocation, policy design and performance measurement.

THE LEGACY OF CONSTRAINED DISCRETION

At the Labour Party conference of September 2005, referring to the 7 July 2005 bombings of the London transport system, Gordon Brown referred to the emergency services as 'the quiet heroes of our country', examples of 'public service at its best, not just a career but a calling, the ethic of duty, care, compassion and service'.[79] Brown further asserted that the Labour Party had 'not talked enough about their ethical foundations, of what, at root, gives purpose to our politics and builds trust in public service'.

Brown's moral compass showed him that 'in return for what we received we had a duty to put something back, one moral community of fairness to all, responsibilities from all'.[80] Brown identified the legacy to the public services from a decade of reform and investment as the expansion in the number of people that recruited to improve them; 92,000 more teaching assistants, 36,000 extra teachers and 85,000 additional nurses, compared with 1997.[81] However, there was growing evidence of public disillusionment with, and an imminent political backlash against, the dividend from the investment in and reform of the public services.

As Brown prepared his campaign for the Labour Party leadership, in March 2007, an ICM poll of voting intent found that no fewer than seventy-one per cent of voters questioned thought, in overall terms, that the extra money the government had spent on public services such as health and education during the past decade had been spent badly; only twenty-five per cent thought it had been spent well.[82] The lack of public confidence in the Blair Government's ability to reform the public services was reflected in the March 2007 Ipsos Mori quarterly Delivery Index, which found that fifty-seven per cent of respondents did not agree that its policies would improve the state of Britain's public services, compared to only twenty-nine per cent who did. No fewer than forty-nine per cent of respondents expected the NHS to get worse, far exceeding the nineteen per cent who expected it to get better. In May 2005, just before the General Election, thirty-seven per cent had expected the NHS to improve and only twenty-eight per cent to worsen. Most worryingly, among Labour supporters, an equal number (thirty-three per cent) expected the NHS to improve as did to worsen. This constituted a significant reversal from November 2006, when thirty-five per cent had expected an improvement and only twenty-seven per cent a deterioration.[83]

An Ipsos MORI opinion survey conducted to mark the tenth anniversary of the Blair Government also found that public belief in the government's policies to improve the state of the public services had declined since the 2005 General Election: the number of people agreeing that services would be improved (forty-three per cent) was only narrowly exceeded by the number disagreeing (forty-five per cent). By March 2007, the number agreeing had declined to twenty-nine per cent, compared to fifty-seven per cent who thought public services would not be improved. No fewer than forty-nine per cent of respondents thought the NHS would get worse over the next few years, compared with nineteen per cent who thought it would get better. At the time of the 2005 General Election, thirty-seven per cent had thought things would get worse, compared to twenty-eight per cent who thought the NHS would get better. Sixteen per cent thought the NHS would get much worse and only three per cent that it would get much better. In education, the picture was more encouraging. In March 2007, thirty-three per cent of respondents thought that the quality of education would improve over the next few years and only twenty-four per cent that it would get worse, maintaining a positive trend of public opinion sustained over the past four years.[84]

An ICM poll on political trust, conducted at the end of May 2007, recorded that more respondents (forty-one per cent) trusted David Cameron to improve the quality of education in schools, compared to forty per cent support for Gordon Brown. The same poll found Cameron leading Brown by forty-two per cent to thirty-seven per cent in relation to public trust over improvement of the NHS. However, the results revealed that the further south the poll was conducted, the larger became Cameron's lead over Brown – widening in the South to four per cent (forty-three versus thirty-nine per cent) on schools and four per cent (forty-one versus thirty-seven per cent) on the NHS. In the key battleground of the English Midlands, Cameron's lead was much more pronounced; five per cent on schools (forty-two versus thirty-seven per cent) and twelve per cent on the NHS (forty-five versus thirty-three per cent). However, in relation to competence, Brown enjoyed a massive twenty-five per cent advantage (fifty-four versus twenty-nine per cent), a twenty per cent lead in terms of being a strong leader (fifty-three versus thirty-three per cent) and a crushing seventy-eight per cent lead in experience (eighty-five versus seven per cent). Despite these advantages, Brown's overall lead in terms of making a better Prime Minister was only two per cent (forty-five versus forty-three per cent).[85] It is clear that winning the battle of ideas and policies on the reform of public services will be one of the key contests in the run-up to the next General Election.

PERSONALISED PUBLIC SERVICES: THE AGENDA FOR THE BROWN GOVERNMENT

There will be no slackening in the pace of the reform of public services in England under the Brown Government. On the contrary, Gordon Brown indicated that the momentum of the reform process would, if anything, increase. Barely a week after he became Prime Minister, Brown announced a 'once-in-a-generation' review of the NHS. The new Health Secretary, Alan Johnson, promised that there would be 'no further centrally dictated, top-down restructuring to primary care trusts and strategic health authorities for the foreseeable future' (although Johnson did not rule out further top-down restructuring after that); instead, the review would ensure that 'a properly resourced NHS is clinically led, patient-centred and locally accountable'.[86] For his part, welcoming the review, Gordon Brown stated, 'No institution touches the lives of the British people like the NHS. It is part of what makes Britain the place it is'.[87]

Johnson and Brown's statements encapsulated several distinct features of public services reform under the Brown Government. First, nowhere in Johnson's statement (nor in the Department of Health press release which accompanied it) was there any mention that the NHS review would apply only to England. Not for the first time, a quintessentially English policy was presented as being British; a frequent occurrence during the early weeks of the Brown Government. (Ed Balls, Secretary of State for Children, Schools and Families, also portrayed his agenda as if it would apply to schools and children throughout the United Kingdom; the civil servant who edited the accompanying press release had to add a note at the bottom of the page '*This press notice relates to "England"*'.[88])

Second, the NHS review was to be led by Professor Ara Darzi, a leading surgeon, who would become a Health Minister by his appointment to the House of Lords. Once more, whereas devolution in the other constituent nations of the United Kingdom extended the democratic control of citizens over policy design and resource allocation in the reform of public services, in England, the process would be driven by an unelected technocrat, who the citizens of England would be unable to hold to account at the ballot box. Third, despite Johnson's denial of a top-down restructuring, which would be locally accountable, the NHS review in England would be centrally conducted by Whitehall. The nationalisation of policy design and resource allocation would continue.

Brown's conviction is that 'by combining continuing modernisation of our public services with continuing investment, we can better harness the ethos of public services to meet the needs of the people we serve'.[89] He has identified a series of challenges, domestic and external, which confront the public services. Externally, issues arise from globalisation: security, economic and environmental challenges. Domestically, Brown has identified:

> ... the challenge of ever-rising individual aspirations, people's desire for an individual, often personalised tailor-made service that is customised to meet their needs and their requirements, allied to a new range of public needs and the continual quest for value for money.[90]

This challenge will be met by cutting administration budgets by five per cent in real terms and re-allocating the one billion pounds saved into front-line services. These changes will be augmented by selling thirty-six billion pounds of surplus assets and saving an additional two billion pounds a year by setting unchanged or reduced figures for the 2007 Spending Review settlements for government departments including the Cabinet Office, Treasury, the Department of Constitutional Affairs and the administration of the Department for Work and Pensions.[91]

For Brown, the next stage of reform entails 'personalised services tailored to people's needs'. In practice, his Government has committed itself to:

> ... exciting and innovative new areas of policy, greater choice, greater competition, greater contestability, there will be greater accountability, there will be new approaches to the responsibilities as well to the rights of citizens, there will be a coming together with the third sector and social enterprise so that we can do more.[92]

We should note that while Brown developed these ideas within a discourse about Britain and Britishness, devolution means that this agenda will apply only to England, unless the devolved institutions of the other constituent parts of the United Kingdom decide to follow his lead. Brown has promised 'reforms that create greater citizen empowerment and accountability so that people have more control over the services that serve them'.[93] His problem is that the legacy of the principles and practice of constrained discretion is that the nationalisation of policy design and resource allocation in

England is still based on the denial of precisely that empowerment and accountability, at the community level.

Brown has described a model of 'the double devolution of power from Whitehall to the Town Hall and then from the Town Hall to citizens and communities'.[94] But this model only devolves the power to take decisions over the administration of public services within the constrained discretion (or limited freedom) of the nationalised framework of the Spending Reviews and Public Service Agreements. The greater choice and competition that will come from personalising and individualising public service delivery will empower people as consumers, rather than as citizens.

This personalisation and the double devolution of administrative power was initially planned within the context of the 2007 Second CSR. Although this would allocate resources only for 2008–2009 until the end of 2010–2011, it would set the framework for public services reform (at least in England) for the next decade. In quantitative terms, the major financial challenge to Gordon Brown as Prime Minister would remain the deceleration of the overall increase in public spending. Until 2010–2011, spending was planned to increase by an average of only 1.9 per cent per year in real terms, a slower rate of increase than under the previous two Spending Reviews; a pattern which would be repeated in the planned spending for individual programmes. For example, the Department for Education and Skills would increase average education spending in England by 2.5 per cent a year in real terms (5.3 per cent in nominal terms) during the period of the CSR.[95] This was a significantly lower level of planned spending compared to the average 5.6 per cent per year real increases during the 2000 Spending Review, the 6.0 per cent annual real growth during the 2002 Spending Review and the 4.4 per cent annual real terms increase during the 2004 Spending Review.[96]

The fat years are over for the public services. Reforms will have to be implemented in a context of tighter budgets. One of the key doubts surrounding the 2007 CSR is whether it can deliver the anticipated 2.5 per cent annual efficiency savings needed to fund the reallocation of resources into front-line services. When Brown reported the findings of the July 2004 Spending Review, they were accompanied by the publication of the Gershon Review of public sector efficiency. This identified potentially twenty billion pounds of efficiencies in public spending by 2007–2008.[97] However, by the end of September 2006, departments and local authorities had reported annual efficiency gains totalling only £13.3 billion.[98]

Considerable scepticism has surrounded whether these amount to actual tangible savings that can result in the reallocation of resources to front-line services. A report from the Work Foundation pointed out a potential contradiction in the Treasury's agenda for the public services.[99] On the one hand, the Gershon Review's efficiency programme would result in significant cuts in staffing in public services. On the other, if the Brown Government continued to emphasise the importance of choice and the personalisation of services, there would need to be enough spare capacity in those services to make the exercise of individual choice feasible.

This was painfully demonstrated by the inability of English NHS Trusts to reduce possible infections by isolating new patients, because of the lack of hospital beds. In 2006–2007, no fewer than fifty-five (fourteen per cent) of English NHS Trusts stated that they could not keep their patients, staff and visitors safe by ensuring the risk of hospital-acquired infection was reduced, compared to only 7.2 per cent of Trusts in the previous year.[100] The imperatives of greater choice and greater efficiency contradicted one another. Moreover, there remain significant, but as yet unaddressed, practical obstacles to meeting the objective of efficiency, not least because of weaknesses in recruitment and the threat of 'significant industrial relations problems in the future'.[101]

In his March 2007 Budget statement, Brown announced that for public sector workers covered by the independent Pay Review Body, the overall headline awards in 2007–2008 would average 1.9 per cent, their lowest level for a decade.[102] Public service trades unions were particularly angered by the fact that while the Pay Review Body's recommendation of 2.5 per cent for NHS workers was accepted by the government, Brown chose to stage the pay award in England and Wales (an extra 1.5 per cent from 1 April 2007 and an additional one per cent from 1 November 2007) to keep the award within his two per cent target for public sector pay increases. Members of UNISON, the largest public sector union, unanimously voted to reject the offer. The unions' anger at the staging of the award was exacerbated when it was announced that the NHS in England had recorded a net surplus of £510 million in 2006–2007, compared to a deficit of £547 million during the previous year.[103]

Although trades unions such as UNISON actively supported Gordon Brown's candidature for Labour Party leader, they have demonstrated that they do not share his vision for the reform of the public services. One union-sponsored study asserted that 'the discussion around public service reform has been distorted by a distracting emphasis on market mechanisms and private sector involvement'. However, while 'In theory, such reforms have been thought to offer a route to consumer choice, competitive discipline and managerial innovation', in practice the reforms had 'foundered on the fact that such solutions are not readily applicable to the practical realities of public services'. In particular, such reforms left a legacy of fragmented services, disrupted collaborative relationships, poorer working conditions, higher costs and monopoly profits, 'short-term cost-cutting and distortion of priorities' and the compromising of 'the principles of social equity and public accountability that should underpin all public service reform'.[104] The trades unions maintained that a distinction must be drawn between public services and the private provision of consumer goods and the government must acknowledge the different expectations of each. UNISON has continued to maintain that 'markets will at best only ever be marginal and at worst could be a serious obstruction to the real challenges of public service improvement'.[105]

Venting his frustration at the slow pace of change in the reform of the public services, Tony Blair famously stated, 'I bear the scars on my back after two years in government' and frequently thereafter referred to 'the forces of conservatism' that were threatening modernisation.[106] When he singled out the need to 'take on the forces of conservatism in education' and urged teachers to end the 'culture of excuses', he received a furious reaction from the representatives of professional groups and trades unions representing public sector workers.[107] Gordon Brown's insistence on maintaining – and possibly accelerating – the pace of reform in the public services means that as Prime Minister he can expect similar scars from the 'forces of conservatism'.

BALANCING PERSONAL ASPIRATIONS AND PUBLIC EXPECTATIONS WITH RESOURCES

One of the biggest challenges confronting Gordon Brown as Prime Minister is how to meet the greatly increased public expectations generated by a decade of investment in the public services and the Blair Government's consumer-led approach to reforming service delivery. Despite the fresh momentum that the 2007 CSR brought to the process of public services' reform, the Brown Government did not start with anything resembling a clean sheet but had to work within the restrictions of the legacy of a decade of constrained discretion.

Following Tony Blair, and the Third Way's example of the knowledge-based economy, Brown identified education as the future basis of economic success and what was going to make Britain great in the modern world. His problem is that, because education policy is devolved to the Scottish Parliament and (to a lesser extent) the National Assembly for Wales, his power to intervene can only affect England's schools. Once more, the fact that he represents a Scottish constituency could be used against him by political opponents, both at Westminster and in the media. Brown used a succession of Budgets during New Labour's second and third terms to by-pass local authorities and allocate funding directly to head teachers. For example, Brown's 2006 Budget speech announced new direct payments to schools (worth £270 million in 2006–2007 and £440 million in 2007–2008), which meant that total per-pupil spending in the state sector increased by an annual average of 5.3 per cent between 1996–1997 and 2007–2008.[108] In a television interview in January 2007, Brown said that education is:

> ... the priority, it will have pride of place and indeed it's my passion ...
> We used to talk about education, education, education [but now] If
> anything it's excellence, excellence, excellence, for the next few years.
> Excellence for all.

Brown also said he believed that Britain (in effect, England) 'can move to a world-class education system over the next few years'; one that concentrates on individual tuition.[109] Furthermore, Brown stated that 'our education system should keep people in part-time or full-time education until at least eighteen'.[110]

Brown's ambition for schools in the United Kingdom was, once again, open to being disrupted by devolution. The school leaving age in Scotland and Wales could be raised only with the consent of their Parliament and National Assembly. At best, the Scottish Parliament might anticipate possible reform in England by introducing such a measure at an earlier date, thereby embarrassing the Prime Minister. At worst, the devolved institutions might adopt an alternative policy, to assert their genuine political autonomy and resist any attempt to orchestrate policy from Westminster and Whitehall, in pursuit of a 'British Way' of United Kingdom-wide public services' reform.

Brown also indicated that, through the introduction of more Foundation Schools and Academies, he would continue the unpopular trend towards greater diversity of education provision in England and the dilution or dismantling of the comprehensive system. Brown believes in greater variety and diversity of education institutions because 'It puts pressure on the other schools to do better'. He has further identified 'more choice also within the school, within the classroom itself, as being the next stage'[111] Brown claimed that the Blair government had reached only the foothills of educational progress and he looked forward to 'exciting new innovative areas, whether it be greater choice, greater competition, greater contestability and greater local accountability'.[112]

In effectively reiterating Tony Blair's famous mantra 'education, education, education' and embracing the Blairite faith in consumer choice and market competition as the key agents for modernisation in England's public services, Gordon Brown confronted an immediate fiscal challenge to the affordability of his ambition of educational excellence for all. In his 2006 Budget speech, noting the £3,000 disparity between spending per pupil in state schools (£5,000) and in private schools (£8,000), Brown declared, 'our long term aim should be to ensure for one hundred per cent of our children the educational support now available to just ten per cent'. To deliver, by 2011, the same level of capital investment per state pupil enjoyed by private school pupils in 2006, Brown announced 'a total of thirty-four billion pounds new investment over five years'.[113] However, the misleading nature of this statement and the disparity between Brown's aspirations for educational attainment and spending and the cost of translating that aspiration into an actual policy commitment was highlighted in research prepared by the Institute for Fiscal Studies (IFS) for the House of Commons' Education Select Committee.

The IFS noted that Brown's statement led to tabloid newspaper headlines such as '£34 Billion Schools Bonanza'.[114] However, that figure could only be arrived at by adding together the entire planned capital spending for the period between 2006–2007 and 2010–2011. The implication of Brown's speech had been that there would be 'a significant increase in the rate of growth of new school capital spending in the public sector'. This was not the case. In truth, school capital spending in 2010–2011 would be only £0.9 billion higher in real terms than in 2007–2008, a very different figure from Brown's thirty-four billion pounds.[115] By presenting a cumulative total as if it were an annual increase, Brown had repeated the same trick that he had played eight years earlier when announcing the July 1998 CSR.[116] More damningly, the IFS calculated that to raise per capita education spending on the United Kingdom's projected 7.2 million state pupils in

2010–2011, to the level enjoyed by private school pupils, would cost an extra seventeen billion pounds a year in real terms. If, under a Brown Government, state school spending were to increase at the Treasury's projected 2.25 per cent underlying the real annual rate of growth of the economy, it would take until 2024 to close the gap between the public and private sectors.[117] A pupil aged eleven when Brown first announced his aspiration would be twenty-nine years old by then.

Challenged on the apparent lack of progress on educational attainment during a decade of New Labour government, Brown disputed that the educational glass was half empty rather than half full. Having claimed that the number of pupils achieving the benchmark of five 'good' GCSE A* – C grades had improved from forty-five per cent to sixty per cent, he was reminded that when two of those five had to be in mathematics and English, the percentage fell to forty-five per cent. Brown retorted that that still meant 'a big improvement' in overall terms and that he didn't think 'any parent looking at the schools today will doubt there's been improvement'.[118] The problem for Brown, with all New Labour's public service reforms, is whether the electorate thinks there has been enough improvement, given the additional taxpayers' money invested in education and health. As the aforementioned trends in opinion polls suggest, the legacy of a decade of constrained discretion is not necessarily promising.

THE NEW AUSTERITY

On becoming leader of the Labour Party, Gordon Brown affirmed his commitment to the personalization of public services in England and meeting 'aspirations that are about higher standards tailored to people's individual needs'. Echoing Tony Blair's priorities a decade earlier, Brown claimed, 'Our national mission is to be world class in education', but also stated that 'the NHS will be my immediate priority'.[119] The next stage of what Brown depicted as the 'transformation' of the public services would not just deliver basic services but high quality care, available to all at an affordable price. Brown wanted 'an NHS: personal to you'.[120] His stated intention was 'to put more power in the hands of patients and staff in the NHS in England, not least through early legislation to create 'a new integrated regulator for health and adult social care, called Ofcare, with a stronger focus on ensuring the highest quality and safety standards are maintained across the NHS'.[121] Despite his continuation of the permanent revolution in England's public services that had characterised the Blair Governments, subsequently Brown promised that the pace of reform would be picked up even further in 'the next stage of delivery. This would make services more responsive to users' wants, and both personal requirements and the demand for excellence. Services which are shaped by the user'.[122] The personalisation and improvement of the public services would be implemented through an Education and Skills Bill for England, to 'provide powers that every school is a good school', and an NHS Reform Bill to establish an NHS Constitution for England, setting out the rights and responsibilities of staff and patients.[123]

Despite Brown's commitment to 'a new settlement for new times', in which England's public services would be 'not only available to all, but personal to each',[124] his government's tenure has been marked by a stream of critical reports from parliamentary select committees and professional bodies highlighting the continuing failure of reforms to achieve their set targets and standards. This marks an essential continuity with the under-performance of services that had characterised the Blair Governments. For example, despite the estimated sixty-six per cent real terms increase in revenue funding per student/pupil in England between 1997–1998 and 2007–2008,[125] a major review of primary education by Cambridge University had identified a politicisation of basic skills; an over-emphasis on short-term learning of literacy and numeracy at the expense of pupils' longer-term development; and the need for the existing curriculum to be scrapped.[126] Deficiencies had also been identified in the improvement of adult literacy and numeracy in England, despite the investment of £5 billion between 2001 and 2007. In 2003, 5.2 million people lacked functional literacy and 6.8 million lacked functional numeracy. The Brown Government's response was to announce a new objective of helping ninety-five per cent of the adult population achieve functional literacy and numeracy by 2020, a very distant target and one that, if achieved, would only match the existing performance of the top twenty-five per cent of OECD member countries.[127]

In a similar vein, in the NHS in England, the change from Blair to Brown did not manufacture any significant improvement in the pace of implementing the National Programme for IT (Information Technology), designed to improve the use of information in the delivery of services and the quality of patient care. Indeed, recent progress was deemed to be 'very disappointing', with just six deployments in total during the first half of 2008–2009. By January 2009, the project's estimated cost had soared to £12.7 billion, and its completion date of 2014–2015 was no fewer than four years later than originally planned.[128] Where the project[129] had been implemented, staff had been 'incredibly disappointed' with its performance, because it had cost one trust an extra £10 million and meant fewer patients could be seen. In the case of the new contract for general practice (GP) services in England, in its first three years the contract had cost £1.8 billion more than planned, because GP partners' pay had increased by fifty-eight per cent on average, compared to the expected fifteen per cent. Paradoxically, GP productivity had actually decreased, on average, by 2.5 per cent during the contract's first two years, when it was supposed to deliver 1.5 per cent productivity gains year-on-year.[130]

In addition to the continuing failure to achieve the expected return, in terms of improvement in the quality of services, on its sustained investment and reform programme, Gordon Brown has confronted the challenge of having to introduce his agenda for achieving 'world-class public services' in England, against the backdrop of rapidly deteriorating public finances. For Brown, world-class public services require the empowerment of citizens, through the extension of choice and personal budgets; a new professionalism among the public service workforce; and stronger strategic leadership from central government, through direct intervention to tackle underperforming organisations.[131] Strategic leadership by central government also requires 'clear direction and sustained investment for public services'.[132] The likelihood of the latter has appeared increasingly uncertain given the new austerity confronting the United Kingdom, following its transition from economic boom to bust.

The 2008 Pre-Budget Report indicated that current spending would grow by an annual average of only 1.2 per cent in real terms from 2011–2012 to 2013–2014, and total spending by only 1.1 per cent per annum in real terms over this period.[133] As the Institute for Fiscal Studies (IFS) noted, this would be 'less than a third of the average growth rate seen under the previous five Labour Spending Reviews, and lower than the average growth rate seen during the 18 years of Conservative governments from 1979 to 1997'.[134] If implemented, such a slow growth rate for expenditure would 'cut public spending by 2.5% of national income over three years – £37 billion in today's terms'.[135] The Pre-Budget Report also announced lower than previously planned expenditure for 2010–2011, incorporating an additional £5 billion 'Value for Money' efficiency saving and a cut in the capital expenditure budget for the NHS in England of £1.4 billion.[136] The IFS has concluded there is a very real danger that the Brown Government will have to implement its proposals for further public services reform in England against a backdrop where overall departmental spending will have to remain frozen in real terms, and spending on both education and health will have to fall as a share of national income.[137]

CONCLUSION

After a decade of constant reform and significant investment in the public services, Gordon Brown was able to point to a major legacy. For example, by 2007–2008 (compared with 1997–1998), health spending in the United Kingdom would be eighty-five per cent higher in real terms. Where a quarter of a million patients were waiting for more than six months for an operation when New Labour took power in May 1997, a decade later almost no one had to wait that long.[138] Despite this investment, as the trend in the public opinion polls has suggested, there remains widespread public dissatisfaction at the dividends of a decade of reform.

This is understandable, given the regularity with which the media has been presented with reports questioning the efficiency and equity of the allocation of public resources. Public confidence is unlikely to be enhanced when a parliamentary select committee identifies that, despite record investment and succession of massively expensive administrative reorganisations, the Department of Health still lacks the present-year information needed to manage NHS finances 'in the most effective manner'. Within the wider NHS, 'there is a lack of financial management expertise ... a need to strengthen communication between those responsible for the finances and for the delivery of local health services'.[139] Such weaknesses in financial management and accounting led to a £560 million shortfall in 2005–2006 of the resources needed for the 'Agenda for Change' pay initiative. This resulted in an overall deficit for the NHS in England, at a time of record real terms investment.

This is not a proud legacy of a decade of the Treasury's model of constrained discretion. The nationalisation of policy design and resource allocation in England meant that public services in general, and the NHS in

England in particular, had become ever more centralised. Patricia Hewitt, the former Secretary of State for Health acknowledged that with its net budget for England planned at 90.7 billion for 2007–2008:

> If the NHS were a country, it would be the 33rd biggest economy in the world, larger than new European Union transition economies like Romania and Bulgaria ... The NHS is four times the size of the Cuban economy and more centralised.[140]

While it may have suited the Treasury, little in organisational theory or empirical evidence suggested that maintaining such a centralised structure could necessarily plan policy, allocate resources or deliver services in the most effective manner. There was also the additional legacy of the huge deficit in, and cost to, democratic citizenship rights which constrained discretion bequeathed to the people of England. There has been taxation but insufficient representation of the views of citizens in their communities. As one parliamentary select committee concluded, 'with the powers already conferred on unaccountable regional bodies there is a democratic deficit and with the existing devolution of powers and resource allocation to Scotland, Wales and Greater London', devolution in England must be addressed'.[141]

Despite a decade of frenetic reform, it is evident that the pace of renewal of the public services in England is not going to slacken under the Brown Government. On the contrary, he has indicated that the intensity of reform will, if anything, increase under his leadership. Brown wholeheartedly endorsed the Blair Government's Policy Review of the public services; therefore, in future, citizens will experience public services that are 'increasingly personalised to meet their needs'. The vision that Brown has embraced is of government creation of 'self-improving institutions of public service, independent of centralised state control, drawing on the best of public, private and third sector provision ... a new concept of modern public services: one built around the user of the service'.[142] This choice-based vision is rooted in the belief that 'the UK is also now a consumer society', in which consumers are 'highly educated and sophisticated'.[143]

It is also a vision for England's public services founded on the empowerment of individuals through deliberative forums and participation in third-party organisations, rather than through the extension of citizenship rights via directly elected, devolved institutions, as in the other constituent nations of the United Kingdom.[144] The Treasury hopes that a greater reliance on voluntary organisations, families and individual responsibility for the provision of social welfare will reduce the future burden on the hard-pressed taxpayer. The need to limit the tax burden on corporations and entrepreneurs, to maintain their international competitiveness in global markets, is being used as a powerful rhetorical device to reduce expectations of the role of the state in service provision. The role of the voluntary sector is being championed as a source of individual and community empower-ment, an effective partnership between the state, society and the individual and a means of enhancing the moral virtues of duty and service to others.[145]

The danger for the future of the public services is that this model has overly focussed on the individual as consumer and is too far removed from the public domain of citizenship, equity and public service. The Brown Government has trusted individual consumer choice, the entrepreneurship of private corporations and the social entrepreneurship of voluntary organ-isations as the prime agents of reform and modernisation in the public ser-vices. This risks perpetuating the hollowing out of democratic citizenship and public trust in England. Citizens will only trust the public domain if they believe that public services are governed by an ethic of equity and ser-vice.[146] If people believe that the provision of health care and education is governed by an ethic of competition and profiteering no different from ser-vices provided in private markets, even more Labour Party members and voters may desert a political party whose history is bound up so closely with the provision of public goods and services by public agencies.

The good news for Gordon Brown was that there was early evidence of a (at least short-term) 'leadership bounce' in public opinion on the reform of public services, before he became Prime Minister. This trend continued dur-ing the early weeks of his government. The Ipsos MORI May 2007 Government Delivery Index reported that the number of people agreeing that the government's policies would improve the state of Britain's public services had risen to thirty-eight per cent, while the number disagreeing had fallen to fifty-one per cent. This meant that the figure for net optimism had improved to –fourteen per cent, compared to –thirty per cent in March 2007. Specifically, the net optimism figure for the NHS had improved to –fourteen per cent (twenty-four per cent versus thirty-eight per cent). However, there was be no room for complacency; the net optimism figure for the quality of education had fallen from nine per cent to seven per cent.[147]

The public's priorities remained the same during the early weeks of the

Brown Government as they were during the decade of the Blair Government. In May 2007, a YouGov poll found that cutting NHS bureaucracy was the highest-ranked objective for the Brown Government, with eighty-seven per cent of people advocating it. Eighty-eight per cent of respondents thought it desirable that a Brown Government should focus on policy and delivery, not celebrity, seventy-six per cent that pharmacists should be able to carry out routine procedures such as blood-pressure tests, seventy-two per cent that general practitioners should be required to extend the opening hours of their surgeries and seventy per cent that arrangements should be made for school pupils who struggle with mathematics to have one-to-one tuition.[148]

The bad news for Brown was that, after eighteen months of his government, public faith in the efficiency of his reforms of the public services had diminished significantly. In February 2009, with public services and taxation identified as the second most important issue (behind the economy generally) for determining votes at the next General Election, an ICM poll found the Brown Government (thirty-one per cent) enjoying an eight percentage point lead over the Conservatives (twenty-three per cent) on health policy. However, on education policy, the Labour Party (twenty-six per cent) trailed the Conservatives by one per cent, while the Conservative Party (twenty-seven per cent) enjoyed a four per cent lead on policies concerning public services and taxation.[149] Ironically, at the time of the 'Brown Bounce', the Labour Party had been rated as the best political party on both education policy (with a thirteen per cent lead) and health policy (with an eleven per cent lead) in September 2007, but Gordon Brown had chosen not to call an early General Election.[150]

The greatest challenge confronting the Brown Government remains its capacity to meet the public's high expectations of what public services can deliver for them as individuals, when confronted by the deepest recession since the 1930s, and the need to cut spending and raise taxes. The greatest political legacy of a decade of reforms in England's public services – reforms that enhanced the role of the individual as consumer within internal markets and through competition among providers but weakened the ethic of public service – is that people now expect a lot more. They have paid more tax. They want more for it. Brown has reaffirmed that his agenda 'will mean greater choice. It will mean greater control of the services by the citizens who use it. It will mean personal budgets'.[151] It is hard to reconcile these promises with Brown's economic legacy of the worst public finances in living memory.

Chapter 5

The British Way of Identity and Citizenship

INTRODUCTION

During the Blair Government's second term, one of the most conspicuous features of Gordon Brown's speeches was his gradual switch from a preoccupation with macro-economic stability and fiscal prudence to a fixation with Britain and Britishness. Recent speeches to the annual Labour Party Conference were replete with references to Britain, Great Britain or Britishness (fifty-nine in 2003, fifty-one in 2004, fifty-four in 2005 and forty-two in 2006). Whether at home, attending the 'Great Britons' Awards or delivering the British Council Annual Lecture or abroad, during visits to Africa, Brown missed no opportunity to associate himself with Britain and Britishness. To restore a shared sense of national patriotic purpose, which he believes Britain and the British to have lost, in various speeches he has proposed a series of measures, including the establishment of a British youth national community service, a British Day, the reclaiming of the Union flag 'as a flag for Britain, not the British National Party' to be honoured and not ignored, a national Veterans' Day, the introduction of a biometric British National card, and English language and British history lessons for immigrants.[1]

In this chapter, I shall explore the definition and rationale of the British Way and consider its fundamental flaws. The 'British Way' is Brown's attempt to refine the political asymmetries of citizenship, identity and power that arise from the unique nature of the British Union and have been deepened by the Blair Government's constitutional reforms in general and its devolution agenda in particular. It is also Gordon Brown's means of maintaining the unprecedented Treasury control over policy design and resource allocation in England that was entrenched during Brown's tenure as Chancellor of the Exchequer and would be maintained during the first eighteen months of his tenure as Prime Minister.

The British Way is fundamentally flawed: not only did the Blair Government fail to deliver (in England) its tenets but it is also sustained by historical illustrations and literary references that are almost exclusively about England and Englishness, conflated or misconstrued to become examples of Britishness and British history. Brown has attempted to confine expressions of English identity to the realm of sport but his attempts to ingratiate himself with English football supporters have led to ridicule.

The legacy of the British Way is to have denied the citizens of England the liberty for all, responsibility from all and fairness to all that Brown has identified as the defining characteristics of Britishness. The historical and literary examples Brown has used to substantiate it actually point towards the possibility of an alternative 'English Way', based on an inclusive civic identity and a devolved and more plural approach to politics, policy design and resource allocation.

THE BRITISH WAY: LIBERTY FOR ALL, RESPONSIBILITY FROM ALL, FAIRNESS TO ALL

From the beginning of the Blair Government in May 1997, the New Labour project was characterised by significant similarities and differences in the politics and political economies of Gordon Brown and Tony Blair. One notable difference was the manner in which Brown deliberately shunned the concept of the 'Third Way'. He used the term only once, in an early speech on Britain's role in Europe where 'the third way of economic reform' was contrasted with New Labour's rejection of 'both the federal way and the regulatory way ahead'.[2]

In ideological and rhetorical terms, as I tried to show in Chapters Two and Three, the quintessential characteristic of the British Way is the liberalism of the political philosophy and economy which underpins it. The British Way does not reflect the history and ideas of the Labour Party and its socialist and social democratic traditions; Brown has drawn much more heavily on liberalism, citing the work of John Locke, Adam Smith, Alexis de Tocqueville, John Stuart Mill, T. H. Green and J. A. Hobson. On one notable occasion, when the British Way did actually draw on the work of a prominent socialist, Brown wrongly attributed the quotation 'a poverty of aspirations' to Aneurin Bevan; as Alan Johnson noted, it was in fact said by Ernest Bevin.[3]

As I showed in Chapter Two, Brown has used Himmelfarb's analysis of the paths to modernity in Britain, the United States and France to highlight the superiority of the British reformist 'sociology of virtue', rooted in Enlightenment liberal moral philosophy and characterised by a social ethic and moral sense, over its American 'politics of liberty' and French 'ideology of reason' rivals. Himmelfarb argued that Adam Smith's moral vision of political economy is characteristic of the contemporary United States and has supported George W. Bush's Administration's vision of compassionate conservatism.[4] Brown has endorsed the work of the one of the most prominent American conservative philosophers, James Q. Wilson, precisely because he draws on the Enlightenment notions of moral sentiments and moral sense.[5]

Another salient feature of Brown's British Way, visible during his tenure as Shadow Chancellor and Chancellor of the Exchequer, was his very distinct statecraft. The desire to micro-manage and centrally prescribe policy design and resource allocation in England placed Brown firmly in the technocratic tradition of managerial modernisers. The British Way does not contemplate or sanction the 'marked bias towards individual autonomy' characteristic of Dennis and Halsey's description of English ethical socialism as 'a theory of personality and society which places moral motivation as the mainspring of individual conduct and social organisation'.[6] While maintaining the link between moral motivation and human conduct, only rarely has the British Way drawn on the work of R. H. Tawney or other Labour Party thinkers.[7] Nor have Brown's examples of best practice in public policy or civil society been drawn from the European social democratic tradition. On the contrary, his notion of 'moral sense' comes from liberalism and the thinking of Adam Smith and Adam Ferguson, while the British Way's examples of best practice in civil society have been predominantly North American.

The thesis of the British Way was developed first in Brown's November 1997 Spectator/Allied Dunbar Lecture. Rejecting both the idea of the declining relevance of national identity and the alternative political project of supranational federalism, Brown sought to define British identity in terms of a distinct national character and three 'qualities of a people, of the collective experience they have shared over time'. First, the British Way was manifest in a commitment to liberty through the protection of the individual against the arbitrary power of the state. This was achieved not by the pursuit of crude individualism but by the exercise of mutual responsibility and duty, initially through civil society associations and latterly through the welfare state and NHS. Second, the British Way was adaptable, including the willingness 'to embrace, not fear, constitutional reform ... to break up centralised institutions that are too remote and insensitive and so devolve power'. Third, the British Way was to pursue an outward-looking and internationalist patriotism.[8]

Brown did not develop this theme further until April 1999, when, in a speech at the Smith Institute, he claimed that 'throughout the centuries' the British Way had been 'to foster a uniquely rich and continuously evolving relationship between individual community and state, a strong vibrant civil society where there is opportunity for all'. Casting aside the narrower neo-liberal and Thatcherite concept of Britishness as individualism, the shared British values to be rediscovered were 'creative enterprise and hard work, of outward-looking tolerance and fairness' and also 'public service and a practical outward-looking internationalism'. Brown conceded that these values were 'not necessarily unique' to Britain but none the less, their combination could give rise to 'a special and unifying identity'. Through the rediscovery of these values, Britain could move 'from an over-centralised and uniform state – the old Britain of subjects – to a pluralist and decentralised democracy – the new Britain of citizens'.[9]

However, the definitive statement on the British Way was not articulated until July 2004, when Brown gave the British Council Annual Lecture. In his speech, he sought to weave what he depicted as three muscular and robust 'core values of Britishness' with three distinct national qualities. These six values and qualities: 'being creative, adaptable and outward looking, our belief in liberty, duty and fair play' had, he declared, combined to fashion both 'a distinctive Britishness' and a unique British political settlement, balancing the rights and responsibilities of individuals, communities and the state.[10]

Brown further asserted that these values and qualities should be mobilised both to organise Britain's institutions and to generate a specific political agenda. First, the 'British desire for liberty' and its attendant 'strong sense of civic duty and fair play', which had engendered the British Way of encouraging and enhancing the status of voluntary and community organisations, should now be used to 'refashion the settlement between individual, community and government'. Second, to complement and augment the British Way's restoration and enhancement of local initiative and mutual responsibility in civic affairs, the local institutions of government should be strengthened 'to empower people in their own neighbourhoods'. Third, the British Way's strong sense of duty, fair play and commitment to public service should be harnessed to make citizenship serious.

For Brown, this meant a national debate about the responsibilities and rights of citizenship, embracing 'new literature, new institutes, new seminars, new cross-party debate' and the reclaiming of the Union flag from the British National Party to become 'a flag for all Britain – symbolising inclusion, tolerance and unity'. Britishness would embrace a commitment to 'liberty for all and responsibility from all but fairness to all'.[11]

A MATTER OF POLITICAL ASYMMETRY

One of the principal motives for Brown's increasingly frequent promulgation of his British Way is simple electoral arithmetic. In the seventeen United Kingdom General Elections held since 1945, the Labour Party has won a majority of seats in England on only five occasions (1945, 1966, 1997, 2001 and 2005). Its average of 241 seats and 40.8 per cent of the vote in England compares with the Conservative Party's average of 262 seats and 43.3 per cent of the vote. In the 1997 and 2001 General Elections, the Labour Party won almost twice as many seats in England as the Conservative Party. However, at the 2005 General Election, in winning 286 seats (thirty-seven fewer than in 2001), the Labour Party polled 65,000 fewer votes than the Conservatives. Should it lose a further twenty-one seats at the next General Election, to have a majority on any legislation affecting England the Labour Party would have to rely on its (currently sixty-eight) MPs from Scottish and Welsh constituencies or the votes of other political parties. Such a scenario would appear unsustainable.

While this might have been tolerated in pre-devolution times, Brown appears to comprehend only too readily that this is unlikely to be the case post-devolution. Having campaigned at the 2001 and 2005 General Elections with the policy of 'English votes for English Laws', the Conservative Party has increasingly questioned the legitimacy of the Brown-led Labour Party's right to govern England while holding only a minority of English seats.[12] In February 2006, in a speech entitled 'Modernisation with a purpose' (aping Brown's frequent references to 'prudence with a purpose'), David Cameron announced the creation of a Democracy Task Force, chaired by the former leadership candidate Kenneth Clarke MP.[13] The Task Force addressed a number of key constitutional questions, including the case for equality arising from 'the West Lothian Question (or more accurately) the English question'.[14] Brown has seized every available opportunity to deflect demands for English devolution by trying to convince the English that their political identity must be British and that they should not demand the equivalent political and citizenship rights to their compatriots within the British Union. His task has been made more difficult by a series of hostile opinion polls. For example, an ICM opinion poll in May 2006 showed that fifty-five per cent of those questioned in England (and fifty-two per cent in the United Kingdom) opposed the idea of an MP for a Scottish constituency becoming Prime Minister.[15]

Public disquiet had been fuelled by the thousands of job losses and budget deficits in the NHS in England, a pattern conspicuous by its absence elsewhere in the United Kingdom. The Government would have lost important votes on policies for England (notably health and social care in July and November 2003 and higher education in January and March 2004) had voting been restricted to English MPs. The ban on smoking in public places in England was affected by the votes of 93 MPs from other parts of the United Kingdom. Above all, Tony Blair's final Cabinet contained the anomaly of John Reid, Home Secretary (and former Health Secretary), with responsibility for prisons, police and the criminal justice system in England but not in his native Scotland and Douglas Alexander, Transport Secretary, responsible for England's railways, roads and airports but not those in his Paisley and Renfrewshire constituency.

These imbalances in accountability highlight the peculiar political asymmetries of the United Kingdom. England accounts for almost eighty-four per cent of the UK's population and almost eighty-six per cent its income. If England were an independent state, its population of 50.1 million and GDP of £861 billion (figures from 2004) would make it both one of the largest member states of the European Union and a prospective member state of the G7/G8. Yet paradoxically, within the British Union, England has not enjoyed an identity as a distinct political community. As an adjunct of the British state (and as the Encyclopædia Britannica states), 'Constitutionally, England does not exist'.[16] This lack of identity ferments the long-standing discontent over the iniquities of the Barnett Formula, the pre-Thatcherite mechanism for the territorial allocation of public spending between the constituent nations of the United Kingdom, which was left unchanged by the legion of reforms unleashed by Brown's British model of fiscal policy. A further source of discontent is that, on a strictly pro rata basis, England's population should be represented by 549 rather than 529 Westminster constituencies. These asymmetries made for a potent undercurrent of English discontentment under the three-hundredth anniversary (in 2006) of the Union of the English and Scottish Parliaments.

The implications of these asymmetries were acknowledged in 1973, when the report of the Royal Commission on the Constitution concluded that such political asymmetries could not be redressed by a United Kingdom federation, with a federal Parliament and a Parliament in each of the constituent countries, because of domination by 'the overwhelming political importance and wealth of England'. Nor could the constitutional imbalances embraced by the United Kingdom be corrected by artificially dividing England into a number of federal provinces of equal status; 'this would be unacceptable to the people of England'.[17] The accompanying Memorandum of Dissent pointed out that to grant significant additional political rights to Scotland and Wales, while denying them to the people of England, would result in an inequality of political rights that would not be 'right or acceptable'.[18]

THE NEGATION OF CITIZENSHIP IN ENGLAND

The British Way has fashioned a uniquely British political settlement. It has balanced rights and responsibilities such that citizens and communities in England are denied the opportunity of an autonomous democratic voice and accountability which the devolved institutions have provided elsewhere in the United Kingdom. Interviewed in the *Guardian* in February 2006, Brown promised 'more power for individuals and for neighbourhoods' but used his May 1997 policy choice of 'making the Bank of England independent' as a specific example of the executive both giving up power and building trust in the public realm. Brown claimed that Britain was ready 'to shape a new constitutional settlement' based on 'a new compact between the local and the national and between the executive and the legislature'. This in turn would be based on 'the primacy of the Commons and the enhanced accountability of the second chamber'.[19]

This constitutional settlement merits closer scrutiny. The Bank of England is not independent. The Monetary Policy Committee (of nine appointed, not elected members), exercises a degree of administrative autonomy over the setting of interest rates but only within the monetary policy framework and inflation target laid down by the Treasury and the Chancellor of the Exchequer. What Brown presented as devolution of political power was, in practice, a delegation of administrative responsibility that provided Brown with an institutional alibi for unpopular economic policies. Brown claimed that the 'British idea of liberty' had found new strength through 'the empowerment of each individual' and through responsibility being exercised through 'new forms of active civic engagement'.[20] However, there could never be a new compact between the national and the local in England until the central executive devolved political power (as opposed to merely administrative responsibility) to directly elected local governments, democratically accountable to local citizens and with no centrally prescribed performance indicators and output targets.

Speaking in 2001, Brown's solution to his English conundrum was 'a Britain of regions and nations', which divides (and thereby conquers) England's political identity as a discrete nation.[21] In his vision, the nations are Scotland, Wales and Britain; the regions are England's. England does not – and must not – exist as an autonomous distinct political community. In an address to the 2005 Sustainable Communities Summit in Manchester, Brown asserted that regional policy was entering a third phase, in which 'the top-down centralised systems of regional and urban policy – the *dirigiste* systems of the mid-twentieth century' would be set aside, in favour of local indigenous capacity'. Brown promised that 'the Treasury and central government generally will continue to devolve power away from the centre'.[22] However, to illustrate this 'true devolution of power', Brown cited the examples of the Regional Development Agencies, the Northern Way, the pilot Local Area Agreements, Sure Start, the New Deal for Communities and the Safer Communities Initiative. The common denominator of these

English (not British nor United Kingdom) initiatives was that they had all been designed by central government and operated within the constrained discretion demanded by the Treasury. Brown's periodically-stated commitment to the reinvigoration of elected local government and to increase openness and transparency by 'reforming undemocratic institutions'[23] (specifically the House of Lords) would leave his power as Prime Minister and that of the Treasury in England unchecked. Local government would continue to function within the national framework of Spending Reviews and Public Service Agreements. The House of Lords would remain a subordinate revising chamber. The British Way envisaged that the identity of England as a nation would be limited to the cultural and sporting.

THE KIRKCALDY AND COWDENBEATH QUESTION

Tam Dalyell MP first posed the 'West Lothian Question' in pre-devolution 1977; the question is a modern incarnation of Gladstone's travails over Irish 'Home Rule'. Dalyell described the 'absurd situation' of MPs representing Scottish constituencies being able to vote on areas of policy affecting England, when MPs representing English constituencies would not be able to exercise similar political rights in the Scottish Parliament.[24]

The political asymmetries and postcode lottery in democratic accountability and citizenship fostered by the Blair Government's constitutional reforms created the post-devolution 'Kirkcaldy and Cowdenbeath Question', to which the British Way was to become Brown's answer. Why should Brown or any member of the Westminster Parliament representing a Scottish (or Welsh or Northern Irish) constituency, be able to exercise unchecked and unbalanced power (including voting rights) over the allocation of resources and the design of policies affecting the people of England, when those same policies do not directly affect their own constituents, their schools and hospitals and when the English electorate cannot directly vote them into or out of office?

The British Way is ultimately about the exercise of political power and the desire to maintain the unprecedented power that Brown's illiberal statecraft of 'constrained discretion' exercises over the design of policy and resource allocation in England, when devolution to the Scottish Parliament and Welsh Assembly denies him such power elsewhere. As Chapter Four illustrated, policy design in England was effectively nationalised through the Comprehensive Spending Reviews and the Biennial Spending Reviews and their accompanying Public Service Agreements. This was allied with New Labour's failure to remove caps on the finances of English local government and to reverse the centralisation (so steadfastly opposed by Old Labour in Opposition) enacted by the Thatcher and Major Governments. Any extension of English citizenship, political rights and genuine democratic autonomy would challenge the power of the Treasury and the right of Prime Minister Brown, as an MP for a Scots constituency, to govern England.

Brown has made the same political calculation as did Blair. Genuine political autonomy over policy and resources might be permissible in the heartlands of Scotland and Wales, where Labour is guaranteed its lion's share of seats but nothing more than administrative devolution can be countenanced in the more volatile marginal constituencies of southern England. Tony Blair's desire to maintain and deepen central control was defined in terms of the application of the concept of 'earned autonomy' to reform of public services. Devolution empowered 'locally-elected representatives to adopt approaches to public services reflecting their own national priorities and concerns' but in England alone Blair prescribed that 'devolved delivery can only operate with national standards and accountability'. By complying with this overall vision of centralised prescription over policy design and resource allocation, England's schools, hospitals, local government and other public services had 'earned autonomy' to administer 'by devolution and delegation to the front line'.[25]

For Brown, Treasury power was exercised through the application of the principle of 'constrained discretion' to the 'British Model' of fiscal policy. Through the biennial Spending Reviews and their accompanying Public Service Agreements, the Treasury was sanctioned only heavily-constrained administrative discretion (as opposed to genuine political autonomy) to public spending bodies in England, in accordance with the Treasury-determined spending totals, policy choices and performance indicators.[26] The price of fiscal discipline for England, purportedly to help maintain confidence among the City of London's investors, was to remove the autonomy and trust characteristic of the genuinely pluralistic and associative democracy envisaged by ethical socialists. For England, 'constrained discretion' was technocrat-speak for 'limited freedom' and the negation of English citizenship.

The constitutional imbalances in accountability and legitimacy raised by devolution in general, and the Cowdenbeath and Kirkcaldy Question in particular, were vividly illustrated by the fate of the project to establish a British youth national community service, modelled on the United States' AmeriCorps. On 17 May 2004, Gordon Brown and the then Home Secretary David Blunkett announced the creation of a commission chaired by the then Chief Executive of Scottish Power, Ian Russell (an interesting choice to lead a commission whose work was intended to help strengthen British identity, given that in March 2002 Russell had led thousands of bag-pipers in a St Andrew's Day parade through the streets of New York). The Russell Commission was asked to draw up plans for a national community service scheme for young people. Brown had intended the 'national' ele-ment of the Commission's work to mean 'British'. However, the Commission's work was pre-empted by the Scottish Executive's launch, a week earlier on 11 May, of 'Project Scotland', a national youth volunteering programme for sixteen to twenty-five year old Scots.

Launching the 'ScotsCorps' programme, Jack McConnell, Scotland's First Minister, stated that Project Scotland was intended to enable Scotland 'to move from a culture of dependence to a culture of responsibility' and to help young Scots to show their national pride and display 'the kind of Scotland that our country will become'.[27] There was no mention of any desire to promote a civic British identity to complement a new Scottish identity. Ironically, one of the founding corporate partners of Project Scotland was Scottish Power and one of the project's principal supporters was none other than Ian Russell. He justified his company's sponsorship as 'the chance to help young Scots attain their fullest potential and the oppor-tunity to invest in people now in order to improve our nation's future com-petitiveness'.[28]

One Scot (Brown) had commissioned another Scot (Russell), in charge of a Scottish company (Scottish Power), to produce a report on a United Kingdom volunteering project that would celebrate the values of a civic British identity, only for it to be pre-empted by another Scot (McConnell) and the Scottish Executive's own project on Scottish volunteering which celebrated instead the values of a civic Scottish (but not British) identity.

The peripheral nature of the influence of the Russell Commission's work on volunteering in Scotland and Wales was demonstrated by the fact that of the Commission's thirty-six public consultations, only one was held in Scotland and one in Wales.[29] When the Russell Commission published its report, *A National Framework for Youth Action and Engagement*, it did not acknowledge that the 'national' in its title now meant 'English', not 'British', because the devolved administrations in Scotland and Wales had chosen to pursue autonomous initiatives. The Commission conceded that its framework 'could be applied throughout the UK but the final decisions regarding implementation will rest with each administration'.[30] While the implementation of the Commission's work in England was to be funded by £45 million of public money matched with £55 million of private sponsorship, the devolved institutions were allocated £19.5 million for implementation. This – significantly more generous – allocation of public money was provided even though the devolved institutions had decided to set aside the Commission's work in favour of their own programmes, notably Project Scotland. Since the publication of the Russell Commission's report, a new charity – 'V' – has been created to fund volunteering among 16–25 year olds. However, it is confined to developing close partnerships with voluntary organisations in England.

Thanks to devolution, the legacy of Gordon Brown's ambitions to promote civic British identity through a culture of volunteering is the highlighting of the manner in which devolution has constrained his power to intervene on questions of citizenship in nations other than England.

THE FLAWS OF THE BRITISH WAY

There are many further flaws in the British Way. Brown has asserted that it embraces adaptability, the willingness to embrace rather than fear constitutional change and the devolution of power, to break up remote, centralised institutions. In April 1999, Brown claimed that the whole of Britain would benefit from 'the birth of new centres of power and initiative'; that this new Britain would embrace a 'commitment to participatory democracy' and that it would be built on 'a new set of constitutional arrangements and a unifying and inclusive idea of citizenship'.[31] However, the greatest political asymmetry in and anomaly of devolution is that it has (so far) circumvented the vast majority of the electorate in England (and by extension, the United Kingdom). Only the electorate of Greater London has its own Mayor and Assembly, which leaves 86.4 per cent of England's electorate (72.3 per cent of the United Kingdom electorate) still beyond the pale of devolution. Even if the electorate of the North East of England is taken into account (an electorate which overwhelmingly rejected a Regional Assembly with few meaningful powers in a referendum in November 2004), devolution has still by-passed 81.2 per cent of England's voters and 68.0 per cent of the United Kingdom's electorate.

The British Way identifies the NHS as quintessentially British, where 'national is unquestionably "British" '.[32] This ignores the fact that, with the onset of devolution elsewhere, only in England does the internal market continue to operate. (Similarly, in relation to education, only in England have schools continued compulsory Standard Assessment Tests.) This is a significant divide in the reform of public services; for the NHS in England, 'national' now unquestionably means 'English', not 'British', unless the Government needs 'British' votes from Scots, Welsh and Northern Irish MPs to pass unpopular English reforms.

Further flaws and contradictions in the British Way arise in relation to the pursuit of an outward-looking and internationalist patriotism, which was criticised both at home and abroad. In the majority of his speeches about Britain and Britishness, Brown has tended to avoid the question of the legacy of the British Empire. However, in a speech at the British Museum, many of whose most important artefacts attest colonial plunder, Brown asserted that 'we should be proud ... of the empire'.[33] During a visit to Tanzania in January 2005, Brown told a BBC *Newsnight* film crew, 'the days of Britain having to apologise for our history are over ... we should celebrate much of our past rather than apologise for it and we should talk, rightly so, about British values'[34] Brown specifically linked imperialism with enduring British values of enterprise and internationalism by claiming that the Empire gave Britain a greater global reach than any other country. Drawing on his belief in a moral sense of duty, Brown also asserted that missionaries had been driven to Africa by their particular sense of duty.[35]

The hostile reaction to Brown's defence of the British Empire was led by Thabo Mbeki, President of South Africa. Mbeki described Brown's comments as 'a real surprise and a matter for serious concern' and noted that the United Kingdom had never apologised to those whom it had colonised. Mbeki endorsed an alternative depiction of the British Empire: 'genocide, vast ethnic cleansing, slavery, rigorously enforced racial hierarchy and merciless exploitation'. As an alternative to Brown's vision, Mbeki preferred 'to celebrate those who campaigned for colonial freedom rather than the racist despotism they fought against'.[36] Brown's favourable disposition towards the Empire might be understandable in terms of the high profile of Scots in the Empire's construction but it is somewhat contradicted by his tendency regularly to cite the work of the English radical liberal theorist, J. A. Hobson, one of the greatest critics of imperialism.[37]

THE CONFLATION OF ENGLAND WITH BRITAIN

The most intriguing element of and greatest flaw in Brown's British Way is the extent to which it can only be sustained by drawing on examples of English history or writings specifically about England and the English and reinventing them as if they were about Britain and the British. For example, identifying the British affirmation of freedom and liberty and commitment to fairness for all, Brown cited the signing of the Magna Carta at Runnymede in 1215. He also quoted 'from early opposition to the first poll tax in 1381 to the second', 'the civil war debates – where Rainborough asserted that "the poorest he that is in England hath a life to live as the greatest he" ' and the Bill of Rights in 1689.[38] These are all examples of English history, predating the Act of Union and the creation of the United Kingdom.

While its historical significance and political, social and religious implications have been widely debated, the salient feature of the Peasants' Revolt of 1381 against the third poll tax (following those of 1377 and 1379) is that it was quintessentially English. It was a revolt led by Englishmen (notably Wat Tyler) against the English Exchequer's attempts to meet the costs of England's war with France and arose in the English counties of Essex, Kent, Norfolk, Suffolk and Hertfordshire and did not spread any further north than York, Beverley and Scarborough. Similarly, the Putney Debates of 1647 were conducted by the General Council of the New Model Army at the end of the first English Civil War. They were debates conducted among Englishmen about what actually constituted the English nation and had nothing to do with Britain or Britishness. The debates brought forward 'utterly irreconcilable notions of English particularity, what amounted to two different claim-rights to the kingdom, two different notions of what it was to be English'. Colonel Thomas Rainborough was a member of a very small Republican faction in the Commons who spoke up for the aspirations of ordinary English soldiers. He claimed that law limiting the franchise was 'the most tyrannical law under heaven'; pondering 'what we have fought for ... if it was not to free the population from "the old law of England ... that enslaves the people of England" '.[39]

The British Way is even more dependent on reinventing literary Englands as if they were about Britain and Britishness. Identifying liberty as the primary British value, Brown claimed that Voltaire said that Britain had given to the world the idea of liberty.[40] What Voltaire actually wrote in his *Letters concerning the English nation* was that 'the civil wars of *Rome* ended in slavery and those of the *English* in liberty. The *English* are the only people on earth who have been able to prescribe limits to the power of Kings by resisting them'. Moreover, Voltaire noted that the English were 'not only jealous of their own Liberty but even of that of other nations'[41]. Voltaire identified an essentially English tradition that had nothing to do with Britain or Britishness. In his July 2004 British Council lecture, Brown also cited Montesquieu's statement that 'ours was "the freest country in the world" '.[42] 'Ours' was not Britain. Montesquieu wrote, about England and its constitution, 'England is the freest country in the world'.[43] Cronk, in his 1994 'Introduction' to Voltaire's *Letters*, describes their true importance as that they constitute 'the earliest expression of Enlightenment thinking' and describe 'the rise of empiricism from Bacon to Locke as an English phenomenon in opposition to the French tradition of rationalism'.[44] Likewise Montesquieu, because of his focus on the effectiveness of the balance of power and checks and balances in its constitution and the importance of its commerce to its general spirit, has been described by Pangle, in *Montesquieu's Philosophy of Liberalism* as 'the most influential foreign champion that England ever had'.[45]

Brown further suggested that Edmund Burke's 'little platoons' reflected 'both a British desire for liberty and a strong sense of civic duty and fair play'. However, when Burke stated that 'to love the little platoon we belong to in society, is the first principle (the germ as it were) of public affections', he was comparing revolutionary France specifically with England, and his native Ireland, rather than Britain.[46] In asserting that the superiority in the wealth of England, compared with pre-revolutionary France, could be attributed to the English form of government, Burke specified 'I speak of England, not of the whole British dominion'. When the nation contemplated the French revolutionary model of government, Burke was also adamant that the nation 'must feel as Englishmen and feeling, we must provide as Englishmen'.[47] Burke sought to advance a conservative nationalism, based on 'the whole representative majesty of the whole English nation', to counter a flourishing radical Enlightenment version of English nationalism. Despite his Irishness, Burke sought not only to become 'an *embodiment* of the English national character' (Furniss, in *Cementing the Nation*) but also to redefine that national character, based on a reinvention of the English constitution.[48] That reinvention embodied an explicit rejection of the 1689 Bill of Rights, which Brown had identified as an exemplar of the British 'golden thread of liberty'. Far from Burke's work amounting to an endorsement of the Act of Union between Britain and Ireland, if the predictions about the dangers of the future in Burke's *Reflections on the Revolution in France* are taken seriously, the Act of Union can be seen as 'a disruptive and even revolutionary moment' and 'a precarious political gesture'.[49]

Constructing the British Way, Brown misquoted or misrepresented as exemplars of British qualities and values, literature about England and Englishness provided by Thomas Gray, William Wordsworth, William Hazlitt, Lord Henry Grattan, Alexis de Tocqueville, George Orwell and Winston Churchill. To illustrate both the triumph of human spirit and the tragic waste of human potential in British history, Brown elected to cite Thomas Gray's *Elegy in a Country Churchyard* and its reference to 'Some mute inglorious Milton'.[50] To celebrate Britishness, Brown had chosen an English elegy, by an English poet, written in an English rustic setting. Referring to another English poet, William Wordsworth's 'flood of British freedom', Brown did not indicate that the quote came from a poem entitled *England, 1802*. In this particular poem, Wordsworth declared, 'Milton! Thou shouldst be living at this hour: England hath need of thee' and duly summoned up a string of English authors, including Shakespeare.[51] Brown also cited the English political essayist William Hazlitt: 'we have and can have "no privilege or advantage over other nations but liberty" '.[52] Hazlitt's exact words were not 'we' (Britons) but 'an Englishman has no distinguishing virtue but honesty: he has and can have no privilege or advantage over other nations but liberty. If he is not free, he is the worst of slaves, for he is nothing else'.[53]

Another prominent example of misquotation and misrepresentation in the cause of the construction of New Unionism came when Brown noted that the nineteenth-century Irish statesman Lord Grattan said, 'we can get a Parliament from anywhere ... we can only get liberty from England'.[54] A member of the Irish Parliament (and who served as a member of the British Parliament for fifteen years until his death in June 1820), Henry Grattan actually said, 'you can get a king anywhere, but England is the only country with whom you can participate in a free Constitution'.[55] This statement formed part of Grattan's famous 'Declaration' speech to the Irish Parliament of the 16 April 1872.[56] It was not a tribute to British liberty was but an impassioned demand for Irish freedom and legislative independence from Great Britain. The following month, the Lord Lieutenant, the Duke of Portland, proclaimed that the British legislature had agreed a resolution to remove the causes of Irish discontents and jealousies. This led to the repeal of both the English Declaratory Act, which had asserted the right of Westminster to legislate for Ireland and the Irish Act (Poynings' Law), which had meant that all bills passed in the Irish Parliament, with the exception of money bills, were subject to revision by the Privy Council of England.[57]

Delivering the 2005 Hugo Young Memorial Lecture, Brown cited the French political philosopher, Alexis de Tocqueville. Brown claimed that de Tocqueville had identified civic associations 'at the heart of America'.[58] In fact, in *Democracy in America*, de Tocqueville stated that 'the right of association was imported from England ... the liberty of association has become a necessary guarantee against the tyranny of the majority'.[59] Throughout, de Tocqueville's comparison was between America and England, rather than America and Britain; he saw a symbiotic relationship between political association and civic association, contending that 'civil associations, therefore, facilitate political association; but, on the other hand, political association singularly strengthens and improves associations for civil purposes'.[60] While Brown's British Way had permitted civic associations to sit alongside political associations in his native Scotland, strengthened and deepened through the restoration of the Scottish Parliament, Brown's vision of English democracy championed civic association but negated any suggestion of political association through English devolution: such a move would challenge the power and authority of constrained discretion. Paradoxically, de Tocqueville noted that England had never centralised its administration and believed that centralisation in nations could only exist 'by incessantly diminishing their local spirit'.[61]

Brown's use, and misquotation, of the work of George Orwell to substantiate the British Way is particularly important, because Orwell is the only significant figure from the Labour Party's history of ideas who Brown quotes regularly. Brown claimed that 'Orwell talked of a Britain known to the world for its "decency" ' and believed Britain in 1951 was 'still a country of fixed certainties – echoing Orwell's *Lion and the Unicorn*'. In this book, Orwell asserted, 'in England such concepts as justice, liberty and objective truth are still believed in'.[62] Orwell subtitled that particular work, *Socialism and the English Genius* but Brown referred to, 'in Orwell's words, the British genius'.[63] Orwell had not been making a statement about British qualities; the work relentlessly focuses on England and Englishness. *The Lion and the Unicorn* ends with an essay on 'The English Revolution', which concludes that:

> ... the task of the bringing the real England to the surface, even the winning of the war, necessary though it is, is secondary ... I believe in England and I believe that we shall go forward.[64]

Gordon Brown's challenge as Prime Minister is that he believes in Britain and that it will go forward, at a time when a decreasing percentage of the population share his perspective. Brown looked for inspiration to the last Westminster major speech of a previous Prime Minister, Sir Winston Churchill. However, Churchill did not, as Brown claimed, state that Britain is defined by its sense of fair play.[65] Churchill made a speech on defence policy, in which he reaffirmed his government's commitment to the development of the hydrogen bomb and the maintenance of powerful conventional armed forces within the framework of the North Atlantic Treaty Organisation. He concluded it by hoping that 'the day may dawn when fair play, love for one's fellow men, respect for justice and freedom, will enable tormented generations to march forth serene and triumphant from the hideous epoch in which we have to dwell'.[66] Brown might also reflect on the fact that Churchill once said, 'there is a forgotten, nay almost forbidden word, which means more to me than any other. That word is England'.[67] The more he tries to forget or forbid it as the basis for an alternative national and political identity to Britain and Britishness, the more likely it will be that England will return to haunt Gordon Brown.

BROWN'S INGRATIATION OF THE SPORTING ENGLISH

One of Gordon Brown's principal tactics for diluting resurgent English nationalism and avoiding the possibility that it will develop into a political consciousness is to confine expressions of English identity to sport and culture. Since November 2005, he has sought to lead England's bid for the 2018 World Cup, just as Tony Blair successfully led the British bid for the 2012 Olympics. The Treasury has intruded on the Department for Culture, Media and Sport's responsibility for English football by conducting jointly with it a feasibility study on England's capacity to host the World Cup. When the study's report was published, in February 2007, it was carefully framed within a Unionist, United Kingdom-centric discourse. Instead of focusing on England's capacity, the study began by stating (in bold type), 'There is little doubt that the UK has the ability, capacity and reputation to host large sporting events'.[68]

The report's principal findings included the (not remotely Earth-shattering) revelations that:

> ... hosting the World Cup is likely to produce a positive economic impact as well as other associated intangible benefits ... there are at least eleven existing football stadia in England that could potentially host World Cup matches – with Wembley National Stadium providing a centrepiece ... there is a solid foundation of public support for England pursuing a bid for hosting a World Cup in 2018.[69]

There can can be few better examples of an expensively commissioned report using taxpayers' money to state the patently obvious, for example, that fifty-six per cent of people were in favour of England making a World Cup bid.[70] Moreover, the study had no tangible output other than to provide 'a basis for further work by The FA to establish whether or not a bid to host the future World Cup should be made'.[71] The report merely served as a vehicle and platform for Brown to intrude on English sport.

Brown has also attempted to ingratiate himself with English football supporters and fans. Asked during a visit to Mumbai which team he would support should England's bid for the 2018 World Cup be successful, initially Brown answered 'I think the host'. When questioned, 'Not Scotland?', Brown responded, 'Well, of course, I want Scotland to do well but let's just see how it all works out'.[72] An embarrassed Brown later issued a statement that 'my ideal scenario is that Scotland play England in the final and Scotland win ... But if we don't qualify or we go out in an earlier round, then I would transfer my allegiance to the other home nation, England'. The absurdity of Brown's position had been exposed. To Alex Salmond, the leader of the Scottish National Party, Brown's comments had made him look 'ridiculous in Scotland and insincere in England'.[73]

During the 2006 World Cup, Scottish Cabinet ministers were surveyed to establish whether they would be supporting England (Scotland having failed to qualify for the tournament). Brown claimed that one of his favourite moments in football was Paul Gascoigne's goal in England's victory over Scotland at Wembley during the Euro '96 Championship. Brown also asserted that more than sixty per cent of Scots would be supporting England's attempt to win the World Cup. The Euro '96 match, together with England's 1997 draw against Italy in a World Cup qualifier in Rome, had been 'the most memorable' England games he had attended.[74]

Brown was the only Scottish Cabinet minister who did not refuse to answer the survey. His comments were met with incredulity by his own countrymen. Alex Salmond warned that 'real English football fans will begin to smell a rat'. Brown's comments were also described as 'a load of rubbish' and an electoral stunt by Turnbull Hutton, the Scottish businessman and former chairman of Raith Rovers, the Scottish League Division Two team based in Brown's constituency. Brown had helped Hutton to save Raith from bankruptcy in December 2005.[75]

Brown's claims appear even more incredible when his contribution to a 1994 collection of essays on football is taken into account. (One of the co-editors of the collection was Alistair Campbell, Tony Blair's future chief 'spin doctor'.) In their essays, MPs spelt out their devotion to football as 'The People's Game'. Brown's contribution was entitled 'Why Scotland Means The World To Me' and included the confession, 'you start young and you can't give up supporting Scotland', which makes a complete mockery of his 1997 claim about Gascoigne's goal in Euro '96.[76] Brown also celebrated the invasion and destruction of the Wembley pitch by Scottish supporters following Scotland's victory over England in the 1977 Home International Championship. Attributing 'the burden of national pride' carried by the Scottish football team on behalf of 'a country that was denied its own parliament', Brown also claimed 'English nationalism flowered on the playing fields of Eton', apparently referring to the reasons for the victory at the Battle of Waterloo wrongly attributed to Arthur Wellesley, the Duke of Wellington.[77] Subsequently, Brown denied that the political settlement that devolved power to the Scottish Parliament, the National Assembly for Wales and the Northern Ireland Assembly should extend to an English parliament. This has fuelled a resurgent English nationalism that extends far beyond the former officer class at Eton.

Brown has vocally supported the idea of a Great Britain football team, which Jack Straw, Brown's campaign manager for the Labour Party leadership, has proposed on a number of occasions. In November 2000, Straw stated, 'I personally look forward to the day when we have a British football team. I think we might start winning some games'.[78] Straw's suggestion was dismissed by Number 10 as a 'personal view' and rejected elsewhere with near universal and vehement condemnation, especially from Scotland.[79] This degree of hostility towards the idea of a Great Britain football team has not diminished. The Scottish Football Association and Football Association of Wales have ruled out their participation in a Great Britain team at the 2012 London Olympics.[80] In the politics of world football, the national associations of the United Kingdom have fought long and vigorously to retain their identity and the right to compete separately, rather than as a single Great Britain or United Kingdom team. The maintenance of four national teams also gives the associations the right to elect one of the vice-presidents of world football's governing body, FIFA. The idea is also loathed by representatives of supporters' organisations, who have no affinity with a politically contrived Great Britain team; it has never featured in the supporters' blueprint for the future of football.[81] In England and Wales, a poll conducted by the Football Supporters' Federation showed fifty-three per cent did not support a combined Home Nations' team.[82]

Beyond football, the 2012 London Olympics has assumed enormous importance to Brown's project to regenerate the United Kingdom and Britishness. In an attempt to avoid the possibility that the Olympics will be seen by the rest of the United Kingdom as a project solely for Londoners, the only consequence of which will be the diversion of £2.175 billion of National Lottery funding away from more worthy good causes, Brown announced two new initiatives in his 2006 Budget statement. First, before the 2012 Olympics, there would be a United Kingdom Schools' Olympics and second, there would be funding of thirty four million pounds for a new National Sports Federation (NSF).

The problem with these initiatives is that the governance of sport (together with arts and culture) within the United Kingdom is largely devolved, reflecting the fact that in most competitions other than the Olympic Games players tend to represent the constituent nations rather than the United Kingdom or Great Britain. For example, in Scotland, sportscotland, the national agency for sport, is accountable to the Scottish Executive and Scottish Parliament. The Scottish Institute of Sport, which provides support for Scotland's elite athletes, is separate from the English Institute of Sport and funded by the sportscotland Lottery Fund.[83] Although Brown's announcement of the new NSF implied that it was a United Kingdom institution, in practice its responsibility would be 'levering new and additional private investment into community sport in England' alone.[84]

AN ENGLISH WAY

Gordon Brown's British Way defined Britishness in terms of liberty for all, responsibility from all and fairness to all. Brown's political legacy, in terms of national identity and citizenship, is the delivery of liberty for some, responsibility from some and fairness to some. The citizens of England have not enjoyed the same liberty, defined in terms of Brown's defence of the individual against the arbitrary powers of the state, as citizens of the other constituent nations of the United Kingdom, where new, devolved, institutional checks and balances on state power have been created. The citizens of England have not been able to exercise the same degree of responsibility, defined in terms of Brown's willingness to embrace constitutional reform and break up centralised institutions. The absence of devolution has denied them the opportunity of extended democratic citizenship rights. The citizens of England have been treated unfairly, compared to citizens elsewhere in the United Kingdom.

Fifty-eight per cent of the White British population describe their national identity as English rather than British (thirty-six per cent);[85] the key challenge for England remains not to contrive a British Way but to define an inclusive and civic political identity or 'English Way'. This way must mirror the multicultural diversity of England's sporting and cultural institutions and the popular reclaiming of the Cross of St George. The task was given greater urgency by the May 2001 Oldham and July 2001 Bradford riots and renewed impetus by the increased electoral support for the British National Party in traditional working-class Labour constituencies in England (notably Burnley and Barking) and the London bombings of 7 July

2005 by three born-and-bred Yorkshiremen. Championing the introduction of British identity cards, Brown warned of 'the obvious vulnerability' to identity theft.[86] However, in articulating the British Way, the real theft being perpetrated by Brown has been that of English identity.

Public opinion turned markedly against Brown's British Way even before he became Prime Minister. An April 2007 YouGov poll for the *Sunday Times* found that seventy-six per cent of respondents thought it unfair that Scottish MPs should be able to vote on matters affecting only England when English MPs cannot vote on matters that affect only Scotland. Only ten per cent thought the situation fair. Asked about the way England should be governed in the light of devolution to Scotland and Wales, the preferred solution (for fifty-one per cent) was to stop Scottish and Welsh MPs voting on matters that affected only England, while twenty-one per cent favoured an English Parliament with similar powers to the Scottish Parliament. Only twelve per cent preferred to keep the current arrangements. In terms of government spending per head being about twenty per cent higher in Scotland than in England, sixty-eight per cent thought this unfair, compared with only sixteen per cent who thought it fair. To resolve this situation, thirty-nine per cent thought Scottish taxes should be raised to pay for the extra spending and thirty per cent that Scottish spending should be cut to English levels. Only fifteen per cent thought the *status quo* the best option. Fifty per cent thought the Scots ungrateful for their extra spending, fifty-nine per cent thought English taxpayers were subsidising the other constituent nations of the United Kingdom and seventy-eight per cent thought it wrong for Scotland and Wales to have lower prescription changes and lower university fees than England.[87]

During the Labour Party leadership campaign, Brown's campaign manager, Jack Straw, sought to breathe new life into the British Way. He asserted that:

> We need a British story [where] there is room for multiple and different identities but there has to be a contract that they will not take precedence over the core democratic values of freedom, fairness, tolerance and plurality that define what it means to be British. It is the bargain and it is non-negotiable.

Straw claimed that 'what we describe as Britishness in our story traces back to our own Civil War, its resolution in 1688 – and the Treaty of Union in

1707' and that at the heart of this story lies 'the narrative of the Magna Carta, the Civil War, the Bill of Rights'.[88] As in Brown's analysis, herein lies a central flaw of the British Way. In using these examples, Straw was citing major events from the history of England and the constitutional development of English law. The 'our' in our own Civil War is England. What Straw described as Britishness was, in truth, his understanding of Englishness. Similarly, when Straw made the absurd claim, 'we are the only European nation', he was thinking of the United Kingdom and the British state but the historical lineage was of England and the English state.[89] One more conflation of England and the English with the United Kingdom and the British.

Straw thus highlighted the contradiction at the heart of the British Way. He noted that one in five neighbourhoods in England was racially mixed (that is, at least ten per cent of the population was from an ethnic minority) and that there was 'increasing integration for most people, in most areas, but increasing segregation for some in others'. He further noted how this divergence was highlighted in 2006 in *The State of the English Cities*.[90] Because of the historic and recent pattern of immigration into the United Kingdom, the challenge of integration and multiculturalism was – not exclusively but none the less predominantly – an English question. Moreover, Straw concluded that 'we can learn much from countries that have a more developed sense of citizenship and what goes with it'. In short, 'what goes with a more developed sense of citizenship' is a written constitution entrenching checks and balances on the power of the central executive, clearly defined civil and political rights and, above all, genuine political autonomy for cities, localities and other communities to raise taxes and allocate resources and design policies according to their own priorities, without their discretion being constrained by relentless centralised prescription and intervention.[91]

It would be possible to construct an alternative politics and inclusive concept of citizenship based on Brown's 'golden thread of liberty', Straw's 'core democratic values of freedom, fairness, tolerance and plurality' and the historical lineage and literary quotations that have been advanced to substantiate the British Way. However, that particular history and literature have given concrete expression to the possibility of an 'English Way'.

It would also be possible to construct a genuinely plural democratic political culture in England, to mirror its ethnic and multicultural diversity: Jack Straw himself once called on the Left to redefine its patriotism in the quest for a new England.[92] As Tony Benn once acknowledged, a radical English democratic tradition stretches from the English Civil War and the Levellers through to the Chartists of the mid-nineteenth century. These ideas, which informed Tom Paine's *Rights of Man* and both the French and American revolutions, might yet be brought home to England.[93] They could be combined with the radical liberalism of John Hobson and his proposals for proportional representation, the reform of the House of Lords and to the checking and balancing of the power of the Cabinet, to resolve the progressive dilemma of the relationship between liberalism and social democracy in the English path to modernity.[94]

The prerequisite for such an 'English Way' would be a written constitution, a Bill of Rights and, above all, an end to the centralised prescription inherent in constrained discretion and a reversal of more than thirty years' erosion of power of English local government.[95] As Prime Minister, Gordon Brown has demonstrated that he is not prepared to give away that political power.[96]

CONCLUSION

Through its *Governance of Britain* agenda, the legacy of the British Way for England remains parallel deficits in citizenship rights, democratic accountability and the denial of the expression of England's national identity as a distinct political community.[97] By virtue of its introduction of an annual house-building target for England of 240,000 houses by 2016, a total of two million new homes for England by 2016 and three million by 2020; the establishment of up to five new English eco-towns by 2016 and ten by 2020; the reform of the planning laws in England through the creation of an unelected Infrastructure Planning Commission, with responsibility for 'examining applications for development consent for nationally significant infrastructure projects'; the creation of a third runway at Heathrow Airport; and the introduction of an NHS Constitution for England, the Brown Government has deepened England's parallel deficits in democratic citizenship and accountability for two reasons. First, these policies have all been drawn up as top-down initiatives, the result of reports or inquiries by an unelected and democratically unaccountable elite, which have omitted any process of participation by the people of England. Such action has not been possible elsewhere in the United Kingdom, because of the democratic checks and balances institutionalised by devolution. Second, none of these policies (especially *The Governance of Britain* agenda for England) were included in the Labour Party's 2005 General Election manifesto.[98] In this way, the British Way has continued to negate English democracy.

Admittedly, *The Governance of Britain* did concede that, after a decade of constitutional reform by New Labour, 'power remains too centralised and concentrated in government'. Therefore, the Brown Government would reinvigorate British democracy by clarifying the role of government, both central and local, and making people 'proud to participate in decision-making at every level'. However, rather than extending the principle of devolution to England, nine Ministers for the English regions would be appointed, to provide 'a clear sense of strategic direction for their region' and to 'give citizens a voice in central government'. To hold these ministers to account, the Government proposed the possible establishment of nine English regional select committees, which would be only indirectly accountable to the citizens of their respective regions.[99] By contrast, when Donald Dewar, the Secretary of State for Scotland, had introduced *Scotland's Parliament*, the White Paper on devolution, he had asserted that the very objective of devolution, i.e. 'entrusting Scotland with control over her own domestic affairs', would be 'a fair and just settlement for Scotland'. Indeed, devolution would not only 'strengthen democratic control and make government more accountable to the people of Scotland', but also 'better allow the people of Scotland to benefit from, and contribute to, the unity of the United Kingdom'.[100] *The Governance of Britain* failed to explain why the very same principles could not be extended south of the border, to entrust England with control over her own domestic affairs to deliver a fair and just settlement for England, strengthening democratic control and enhancing accountability.

When he became Prime Minister, Brown promised he had listened to and learnt from the people. There had been no calls from the people of England for the creation of regional ministers or select committees. In the November 2004 referendum, the people of the North-East had voted over-whelmingly against the neutered form of regional government on offer. Therefore, the Brown Government's extension of the British Way was about the more efficient administration of English territory. There would no enhancement of local accountability, only a limited pledge to 'assess the

merits of giving local communities the ability to apply for devolved or dele-
gated budgets'.[101] This approach was entrenched further in the July 2008
White Paper, *Communities in Control: Real People, Real Power*. Each of its
chapters began with a quotation from famous figures, such as Mahatma
Gandhi, John Milton, Abraham Lincoln, John Stuart Mill and Thomas
Paine, celebrating the virtues of democracy. The substance of the White
Paper, however, could not have been further removed from real power for
the communities of England.

The White Paper commenced with a foreword by Gordon Brown and
an introduction by Hazel Blears, the Secretary of State for Communities and
Local Government, in which, remarkably, neither felt able to mention
England. By contrast, Britain (Brown), and London, Scotland and
Zimbabwe (Blears) were mentioned. Moreover, while the White Paper's
key theme was 'power, influence and control', central government's power,
influence and control would not be redressed. On the contrary, the performance framework for English local government would continue to deploy
no fewer than 198 national indicators, while local authorities would have to
prioritise as many as thirty-five centrally-determined performance indicators, a framework of centralised control without parallel among the major
industrialised economies. This could only be seen as an act of democratic
empowerment when set against the previous regime of 1,200 'centrally-
imposed performance indicators'.[102] In fact, the White Paper cited a
February 2008 opinion poll in which no fewer than six out of ten people
questioned did not think they were being given an adequate say in how their
local councils were being run. As many as nine out of ten thought their
councils could be rendered more accountable.[103]

To govern England, the Brown Government's extension of the British
Way has rolled forward the frontiers of the unelected, appointed quango,
exemplified by the new Homes and Communities Agency, itself the product
of a merger between two existing quangos – the Housing Corporation and
English Partnerships. The establishment of the agency had set the seal 'on a
troika of power that is accountable, though imperfectly, only upwards'.[104]
The British Way would not have been able to furnish such a top-down,
unelected and locally unaccountable architecture in other parts of the
United Kingdom because of the democratic checks and balances provided
by devolution. It was possible in England because 'local government in
England is neither local, government nor representative. Local authorities

are ruled from above by central government departments and major quangos'.[105] The democratic asymmetries and inequities of Brown's British Way could only be redressed through 'a fundamental reversal of existing policies towards local government and the quango state so that elected local authorities can be made considerably more autonomous in terms of their policies, revenues and expenditure and protected against constant central government meddling'.[106] Through *The Governance of Britain* agenda, Brown's legacy is to have ensured that the meddling will continue.

PART III

Gordon Brown's Foreign Policy Agenda

Chapter 6

New Atlanticism: The New Deal for Global Governance

INTRODUCTION: MAKING GLOBALISATION WORK FOR ALL

Gordon Brown has a very clear vision for global governance. He wants to make globalisation work for all, to assist the developing world through a Global New Deal that will tackle poverty in a modern Marshall Plan of multilateral co-operation.[1] During the second half of his decade as Chancellor of the Exchequer and during his first eighteen months as Prime Minister, Brown developed this agenda, to leave a very clear foreign policy legacy to the United Kingdom in relation to its policy on international development and the reform of the multilateral international organisations that were created at the end of the Second World War.

Brown's vision is of a project of restoration. He wants to re-establish the vision of 'a new public purpose based on high ideals' that inspired the inter-war liberalism of the English economist John Maynard Keynes and the Democrat President Franklin D. Roosevelt.[2] This vision gave expression domestically to the New Deal in the United States during the 1930s and internationally to the Atlanticist multilateralism and co-operation of the mid- to late 1940s.

The earlier era witnessed the establishment of the Bretton Woods international economic order, characterised by the dominance of the dollar, fixed exchange rates and political controls on the movement of capital, the creation of the United Nations, the Marshall Plan for post-war reconstruction and the dawn of the 'Pax Americana'. Brown now wants to locate British foreign policy within a twenty-first century *Pax Americana*, where international peace and security is guaranteed by the active leadership and participation of the United States. This is an agenda for peace and security based on multilateral diplomatic and political co-operation, rather than aggressive unilateral military pre-emption. Brown has used this vision to distance himself and his government both from the failed neo-conservative 'war on terror', while retaining the primacy of Atlanticism and the 'special relationship' in British foreign policy and from any concerted attempt to trap the United Kingdom within the narrow confines of a European Union-led common foreign and security policy architecture (see Chapter Seven).[3]

Brown calibrates his vision by the same moral compass that oriented his 'British model' of political economy. He has called for 'a new paradigm which recognises our increased global interdependence and rejuvenates the earlier notion that an acceptable and sustainable international regime requires a moral underpinning'.[4] Like his domestic model, Brown's Global New Deal is based on learning some very important lessons from the errors of past governments, notably that 'neither isolationism nor the old *laissez-faire* will work. In the last fifty years no country has lifted itself out of poverty without participating in the global economy'.[5] As with the British model of political economy, there is no choice about the need to embrace globalisation: the choice is 'whether we manage globalisation well or badly, fairly or unfairly'.[6] Like his nationalisation of policy-making for public services in England, Brown's vision for global governance is top-down, technocratic and managerialist, shaped by his involvement in the work of a series of elite commissions and committees from the International Monetary Fund (IMF) to the United Nations.

Nationally, Brown's interest in foreign policy and issues of global governance is reflected in the triumvirate of White Papers, membership of elite committees and his involvement in commissioning reports on aspects of global governance. His desire to defeat global poverty and make globalisation and governance work for all was given concrete form in the three White Papers that mapped the Blair Government's policies on international development.[7] At Cabinet Committee level, Brown served as a member of the Ministerial Committee on Defence and Overseas Policy, whose remit was 'to set strategies for the Government's defence and overseas policy'. He also served on the Subcommittee on International Terrorism, which kept under review 'the Government's strategy for reducing the risk from international terrorism both in the United Kingdom and to its interests overseas'. (Significantly, Brown sought to distance himself from the consequences of the Blair Government's decision to participate in the invasion of Iraq. He sat neither on the Subcommittee on Iraq, whose remit was 'to set and monitor progress against the strategic objectives for British policy in relation to Iraq' nor the Subcommittee on Conflict Prevention and Reconstruction.[8]) Brown served as a member of the Commission for Africa and the Policy Review Working Groups chaired by Tony Blair on Britain and the World and Security, Crime and Justice.[9] As Chancellor of the Exchequer, Brown commissioned Sir Nicholas Stern to review the economics of climate change.[10]

Internationally, and as Chancellor of the Exchequer, Gordon Brown's longest-standing contribution to global governance was as Chairman of the IMF's most powerful committee, the International Monetary and Financial Committee (IMFC) from September 1999.[11] Under Brown's stewardship, the IMFC acted as the primary advisory committee to the IMF's Board of Governors, reporting on major issues, notably the management and adaptation of the international monetary and financial system, proposals for reform of the IMF's governance arrangements (through amendments to its *Articles of Agreement*) and dealing with 'sudden disturbances' that might threaten the international monetary and financial system.[12] During his tenure as IMFC Chairman, Brown repeatedly endorsed the neo-liberal orthodoxy on globalisation and the benefits of liberalised financial markets, favoured by Alan Greenspan. Despite the substantive evidence before him at home and abroad of increasing debt and imprudence, not least that identified in repeated IMF reports (see Chapters Three and Eight), Brown did nothing to recommend action to curb irresponsible lending or risk-taking which might disturb relations between Her Majesty's Treasury and the United States' Department of the Treasury. Following the September 2005 World Summit, Brown served on the United Nations Secretary-General's High-level Panel on System-wide Coherence, which reported, in November 2006, on how the United Nations could overcome its fragmentation and help deliver the Millennium Development, and other internationally agreed, goals.[13]

The single most important legacy to global governance from Brown's desire to make globalisation work for all arose from the 2005 United Kingdom year-long leadership of the Group of Eight (G8) industrialised economies. During its leadership of the G8, which between 1 July and 31 December coincided with its Presidency of the Council of the European Union, the Blair Government sought to focus international attention on Africa and climate change. Gordon Brown was at the heart of this initiative, which was accompanied by the year-long 'Make Poverty History' campaign, led by an alliance of non-governmental organisations (NGOs). This followed the publication of the report of the Commission for Africa (Brown was one of its seventeen commissioners) and Brown's concerted attempts to attract international support for his International Finance Facility (IFF), a mechanism for accelerating the provision of Official Development Assistance (ODA) to Africa. The high point of this activity was the July 2005 G8 Gleneagles Summit, at which an agreement was reached to double annual world-wide ODA by fifty billion dollars, including an extra twenty-five billion pounds for Africa, and immediately to write off the debts of eighteen of the world's poorest countries.[14]

In this chapter, I shall explore the nature and legacy of Brown's desire to make globalisation work for all. I will evaluate the legacy of the Gleneagles Summit and how the G8 has failed (thus far) to furnish the resources required to deliver the Millennium Development Goals. The chapter ends by focusing on Brown's increasing emphasis, affirmed during the first eighteen months of his premiership, on the need for a new security architecture for the United Kingdom and a modified approach to global governance. This approach, which places increased emphasis on winning the battles of ideas and of hearts and minds in the fight against terrorism at home and abroad has remained implacably Atlanticist in its priorities and orientation, symbolised by Brown's commitment to renew the United Kingdom's independent nuclear deterrent.

My theme throughout this chapter is how Brown's desire has been compromised by his insistence on the market liberalism of the 'Washington Consensus', championing trade liberalisation and the neo-liberal orthodoxy of the IMF, World Bank and World Trade Organisation (WTO) at the expense of a more inclusive approach to global governance and a political economy of human development more attuned to the needs of the poorest countries.[15] (Throughout this chapter, neo-liberalism is used as a convenient shorthand to denote the ideology and policies, popularised during the 1980s by the governments of Margaret Thatcher and Ronald Reagan, which sought to roll back the frontiers of the state and roll forward the frontiers of the market through privatisation and the liberalisation and deregulation of markets.)

THE NEW ATLANTICISM

At first, Brown's focus as Chancellor was on the domestic monetary, fiscal and supply-side components of the British model of political economy, so it is perhaps not surprising that he did not make a major speech about global poverty until January 2000. In 1998, when the United Kingdom held both the Presidency of the Council of the European Union (EU) and the G8 in the immediate aftermath of the Asian financial crisis (which damaged global investor confidence and particularly the economies of South Korea and Thailand), the Blair Government chose to make achieving sustainable economic growth its central priority.[16] Brown focussed the attention of the May 1998 G8 Summit in Birmingham on strengthening the architecture of the international financial system and the identification of seven broad principles for growth and employment in the leading industrialised economies, rather than on the interests of developing countries.[17] When Brown was invited by Oxfam to deliver the Gilbert Murray Memorial Lecture, he identified two of the key facets of his perspective on global governance.

The first facet of Brown's vision for international development was its historical and intellectual debt to American liberalism, rather than the Labour Party's tradition of socialist internationalism or European social democracy. This debt was acknowledged by quotations from addresses by President Kennedy and Martin Luther King, the like of which had informed his father's sermons and helped orient Brown's moral compass. Brown cited Kennedy's invocation that 'If a free society cannot help the many who are poor, it cannot save the few who are rich' and King's belief that 'we are tied together in the single garment of destiny, caught in an inescapable network of mutuality'.[18] Brown also deployed a quote from an American academic, Professor James W. Stockinger, which later appeared in many of his speeches on poverty and development and became the signature statement of Brown's belief in the mutual dependence of humanity:

> It is the hands of others that grow the food we eat, sew the clothes we wear, build the homes we inhabit. It is the hands of others who tend us when we are sick and lift us when we fall. It is the hands of others who bring us into this world and lower us into the grave.[19]

The second facet was Brown's desire to define a new paradigm for international development. He contended that there was a need 'to move beyond the Washington Consensus of the 1980s, a creature of its times which nar-rowed our growth and employment objectives', which had 'proved inade-quate for the insecurities and challenges of globalisation'.[20] As its successor, Brown proposed 'a new 2000 paradigm' which could not be 'a Washington Consensus, but, as we have recognised in the poverty-reduction strategies, countries cannot claim ownership and make it part of their national con-sensus'. The four key elements of this new paradigm might be: recognition of 'the critical role of the public sector as well as the private', macro-economic stability as 'an essential condition for growth' together with the pursuit of 'clear policy codes and principles' to ensure it, participation of the poorest countries in the global flow of capital, technology and ideas in a manner beneficial to their development and a recognition of the total inter-dependence of sustainable economic growth and social justice.[21]

Far from being a new paradigm, Brown's agenda was nothing more than a redefinition of development priorities within the neo-liberal ortho-doxy of the Washington Consensus, with its emphasis on market liberalisa-tion and deregulation. First, his emphasis on the critical role for the public sector appeared to be merely an endorsement of the World Bank's ortho-doxy that the role of the state should be to build institutions for the mar-ket.[22] Second, his insistence on macroeconomic stability as a prerequisite of development and the pursuit of principles and codes to guarantee stability was little more than the sanction of the surveillance of its member states' economies conducted by the IMF. The highly prescriptive conditions of and structural adjustment required for multilateral loans threatened the sover-eignty of the IMF and World Bank's client states by forcing them to under-take major reforms of their economies and societies which their populations had not chosen.

Third, the notion of the poorest economies engaging with globalisation in a manner beneficial to their development ignored the extent to which market liberalisation tended to reinforce the competitive advantage of the richest economies and accentuate global inequalities in income and wealth. Fourth, Brown's insistence on the interdependence of sustainable economic growth and social justice ignored the evidence from major international reports and summits of conflict both between growth and environmental sustainability and between market liberalisation and social justice for poorer economies. In 1987, the World Commission on Environment and Development (the Brundtland Report) concluded that a general acceleration of global economic growth would result in 'a mere perpetuation of existing economic patterns' and would not be sufficient to reduce dependence or inequalities.[23] A decade later, in a similar vein, the June 1997 United Nations General Assembly Special Session (Earth Summit II) identified the 'real risk' that trade liberalisation could 'further marginalise' the least developed economies,[24] and that 'decisions on further liberalisation of trade should take into account effects on sustainable development'.[25]

A GLOBAL NEW DEAL THROUGH A MODERN MARSHALL PLAN

Brown's vision for global governance remains decidedly British and Atlanticist; not in any sense European. Brown sees no advantage whatsoever in contemplating further moves towards an ever-closer European political union with a common security and foreign policy agenda for the European Union. As in many other areas of politics, Brown has not sought inspiration from examples drawn from a European social democratic tradition, which would be a natural choice given the Labour Party's historic commitment to internationalism. Brown has looked instead to American liberalism and the example of the Democratic Secretary of State, George C. Marshall, and his programme for post-war reconstruction in Europe and the broader *Pax Americana*, created by the formation of multilateral institutions, notably the IMF and the World Bank.[26]

The vision for the Marshall Plan was set out in a speech at Harvard University made on the eve of the third anniversary of the D-Day landings. Marshall contended that although the American people were 'distant from the troubled areas of the Earth', nevertheless, the United States either had to provide Europe with 'substantial additional help or face economic, social and political deterioration of a very grave character'. Marshall asserted that the United States' Government's response should not be piecemeal but 'provide a cure rather than a mere palliative'.[27] Brown's preferred basis for global governance is a Labour Government working closely in partnership with a Democratic President of the United States to promote the global public good, prosperity and security.[28] Brown's vision is based on the historical precedent of multilateral co-operation but is a process of governance led by the rich industrialised economies rather than a truly global partnership.

The events of September 11th 2001 provided Brown with an international platform on which to confirm his commitment to establishment a new Marshall Plan and Global New Deal for tackling poverty. In the aftermath of the attack, Brown visited the United States to deliver two keynote addresses, in New York and Washington, setting out his vision for global governance. Brown's thesis was that 9/11 demonstrated that 'in the new global economy we are, all of us – the richest countries and the poorest countries – inextricably bound to one another by common interests, shared needs and linked destinies'. The choice facing the international community was 'whether we manage globalisation well or badly, fairly or unfairly [and] whether we are for social justice'. The opposing temptations of 'outdated protectionism and isolationism ... the old *laissez-faire* attitude of there is nothing that can be done' must be resisted. The alternative was to strengthen international co-operation by 'modernising our international rules and reforming the institutions of economic co-operation'.[29]

Brown claimed that his vision of a new global consensus was feasible. Even those campaigning for fair trade for developing countries must acknowledge:

> ... the importance of markets, the pivotal role of private capital and that while the unfettered power of any vested interest anywhere is unacceptable, private companies and private-not just public investments are crucial to making global economic development work in the interests of the excluded.[30]

This is both something of an over-exaggeration and an over-simplification of the degree of consensus at home and abroad. Fair trade campaigners, such as those who had protested at the WTO ministerial meetings in Seattle in 1999 and Doha in 2001, had acknowledged the importance of markets and the pivotal role of private capital but only to the extent that they believed globalisation to be a means to the extension of the power of transnational corporations.

Despite the weight of opposition, Brown maintained that his Global New Deal could be constructed on four building blocks: first, the creation of 'new rules of the game in codes and standards'. These would drive 'an improvement in the terms on which the poorest countries participate in the global economy and actively increase their capacity to do so'. Second, 'the adoption by business internationally of high corporate standards for engagement as reliable and consistent partners in the development process'. Third, building on the WTO ministerial meeting at Doha, 'the swift adoption of an improved trade regime essential for developing countries participation on fair terms in the world economy'. Fourth, 'a substantial transfer of additional resources from the richest to the poorest countries in the form of investment for development'.[31]

Underpinning each of these building blocks of Brown's modern Marshall Plan was the assumption that private capital, in the form of transnational corporations (TNCs) could be persuaded or manipulated to deliver the Global New Deal by investing in some of the poorest economies. However, the evidence from successive World Investment Reports produced by the United Nations is that the world's 60,000 or more TNCs and their 800,000 affiliates invest only where there is profit to be made. That means investment has overwhelmingly gone to the richest economies or to developing countries with major oil or mineral deposits. In 2000, when global Foreign Direct Investment (FDI) reached a record $1.3 trillion, the EU, United States and Japan accounted for seventy-one per cent of inward investment flow and eighty-two per cent of outward investment. Developing countries received only nineteen per cent of global FDI and the forty-nine least developed countries only 0.3 per cent. Africa's entire total was a paltry $9.1 billion.[32] By 2006, the distribution of private investment to the poorest economies had not altered significantly. During 2005 global FDI stood at $916 billion, of which the United Kingdom was the principal beneficiary, with $165 billion. Developing countries received $334 billion (thirty-six per cent of total FDI) but Africa's share (while a record) was only thirty-one billion dollars for the whole continent.[33]

Brown chose to overlook the growing evidence, manifest at the WTO's biennial ministerial meetings in Seattle and Doha, that the interests of the richest and poorer countries were diverging rapidly over the issue of trade liberalisation. Far from a global consensus, a fissure had developed between the richest economies (including the United Kingdom, who had pressed in Doha for broader and accelerated liberalisation of trade, especially in services) and the developing countries. The latter resisted the liberalisation of services until the richest countries had fully opened their markets for trade in agriculture, textiles and the other areas of trade where developing countries had a comparative advantage.[34] Moreover, the developing countries pointed out (correctly) that at a similar stage of their development, economies like that of the

United States, Japan and the EU member states had all deployed tariff and non-tariff barriers to trade, to protect and nurture the infant industries on which their future prosperity depended. In the interest of fair trade, developing countries should be accorded the same opportunity and the 'one-size-fits-all' approach to trade liberalisation abandoned.

A PILLAR OF THE ESTABLISHMENT

The degree to which Brown's vision for global governance amounted to an adaptation of, rather than a genuine alternative to, the neo-liberal orthodoxy of market liberalisation and deregulation is best illustrated through Brown's most enduring practical contribution to global governance, as the Chairman (from September 1999) of the IMF's most powerful committee, the International Monetary and Financial Committee (IMFC).[35] Under Brown's stewardship, the IMFC acted as the primary advisory committee to the IMF Board of Governors. The IMFC reported on major issues, notably the management and adaptation of the international monetary and financial system, proposals for reform of the IMF's own governance arrangements (through amendments to its Articles of Agreement) and dealing with 'sudden disturbances' that might threaten the international monetary and financial system.[36] Over the fifteen meetings of the IMFC he chaired, Brown became a pillar of the IMF establishment.

From the very first meeting he chaired, in April 2000, at which the IMFC reaffirmed 'its strong support for the Fund's unique role as the cornerstone of the international monetary and financial community', Brown used the IMFC to endorse the neo-liberal orthodoxy of IMF policy and governance.[37] Any limited reforms proposed by the IMFC sought to strengthen and deepen the managerialist and technocratic role of the IMF in surveying the economies of its member states. These reforms were consistent with the desire of the United States' Department of the Treasury, under the Bush Administration, to put an end to the 'mission creep'[38] of the IMF and return it to its core mission of promoting international monetary co-operation and exchange rate stability.[39] In particular, under Brown's stewardship the IMFC adhered to the Bush Administration's objective of focusing the IMF on the prevention, rather than resolution, of financial crises and expanding the role of the private sector in crisis resolution, through the extension of

Collective Action Clauses.[40] The IMFC also endorsed the IMF's role in poor countries, promoting policies such as the Contingent Credit Line (CCL), as 'indispensable' and lauding its interventions in financial crises such as that of Argentina in 2001, where the IMFC considered the IMF-supported programme to be 'an important and decisive step to boost confidence'.[41]

The IMFC's praise of the IMF flew in the face of the fact that not a single member state ever signed up to the CCL.[42] More damningly, in a series of highly critical reports, the IMF's Independent Evaluation Office (IEO) criticised the IMF's policies and prolonged use of its resources in poor countries.[43] The IEO recommended that:

> ... the IMF should strengthen the ability of its staff to analyse political economy issues in order to achieve a better understanding of the forces that are likely to block or enhance reforms and to take these into account in program design.

In particular, where the IMFC under Brown had praised the IMF's intervention in Argentina, the IEO criticised it for supporting Argentina 'despite repeated policy inadequacies'. It further claimed 'the IMF's surveillance and program conditionality were handicapped by analytical weaknesses and data limitations'.[44] Despite the repeated failings in IMF surveillance, the IMFC advocated that 'regional and global surveillance should play an increasingly important role and be better integrated with bilateral surveillance'.[45]

This advocacy of an expanded role for the IMFC was in spite of the fact every IMFC communiqué issued under Brown's chairmanship recommended the need for fiscal balance in the United States (lower public spending and/or higher taxation), structural reform in the European Union (greater liberalisation and deregulation of labour and product markets) and financial and corporate restructuring in Japan (fiscal consolidation and reduction of non-performing loans). The sheer repetition of this advice was indicative of the reluctance of the most powerful industrialised economies to give in to the IMFC's desire to micro-manage their domestic economic policies.[46]

THE INTERNATIONAL FINANCE FACILITY

Gordon Brown used the IMFC to power the spread of the British model of political economy and publicise the enduring success of the Brown Boom.

He also used it to promote his particular agenda for and innovations in international development, the most prominent of which was the creation of an International Finance Facility (IFF).

The fourth building block of Brown's modern Marshall Plan was 'a substantial transfer of additional resources from the richest to the poorest countries in the form of investment for development'.[47] In June 2001, a report prepared for the United Nations calculated that an extra fifty billion dollars a year in aid would be required if the international community were to finance the Millennium Development Goals (MDGs). Drawing on these findings and to make good the aid deficit, Brown initially advocated the creation of an International Development Trust Fund. This would have been overseen by a joint implementation committee of the IMF, the World Bank and possibly some member countries.[48]

By January 2003, the International Development Trust Fund had evolved into the IFF. To provide the additional aid required to meet the MDGs, the IFF proposed an extra fifty billion dollars in aid each year until 2015. As a temporary finance facility, rather than a development bank or aid agency, the IFF would organise the disbursement of aid in four- to five-year programmes, raising the money from international capital markets by issuing bonds, with legally binding commitments from the donors; bondholders would be repaid by the IFF. Aid would be disbursed over fifteen years, with the repayment phase lasting a further fifteen.[49] The additional aid would be disbursed through the existing multilateral and bilateral aid infrastructure. Introducing the IFF, Brown argued that, as the core of the modern Marshall Plan, it was based on 'the Marshall Plan's enduring values'. The IFF was urgently needed; it was known that in poor countries, some 115 million children were not able to go to school, 30,000 infants were dying every day and more than two billion people were living on an income of less than two dollars a day. The IFF could fund development that would mean 'the difference between life and death'.[50] The Treasury argued that the IFF would be a practical and cost-effective measure. Having the financial backing of the governments of leading industrialised economies, the IFF bonds would attract high credit ratings. There was also 'a strong moral case for bringing forward these additional resources'.[51]

The IFF for Immunisation was launched in 2006, to provide funding for health and immunisation programmes in seventy of the world's poorest countries. Its rate of return was estimated at 'well over twenty-five per cent'.[52]

The IFF was publicly welcomed by Kofi Annan, Nelson Mandela, Pope John Paul II and Bob Geldof. Mandela, for example, described the IFF as 'an absolutely necessary and timely initiative and deserves an active response from all members of the international community'.[53] However, the United States' Treasury steadfastly refused to stand shoulder-to-shoulder with Brown in the moral crusade against global poverty, because the IFF was not consistent with George W. Bush's Administration's agenda for fighting the economic dimension of its 'war on terror'.[54]

The IFF was also heavily criticised by influential voices within the NGO community. The influential London-based campaigning NGO, the World Development Movement (WDM), pointed out that, according to the Treasury's own calculations, the IFF was likely to raise, on average, an extra nineteen billion dollars per year (at 2006 prices), rather than the fifty billion dollars target. While WDM estimated that the IFF would provide an additional $209 billion in aid (at 2006 prices) between 2006 and 2017, this sum would be more than offset by the repayments that would have to be made from aid budgets, to IFF bondholders between 2018 and 2032. WDM asserted that there would be (at 2006 prices) $316.6 billion less available for aid during this period, meaning that 'the IFF will result in an overall net loss of some US $108 billion less than would otherwise have been available in total aid between 2006 and 2032'. Moreover, WDM calculated that while the IFF would disburse $500 billion over its lifetime, because of the interest payments to bondholders it would cost $720 billion to finance: a net loss of $220 billion.[55]

Similar criticisms came from the Washington-based think tank, the Centre for Global Development (CGD), which is dedicated to reducing global poverty and inequality. It identified ten myths pertaining to the IFF, including the assertion that the IFF would create additional resources for development and that its additional financing costs were defensible. CGD observed that these costs were probably not justified, because the donors 'will pay *at least twenty-four billion dollars in extra interest costs, over and above the regular interest charges*'.[56] Furthermore, CGD disputed whether, because of the likely backlash against aid in the US Congress, American participation in the IFF was either essential or possible and it questioned the capacity both of the IFF to disburse an extra fifty billion dollars a year and to help achieve the Millennium Development Goals. While the myth of 'doubling aid to halve poverty' might sound attractive, CGD described this as 'utterly implausible'. Consequently, CGD concluded that other options for increasing aid to developing countries merited consideration, 'including a more vigorous appeal for more aid through the normal budgetary processes and long-term constituency building'. While such options might be less exciting than Brown's IFF, they might 'nonetheless [be] more transparent, accountable and democratic'.[57]

THE COMMISSION FOR AFRICA

Scepticism also surrounded another of the Blair Government's major innovations in international development, in which Gordon Brown played a major role. As one of seventeen commissioners, Brown contributed to the production of the report of the Commission for Africa. Chaired by Tony Blair, the Commission was launched in February 2004. Its five formal objectives included a commitment 'to generate new ideas and action for a strong and prosperous Africa'.[58]

Unfortunately, the Commission failed to generate the progressive global consensus Brown envisaged. Before the publication of its final report, the Commission was warned by a parliamentary select committee that it should first do no harm and should focus on policy coherence for development and press 'for action on global governance, to ensure that Africa had a louder voice in international organisations such as the United Nations, the World Bank and the International Monetary Fund'.[59] This call was echoed by the United Kingdom NGO, ActionAid, which asserted that 'the first step in supporting African development must be to do no harm'.[60] Indeed, ActionAid created its own 'African Commission for Britain', an all-African panel whose membership, including Michael Camdessus, the former Managing Director of the IMF and Ralph Goodale, Canada's Minister of Finance, contrasted vividly with the Commission for Africa's majority of white commissioners.[61]

When the Commission for Africa published its final report on 11 March 2005, its recommendations did not receive universal approval. The Commission recommended 'significant transfers of money' from richer countries to fund: improved governance and capacity building (an additional up to £3.5 billion), Education for All (an additional seven to eight billion dollars per year), improved public health services (an additional seven to eight billion dollars), investment in infrastructure (an extra ten billion dollars a year to 2010, rising to twenty billion dollar a year to 2015), increased trade through a completion of the Doha Round of world trade talks by the end of 2006, the elimination of export subsidies and trade-distorting support for agriculture by 2010, 'untied, predictable, harmonised' aid, total debt cancellation 'as soon as possible' and a greater voice for African countries in multilateral institutions.[62] Far from generating a new global consensus, both the Blair Government and the Commission came under sustained criticism.

John Hilary, Director of Campaigns and Policy at the campaigning NGO, War on Want, described the report as a 'damning indictment' of the Blair Government's policies of trade liberalisation and privatisation.[63] Hilary highlighted the discrepancy between the Commission's assertion that 'forcing poor countries to liberalise through agreements is the wrong approach to achieving growth and poverty reduction',[64] and the Blair Government's commitment to trade liberalisation as an instrument, as described in the DTI publication, *Making globalisation a force for good.*[65]

Furthermore, despite running to no fewer than 461 pages, the report made no recommendations about climate change and side-stepped a detailed analysis of the impact of transnational corporations on African development.[66] As WDO concluded, in overall terms the report amounted to a backward step from the much clearer and more extensive commitments arising from the twin reports of the Brandt Commission, which had helped initiate the debate on global governance.[67]

THE LEGACY OF THE GLENEAGLES G8 SUMMIT

The failure of major international agents (notably the Bush Administration) to provide substantial backing for the Commission for Africa's recommendations and the hostile reception of the Commission's report by major United Kingdom-based NGOs were particularly damaging for Brown's ambition to foster a New Deal for global poverty. The Blair Government had made Africa and climate change two key themes of the United Kingdom's Presidency of the G8 in 2005. They also featured prominently in the priorities of the United Kingdom's simultaneous presidency of the European Union.[68] The Blair Government had actively courted the global 'Make Poverty History' campaign, in which United Kingdom NGOs were the prime movers, to mobilise popular support for concerted international action on Africa and climate change. For those very same NGOs to criticise the Commission for Africa's report, one of the focal points of the dual G8/EU Presidencies was, at best, an acute political embarrassment.

At the conclusion of the summit of the G8 leaders in Gleneagles in July 2005, a communiqué was issued that included a commitment to double worldwide official development aid by 2010, providing an extra fifty billion dollars per annum, including an annual increase of twenty five billion dollars for Africa. In addition, there were commitments both to write off the debts of eighteen of the world's poorest countries, at a cost of forty billion dollars, and to end export subsidies.[69] For both Brown and Blair, these commitments amounted to one of their most important legacies to global governance and the attempt to reduce global poverty.

However, the record since the Gleneagles summit has demonstrated Brown's difficulties in generating a new global consensus. The Development Assistance Committee (DAC) of the Organisation for Economic Cooperation and Development (OECD) reported that its twenty-two members provided $103.9 billion in aid during 2006 – but this amounted to 5.1 per cent less than in 2005, measured in constant dollar terms. In real terms, this constituted the first decrease in Official Development Assistance (ODA) since 1997. Most significantly, it meant that the Gleneagles G8 Summit commitment to double aid to Africa by 2010 had become much harder to accomplish. While in 2006 the United Kingdom's $12.2 billion ODA represented an annual increase of 13.1 per cent, reflecting larger contributions to international organisations, the United States' fell by twenty per cent, Japan's by 9.6 per cent, Canada's by 9.2 per cent and Italy's by thirty per cent.[70] Other members of the G8 had not rallied to Brown's quest for a Global New Deal nor been prepared to stand shoulder-to-shoulder to deliver the financial commitment that would make a new Marshall Plan feasible.

One of the institutional legacies of the Commission for Africa was the creation of an African Progress Panel (APP) of six eminent figures, including the former United Nations Secretary-General Kofi Annan, the former IMF Managing Director, Michel Camdessus and Bob Geldof, the founder and Chair of Band Aid, Live Aid and Live8. In its first communiqué, the Panel noted that 'in a globalised world, the stability and prosperity of the world is at risk when an entire continent is lagging behind'. At the midpoint of the Millennium Development Goals (MDGs), 'sub-Saharan Africa is the only region which, at current rates, will meet none of the MDG targets by 2015'. During 2006, the continent of Africa achieved a growth rate of 5.4 per cent, well below the seven per cent annual growth needed to reduce African poverty substantially. Moreover, Africa's share of world trade fell, during 2005, by two per cent, pointing to the failure of the trade liberalisation championed by Brown to yield a significant developmental divided for the poorest economies. The APP further identified the shortfall in international aid, despite the G8 commitments made at Gleneagles: the 'G8 governments need to make urgent budget provisions of more than five billion dollars every year, to find the twenty-five billion dollars which they have pledged by 2010'. At the same time, the Education for All Fast Track Initiative, championed by Brown,[71] confronted 'a funding gap of at least US$2.5 billion'.[72]

The most damning criticism of the failure of the international community to deliver on its pledges for aid and debt cancellation has come from the coalition of NGOs who formed the 'Make Poverty History' campaign. That coalition, and its campaign that accompanied the United Kingdom's Presidency of the G8 and EU (which Tony Blair and Gordon Brown actively courted to rally support for their agenda for international development) was reborn as 'The World Can't Wait'. It has sought to address the issues, surrounding debt cancellation, trade justice, vital public services and climate change, on which the G8 and EU failed to deliver during 2005.[73] In a series of highly critical reports and in damning evidence given to a series of parliamentary select committees, United Kingdom-based NGOs identified the flaws in Brown's agenda. In particular, they criticised his – and the Blair Government's – insistence on trade liberalisation by developing countries. For example, Christian Aid identified how 'trade liberalisation has cost sub-Saharan Africa US$272 billion over the past twenty years', a sum which far exceeds the forty billion dollars of aid agreed at the Gleneagles summit.[74] For its part, the World Development Movement identified the United Kingdom's unjust contribution to global climate change (one of the two priorities for the Presidency of the G8). And ActionAid not only repeatedly highlighted the failure of the G8 to meet its targets on debt, trade and aid but also identified a gap of $8.1 billion in funding in 2007 for achieving universal access to HIV infection prevention, treatment and care by 2010.[75]

Even multilateral international organisations have had to acknowledge the shortcomings in global governance and the lack of progress towards the Millennium Development Goals (MDGs). In their annual Global

Monitoring Report, the World Bank and IMF recognise that, five years after 189 states signed the Millennium Declaration pledge to deliver the MDGs by 2015, 'many countries – particularly in Africa and South Asia – are off track [with] over ten million children dying annually of readily preventable diseases'. Despite this, the G8 commitments on aid 'risk remaining unfulfilled'.[76] In a similar vein, the World Economic Forum's Global Governance Initiative (GGI), which monitors annual progress on a range of internationally agreed human development objectives, vividly demonstrated the failure of the international community to deliver anything like Brown's global New Deal or Marshall Plan. A GGI score of ten out of ten would signify adequate human developmental progress; in its first three annual reports, the GGI failed to register a single mark higher than a paltry five (for progress in addressing health and poverty during 2005). Indeed, during 2005, peace and security could score only three, while progress on human rights and the environment was a lamentable two out of ten.[77] In the face of such sustained failure, the World Bank conceded that, while it still believed Brown's priorities (institutionalised in the British model of political economy) of 'macro-economic stability, domestic liberalisation and openness [to] lie at the heart of any sustained growth process', it had to concede that 'the options for achieving these goals vary widely'.[78]

Despite the legion of evidence that the existing pattern of global governance has failed to deliver the MDGs, Gordon Brown has remained steadfastly committed to strengthening and deepening existing multilateral institutions, because of their Atlanticist provenance and the manner in which their governance and policies have permitted the export of the British model of political economy. While Chairman of the IMFC, Brown remained convinced that 2005 had witnessed: 'the first steps to make poverty history and now we must ensure 2005 is remembered not as a one-off but as the beginning of step change in international development'.[79]

Furthermore, in spite of increasing incidences of major financial crises both in developed economies (South Korea, 1997) and developing countries (Mexico, 1994, Russia, 1998, Argentina, 2001), Brown remained adamant that 'stronger IMF surveillance will be critical to resolving the current imbalances and maintaining global economic stability in the medium term'. In short, the IMF could be reformed to deliver prosperity for all by making it 'fit for purpose', by giving it greater power to survey its member states' economies and financial systems through 'a new approach to multilateral surveillance, taking into account the linkages and spillover effects of one country's policies on others in the global economy'.[80] In a classic conflation of his own agenda with that of other interested parties, Brown claimed to be able to identify 'a new consensus developing that an emerging market country and a developing country responding to globalisation will need to have stability, will need to have private as well as public investment'.[81] However, as the sheer weight of evidence submitted to parliamentary select committees by academics, NGOs and critics of the IMF demonstrated, Brown, in believing that such a new consensus exists, might find himself in a small minority.[82]

RENEWING THE 'SPECIAL RELATIONSHIP' IN THE AGE OF INTERDEPENDENCE

As the likelihood of his succeeding Tony Blair became a strong probability rather than a possibility, Gordon Brown returned to the American liberalism of the 1960s Democratic Party for the inspiration to define the agenda for global governance and international development that would shape the foreign policies of his Government.

Brown asserted that because of the rapid and extensive transformation of the global economy, we are witnessing an 'emerging new world order [which] cannot work unless we recognise that we are in age of interdependence'.[83] The concept of an age of interdependence was deployed by President John F. Kennedy during a speech in July 1963, at the height of the Cold War and in the aftermath of the Cuban Missile Crisis. Just months before his assassination, Kennedy claimed that 'the age of interdependence is here'.[84]

President Kennedy's thesis was that the United States' West European allies in the North Atlantic Treaty Organisation (NATO) were 'committed to the path of progressive democracy – to social justice and economic reform attained through the process of debate and reform'. Kennedy sought to champion progressive democracy as a path, superior to communist dictatorship, to modernisation, growth and prosperity. The age of interdependence had arisen because it was 'increasingly clear that the United States and Western Europe are tightly bound by shared goals and mutual respect', wherein 'the central moving force of our great adventure is enduring mutual trust'.[85] Brown wants to develop this same enduring mutual trust in contemporary global governance. It might appear perplexing that a Labour Prime Minister has chosen to build his vision for the future of global governance on a concept developed by a Cold War warrior, given the Labour Party's strong historic commitments to internationalism and pacificism. If, however, Brown's legacy to global and domestic security is taken fully into account, then it becomes apparent that in his premiership, he is seeking to strengthen and deepen, rather than dilute or abandon the trans-Atlantic 'special relationship'.

While he may have refused to embrace the rhetoric of George W. Bush's 'Axis of evil' or Tony Blair's 'Arc of extremism', Brown, nevertheless, steadfastly remained shoulder-to-shoulder with Number Ten and the White House in their post 9/11 war on terror. Brown was one of the 412 MPs who, on 18 March 2003, voted in favour of the United Kingdom using 'all means necessary to ensure the disarmament of Iraq's weapons of mass destruction'.[86] In November 2006, Brown visited British troops in Basra, describing the Prince of Wales' Royal Regiment (known as 'the Tigers') as 'proud and courageous tigers and everyone in Britain is very proud of you'.[87] In March 2007, Brown flew unexpectedly to Helmand Province, Afghanistan, where he stated that, 'achieving security must be our first priority'.[88] Most importantly and almost unnoticed, given the periodic public furore over alleged equipment shortages and deficiencies, as Chancellor of the Exchequer, Brown financed a significant real increase in the United Kingdom's defence spending.

When the Blair Government first took office, the July 1998 Comprehensive Spending Review noted that the United Kingdom's defence spending had 'fallen by some twenty-three per cent in real terms and the Armed Forces have been reduced by almost a third since 1990'. The Government's Strategic Defence Review envisaged 'a radical modernisation of the United Kingdom's defence forces', to be achieved while delivering 'real savings to the taxpayer' from 'within a defence budget that will continue to fall as a share of GDP'.[89] By July 2000, Brown's second Spending Review reflected a changing security agenda. The involvement of British armed forces in Kosovo, East Timor and Sierra Leone meant that defence spending would increase in real terms for the first time in more than a decade, albeit at only 0.3 per cent in real terms per year.[90]

The events of 9/11 marked a sea change in the security agenda: Brown contended that 'Britain's international engagement ... has assumed new importance'.[91] In the July 2002 Spending Review, Brown announced a 1.2

per cent real terms increase, the largest sustained increase in defence spending for twenty years. This was accompanied by parallel increases in the budgets of the Foreign Office, the British Council and the BBC World Service, together with a huge increasing in spending on international development, yielding 'A thirty-five per cent real terms increase since 2001, a ninety-three per cent real terms increase since 1997'.[92] Reflecting this change in the commitment to security at home and abroad, the 2002 Pre-Budget Report redefined the Blair Government's central objective to include 'security for all' for the very first time (a commitment that has remained).[93]

The fiscal prudence of the British model of political economy during the Blair Government's first term left a significant legacy to the United Kingdom's expenditure on both cultural and indirect influences (soft power) and military action (hard power) during New Labour's second term.[94] The greatest dividend of Brown's prudence came after the March 2003 invasion of Iraq. While he maintained a conspicuous public silence on the conduct of the war and its aftermath, in subsequent Budget statements and in the Pre-Budget Report, Brown highlighted the commitment of additional resources to the wars in Iraq and Afghanistan. Not once did he question the efficacy or legitimacy of this expenditure. Having allocated three billion pounds for the war in Iraq in his April 2003 Budget, together with an extra £330 million for additional domestic counter-terrorism measures, in December 2003 Brown announced the 'money set aside for the war against terror including in Afghanistan and for our action in Iraq is £5.5 billion'.[95] In his July 2004 Spending Review statement, Brown announced a further annual average increase of 1.4 per cent, equivalent to an additional £3.7 billion a year by 2007–08 but supplemented by £2.8 billion of efficiency savings over the 2004 Spending Review period.[96] Whenever resources have been needed, Brown's fiscal legacy for global governance has been to make fighting the war against terror overseas a core priority.

THE BATTLE FOR HEARTS AND MINDS

9/11 brought about a sea change in the priority Brown gave to security issues overseas; the terrorist attacks on the London transport system on 7 July 2005 brought about a similar change to his perspective on the implications of global terrorism for domestic security. Brown asserted that since 9/11, the Treasury had, in effect, become a department of security. Indeed, he claimed that 'it is not just the Treasury that is a department of security. So too is almost every other department'. This was because 'addressing the reality, causes and roots of international terrorism is one of the greatest new challenges of our times'.[97] For this reason, the second 2007 Comprehensive Spending Review, the framework for the expenditure priorities not only for the three years until 2009–2010 but also for the policy priorities of the Brown Government for the next decade, identified global uncertainty as one of the principal long-term challenges facing the United Kingdom.[98]

As in other areas of global governance, Brown asserted that the 'British way' to act together, both globally and nationally, is through the construction of 'a unified national consensus'. Because globalisation afforded new opportunities to terrorist networks, Brown advocated steps 'to isolate extremists from the moderate majority'. The model for the fight against international terrorism must be the 'cultural Cold War – a Cold War of ideas and values – and one in which the best ideas and values eventually triumphed'.[99] The Internet has allowed terrorist networks to exchange ideas; Brown has urged that these ideas be openly discussed, so that the moderate majority can 'win the global battle for hearts and minds'.[100]

Although the full forces of the mass media, the arts, literature, foundations, trusts, civil society and civic organisations must be engaged in this battle for hearts and minds, Brown looks to the resources of the state to lead the war against terrorism, noting the investment of two billion pounds a year on counter-terrorism and resilience, a doubling of expenditure since 9/11. Brown has strongly affirmed the introduction of biometric passports, the United Kingdom's movement towards 'an integrated electronic border security system', the extension of pre-charge detention powers from fourteen to twenty-eight days (and beyond, if warranted) and, above all, the introduction of national identity cards. Brown has, opportunistically, linked the war against terrorism with his desire to strengthen the celebration of British national identity by advocating 'the ideals of Britishness' as another bulwark against extremism. In short, 'global terrorism must be fought globally – with all the means at our disposal: military, security, intelligence, economics and culture'.[101]

Drawing on the insights of another eminent American Democratic politician from the Cold War era, Dean Acheson, the former Secretary of State in the Truman Administration, Brown concluded that if the battle for hearts and minds is to be won, peace and prosperity must be seen as indivisible.[102]

Ironically, it was Acheson who famously observed that 'Great Britain has lost an empire and has not yet found a role'.[103] For Brown, the quest for a new global role for the United Kingdom in the twenty-first century means, above all, that the 'special relationship' with the United States will endure. Brown's determination to maintain this primacy in the United Kingdom's Atlanticist foreign policy has been demonstrated by his stance on the UK's independent nuclear deterrent. When the issue was debated in the House of Commons, Brown voted in favour of renewing the United Kingdom's Trident nuclear submarine system. The Government secured the support of 409 MPs and a majority of 248. No fewer than ninety-five Labour MPs voted for an amendment which stated that the case for renewal had not yet been proven and therefore a decision should be delayed and eighty-eight voted against the Government's motion. The dissenters included sixteen former ministers; four were former Cabinet ministers.[104] Intriguingly, sixty of the ninety-five unconvinced of the case for renewal later nominated Brown as Blair's successor, as did forty-eight of the eighty-eight rebels who voted against the Government.[105] There may be trouble ahead in future Parliamentary votes on Trident's renewal.

BRITAIN AS A GLOBAL HUB

On becoming Prime Minister, the most immediate challenge in foreign policy confronting Gordon Brown was whether and how to extricate his government from the damaging legacy of the war on terror in Iraq. Interviewed on BBC television in January 2007, Brown said there were two clear lessons to be learnt from the war in Iraq. The first lesson, related to Iraq itself, is that there should have been a much earlier 'passage of authority to the local population'.[106] In May 2007, Brown reminded the Labour Party that in Iraq 'there is only one province left to hand back. There were 44,000 troops in Iraq, there are now 7,000 going down to 6,000' and that therefore there was no need to be hurried into an early announcement on a definitive timetable for a final British withdrawal from Iraq because it had already largely taken place.[107] The fact that Brown chose not to criticise the American decision to dismantle the former Baathist regime or the slow pace of reconstruction – and thereby to forget the lessons learnt in Japan and Germany at the end of the Second World War – was indicative of the underlying strength of Brown's faith in Atlanticism. Indeed, the actual announcement to withdraw the remaining United Kingdom forces from Iraq by the end of July 2009 was not made by Brown until 17 December 2008.[108]

Brown claimed the second lesson, related to the more general war on terror, would be both 'of huge significance in the years to come' and 'almost a big change in the way we've got to look at these issues'. The lesson was that while military action, policing, intelligence and security work 'can achieve a great deal', they would not be sufficient by themselves. The core of British foreign policy under his government would be the Brown doctrine that 'you will not win against extremist terrorist activities and in particular the propaganda activities, unless you have this battle of hearts and minds that is won'. In his major speeches on security, Brown repeated the mantra that this battle is like the Cold War: the 'cultural war that had to be fought against communism from the 1940s and 50s onwards'. For Brown, that is 'in a sense the model for what we've got to do here'.[109] This view has been shared by David Cameron, who in a point of foreign policy convergence, has built the liberal conservatism of his foreign policy on the recognition that communism was defeated 'in the battle of ideas', rather than by the military.[110]

Continuity in British foreign policy under a Brown Government has come from the priority afforded to Atlanticism and the continuation of the 'special relationship' over European integration and stout opposition to a revival of the European Union constitution to facilitate closer political union. Brown has claimed that 'The British national interest is what I and my colleagues are about' and the tacit assumption has been that the pursuit of that interest overseas is synonymous with Atlanticism. Brown stated how he looked forward to working with President George W. Bush (a statement he was to repeat, with much greater conviction, on the election of President Barack Obama) and reminded interviewers that he had already worked with 'major figures' in previous United States' administrations, notably Alan Greenspan, Robert Rubin and Larry Summers.[111]

The Brown Government wasted little time in setting out its commitment to a New Atlanticism in British foreign policy. David Miliband, the Foreign Secretary, confirmed that the United Kingdom would bring together 'a unique set of alliances' in Europe; alliances with the United States and 'some vital developing countries like India'. At its heart, Britain and its cities would serve as a global economic hub, through the City of London, a global cultural hub, not least through the work of the British Council, and have the potential to be a global hub for political and scientific collaboration.[112] The interdependence of domestic and foreign policy would be reflected in a foreign policy that sought to win the battle of ideas by using British strength in international engagement to be 'a force for good in the world'.[113] To become that force, the Brown Government would acknowledge the growing power of India and China and the 'growing mismatch between national power and global problems', combining in its foreign policy 'the soft power of ideas and influence and the hard power of economic and military incentives and interventions'.[114]

In effect, the Brown Government returned to the multilateralist principles identified in Robin Cook's vision of an ethical dimension to British foreign policy and more fully elaborated in Tony Blair's doctrine of an international community.[115] British power in foreign policy would be derived from winning the battle of ideas, exercising influence within multilateral institutions and the European Union to give them a strong sense of purpose, providing incentives and sanctions through the use of harder power and engaging in direct intervention when appropriate, as in Kosovo in 1999.[116] However, in advancing this vision of a New Atlanticism, the Brown Government offered no guarantee that it would not be prepared to back military sanctions against Iran, should it continue to defy diplomatic pressure from the United Nations to close its uranium enrichment programme.

A key appointment that demonstrated the Brown Government's commitment to a New Atlanticism based on proactive multilateral co-operation, rather than British support for pre-emptive, unilateral action by the United States, was that of Lord Malloch Brown to the new ministership for Africa, Asia and the United States. During his tenure as the United Nations' Deputy Secretary-General and Chief of Staff to the former United Nations' Secretary-General Kofi Annan, Malloch Brown had angered the Bush Administration by his repeated criticism of the United States' policy towards the United Nations. In June 2006, Malloch Brown contended that 'even as the world's challenges are growing, the UN's ability to respond is being weakened without US leadership'. He further asserted that no President since Harry Truman in the late 1940s had thought 'managing global security and development issues through the network of a United Nations was worth the effort' and the Bush Administration had adopted counter-productive 'maximalist positions when it could be finding middle ground'.[117] John Bolton, the United States' Ambassador to the United Nations retorted that such remarks by a senior United Nations' official were 'a very, very grave mistake' whose 'condescending and patronising tone' had delivered 'a very serious affront' to the American people.[118]

Shortly after his appointment at the Foreign Office, Malloch Brown stated his belief that British foreign policy should not be so reliant on the United States.[119] This followed a major speech given in Washington DC in July 2007 by Douglas Alexander, the Secretary of State for International Development, in which he set out the Brown Government's vision of 'an alliance of opportunity'. According to this vision, the whole international community must rally to the Brown Government's cause of advancing change through common values and new alliances must be formed based on those values. Words and actions alike must demonstrate that 'we are: internationalist not isolationist, multilateralist not unilateralist, active not passive and driven by core values consistently applied, not special interests'. Because isolationism did not work in an interdependent world, global civilisation must be guaranteed by a multilateralist, not unilateralist, approach to 'a rules-based international system'. Global challenges must involve the active engagement of the United States and a global community capable of acting together 'through modern effective institutions, including a reformed United Nations, International Monetary Fund, World Bank, World Trade Organization and European Union'.[120]

Douglas Alexander claimed that the Brown Government's foreign policy would be driven by core values, such as opportunity, responsibility and justice, rather than special interests. However, the Brown Government's vision of the United Kingdom as a global hub was largely built on a desire to defend the special interests in global commerce of the City of London's financial markets. Furthermore, the Government's announcement of its commitment to increase defence spending from £34 billion in 2008–2009 to £36.9 billion in 2010–2011 and to order two 65,000-tonne aircraft carriers at an estimated cost of £3.9 billion, each equipped with 36 Joint Strike Fighter aircraft at a further estimated cost of more than £5 billion, reflected the continuing influence of the special interests of the United Kingdom's warfare state in British foreign and security policy.[121]

Some interpreted Alexander's speech as a veiled critique of the Bush Administration and a signal that the Brown Government would distance itself from the 'special relationship'. However, on 25 July 2007, two days before the Summer Recess and with no debate, the Government announced to Parliament that it had agreed to a request from the Bush Administration to upgrade the Ballistic Early Missile Warning System radar at RAF Fylingdales in North Yorkshire, to enable it to contribute to the controversial United States' ballistic missile defence system. This confirmed that the 'special relationship' would be strengthened and deepened, rather than weakened, in Brown's New Atlanticism.[122]

Brown has described his approach to foreign policy as 'hard-headed internationalism'. It must be internationalist 'because global challenges need global solutions and nations must cooperate across borders – often with hard-headed intervention – to give expression to our shared interests and shared values'. It must be hard-headed 'because we will not shirk from the difficult long term decisions and because only through reform of our international rules and institutions will we achieve concrete, on-the-ground results'. The objective must be the construction of a global society 'no longer just based on the power of states delineated by borders but on the aspirations of people that transcend ideology; a global society no longer founded just on balancing competing interests but on building institutions that foster mutual interests because they are grounded in common values'.[123]

In order to achieve this global society, and to construct 'not just security but environmental stewardship and prosperity free of global poverty', Brown wanted 'a G8 for the 21st century, a UN for the 21st century, and an IMF and World Bank for the 21st century'.[124] This would entail a reformed and 'more representative, more credible and more effective' permanent membership of the United Nations' Security Council; an increasingly broadened G8 (to become the G20) 'to encompass the influential emerging economies now outside but that account for more than a third of the world's economic output'; and 'a new coalition of democracies and civic societies joining together as allies for progress, with leaders in politics, economics and civil society all pushing forward reform'.[125] In its foreign policy language, the Brown Government would no longer speak of 'the war on terror'.

Like Tony Blair before him, as Prime Minister Brown has chosen to make his most important keynote speeches to American audiences. Thus, in giving the Kennedy Memorial Lecture in April 2008, Brown told his audience in Boston that the special relationship between Britain and the United States remained 'strong and enduring – so firmly rooted in our common history, our shared values and in the hearts and minds of our people that no power on earth can drive us apart'. Global problems required global solutions, 'the boldest of global reforms', and global cooperation to tackle the challenges of economic globalisation, climate change and 'the risk of violence and instability originating in failed and rogue states'. Brown believed 'a new global deal as bold as the Marshall Plan of the 1940s' was possible, but it would require American leadership redolent of John Kennedy's Declaration of Independence and the spirit of Bretton Woods.[126] In so stating, Brown had anticipated the election of Barack Obama as President of the United States. Obama had repeatedly committed his future administration to providing the necessary American leadership. Brown further suggested that a global society could be created by the New Atlanticism but it would require in turn nothing less than 'more systematic use of earlier Security Council action'; a strengthening of the role of international institutions 'in ensuring a unified global response to terrorism'; and new global agreements and strengthened global institutions 'to protect and safeguard essential global resources'.[127] This agenda seemed entirely feasible since Obama had already declared, 'No country has a bigger stake than we do in strengthening international institutions – which is why we pushed for them in the first place, and why we need to take the lead in improving them'.[128]

CONCLUSION

From his tenure as Chancellor of the Exchequer, Gordon Brown's legacy to global governance is a vision rooted in the ideology and institutions of the American liberalism of the 1930s' New Deal and the post-war multilateralism of the Marshall Plan and the *Pax Americana*. Brown looks to that particular ideological and institutional legacy as a model for global governance in the twenty-first century. He is as determinedly, if not more, committed as Tony Blair to writing new chapters in the 'special relationship' with the White House. The only significant difference so far has been the greater emphasis that Brown has placed on issues of international development and economic governance, compared to Blair's more vigorous espousal of the legitimacy of the 'war on terror'.[129] While some of Brown's proposals, notably the International Finance Facility, have been imaginative, they have been cast firmly within the tenets of the neo-liberal Washington Consensus, with its unassailable faith in the merits of liberalisation, deregulation and privatisation as the basis for development. During his tenure as Chairman of the IMFC, Brown steadfastly toed the establishment line in relation to the governance of the IMF and other multilateral institutions. During his tenure as Prime Minister, Brown has been equally steadfast in his desire to strengthen and deepen Atlanticism, but has seen the election of President Barack Obama as an opportunity to rebuild a sense of public purpose in global governance, based upon the values of American liberalism which he and Obama share (see Chapter Nine). Brown's desire to cement that relationship was reflected in his offer to host the vital G20 Summit in London on 2 April 2009, his securing of the first visit by a European Union leader to the White House to meet President Obama, and his invitation to address both Houses of Congress.

Through international co-operation and the reform of international institutions, notably the United Nations, the North Atlantic Treaty Organisation, the IMF and the World Bank, Brown continues to believe that globalisation can be made to work 'to ensure prosperity and opportunity for not just some people but all people'.[130] His thesis is that the global public good, notably in energy and natural resources, the environment and the fight against terrorism, will only be secured through co-operation. For international co-operation to be feasible, there must be both 'reformed international institutions and more effective multilateral networks'. While the post-1945 Bretton Woods system of international institutions, crafted for 'a world of sheltered economies and just fifty states, is not yet broken', it is nevertheless 'urgently in need of modernisation and reform [for] a world of two hundred states and an open globalisation'.[131]

Brown does not envisage that the United Kingdom will stand down from its permanent seat on the United Nations' Security Council to make way for new twenty-first century powers, such as India and China. Speaking during an official visit overseas while 'Prime Minister-in-waiting', Brown acknowledged India's 'right to an increased voice, side by side with the responsibilities of an economic openness and enhanced international co-operation that come with it'.[132] His balancing of India's rights with its responsibilities sent a clear message about twenty-first century global governance and the contribution that British foreign policy will make to it. India must open up its protected markets to foreign (not least British) investment, in the same way that the United Kingdom has liberalised its markets. India and other developing economies must join the international club on his terms. Just like the European Union, they must converge towards the British model and embrace the Brown Government's agenda for global governance.

Chapter 7

Global Europe: Convergence Towards the British Model

INTRODUCTION

If control over the agenda for the reform of public services in England was the greatest source of friction in domestic policy between Tony Blair and Gordon Brown, the United Kingdom's attitude towards the European Union (EU) was the greatest source of tension in foreign policy. While committed wholeheartedly to the United Kingdom's membership of the EU, Brown is, nevertheless, a confirmed Euro-sceptic and in his pro-European realism, wants the EU to converge towards the British model of political economy. The necessity of that convergence has been institutionalised in the 'Five Tests' that must be passed before the people of the United Kingdom are invited to vote in a referendum on participation in the single European currency. Brown, in his vision of a Global Europe based on pro-European realism, has explicitly rejected the idea of ever closer political union as the future for the EU. Indeed, he has designated that earlier model as merely the first, past and completed phase in the history of European integration.

Brown's political legacy as Chancellor of the Exchequer was the obstruction – repeatedly and successfully – of Tony Blair's stated ambition to place the United Kingdom at the heart of Europe. The United Kingdom did not participate in the first wave of European Monetary Union (EMU). During New Labour's first term, Brown quickly, and decisively, ruled out the United Kingdom's participation in the Single European currency for the lifetime of that Parliament. During the Blair Government's second term, Brown devised a complex array of detailed studies and tests to evaluate progress towards convergence between the United Kingdom economy and the euro-zone. Those studies concluded that it was not then in the United Kingdom's national interest to replace the pound with the euro. Nor is there any prospect, in the immediate or foreseeable future, that the Brown Government will do so. Brown's British model of political economy and unprecedented political power as a peace-time Chancellor was built on the foundation of the national rather than the supra-national control of monetary, fiscal and enterprise policy. The Treasury, under Gordon Brown and outside the euro-zone, not the European Central Bank within it, shaped the United Kingdom's engagement with the European single market. For Brown and his political allies, the vindication of that strategy has been the sustained growth of the national economy outside the euro-zone.

Gordon Brown became Prime Minister at a particularly sensitive time for the EU. Having marked the fiftieth anniversary of the creation of the European Economic Community on 25 March 1957, the European Council held a summit meeting in Germany on 21 and 22 June 2007, to debate the future of the *Treaty Establishing a Constitution for Europe*. The summit was held just after the second anniversary of referendums in which the French and Dutch people had voted 'no' to the Treaty and the European Council's call, in the aftermath of the Constitution's rejection, for a 'period of reflection'.[1]

Brown's reflection on the first fifty years of European integration is that its first phase is over. That phase, of regional economic integration, reconstruction of trade and investment links, development of 'new policies and institutions as the foundation of a common market' and the strengthening and then enlargement of the Single Market, has been supplanted by a second phase. For Brown, the EU must 'move on from the older, inward-looking model to become a more flexible, reforming, open and globally-oriented Europe'.[2] As with so many other aspects of his domestic and international political agenda, Brown has identified globalisation, and the competitive challenge posed by the United States, Japan, China and India, as the justification for major institutional and policy changes at the supra-national level.

The challenge which confronted the Brown Government was that both the European Commission and the political elites of many of the other EU member states remain convinced that the European Constitution can – and should – be revived. For many in France, the principal reason for voting '*non*' in the May 2005 referendum was that the document before them amounted to what Andrew Rawnsley called '*une constitution Blairiste*'.[3] Despite the fact that the EU Constitutional Convention was led by the former French President, Valéry Giscard d'Estaing, there was a widespread belief on both the French Left and Right that the Blair Government had subverted the Constitution. Rather than a further step towards an ever-closer political union, the '*non*' camp was convinced that the Constitution represented a drift towards the Anglo-American model of capitalism and a dismantling of the European social model of comprehensive welfare benefit entitlements. At the same time, high-profile representatives of foreign manufacturers in the United Kingdom criticised the Blair Government's failure to adopt the single European currency and identified how the resulting uncertainty about the pound's future value against the euro had threatened future investment.[4]

For its part, and in the debates held during the period of official reflection under its 'Plan D for Democracy, Dialogue and Debate', the European Commission concluded that there is 'a strong wish by Europe's citizens for more EU action in many areas: on creating jobs, managing globalisation, fighting terrorism and organised crime, promoting sustainable development and solidarity'.[5] The Commission conceded that only forty-seven per cent of its citizens had a positive image of the EU and only forty-four per cent trusted the EU but nevertheless asserted that 'the European Union has never been more needed but rarely more questioned'.[6] It has therefore sought to identify 'A Citizens' Agenda' for Europe, to 'deliver peace, prosperity and solidarity in a new context, globalisation'. Brown's problem is that although the political rhetoric might appear to be converging towards his vision of a 'Global Europe', in practice large parts of the European Commission still believe that globalisation is best addressed by sustaining 'publicly funded health care, social protection and pensions'; somewhat distant from the proposals for wholesale structural reform advanced by the Treasury during Brown's tenure as Chancellor.

As in other areas of domestic and foreign policy, Gordon Brown has sought vigorously to engage in and win the battle of ideas about the future of the EU. There is little sign of any progressive consensus about the future pattern of European integration. In this chapter, I shall set out Gordon Brown's particular vision for the European Union and the United Kingdom's position within it and document how Brown's development of the British model of political economy and broader advocacy of the Anglo-American model of capitalism led to the development of a vision for Europe that is, largely, in accordance with the tenets of Margaret Thatcher's Bruges speech to the College of Europe. I shall then explore the 'Five Tests' for sterling's entry to the single European currency and how Brown, and Ed Balls, developed a very precise agenda for reform of the economic policies of the EU and European Central Bank and in particular the Growth and Stability Pact. The Treasury used the March 2000 Lisbon Summit of the EU as a platform to legitimise Brown's agenda for wholesale structural reform of the Single Market towards a more liberalised and deregulated model. This culminated in Brown's vision of a 'Global Europe' for the twenty-first century and the desire for the other member states of the EU to converge towards the British model of political economy.

THE LESSONS OF 'BLACK WEDNESDAY'

For many eminent social democratic commentators, whether the United Kingdom should align its strategic political and economic interests more closely with those of the United States or the EU is far more than a simple foreign policy choice. The inability of successive post-war British Prime Ministers (including Clement Attlee, Harold Wilson and James Callaghan), to cast off the cloak of the British Empire and move the United Kingdom closer to Europe, was described by Young, in *This Blessed Plot*, as Britain's failure 'to reconcile the past she could not forget with the future she could not avoid'.[7] According to Professor Andrew Gamble, for the British state, 'it is not a matter simply of economics or of politics or of international relations: it goes to the heart of the political identity and political economy of this state formed over a very long period of development';[8] the Labour Party should embrace Europe 'as a model both for capitalism and for welfare and for democracy, to join the euro and to participate fully in developing Britain's European identity and deepening the integration of Europe'.[9] For the *Observer* columnist Will Hutton, 'the quest for European Union is one of the great rousing and crucial political projects of our time' and therefore the United Kingdom should join the euro.[10] For these commentators, the United Kingdom's stance towards European integration is much more than simply a question of whether or not to join the euro. It should be seen as 'a question about what values should underpin the building of Britain's economic and social model'.

This is not a view currently shared by Gordon Brown but it was not ever thus. Speaking at the Trades Union Congress on 8 September 1988, Jacques Delors, the President of the European Commission, appeared to provide the Labour movement with a means to roll back the frontiers of a decade of Thatcherism by embracing the European Community's economic and social model of 'co-operation as well as competition'.[11] During the 1992 General Election campaign, the Labour Party promised to 'promote Britain out of the European second division into which our country has been relegated by the Tories'. Having cast off its overt Euro-scepticism of a decade earlier, the Party would keep the pound within the European Exchange Rate Mechanism (ERM) but play an active role in negotiations on the EMU.[12] However, on 16 September 1992, the United Kingdom suffered the national humiliation of 'Black Wednesday' when currency speculators operating on the City of London's foreign exchange markets drove the pound out of the ERM's fixed exchange rate regime. This happened despite the Major Government's having, within less than four hours, raised interest rates from ten per cent to twelve per cent and then to fifteen per cent, and spent billions of pounds of foreign exchange buying sterling in a vain attempt to maintain the pound within the permitted variation from its central parity of DM2.95.[13] The Major Government's counter-inflationary strategy was destroyed at a stroke, together with its reputation for economic competence. The Chancellor of the Exchequer, Norman Lamont, paid for the crisis with his job.

Gordon Brown and Ed Balls learnt important lessons about the future conduct of British economic policy and its relationship to EMU from the events of 'Black Wednesday'; lessons that provided the foundations of the British model of political economy (as I outlined in Chapter Three). Brown's initial reaction was to suggest that 'Black Wednesday' had demonstrated that Europe was still the answer.[14] More, rather than less, European co-operation was needed 'to diminish the power and role of speculators'. Brown explicitly rejected the idea that a freely-floating pound, outside the

ERM, could provide the 'managed and stable exchange rate essential for sustainable growth'. Brown argued that 'The credibility of Europe depends on the ability of Governments to act together to deal with the problems of the economy'.[15] Above all, Brown wanted to avoid the Labour Party being once more depicted as 'the party of devaluation'.

At this time, Ed Balls did not share Brown's analysis. His lessons from the debacle were much clearer: the ERM had ensnared the pound in a Euro-monetarist trap. The key challenge for the Labour Party was to provide the United Kingdom with an 'alternative but credible policy framework and promote growth and full employment at the same time'.[16] The United Kingdom could not rejoin EMU until there was convergence between a British 'new economic deal for the 1990s' and a non-monetarist 'European policy which puts growth, employment and political integration before over-rigid attachments to fixed monetary rules'.[17] This would rule out the United Kingdom's participation in EMU indefinitely, because of the irrec-oncilable nature of the projects of Labour's domestic modernisation and EMU, unless the latter was prepared to converge towards the former.

Brown was duly persuaded by Balls, and by the policies pursued by the Clinton Administration in the United States, that priority should be given to the construction of a non-monetarist economic policy based on national economic choices rather than supra-national co-operation through EMU. He began to cast off his previous attachment to supply-side socialism, with its roots in continental European national political economy and embrace supply-side liberalism, with its roots in North American capitalism. For Brown, the key point of the victory of the New Democrats in Congress was that:

> Clinton found an echo throughout America for his central idea that government had responsibilities to the whole community to deal with the huge problems of unemployment, the weakness of the American manufacturing sector and training in skills and, of course, for the argu-ment that there were entrenched elites in American society, that were denying people opportunity.[18]

Drawing on the lessons from the New Democrats and the nascent 'Clintonomics', Labour's new economic policy could more effectively secure macro-economic stability and fiscal discipline and confront the challenges posed by globalisation and the impact of new information and communication technologies from outside the ERM and EMU. In New Labour's economic policy, EMU would be subordinate to national monetary and fiscal policy choices.[19] Labour would continue to support EMU but with the strong qualification that 'convergence of the real economic performance of member states is a vital pre-condition of any moves towards economic and monetary union'.[20]

THE 'FIVE TESTS' (PLUS TWO)

In its 1997 General Election manifesto, the Labour Party promised 'a fresh start in Europe, with the credibility to achieve reform'. British leadership in Europe would be based on the vision of Europe as 'an alliance of independent nations choosing to co-operate to achieve the goals they cannot achieve alone'. (This particular section of the manifesto was headed by a picture of Tony Blair taking the lead in talks with an attentive Jacques Chirac.) However, there was also an equivocal statement of opposition to a European federal super-state and a commitment to basing participation in the single currency on 'a hard-headed assessment of Britain's economic interests'.[21] Moreover, the manifesto recognised 'formidable obstacles' in the way of British participation in the first wave of EMU. The economic prerequisite would be 'genuine convergence' among participating economies. The political prerequisites would be Cabinet and Parliamentary approval before a 'Yes' vote in a future referendum.[22]

The United Kingdom's presidency of the European Council (for six months from 1st January 1998) was an opportunity for Brown and the Treasury to ensure the priority of national economic policy over EMU. Any ambitions for sterling to make a belated bid for participation in the first wave of EMU that Tony Blair might have harboured were quickly dashed in a series of decisive moves Brown made.[23] First, he announced the decision to give the Bank of England operational independence over the implementation of monetary policy. Second, his statement of the Blair Government's central economic objectives did not include sterling's participation in his first wave of EMU. Third, in his first major statement of New Labour's European agenda, Brown made it plain that Britain wished to exercise leadership in Europe on New Labour's terms, rather than those of its EU partners.

This speech appears to have been the only occasion during his Chancellorship when Brown actually used the term the 'third way', referring to New Labour's 'third way of economic reform' as an alternative to 'the old choices between a federal versus non-federal Europe and between a social market and a free-market Europe or old style regulation versus crude deregulation ... We reject both the federal way forward and the regulatory way ahead'.[24] Brown based Britain's claim to leadership in Europe on what he termed 'British genius': uniquely British values and qualities such as a commitment to openness to trade, outward-looking and internationalist instincts, connections which stretched across the world, creativity and adaptability as a nation, insistence on the importance of public services and openness in the running of institutions. Brown conceded that Britain shared certain qualities with other European states, such as the importance attached to hard work, self-improvement through education, fair play and opportunity for all but the others, he claimed, were 'uniquely British'.[25] Asserting that Britain had a unique claim to such qualities was flying in the face of centuries of European history, and not least of developments since the end of the Second World War. Many EU states could stake at least an equal claim to such qualities in their national character and political cultures. For example, the much higher share of national income devoted to public spending in general and key public services such as health care in particular, and the resistance to privatisation and deregulation might have suggested that France and Germany had a stronger claim to reverence for the importance of public services.

The most important aspect of Brown's speech was the specification of five tests that would provide 'a hard-headed assessment of Britain's economic interests' and a basis on which to decide whether it was appropriate for the United Kingdom to join EMU. These tests were: first, whether joining EMU would create better conditions for firms contemplating long-term investment in Britain, second, whether joining EMU would benefit the United Kingdom's financial services, third (and notwithstanding long-term benefits from EMU), whether there was sufficient compatibility between business cycles and economic structures in Britain and Europe to enable euro interest rates to be permanently lived with, fourth, whether there was sufficient flexibility within EMU to deal with emergent problems and fifth ('the bottom line'), whether joining EMU would promote Brown's central economic objectives of 'higher growth, stability and a lasting increase in jobs'.[26]

Brown's claims, as the basis for Britain's agenda in Europe, were likely
to offend some EU states, because of their rather arrogant and imprudent
nature. However, Brown's speech was designed to appeal to a domestic
audience, not a continental European one. He had spelt out five economic
tests for determining whether it was in the United Kingdom's interest to
participate in EMU but Brown's strategy was really dictated by a sixth and
seventh pair of hidden (and political) tests that were the true 'bottom line'.
The sixth was whether a United Kingdom referendum on EMU could be
won . This was far from a foregone conclusion. In November 1997, an opinion poll revealed that fifty per cent of those questioned opposed United
Kingdom participation in the euro. Furthermore, sixty-five per cent of
respondents thought such participation would mean the United Kingdom
having to stay in the EU forever. No fewer than thirty-five per cent favoured
outright withdrawal from the EU.[27] The seventh – and most important – test
was whether EMU would fatally undermine the Treasury's control over
domestic economic and social policy choices by taking away discretion over
the design of monetary and fiscal policy. Since it would, there could be no
question of the United Kingdom participating in EMU.

Brown's speech was, in effect, a justification for not taking advantage of
Labour's landslide General Election victory to set an early referendum on
the principle of entry to the euro. The radicalism of Brown's immediate
reforms to monetary and fiscal policy, through the new role for the
Monetary Policy Committee of the Bank of England and the Government's
'golden rules' and spending review, was not matched by similar radicalism
in his attitude to Europe. For the Treasury to have agreed to an early referendum would have meant threatening Brown's unprecedented control
over domestic policy. Becoming a party to the European Central Bank's
Stability and Growth Pact would have meant constraints on his freedom to
use fiscal policy to drive New Labour's domestic modernisation agenda. By
making the United Kingdom's participation in the euro-zone dependent on
major structural reforms to its EU partners' economies, so that they converged towards the British model, Brown knew full well that the United
Kingdom was effectively ruling itself out of joining the euro for at least a
decade.

Brown claimed that 'the Government is throwing open the EMU
debate' but in effect he was closing it down.[28] This was confirmed in his first
major Westminster statement on EMU, in which he asserted that Britain

had faced 'no question more important and more contentious than that of our relationship with Europe ... The decision on a single currency is probably the most important this country is likely to face in our generation'. While there were obvious benefits from EMU, 'in terms of trade, transparency of costs and currency stability', there were three 'issues of principle' that had to be surmounted before Britain could join the euro: whether EMU would work economically, whether a common monetary policy would represent an unconstitutional loss of economic sovereignty and whether the consent of the British people could be secured in a referendum.[29]

Brown confirmed that the Blair Government's conclusion on EMU, based on an application of the five economic tests, was that 'there is no proper convergence between the British and the other European economies now'. The Treasury study revealed important structural differences between the United Kingdom economy and those of other European countries: trade patterns, North Sea oil, company finance, the housing market and notable weaknesses 'in the level of skills, the high numbers of workless households and high levels of long-term unemployment'.[30] Therefore, the United Kingdom did not seek membership of the single currency on 1st January 1999. While there was 'no need, legally, formally or politically, to renounce our option for the period between 1st January 1999 and the end of the Parliament, nor would it be sensible to do so', Brown effectively ruled out United Kingdom entry to EMU for the lifetime of the Parliament, because there was 'no realistic prospect' of the demonstration of 'convergence which is sustainable and settled rather than transitory'. The policy would not change 'barring some fundamental and unforeseen change in economic circumstances'. Brown claimed: 'the essential decision is economic'.[31]

On the contrary, for Brown the essential decision was and always would be, political. Brown had guaranteed Treasury control over monetary and fiscal policy for the duration of New Labour's first term. More importantly, he had, at Tony Blair's expense, entrenched his political control over resource allocation and domestic policy design in England.

THE POLITICS OF 'PRO-EUROPEAN REALISM'

Although Gordon Brown claimed that the Blair Government was 'the first British government to declare for the principle of monetary union. The first to state that there is no over-riding constitutional bar to membership', he had, simultaneously, ruled out the practice of monetary union and constructed an effective Treasury bar to membership.[32]

Brown undermined Blair's oft-stated ambition to place Britain at the heart of Europe. On 5th April 1995, Blair had made a speech on 'Britain in Europe' to the Royal Institute of International Affairs (RIIA) at Chatham House, in which he stated that 'Europe is the only route through which Britain can exercise power and influence. If it is to maintain its historic role as a global player, Britain has to be a central part of the politics of Europe'.[33] Brown's speech to the RIIA at Chatham House two years later crushed that Prime Ministerial vision and weakened Blair's authority. There had been no mention of the 'five tests' during the 1997 General Election campaign or in the Labour Party manifesto. The tests were contrived by Balls and Brown without Blair's involvement. Blair's economic advisor, Derek Scott, later confirmed that Number Ten found it extremely difficult to secure information on key economic decisions from the Treasury. Scott claimed 'the Chancellor's office had instructed all officials within the department that any contact they had with me to be reported, together with the subject discussed'.[34]

The source of the greatest friction between Blair and Brown came on 18th October 1997. The *Times* newspaper carried the headline, 'Brown Rules Out Single Currency for Lifetime of this Parliament'; the *Sun* 'Brown Says No to the Euro'.[35] This information had been leaked to the media by Charlie Whelan, Brown's 'spin doctor'. A vital decision on British government policy had been made without the express knowledge or authorisation of the Prime Minister or the Foreign Secretary or any discussion by the Cabinet. As one influential commentator on New Labour suggested:

> Manoeuvring between its two leading men, exacerbated by the mutual loathing and paranoia of their entourages and further aggravated by the government's haphazard forms of decision-making, was creating mayhem in the most fundamental area of foreign and economic affairs.[36]

The political legacy of this confusion further poisoned the working relationship between Brown and Blair. Personally, the EMU debacle led to weeks of political backbiting between the Blair and Brown camps carried out through their media proxies, culminating in the reported allegation that

Blair believed Brown to possess 'psychological flaws'.[37] On policy, Brown was happy to announce to Parliament both the United Kingdom's Action Plan to create lasting employment and the Treasury's Guide to the Single Currency.[38] However, when it came to the announcement of the United Kingdom's National Changeover Plan for the introduction of the euro (which would come after a referendum vote in favour of EMU), Brown was insistent that Blair make the statement at Westminster.[39]

Brown wanted to distance himself from EMU and for Blair to make a statement to Parliament that would vindicate the Treasury's strategy towards the United Kingdom's participation. Blair's statement, on 23 February 1999, on the National Changeover Plan served precisely those purposes. By affirming that the five tests would have to be passed before a referendum could be held, Blair effectively confirmed that the Treasury, not Number Ten, would decide on the United Kingdom's entry into the euro.[40] In its 2001 General Election manifesto, the Labour Party reiterated its commitment in principle to join a successful single currency but promised an assessment of the UK's standing in the five tests early in the next Parliament.[41] Blair stated, in answer to a parliamentary question, that 'early in the next parliament would of course be within two years'.[42] When the General Election was held on 7th June 2001, it appeared Blair had for once entrapped Brown into a definitive timetable for an assessment that could lead to eventual United Kingdom entry to the euro-zone. However, Blair had not anticipated the lengths to which Brown and the Treasury would go to demonstrate that there was not a clear and unambiguous case for joining EMU.

When the Treasury published its assessment of the five tests for United Kingdom membership of the single currency on 9th June 2003, it produced not one report but eighteen studies that analysed the economic implications of joining the euro-zone in the minutest detail.[43] Their excessive length was an elaborate smoke-screen for the fact that the United Kingdom's participation in EMU was quintessentially a political decision that would be made by Brown and the Treasury, not by Tony Blair or the Cabinet collectively. In the two years before the studies' publication, Brown and Balls delivered a series of keynote speeches and lectures in which they set out, with increasing confidence, the principles and policies of their 'British model' of political economy, reiterated the importance of the five economic tests and identified a series of major structural reforms that would have to be undertaken before the United Kingdom could participate in EMU. Most importantly, they made it increasingly apparent that, with the British economy out-performing its major continental European rivals in employment growth, the convergence would have to predominantly be of the euro-zone economies towards the British model, rather than vice versa.

Immediately after the June 2001 General Election, in a major speech to a City of London audience, Brown defined his approach to EMU as 'one of pro-euro realism'. He claimed that 'a Europe reformed is a Europe that serves Britain and Europe best'. There would have to be urgent reform of the EU budget and the Common Agricultural Policy. The future of the EU must be 'not a federalist one but one in which independent nation states work together to shape the decisions', with increasing 'mutual recognition of national standards and solutions based on exchange of information, peer review and benchmarking rather than the central imposition of "one size fits all." ' While the EU single market must 'rightly, have a social dimension', at the same time, it must make 'subsidiarity or national decision-making the way forward'. There must be 'tax competition not tax harmonisation', with the new Europe being 'outward-looking rather than inward-looking' on trade policy.[44] The message of Brown's speech was clear. Major reforms to the EU would be needed before the United Kingdom could contemplate its involvement in EMU, including structural convergence towards the British model of market liberalisation and deregulation.

Speaking in Oxford in 2002, on the tenth anniversary of the publication of his path-breaking analysis of Euro-monetarism, Ed Balls sought to give the Treasury's five tests greater historical gravitas by locating them within a broader analysis of Britain's relative economic decline. He claimed that the five tests were based on four vital lessons the Treasury had learned from the United Kingdom's return to the Gold Standard in April 1925. First, in 1925 the British Government had not ensured that 'economics, not politics, was the deciding factor on the timing and manner of decision'. Second, this particular decision had been made 'not from a position of strength but from weakness'. Third, the decision had not been based on 'a proper assessment of the long-run economic consequences'. Fourth, at the time, the government had not undertaken 'a full economic analysis of the economic consequences, including any short-term transitional issues so that the economic consequences were fully understood'. For Balls, the lessons of history for the Treasury's assessment of the five tests were clear.[45] The assessment would be based on economics, not politics, made from a position of strength (delivered by the British model) and follow a proper assessment of the long-term consequences of EMU. Pro-European realism would rule the Blair Government's policy.

When the Treasury published a major assessment of the five economic tests, it concluded, in overall terms, the United Kingdom had indeed:

> ... made real economic progress towards meeting the five economic tests. But, on balance, though the potential benefits of increased investment, trade, a boost to financial services, growth and jobs are clear, we cannot at this point in time conclude that there is sustainable and durable convergence or sufficient flexibility to cope with any potential difficulties within the euro area. So, despite the risks and costs from delaying the benefits of joining, a clear and unambiguous case for UK membership of EMU has not at the present time been made and a decision to join now would not be in the national economic interest.[46]

Brown's statement to Parliament confirmed that only the third and fourth of the five tests, on investment and financial services respectively, had been passed. The first test on convergence, the second test on flexibility and the critical fifth test on employment, stability and growth had not. Price inflation in the British housing market (a source of economic volatility during the past fifty years) was a particular structural difference between the United Kingdom and the euro-zone remained and dictated 'a cautious approach'.[47] Therefore, the United Kingdom would not be joining the euro-zone for the foreseeable future, especially since the housing market was one of the principal engines of the consumption-led growth which characterised the British model of political economy.

CONVERGENCE TOWARDS THE BRITISH MODEL

Gordon Brown used his statement on 9th June 2003 on the Treasury's assessment of the five tests to announce the implementation of further major reforms of the United Kingdom economy, to promote the process of 'sustainable and durable convergence'.[48] With increasing confidence in the British model of political economy, arising from the Treasury's rejection of a clear and unambiguous case for EMU, Brown and Balls developed a major critique of the European Central Bank (ECB) and the European Stability and Growth Pact, as supra-national instruments of macro-economic stability. Balls developed the thesis, which underpinned the Treasury's June 2003 assessment, that operating outside the euro-zone, the British model enjoyed a much greater range of macro-economic policy options and was able to respond to any shock which might threaten domestic growth and stability. Outside the euro-zone, the Treasury had recourse to monetary policy, exchange rate adjustment, fiscal policy and flexibility in wages and prices if it wished to respond to an economic shock. Balls asserted that the British model of monetary and fiscal policy had institutionalised the 'principles of modern macro-economic policy' and that the European Growth and Stability Pact should be modernised to embrace them.[49] The British model's range of policy instruments would narrow significantly if the United Kingdom were to join the euro-zone.

Balls asserted that the monetary policy, as a country-specific stabiliser, would be diluted in the euro-zone because the ECB, unlike the Treasury, would respond to an overall euro-inflation objective, rather than one for the British economy alone. In the euro-zone, the Treasury would no longer have the pound's nominal exchange rate as a tool of exchange rate adjustment. The only remaining macro-economic policy options would be flexibility in prices, quantities and capital movements or a greater use of fiscal policy as an instrument for domestic stabilisation. Balls was convinced that, because an over-reliance on flexibility in wages and prices could be potentially damaging for both stability and growth, the ECB and European Growth and Stability Pact must place a greater emphasis on fiscal policy as a source of stability.[50] Therefore, the United Kingdom – and all the other existing euro-zone member states – must consider how a flexible and legitimate national régime for fiscal policy might be designed to operate in the euro-zone. The clear implication was that the existing European Growth and Stability Pact was insufficiently flexible and illegitimate.

Despite the Treasury's reticence, the United Kingdom might be able to join the euro, through the modernisation of the European Growth and Stability Pact so that it converged towards the Treasury's model of constrained discretion. To extend the first principle of constrained discretion, the specification of long-term objectives, to fiscal policy within the euro-zone, Balls proposed that, subject to the ECB's inflation target, the objective should be to minimise deviations of national output and employment from the national economy's trend growth rate. To avoid the possibility of confusion and conflict between national fiscal policy and that operating in the wider euro-zone, Balls proposed that there should be a mechanism to trigger adjustments in national fiscal policy, if there were a prospect of significant deviation of the national economy from a stable path.[51] In its assessment paper, *Fiscal Stabilisation and EMU*, the Treasury proposed a rule for fiscal policy based on an output gap of 1–1.5 per cent.[52] In other words, if the national economy were to deviate from its sustainable path of growth by more than 1–1.5 per cent, a fiscal policy response would be triggered. This trigger would operate subject to the two elements of the Treasury's existing rules-based approach to fiscal policy: the 'golden rule' and the sustainable investment rule.

Balls contented that there were four reasons why this trigger would work effectively for the United Kingdom and other member states within a modernised European Growth and Stability Pact. First, it would avoid excessive instability in national output. Second, because the fiscal trigger would be symmetrical, it could equally be triggered to induce fiscal tightening, should a national economy be growing in an inflationary manner. Third, the trigger, while predictable, would not be automatically implemented: the sole obligation of national governments would be to justify to their Parliament and financial markets why they had chosen to act on fiscal policy or not. Fourth, the trigger would create an explicit link between flexibility and sustainability across the economic cycle and the level of net debt, because it would only operate subject to the existing net debt and sustainable public finances rules in British model of fiscal policy.[53]

The British model provided the European Growth and Stability Pact with a blueprint for its modernisation. The Pact must ensure that within EMU, fiscal activism by individual countries was 'predictable, exceptional and confined to low debt countries'. Members must be committed to 'fiscal discipline, symmetrical over the cycle for all countries', allowing low debt countries only to use fiscal stabilisation measures to ensure stability and growth, consonant with low debt and sustainable public finances and 'effectively enforced fiscal co-ordination between national governments'.[54] To achieve this, the mechanistic and asymmetrically applied annual rules of the European Growth and Stability Pact, with their target of annual reduction of budget deficits by 0.5 per cent of gross domestic product (GDP), should be replaced by guiding principles allowing for constrained discretion, that is, the British model's 'clear pre-commitment to flexible operating rules'.

Balls called for a more prudent interpretation of the European Growth and Stability Pact; an evolution in its institutional design that would give greater flexibility by allowing low debt economies to use discretionary fiscal policy to support stability and growth. This would mean agreement by the Council of the ECB that low debt economies, like the United Kingdom, should be able to breach the three per cent of GDP deficit rule for 'exceptional and temporary reasons'. There would need to be greater fiscal co-ordination within the Council of the ECB and a strengthening of independent monitoring, surveillance and transparency, possibly by creating an inter-governmental 'fiscal surveillance committee ... staffed by Member State and European Commission representatives, with delegated authority to conduct analysis and surveillance of national fiscal policies and advise the Council'.[55]

Balls and Brown wanted the euro-zone to converge towards the British model of monetary and fiscal policy. Just as, under their stewardship, British economic policy had evolved from the flawed policies of Lawson, Major and Lamont into the British model, so now EMU must cast off European monetarism. Their conceit was that, having worked nationally, the British model 'can be made to work in monetary unions too'.[56] Balls first advocated this expansion of the British model at a time when he could confidently predict that the Government would meet its 'golden rule' of fiscal policy, with an annual average surplus over the economic cycle of 0.2 per cent of GDP (fourteen billion pounds) and meet the net debt rule with a margin of 4.5 per cent of GDP (sixty-four billion pounds). This was before Brown had three times had to redefine his definition of the United Kingdom's economic cycle to meet his own fiscal rules (see Chapter Three).

GLOBAL BRITAIN, GLOBAL EUROPE

Gordon Brown and Ed Balls's ambition to export the British model of political economy to the euro-zone was not confined to monetary and fiscal policy. Brown attempted to press other EU economies to transform their prospects for more rapid growth and employment by converging towards the supply-side liberalism of the Anglo-American model of capitalism. Much of the political momentum for this initiative arose from the

European Council's Lisbon Summit of 23–24 March 2000. This Summit marked a turning point in supra-national policy, in that it committed the EU 'to strengthen employment, economic reform and social cohesion as part of a knowledge-based economy'.[57] This agenda sought to draw the EU into a process of political, economic and social renewal whose rhetoric, language and content bore, in many respects, a marked similarity to New Labour's domestic modernisation agenda. The Summit's agenda was based on the conviction that the EU was faced by 'a quantum shift resulting from globalisation and the challenges of a new knowledge-driven economy' which was 'affecting every aspect of people's lives' and which would require 'a radical transformation of the European economy'[58].

Confronted with this challenge, the European Council set the EU the new strategic goal of becoming 'the most competitive and dynamic knowledge-based economy in the world, capable of sustainable economic growth and better jobs and greater social cohesion'.[59] This meant three things for supra-national policy. First, preparation for the transition to a knowledge-based economy and society through better policies for the information society and for research and development and an acceleration of the process of structural reform for competitiveness and innovation and the completion of the internal market. Second, the modernisation of the European social model through investment in people and the combating of social exclusion. Third, the application of 'an appropriate macro-economic policy mix' to sustain the healthy economic outlook and favourable growth prospects for the EU.[60]

From the perspective of Brown's agenda of supply-side liberalism for enhancing competitiveness, the key insight was the recognition granted to the role of the entrepreneur, enterprise, innovation and productivity growth in this new strategic agenda for the EU. The Lisbon Summit acknowledged the direct dependence both of the competitiveness and dynamism of businesses on 'a regulatory climate conducive to investment, innovation and entrepreneurship'. It also recognised the need to redirect public spending 'towards increasing the relative importance of capital accumulation – both physical and human' and the need to adapt the European model of developed systems of social protection to create an 'active welfare state' which would ensure that work was worth it. The Summit agreed that this agenda should be pursued through 'A fully decentralised approach', which would accord priority to the states and regions of the EU and through the development of 'variable forms of partnership'.[61] In short, the supra-national agenda of social and economic renewal was moving much closer, at least in rhetoric, towards New Labour's modernisation agenda.[62]

The confirmation that the EU agenda on competitiveness could converge with that of Brown and the Treasury came with the publication of the EU's programme for enterprise and entrepreneurship for the period which would cover the Blair Government's second term. The European Commission proposed 'a systematic approach to foster entrepreneurship in the new economy', by encouraging 'risk-taking and the spirit of enterprise', because 'Entrepreneurship is the key to the new economy'.[63] The EU must become 'Enterprise Europe', where 'anyone with a commercially feasible idea should be able to realise it, with access to the best technology, and then deliver it, by the best possible means, to the appropriate market'.[64]

This approach to creating a more dynamic European enterprise culture brought supra-national policy closer to the British model. Since the mid-1990s, it had sought to benchmark national economy performance against a range of indicators of enterprise, productivity and innovation; a trend which was widened and deepened by New Labour's fixation on performance and output indicators. Throughout, the United States was identified as the model to follow. It was to the Treasury's advantage that the EU's Action Plan for Entrepreneurship also identified a widening productivity gap between the EU and the US. It lamented the fact that (in October 2003) only four per cent of Europeans stated that they had been engaged in creating a business or being an entrepreneur, compared with eleven per cent of Americans. While forty-four per cent of Americans thought that a business should still be started if there were a risk of failure, only twenty-nine per cent of Europeans concurred.[65]

Gordon Brown sought to exploit this favourable environment for policy by developing an analysis of EU economic performance and competitiveness policy based on his vision of 'Global Europe'. Repeating the pattern of the British model, globalisation became a political weapon in a series of Treasury reports justifying major structural changes and supply-side reforms of continental European economies.[66] In a speech at a Confederation of British Industry conference on 'Competitiveness in Europe-Post Enlargement', rather than setting out how the United Kingdom would seek to converge with the euro-zone, Brown provided his audience with an agenda on how the newly expanded EU should converge with the 'British model' of stability and enterprise.

Brown claimed that globalisation had placed Europe's competitive advantage under a severe, triple, threat that came first from the developing economies, which he claimed could account for half of all global manufacturing exports in twenty years; second, from Asia, to which five million European and American jobs might be out-sourced and third, from China, which was already a larger market for Volkswagen than Germany.[67] Brown portrayed the history of supra-national integration as a process which had created the world's first modern trade block but which had now entered a second phase of 'Global Europe': a Europe facing global competition. Brown did not acknowledge that European integration might fundamentally have been about the vision of an ever-closer political union rather than simply a matter of economics. Instead, he claimed that globalisation demanded 'a programme of liberalisation, tax reform, new employment policies, the opening up of trade and commerce and a modern monetary and fiscal regime'[68].

Brown set out a five-point framework to enable the EU to converge with the supply-side liberalism of the Anglo-American model of capitalism. First, the EU must follow the British example of delegating responsibility for liberalisation to competition authorities, rather than politicians, to accelerate the creation of more open and flexible markets. Second, accelerated liberalisation would require openness, flexibility and competition in taxation. Notions of tax harmonisation, underpinning the idea of an ever-closer political union must be abandoned, not only because they would reduce competitiveness but also because they would be 'unacceptable to the peoples of Europe because decisions on what to tax, and how, reflect national choices and cultures'.[69] Despite this emphasis on the importance of national cultural factors, Brown contended that harmonisation of corporation tax and Value Added Tax must also be abandoned because of the constraints imposed by open global markets.

Brown's third prerequisite for the more competitive enlarged Europe was for it to copy the British example of the New Deal. Passive labour markets, with their implicit inflexibility and welfare dependency, must be abandoned in favour of an active labour market policy. In this way, certain EU states might cut their levels of forty to sixty per cent of unemployment lasting for more than a year and converge on the American figure of only twelve per cent. Fourth, the enlarged EU should meet the competitive challenge posed by globalised trade by abandoning what Brown portrayed as its 'Fortress Europe' approach in favour of leadership of the World Trade Organization, in partnership with the US. Brown claimed that a 'properly sequenced' programme of reforms might create a million jobs in the US and EU, boosting Europe's growth rate by two per cent and the US's by one per cent.[70]

The fifth and final prerequisite was a 'proactive and forward looking' monetary and fiscal policy to address the challenge posed by globalised markets, which the United Kingdom had achieved this through the rules-based approach of the 'British model' for stability. The existing terms of the European Central Bank's Stability and Growth Pact were inappropriate. It was wrong for the European Commission to penalise countries for using fiscal policy to support monetary policy, by making 'sensible investments to improve infrastructure and public services' and thereby combat low growth, especially where countries had 'a position of low debt and of consumption covered by revenues'.[71] In an enlarged EU of 25 member states, Brown's conclusion was that reform was 'not just desirable [but] an urgent necessity'. Liberalisation, flexibility and economic reform should be accomplished through 'inter-governmental co-operation' and not, he clearly implied, through closer political union or endorsement of the draft EU Constitution.[72]

GLOBAL EUROPE AND THE 2005 UNITED KINGDOM EU PRESIDENCY

Gordon Brown's commitment to pro-European realism and his vision of a Global Europe was demonstrated during the United Kingdom's presidency of the European Council which ran from 1st July–31st December 2005, forming the twin themes of his contribution to it.

Brown developed the thesis that the EU was entering a second phase of its history. Flows of capital, companies and brands, which had, during an earlier era of European integration, moved from the national to the European level were becoming increasingly global. The inward-looking 'old trade bloc Europe', with its outmoded vision of 'a single currency and perhaps even a federal fiscal policy with tax harmonisation and then ... a supranational state', must urgently make the transition to an outward-looking Global Europe.[73] This change was made necessary by a circumstance unforeseen by the founders of European integration: the rise of China and

India and other Asian economies from which goods can be obtained and to which investment may flow.

Brown's contention was that Europe was still less competitive in the five key areas of growth, labour market performance, skills, innovation and enterprise. His remedy was the extension of the supply-side liberalism of the British model to the whole EU. Globalisation must be managed well and equitably, through economic and social policies designed to provide the requisite flexibility and fairness to deliver full employment for the twenty million unemployed in Europe.[74] With China and Asia engaged in 'a race to the top', Europe 'must continuously upgrade skills and technology and raise our game'. For Brown, full participation in the new global economy offered the double dividend of efficiency and productivity gains for companies and lower prices for consumers.[75]

In Brown's vision of Global Europe, the United States remained the benchmark for unfavourable comparisons of European economic performance. In terms of growth, Brown asserted that American living standards were more than 30 per cent higher than in the EU. Annual average growth in per capita GDP since 1996 was 0.5 per cent lower in the euro area than in the United States and poor labour market performance was estimated to account for two-thirds of this gap in living standards. Brown highlighted the paltry level of 40.2 per cent employment for Europeans aged 55–64 in 2003, compared with sixty per cent in the United States and sixty-two per cent in Japan. The EU needed to create 22 million jobs by 2010 to meet the targets established at the Lisbon Summit. There was a huge disparity between the EU's 41.8 per cent rate of long-term unemployment (those out of work for more than twelve months) and the 12.7 per cent rate in the United States.[76] Brown did not mention that this might be due to the more generous pension entitlements in the EU member states but the clear implication was that in Global Europe, people would have to work longer.

Brown noted that the EU states had created more than seven million new jobs between 1997 and 2002 in knowledge-intense services but that skill levels were higher in the United States, Canada and Japan and were rising more quickly in emerging markets. In terms of innovation, the EU states had less than half the number of patent applications (per capita) in 2002 than the United States and Japan, while business research and development was almost fifty per cent higher in the United States. (Brown did not supply sources for these statistics.) In terms of enterprise, Brown claimed that total entrepreneurial activity in the United States, Canada and China was 'double or treble that in the large EU member states'.[77]

The message was clear. Europe faced an actual or potential gap in its economic performance and international competitiveness in growth, labour market skills, innovation and enterprise. To create prosperity, full employment and security for all European citizens, the older, inward-looking model of European integration must be supplanted by 'a more flexible, reforming, open and globally-oriented Europe', embracing 'flexibility, dynamism and entrepreneurship supported by an active and responsive labour market policy'.[78] This was something to which Margaret Thatcher or the late Lord Keith Joseph could have objected little.

To deliver Brown's 'full-employment Global Europe', the EU must embrace the economic and social reforms characteristic of the British model of political economy developed by Brown and Balls at the Treasury. Brown emphasised the importance of learning from international practice: for both macro-economic and micro-economic policy, the EU must draw the same lessons from the political economy of the United States as the British model. He insisted that 'there can be no security without change'.[79] However, this strategy must be carried out by the co-operation of national governments rather than through the deepening of supra-national political integration. Brown was equally adamant that policies 'must reflect national traditions and electoral preferences'.[80] Global Europe could be achieved only through 'a new commitment to reform – to complete the Single Market, promote better regulation, encourage innovation and refocus the EU budget'.[81]

In terms of the policy priorities of the United Kingdom's presidency, the first step for the achievement of Global Europe was a political commitment to the completion of the Single Market. For Brown, this entailed liberalisation of EU markets for telecommunications, electricity, gas and commercial services, the elimination of inefficient state subsidies and the implementation of 'an independent and pro-active competition policy'. Furthermore, the EU should deliver 'open, flexible and competitive tax systems across the EU', because 'neither the demands of the modern global economy, nor the principles of subsidiarity and political legitimacy can justify harmonisation of tax rates or bases at an EU level'. Brown held that fair tax competition, rather than harmonisation reflected 'the realities of the global economy' and respected 'the fundamentally national nature of

public services needs and economic management challenges that governments face'.[82] The EU must adopt 'a risk-based approach to regulation' and
reduce the burden of regulation, including the Union's 'enormous and
unwieldy rulebook'. Brown's demand for greater investment in research
and development and policies to stimulate private investment and innovation led him to the thorny issue of reform of the EU budget which, for him,
was 'also key' and must become 'fit for purpose' to meet 'the science, skills
and infrastructure challenges of global change'.[83]

To ensure that Global Europe was outward-looking, Brown was
adamant that the EU must not retreat behind protectionist policies but
must see America, Asia and the rest of the world as partners in a discussion
about 'common approaches to regulation, competition and transatlantic
commerce'. Global Europe would only be possible through a long-term
programme of economic reform in five key areas: structural, budgetary,
social, regulatory and trade reform.[84] Brown consigned political integration
to history but, as with many other areas of his politics, his analysis was built
on weak arguments. For example, he claimed it was 'an implicit assumption
of European development that what happened within the European Union
mattered far more than what was happening outside it'[85] but, by definition,
integration could hardly be anything other than inward-looking.

Conspicuously absent from Brown's vision for the EU was any notion
that the way forward might be to develop a common European citizenship
and identity based on shared values. Brown's preoccupation in his 'British
Way' was the reinvention of British citizenship and identity based on shared
British values: a task which had no supra-national dimension. For the EU,
the challenge of globalisation demanded rethinking of 'the most basic of
political assumptions that have underlain 50 years of development'.
Specifically, two assumptions that must be rethought were 'that we would
move from being economically integrated at a national level to being economically integrated at a European level [and] that cultural and political
integration would follow economic integration'.[86] Brown specifically
rejected the assumption that 'a European identity could supersede national
identities' because of the dominance of globalisation over Europe and the
assumption about the old European model both because of the EU
Constitution referendum results in France and the Netherlands and the
reaction across the EU to a period of low growth. For Brown, the referendums demonstrated how identities had 'remained rooted in the nation state

– and that familiar national, cultural and political attachments are important', not least in relation to 'issues of what is taxed and by whom'. Brown's 'pro-European realism' remained based on 'the founding case for the European Union, the benefits of co-operation among nation states for peace and prosperity but strengthened by the insistence that Europe looks outwards as a Global Europe'.[87]

THE SUPRA-NATIONAL PRIORITIES FOR A BROWN GOVERNMENT

To consolidate his influence over the Blair Government's policy on Europe, Brown sat on two Cabinet Committees: the Cabinet Ministerial Committee on European Policy, whose remit was to determine the United Kingdom's policies on European Union issues and to oversee the United Kingdom's relations with other member states and principal partners of the European Union and the Ministerial Committee on European Union Strategy, whose remit was to oversee the Government's European strategy and the presentation of the Government's European policy.[88] Long before he acceded to the role of Prime Minister, the priorities of a future Brown Government's EU reform agenda were identified.

The central objective of Brown's strategy is maintaining the pressure on the EU to converge towards the British model of political economy.[89] In a joint paper with the Department of Trade and Industry, the Treasury spelled out its vision for the EU Single Market in the twenty-first century. The Treasury contended that progress towards greater employment, growth, choice and prosperity for Europe's citizens and businesses had been slowing and so wanted the EU to embrace Brown's vision of a Global Europe by adopting 'a much more outward-looking, global perspective'. This would require a rethinking of 'the traditional model for the Single Market – one that seeks to achieve integration through legislation and the harmonisation of rules'. The Treasury wanted 'a new strategy for the Single Market that calls for a renewed focus on its core purpose – to provide jobs, growth and prosperity for Europe's citizens'. This would mean an emphasis on action 'in those areas where the economic benefits are greatest'. Policy must become 'more tailored, proportionate and flexible'.[90]

The Treasury approach to the Single Market was based on four principles. First, the EU must 'be clear about the purpose – focusing policy on outcomes of promoting jobs, growth and prosperity, by creating a dynamic and competitive Single Market'. The EU must copy Brown's output-centric approach to policy-making and delivery of services. Second, the EU must 'be focused on priorities – adopting a more systematic approach with policy priorities set according to sound analysis of where the economic benefits are greatest'.[91] In other words, the EU must both converge towards the British model (with its emphasis on constrained discretion and evidence-based reforms) and simultaneously abandon the political project of an ever-closer union through, for example, harmonisation of fiscal policy.

Third, the EU must 'take action at the right level – emphasising co-operation and applying the principle of subsidiarity'. Responsibility for policy design and resource allocation must be taken by national government and, where necessary, taken back from supra-national bodies. Fourth, the EU must 'deliver a modern and flexible framework – policy makers should embrace a wider range of policy tools, including more pro-active use of competition policy'.[92] The EU must continue with the Anglo-American model of capitalism, through accelerated market liberalisation, deregulation and privatisation. Taxes on businesses, both large and small, must be cut and the costs of social welfare, in the context of an ageing population, must be transferred from the general taxpayer to the individual consumer.

The Treasury contended that the benefits of convergence towards the British model would be significant. For example, insufficient liberalisation of EU gas markets was estimated to have cost Europe's energy consumers forty billion pounds during 2007, while the European Central Bank calculated that further competition reform could yield energy price cuts of up to thirty-six per cent.[93] The maintenance of costly subsidies and barriers to external trade and investment arising from protectionist 'tariffs, quotas and unjustifiably restrictive standards' may have cost Europe's consumers 600–700 billion euros (seven per cent of EU GDP) during 2007.[94] Opening up the EU's network industries, for example airlines, electricity, gas, post, rail-freight and passenger services and telecommunications could increase EU welfare by 1.3–1.7 per cent. This would mean an extra seventy-five to ninety-five billion euros of income for the EU economy and the creation of 140,000 to 360,000 jobs.[95] In telecommunications alone, the Treasury noted that liberalisation across the EU might cut prices by about eleven per cent, expand the market by four per cent and increase cross-border trade by twenty-nine per cent.[96]

Having helped, some fifteen years earlier, to initiate Gordon Brown's intellectual reflection on British economic policy and its relationship to European integration, in the weeks before Brown became Prime Minister, Ed Balls published a new essay about the future direction of policy towards the EU. Although he modestly subtitled his essay, *A City minister's perspective*, given the timing of its publication there was little doubt that it fully reflected Brown's agenda for the future of the EU, especially since Balls underlined the case for Brown's 'hard-headed pro-Europeanism'.[97]

Balls's position as City minister was doubly significant; for both Brown and Balls, the City of London's innovative and liberal markets were their blueprint for the future liberalisation of the EU single market. Particularly conspicuous in Balls's agenda was the open dismissal of further consideration of deeper integration and closer European political union. He depicted the advocacy of 'a continental identity both economically and politically' as an outdated product of the Cold War.[98] There was no attempt to engage with, for example, the ambitions of the German Chancellor, Angela Merkel, to revive a slimmed-down version of the European Constitution. Balls looked to a Europe based on 'an inclusive globalisation', where EU-level action is taken, only if it is appropriate, proportionate and flexible and in the national interests of its member states.[99]

The Brown Government's commitment to the pro-European realism of Global Europe was illustrated during his first month in office. David Miliband, the Foreign Secretary, affirmed the United Kingdom's commitment to the EU as an asset in economic terms, an asset in tackling crime and 'a greater asset in foreign policy – not substituting for nation states but giving better expression to the common commitments of nation states'.[100] In the foreword to his Government's White Paper on the British approach to the July 2007 Intergovernmental Conference, Gordon Brown stated that the Blair Government had set out its 'red lines' at the June 2007 European Council, which had ensured that 'there would not be a transfer of power away from the UK on issues of fundamental importance to our sovereignty'.[101] The mandate Brown specified for the Intergovernmental Conference would ensure the intact maintenance of the United Kingdom's labour and social legislation, the protection of its common law system, police and judicial processes, the protection of its tax and social security systems and the preservation of its independent foreign and defence policy. Furthermore, the proposed EU Reform Treaty would, for the first time, make it clear that national security would remain a matter for member states. This agenda would enable the EU 'to move on from debates about institutions to creating the outward-facing, flexible Europe that we need to meet the fundamental challenges of globalisation'.[102] The EU would be aligned with the Brown Government's pro-European realism.

As Prime Minister, Gordon Brown soon discovered that his government's commitment to the pro-European realism of its 'Global Europe' agenda would not only leave him isolated among the leaders of the European Union's member states, but also unable to prevent the European Union taking a further significant step towards an ever closer political union. Having promised in the Labour Party's 2005 General Election manifesto to give the British people a referendum on the Union's Constitutional Treaty, Brown refused to proceed with a referendum when the Lisbon Treaty brought into effect an almost identical set of constitutional and policy reform measures. Brown's refusal was founded upon the claim that in the Lisbon Treaty 'the constitutional concept was abandoned', and so it was 'no longer a constitutional treaty, it is an amending treaty'.[103] However, while the title of the treaty had changed, most of its substantive constitutional and policy reform measures remained in place. This was demonstrated by Brown's strategy of having to negotiate 'red line' safeguards of legally binding protocols, opt-ins and emergency breaks to protect the United Kingdom's sovereignty over justice and home affairs matters, social security, and foreign and security policy.[104]

In the event, the signing of the Lisbon Treaty proved to be a huge political embarrassment for Brown. Initially, the Prime Minister refused to travel to Portugal to sign the Lisbon Treaty with all of the other leaders of European Union states. In his absence, the treaty was signed by David Miliband, the Foreign Secretary. Brown claimed to be unable to attend because of having to appear before the House of Commons Liaison Committee, but the idea that this appearance should take precedence over the signing of a major supranational treaty was seen not only as a huge political misjudgement, but also insulting to other European Union member states. At the last minute, Brown decided belatedly to sign the treaty, but he did so alone and in private. In an attempt to cover his obvious embarrassment, Brown issued a statement prior to signing the treaty. In this, he once again rehearsed his thesis that, rather than looking inward (as by implication, the signing of the Lisbon Treaty had done), the European Union should instead 'demonstrate that the EU is open and outward looking, and focused on the opportunities and challenges of globalisation'.[105] A heavy price had been paid for Brown's steadfast refusal to hold a referendum. As Prime Minister, he had promised to listen to and learn from the British people, but despite the fact that opinion polls repeatedly showed overwhelming public support for a referendum on the Lisbon Treaty, on this occasion he chose not to listen and learn.

CONCLUSION

One of Gordon Brown's most important political and economy policy legacies is the fact that the pound is not part of EMU. By keeping it out, Brown retained control over the United Kingdom's monetary and fiscal policy and thereby consolidated the British model of political economy. In the process, he frustrated Tony Blair's desire to place the United Kingdom at the heart of Europe and ensured that Europe continued to be subordinate to Atlanticism in British foreign policy. In his pro-European, realist vision of Global Europe, Brown staked out the terms of future engagement with European integration during his premiership.

The United Kingdom will not be joining the euro; neither will it be seeking to revive the European constitution nor move towards closer political union. Brown's 'British Way' is focussed on shoring up the British Union, not deepening the European Union. The path to modernity lies with the market liberalism of the United States rather than the social democratic traditions of continental Europe, even though the latter's philosophical roots are much closer to the Labour Party's historical development. Atlanticism will continue to take precedence over European integration in British foreign policy. The Anglo-American model of capitalism will continue to enjoy supremacy, both moral and political, over its inflexible continental European rival.

Brown's stance means that the Labour Party will find it more difficult to portray the Conservative Party as being more Euro-sceptic. Brown's perspective on the challenges of globalisation and European integration is very similar to David Cameron's, in his vision of 'The 3G Europe', with the priorities of 'Globalisation, Global Warming, Global Poverty'.[106] This is a prime example of British politics having become stranded on an ideological common ground. Brown remains wedded to a vision of Europe that encompasses willing and active co-operation between sovereign EU member states, the tackling of present problems in a practical manner, however difficult that might prove, the encouragement of enterprise, the avoidance of protectionism and the maintenance of British and European security through Atlanticist structures like NATO.

The irony is that these are the guiding principles of a vision of Europe set out by a previous British Prime Minister in 1988, speaking to the College of Europe.[107] The author of that infamous Bruges speech was none other than Margaret Thatcher.

Chapter 8

The Brown Government: From Boom to Bust

INTRODUCTION

During his decade as Chancellor of the Exchequer, one of Gordon Brown's most frequent claims was that his economic policies had locked in and entrenched a culture of macroeconomic stability and fiscal prudence in the United Kingdom economy, and moved on decisively from the 'boom-bust instability of the past'.[1] From his inaugural 1997 Pre-Budget Report statement, during a decade of speeches to the Labour Party's annual conference, and in his final Budget statement, Brown was adamant that Britain was 'No longer the boom-bust economy' and there would be 'No return to boom and bust'.[2] The Brown Boom was entrenched. Brown's British model of political economy appeared unassailable.

Brown attributed this apparent transformation in the United Kingdom's economic performance to the new monetary and fiscal policy regime, and its foundation upon 'stability first, foremost and always, stability yesterday, today and tomorrow'. He also celebrated 'our light touch system' of financial regulation which was 'fair, proportionate, predictable and increasingly risk-based'.[3] The tripartite system of regulation he had engineered through the Financial Services Authority (FSA), the Treasury and the Bank of England had enabled the City of London to secure more than 40 per cent of the trade in the world's foreign equities, and 30 per cent of the trade of the world's currency exchanges. Indeed, as he prepared to leave the Treasury to become Prime Minister, Brown predicted 'an era that history will record as the beginning of a new golden age for the City of London'. A 'new world order' was being created, but by openly embracing liberalised financial markets and globalisation, Britain could become 'one of the greatest success stories in the new global economy'.[4]

Brown had seen an economic mirage. There was not a new golden age. Within fifteen months of Brown becoming Prime Minister, the United Kingdom had witnessed the end of the Brown Boom. On 23 January 2009, official statistics revealed that the United Kingdom's GDP (in a preliminary estimate of its chained volume measure) had decreased by 1.5 per cent during the fourth quarter of 2008. Because GDP had fallen by 0.6 per cent in the previous quarter, the UK economy was now technically in recession.[5] In practice, the stark truth was that economic stability and fiscal prudence had long since departed, to be replaced by volatility and imprudence.

The City of London experienced its first run on a domestic bank for 129 years. Rather than celebrating the success of its liberalised financial markets, Brown found himself having to nationalise and bail out many of the United Kingdom's major banks. To finance these rescues, government borrowing soared to its highest level since 1946. At the end of December 2008, public sector net debt, which had stood at £512.9 billion or thirty-six per cent of GDP when Brown had left the Treasury, had soared to £697.5 billion or 47.5 per cent of GDP, an annual increase of £63.5 billion or 3.4 per cent of GDP. Even if the Government's financial sector interventions were excluded, public debt had risen to £594.3 billion or 40.4 per cent of GDP, up by £60.2 billion or 3.2 per cent of GDP.[6] Brown's fiscal rules were suspended, but independent forecasters suggested that public sector debt would be unlikely to fall below forty per cent of national income 'until the early 2030s'.[7] Brown's Sustainable Investment Rule would be transgressed, at the very least, for the whole of the next generation.

In response to the rapidly deteriorating economy, and the widespread market uncertainty, the Bank of England cut interest rates to 0.5 per cent, their lowest ever level since the Bank's foundation in 1694, but it was too little, too late. Having grown for sixty-two consecutive three-month quarters, from April to June 2008, the economy stagnated, and then contracted by 0.6 per cent and 1.5 per cent during the next two quarters.[8] Recession had officially arrived. Unemployment rose to 6.1 per cent in the three months to November 2008, up by 0.9 per cent or 290,000 from a year earlier.[9] Consumer price inflation rose suddenly to 5.2 per cent in September 2008, but then fell back dramatically to 3.1 per cent in December, raising fears of the onset of deflation.[10] The housing market collapsed. Gross mortgage lending fell by forty-seven per cent in a year, to the lowest annual level since 1974, with average property prices falling by 16.6 per cent in a year.[11] The value of the pound reflected the broader economic weaknesss, falling to near parity with the euro, and a twenty-four year low against the dollar. Where once it praised 'the UK economy's remarkable performance that has lasted for more than a decade',[12] the International Monetary Fund (IMF) now forecast that the United Kingdom would record the weakest economic performance among the major industrialised economies, during the worst year for global growth since 1945.[13] The British model of political economy was in ruins.

FROM THE BROWN BOUNCE TO NORTHERN ROCK

Gordon Brown's tenure began promisingly. By-election and opinion poll results had seemed to reflect a general public mood of confidence in and growing satisfaction with the Brown Government. On 19 July, the Labour Party had won by-election victories in Ealing Southall, following the death of the sitting Labour MP Plara Khabra, and Sedgefield, following the resignation as an MP of Tony Blair. Opinion poll trends also appeared to suggest a 'Brown Bounce' in popularity for the Labour Party. A YouGov poll for *The Sunday Times* on 10 August had given Labour (forty-two per cent) a sufficiently wide lead over the Conservatives (thirty-two per cent) to fuel growing rumours in the media of an imminent General Election.[14] The Labour Party was reported to have appointed Ed Miliband, the Cabinet Office minister, to work on a General Election manifesto.

Brown himself had done nothing to quash such rumours of an election. Indeed, he did nothing to deny reports that he had ordered his party to prepare for a snap autumn election. Further opinion polls which coincided with the annual Labour Party Conference saw the Labour Party's lead over the Conservatives at between ten and thirteen per cent, reflecting a share of the vote at between forty-one and forty-four per cent, compared to the Conservatives' thirty-one to thirty-four per cent.[15] A similar result at an autumn General Election would not only have delivered an historic fourth consecutive General Election victory and term of office for the Labour

Party, but also with a much larger share of the vote and parliamentary majority than in June 2005. But then Brown hesitated. An ill-judged and ill-timed visit to British troops in Iraq was interpreted by many in the media and Opposition political parties as open electioneering. Ironically, it was on the question of the health of the United Kingdom's economy that the former 'Iron Chancellor' was unsettled.

In the first instance, from 14 to 17 September 2007, the first run on the deposits of a United Kingdom bank since 1878 had led to long queues of depositors outside the branches of the Northern Rock bank, urgently seeking to withdraw their funds. This had prompted an initial intervention by Chancellor Alistair Darling to guarantee all such deposits. The accompanying volatility in London's financial markets had resulted on 20 September in an injection of £10 billion of liquidity by the Bank of England to lower the cost of inter-bank lending.[16] Brown's role as champion of the City of London and its 'risk-based' approach to financial regulation would now come under increasing scrutiny. Furthermore, on 1 October, Shadow Chancellor George Osborne had used his speech at the Conservative Party annual conference to announce that his party would both raise the inheritance tax threshold to £1 million, and abolish stamp duty on properties bought for less than £250,000 by first-time buyers. This would be financed by a £25,000 flat rate Offshore Domicile Levy on wealthy foreigners living in the United Kingdom. Brown was portrayed by Osborne as the Prime Minister who 'still thinks he can command, control, dictate, regulate and tax'; as the architect of a regulatory system 'designed to stop a run on a bank – and it failed'; the administrator of 'the system that was supposed to reassure savers – and it failed'; and the creator of 'an economy built on debt' which was now 'living on borrowed time'.[17] Brown's British model of political economy was now under its heaviest Opposition attack for a decade.

When an ICM poll of marginal constituencies for *The News of the World* revealed that the Conservatives (forty-four per cent) had a clear lead over the Labour Party (thirty-eight per cent), the moment to call a General Election, and to be certain of a fourth consecutive victory, had passed. Brown had waited too long. However, it was not until 7 October, during a BBC television interview, that Brown confirmed that he would not be calling a General Election.[18] Further damage was inflicted upon Brown the very next day by his denial, at a Downing Street press conference, that he had decided not to hold it because of the reversal in the favourable trend in opinion polls which had marked the 'Brown Bounce' from July to September 2007. Brown conceded:

> Yes, I considered holding an election. Obviously I saw the opinion polls. I also learned from my marginal seat Members of Parliament that if we had had an election they would have won their seats, and I believe and I still believe that we will win, and would have won a majority and will win a majority whenever the election is called. But I had to take a bigger view of the situation.[19]

Few believed the Prime Minister. The moment to secure a mandate from the electorate for his Government's programme had passed. The opportunity had presented itself to convey his vision, clearly and succinctly, in a Labour Party General Election manifesto. Brown had hesitated, and missed that opportunity. A year later, when Brown began his speech to the 2008 Labour Party annual conference, he stated, 'I want to talk with you today about who I am, what I believe, what I am determined to lead this party and this great country to achieve'.[20] Not only was this an admission that his 2007 conference speech had been too long and rambling, for all of his claims to be a 'conviction politician' driven by a moral compass.[21] It was also a recognition that he had failed during the previous year to convey his vision of progressive change to both the Labour Party itself and the electorate at large.

FROM STALIN TO MR BEAN: BROWN'S SEASONS OF DISCONTENT

Following his decision not to call an autumn 2007 General Election, Gordon Brown experienced a nine-month period during which both he and his government appeared to become less sure-footed and increasingly accident-prone. Important figures from within his own party began to doubt Brown's competence as Prime Minister. For example, an embarrassing series of losses of laptop computers, disks and memory sticks was marked by Her Majesty's Revenue and Customs losing the personal data of no fewer than twenty-five million people. The Work and Pensions Secretary, Peter Hain, had to resign following damaging accusations concerning donations made to his (unsuccessful) campaign to become Deputy Leader of the Labour Party. Brown himself ended up signing the landmark

Lisbon Treaty on his own, without the company of the European Union's twenty-six other heads of state. The explanation given was an unfortunate 'diary clash'. Few believed this crass attempt to cover up Brown's reluctance to sign such a controversial document, given the Labour Party's refusal to hold a Treaty referendum, despite its pledge in its 2005 General Election manifesto to do so for the Treaty's almost identical draft predecessor.

For its series of policy blunders and general impression of a tired third term government adrift, the Labour Party was rewarded by the by-election loss of the previously safe Labour seat of Crewe and Nantwich and the worst local government election results in England for forty years, involving the loss of more than 300 seats. It garnered only twenty-four per cent of the vote. Brown himself was the subject of frequent ridicule at Prime Minister's Question Time. This reached its height when Vincent Cable, the Liberal Democrats' Treasury spokesman and acting leader (following the resignation of Menzies Campbell), who had enjoyed a rapidly rising reputation and media profile because of his prediction of and sage commentary on the growing financial crisis, claimed that Brown had undergone 'a remarkable transformation in the past few weeks from Stalin to Mr Bean'.[22]

The greatest political damage inflicted upon Brown once more arose from economic policy. In his final Budget statement in March 2007, Brown had announced that from April 2008 the basic rate of income tax would be cut from twenty-two pence to twenty pence to achieve 'the lowest basic rate for 75 years'.[23] However, in order to finance this tax cut, the lower ten pence rate of tax would be abolished, immediately raising the tax burden on the lowest wage earners. However, when added to the other tax and benefit measures announced in the April 2007 Budget, it was calculated that no fewer than 5.3 million families would be made worse off.[24] As the Brown Government's rating in successive opinion polls deteriorated, speculation gathered of a challenge to Brown for the leadership of the Labour Party and the office of Prime Minister. The clearest challenger, David Miliband, the Foreign Secretary, did nothing to dampen media speculation that he would mount a challenge. In a thinly veiled critique of Brown's record as Prime Minister, he asserted:

> So my message is simple. We can win the next general election because it is our party that has the right values to deliver security and opportunity. We must defend our record, by being candid about its strengths

and weaknesses. We must set out a bold vision. And we must show why conservative means cannot deliver our progressive ends.[25]

In the event, a leadership challenge did not materialise. Brown apologised belatedly for the ten pence debacle, and promised to do better, but the damage to his political authority, especially when challenged in Cabinet by other ministers, would be a lasting legacy. This damage was to be compounded by the disintegration of his British model of political economy.

THE BRITISH MODEL OF MONETARY POLICY: AN END TO GROWTH AND STABILITY

Gordon Brown's reputation as the prudential 'Iron Chancellor', who had successfully 'locked in' low inflation and macro-economic stability, was substantially based upon the British model of monetary policy devised by Brown and Ed Balls, his chief economic adviser, during their decade at the Treasury. Consequently, it was hardly surprising that the Brown Government should have chosen to adhere steadfastly to the principles and practice of the British model. In accordance with these principles, Alistair Darling began his inaugural Budget statement by affirming that 'the core purpose of this Budget is stability'.[26] However, whereas his predecessor had been able repeatedly to boast that his monetary policy stance had locked in macro-economic stability, delivering from 1997 to 2007 'more stability in terms of GDP growth and inflation than in any decade since the war',[27] Alistair Darling was unable to maintain such claims.

On 9 October 2007, in his inaugural Pre-Budget Report statement, and in announcing the conclusions of the second Comprehensive Spending Review, Darling had maintained that 'decisive action' had cut inflation to below the Government's target of two per cent, and that inflation would 'again be on target next year and the year after'.[28] However, it soon became evident that the Treasury under Darling was repeating its proclivity under Brown for being over-optimistic about the prospects for the United Kingdom economy, especially in the face of growing global market uncertainty. Consequently, Darling's first Budget was able only to promise that the Brown Government would 'do everything in our power to maintain stability'. Moreover, Darling's statement was notable for the extent to which it preferred to look backwards to the 'hard-won stability' achieved by the

British model during the Brown decade, which had delivered inflation of just two per cent since 2002, rather than to look forward into the abyss of global instability.[29] The macro-economic stability and low inflation about which Brown boasted during his final months at the Treasury had gone. The degree to which the British model had locked in macro-economic instability was now becoming evident.

THE BRITISH MODEL OF FISCAL POLICY: AN END TO PRUDENCE

While Gordon Brown as Prime Minister was unable to boast the same record of macro-economic stability as he delivered as Chancellor of the Exchequer, his government was even more troubled in the field of taxation and public expenditure. The full economic and political implications for low income earners of the abolition of the ten pence rate of taxation were identified as major contributory factors not only to disastrous opinion poll ratings for both Brown as Prime Minister and his government, but also consecutive by-election defeats for the Labour Party. Alistair Darling was duly forced to deliver a mini-Budget on 13 May 2008 which provided £2.7 billion of personal allowances to basic rate taxpayers. When Darling announced four months later the postponement of the two pence increase in road fuel duties scheduled for 1 October 2008, he had foregone a further £550 million in revenue. This followed the net tax cut of £6.3 billion in 2008–2009 arising from the measures announced in the 2007 and 2008 Budgets, and the 2007 Pre-Budget Report.[30]

The degree to which the public finances had deteriorated under the Brown Government became fully evident when, during the first six months of the 2008–2009 financial year, public sector net borrowing was £37.6 billion – a 75.2 per cent increase on the £21.6 billion borrowed during the equivalent period in 2007–2008, and more than the total borrowing for the previous financial year.[31] The Institute for Fiscal Studies (IFS) calculated that, on this basis, borrowing during the current financial year would soar to a total of around £64 billion, compared to Alistair Darling's March 2008 Budget forecast of £43 billion, a margin of error in excess of fifty per cent.[32] Net debt (excluding the Government's financial sector interventions) stood at £594.1 billion at the end of December 2008, equivalent to 40.4 per cent of

GDP. However, with the inclusion of the Government's financial sector interventions to rescue British banks, net debt was £703.4 billion, equivalent to 47.8 per cent of GDP.[33] With the onset of recession and the consequent increased expenditure on benefits and falling tax receipts, the Sustainable Investment Rule (where national debt should not exceed forty per cent of GDP) would be broken in successive years. Indeed, the IFS predicted that the economic slowdown arising from the collapse of the Brown Boom might push net debt 'closer to 50% of national income'.[34] The IFS also concluded that the British model's Golden Rule, namely that public sector current spending should be financed entirely from public sector receipts over the economic cycle, and borrowing should only be used to finance capital expenditure, was also 'likely to be breached unless the government chooses to accrue current budget surpluses during periods when the economy is weak'.[35]

Gordon Brown could not claim that he had not been warned many years earlier about the likely longer term consequences of his earlier imprudence, when he had chosen to accelerate the rate of increase in public spending from 2002, at a time when the economy was experiencing its longest period of sustained growth since records began. The IMF, the Organization for Economic Co-operation and Development (OECD) and European Commission had all warned repeatedly in their respective surveys of the United Kingdom economy of the dangers posed by the sustained imprudence of the British model of fiscal policy. For example, as early as 24 November 1999, the concluding statement of an IMF staff mission to the UK had warned of 'a need for vigilance in the public finances not only in the short term, but in the long term as well'.[36] In March 2000, the IMF cautioned that Brown's fiscal rules 'did not adequately constrain policy at present and left scope for sizable spending initiatives'.[37] In its February 2001 staff report, the IMF noted that Brown's 'planned expansion during the second half of 2000/01 and in 2001/02 was not without risks', and that above all this would require 'great prudence in fiscal policy in 2001/02'.[38]

This message was reinforced in March 2003, when IMF Directors had noted that there were 'appreciable risks' to continued economic recovery arising from 'both external and domestic uncertainties', and 'In particular, domestic demand is being sustained by high and increasing levels of household debt, fuelled by house price inflation and low interest rates, which increases vulnerability to potential adverse shocks'. Moreover, with prescient foresight of events some five years later, the Directors had called for 'heightened vigilance to these risks by the authorities, especially regarding the possible existence of a housing price bubble with its potential deflationary consequences'.[39] Brown had chosen not to heed these warnings. He was imprudent for the purpose of increasing expenditure on public services with a view to securing a third consecutive General Election victory for New Labour. It was only after the 2005 General Election victory that fiscal policy began to be tightened, but by then Brown's actions were too late to restore fiscal prudence. The IMF had warned consistently of the United Kingdom's particular vulnerability to 'low probability, but potentially high-impact risks, particularly as the global financial centre could transmit shocks to the domestic economy'.[40] Regrettably for Brown as Prime Minister, the good fortune which had marked his decade as Chancellor ran out. The 'low probability, but potentially high-impact risks' arrived during the summer of 2007 to wreck the British model, at precisely the moment Brown left the Treasury for Number Ten Downing Street.

THE BRITISH MODEL OF COMPETITIVENESS POLICY: AN END TO RISK-BASED REGULATION

Brown's British model of political economy from May 1997 to June 2007 consistently championed the liberalised financial markets of the City of London and their 'light-touch' and 'risk-based' regulatory structure, not only as a blueprint for how the United Kingdom should seize the opportunities arising from the competitive challenges posed by globalisation, but also as a model for the future political economy of the European Union.[41] The City had been praised by both Brown and Ed Balls as the location for forty per cent of the over-the-counter derivatives market, and seventy per cent of the global secondary bond market,[42] and other forms of financial trading. Risk was originated by London's traders but then distributed throughout the world's financial markets through securitisation and other financial instruments, so that it was spread among a wide range of investors and traders. For his part, Brown drew upon the example provided by the City to contend that 'we can demonstrate that just as in the nineteenth century industrialisation was made for Britain, in the twenty-first century globalisation is made for Britain'.[43]

Brown's competitiveness policy had encouraged United Kingdom-based financial institutions to engage in innovative product development and thereby rapidly to increase their market share and exposure to risk. For example, the former building society, Northern Rock, had de-mutualised in 1997 and then expanded its assets six-fold to £101 billion within the decade of Brown's tenure at the Treasury. That rapid expansion had been financed by borrowing and debt, reflecting the same trends that had characterised the rapid growth of personal consumption and rising property prices. As a consequence, only a quarter of Northern Rock's rapid expansion in the mortgage market had been funded by its depositors' savings, compared with almost two-thirds at the time of its de-mutualisation. Moreover, the remaining three-quarters of expansion had been funded by the City of London's financial markets, with more than forty per cent of Northern Rock's borrowing being financed by mortgage-backed securities. During the first half of 2007, Northern Rock's aggressive marketing meant that it had accounted for nearly ten per cent of gross mortgage lending in the United Kingdom.[44]

The originate-and-distribute, debt-based business model was unsustainable without continuing and continual access to new funding, but when market concerns arose about the scale of losses arising from the US sub-prime mortgage market, Northern Rock's supply of capital was cut off. The bank was therefore forced to seek liquidity support from the Bank of England. Although the Financial Services Authority (FSA) indicated that it regarded Northern Rock as solvent, this was not sufficient to prevent the first major retail run on a British bank since 1878.[45] The 'light-touch' and 'risk-based' approach to financial regulation, upon which the British model of competitiveness had been founded, began to fall apart during the course of the next five months. The Treasury and Bank of England announced the extension of depositor protection on the first £35,000 of losses for all UK banks and the provision of a further facility for Northern Rock until February 2008, with no specific borrowing limit. However, none of these measures was sufficient to attract a private sector buyer for Northern Rock. The two offers tendered from the bank's own board and Virgin Group were deemed by the Government to offer insufficient protection to the taxpayer. Therefore, on 17 February 2008, Alistair Darling announced that Northern Rock would be taken into temporary public ownership, but, in the process, the British model of fiscal policy had been damaged, perhaps fatally.

ZOMBIE BANKS AND A ZOMBIE GOVERNMENT

On its own, the demise of Northern Rock would have been sufficient to undermine the political and market credibility of Brown's Government. However, the sheer scale of the financial bailout of Northern Rock was soon dwarfed by the announcement on 8 October 2008 of a £500 billion package of support for British banks, in the face of continuing volatility in global financial markets. Introducing the package, Brown stated, 'This is not a time for conventional thinking or out-dated dogma, but for the fresh and innovative intervention that gets to the heart of the problem'.[46] At a stroke, the old discredited British model was being abandoned, and a radically different model of political economy was being fashioned to take its place. First, the Bank of England would extend the loans available to banks under its Special Liquidity Scheme from £100 billion to 'at least' £200 billion. Second, the taxpayer would extend at least £25 billion and up to £50 billion of capital to the major British banks. Third, for a commercial fee, the Government would provide 'at least' £250 billion of guarantees to allow United Kingdom banks to raise their own money on the private capital markets.[47] In addition, in its Pre-Budget Report, the Government announced a temporary reduction in Value Added Tax from 17.5 per cent to fifteen per cent from 1 December 2008 until 31 December 2009, to inject £12.4 billion or around £275 into the pockets of the average household.[48] Brown believed the restructuring would deliver 'a fairer, more equitable and reliable financial system'. Indeed, in making such interventions, Brown claimed, 'We have led the world'.[49] In reality, the liberalised market, which the British model promised to make work more effectively in the public interest, had failed spectacularly. Enormous risks, based upon huge borrowing and debt, had been taken by private market actors, threatening the entire banking system. The taxpayer had been forced to intervene. Profit had been privatised, but risk and losses had been socialised, and eventually nationalised.

As the full impact of the credit crunch became apparent upon the domestic economy in general and the United Kingdom's major banks in particular, the Brown Government reacted with two further financial rescue packages. Each was unprecedented in its scale. Each was an admission that previous measures had been insufficient both to reduce market volatility and uncertainty and to restore sufficient confidence for bank lending to resume. However, in advance of the Group of 20 (G20) Summit of industrialised economies, to be held in London on 2 April 2009, the Brown Government attempted to give retrospective coherence to its on-the-hoof interventions by portraying them as a coherent economic recovery plan.[50] In truth, the approach to the growing financial crisis had been reactive rather than proactive, event-driven rather than principle-based.

When its initial package of measures failed to restore confidence and bank lending, on 14 January 2009, the Brown Government announced a range of measures intended to address the cash flow, credit and investment needs of small and medium-sized enterprises. These measures included a £10 billion working capital scheme, which would secure up to £20 billion of lending. However, less than one week later, on 19 January, Alistair Darling announced a second major package of financial intervention to support lending in the economy. In addition to an extension to its existing Credit Guarantee Scheme, the Government would introduce from April 2009 a new guarantee scheme for asset back securities, in an attempt 'to improve banks' access to wholesale funding markets, help support lending, and promote robust and sustainable markets over the longer term'.[51] Furthermore, in order to enhance the availability of corporate credit, and to reduce the illiquidity of the underlying financial instruments, the Bank of England would establish an asset purchase programme of up to an initial £50 billion, financed by Treasury bills. Finally, the Government would launch an Asset Protection Scheme 'to offer capital and asset protection on those assets most affected by the current economic conditions'.[52]

In effect, to rescue the banks from the consequences of their irresponsible lending and risk-based financial products, the Brown Government had introduced a retrospective insurance scheme whereby the taxpayer would underwrite the risky loans that the banks had made during the Brown Boom. While the Government would be able to charge an insurance premium payment for insuring these loans, the taxpayer would be responsible for meeting the bill should borrowers default on their loans. No upper limit had been set on the taxpayers' exposure to 'toxic' loans. In the event, the fact that the Government had not yet negotiated all the details of its various measures, and had stopped short of establishing an actual 'toxic' bank to deal specifically with sub-prime loans and assets, served only to decrease rather than enhance market confidence. The major banks' share prices fell sharply as investors feared that the measures might presage full nationalisation, and thereby render their shareholdings effectively worthless.

The failure of its two previous rescue packages to restore market confidence, liquidity and lending to the United Kingdom banking system led the Brown Government to announce a third bailout of the banks on 20 February 2009. On this occasion, the Royal Bank of Scotland (RBS) placed £325 billion of assets into the taxpayer-guaranteed Asset Protection Scheme. In exchange for the taxpayer guarantee, RBS paid £6.5 billion to the Treasury and was responsible for the first £19.5 billion of any losses arising from the insured assets. It would also provide an additional £25 billion of lending during 2009. The taxpayer provided a further £13 billion cash injection to RBS, on top of the £20 billion already provided. Since the taxpayer already owned seventy per cent of RBS, any losses arising from sub-prime, toxic assets would effectively have to be met from future taxes. Lloyds and HBOS, which had already received £17 billion in taxpayers' support, would also place £260 billion of assets into the taxpayer-guaranteed Asset Protection Scheme.[53] The impact of these actions on public sector net debt would be to add 'between 70 per cent and 100 per cent of GDP' to the national debt.[54] The third rescue package coincided with a series of huge financial losses, unprecedented in British corporate history. RBS announced losses for 2008 of £24.1 billion. Lloyds Banking Group, which had acquired HBOS in a shotgun wedding in January 2009, only after the Brown Government agreed to waive the normal competition rules applicable to the mortgage market, reported an annual profit of £807 million, down eighty per cent on the previous year. However, its newly acquired HBOS business reported a loss of £10.8 billion for the same period, as no less than 11.9 per cent of its loans were reported to be bad debts.[55]

The political reaction to the Brown Government's decision to expose the British taxpayer to up to many hundreds of billions of pounds of toxic bank assets was extremely hostile. George Osborne, the Shadow Chancellor, pointed out that RBS's agreement to provide an extra £25 billion of lending during 2009 amounted to only 3.4 per cent of its total lending to non-bank customers, a very small cost to the bank for such a huge taxpayer rescue. Moreover, since its acquisition of a majority shareholding in RBS in October 2008, the taxpayer had lost £16 billion to date, because of the collapse in the bank's shares.[56] Vincent Cable, the Liberal Democrats' Treasury spokesman, who had predicted the credit crunch, was much harsher in his critique. Portraying the Asset Protection Scheme as both 'a disgrace and a betrayal of taxpayer's interests' and 'absolutely dire', Cable claimed it was 'a classic case of privatising profits and socialising loss'. The Brown Government had failed to use its majority shareholding and control of RBS to nationalise the bank. Nationalisation, Cable pointed out, had been recommended the previous week by Alan Greenspan, former chairman of the Federal Reserve Board. Greenspan had argued 'we can't keep on funding zombie banks without gaining public control'. However, for Cable, the real problem was that 'we have not only zombie banks, but a zombie Government: the walking dead, controlled by people who have a strong vested interest in protecting their bonus arrangements and covering up large-scale tax avoidance'.[57]

THE THEORY OF MORAL SENTIMENTS, THE PRACTICE OF IMMORAL ACTIONS

One of the constants throughout the transition from boom to bust was Gordon Brown's continuing belief in Adam Smith's moral sentiments, especially the sentiments of responsibility and duty. Brown expressed his anger at 'the irresponsibility of risk-taking and the irresponsibility of not disclosing things, that has now spread to become not just a financial crisis but an economic crisis'.[58] What Brown failed to acknowledge was that it was his own risk-based and FSA-led approach to financial regulation and bank supervision that had given bankers the license to undertake immoral actions, rather than to practise moral sentiments. In this regard, the greatest political embarrassment for the Brown Government concerned Sir Fred Goodwin, the former chief executive of RBS. He had presided over the disastrous series of takeovers by RBS, which had culminated in the bank's £24.1 billion annual loss, the largest in British corporate history. Despite this wretched performance, Goodwin had retired early at the age of fifty with a pension fund of £16.9 million. Its value had been doubled by the RBS board from the £8.37 million listed in the bank's most recent annual report, paying him around £13,000 a week in retirement. The pension appeared to have been sanctioned with the knowledge of Lord Myners, the minister for the City of London, at a time when the taxpayer was being expected to find billions of pounds to rescue irresponsible bankers from their previous risk-based commercial strategies.

In relation to remuneration and bonuses, Gordon Brown argued that 'where people are enterprising and are responsible in their risk-taking they should be rewarded'. However, if 'irresponsible or excessive risk-taking' took place, action would be taken.[59] What Brown failed to acknowledge was that his FSA-led and 'risk-based' approach to regulation had failed to put in place any checks and balances upon individual remuneration. Market judgements as to the appropriate rewards for enterprise would always be subjective, as would judgements about if and when risk-taking was responsible or irresponsible. Not once did Brown acknowledge that, during a decade as Chancellor of the Exchequer, his 'risk-based' British model had trusted the financial markets to regulate themselves in the remuneration of individuals. Not once did he concede that the liberalised markets, which his British model had claimed could be made to serve the public interest, had failed. Rather than acting decisively, as the Obama Administration was later to do, to curb greedy remuneration, Alistair Darling was initially content to point to the fact that the FSA was 'looking at these things' and 'drawing up a code'.[60] Even in these dire circumstances, market voluntarism was still preferred to statutory intervention.

Alistair Darling blamed the previous Conservative governments for the banking failures, stating, 'The answer for today's problems partly lies in the deregulation of global banking in the 1980s, which was followed by huge financial innovation in the 1990s. This, combined with low interest rates around the world, set the scene for one of the biggest global credit bubbles in history'. Indeed, 'Banks everywhere took on too much risk, and worse, risk that they didn't properly understand'. As a consequence, there were 'many lessons to be learnt – by governments, regulators and by banks themselves', but Darling's silence was deafening on why Gordon Brown's British model of risk-based regulation had failed to identify the credit bubble and excessive risk-taking.[61] New Labour had been in government for nearly twelve years. This, in itself, was more than ample time for Brown to have identified and dealt with any flaws in the deregulation of the 1980s, or financial innovation of the 1990s. After all, the Blair Government's landslide General Election victory had coincided with the onset of the Asian financial crisis, and its 2001 General Election victory with the bursting of the dotcom bubble in the United States.

Darling contended that 'as a condition for putting taxpayers' money into banks, we must also take action to end the old short-term bonus culture – the one-way bet culture – that encouraged banks to make reckless decisions. People want free markets, not value-free markets'.[62] In the future, four principles of fairness would be applied to banking, namely that there would be no reward for failure; no bonuses to be paid unless based on long-term sustainable performance; the right of clawback of bonuses, if performance was not sustained; and the taking into account of pay and bonuses in financial supervision.[63] However, less than a week after Darling's pronouncement, the details of Sir Fred Goodwin's pension were published, demonstrating that the Treasury and Brown Government had been party to the application of the principles of unfairness.

In the face of what he described as 'the biggest collapse in the banking system that the world had ever seen', Gordon Brown identified a clear agenda for his government: 'Our task must be nothing less than to rebuild a financial system where it has failed, and then to create an economy in which banks are no longer serving themselves but are serving the public of this country'.[64] However, the truth was that Brown's risk-based approach to financial regulation had arisen because New Labour had allowed its political economy to become subservient to, rather than the master of, liberalised financial markets and the interests of the City of London. Brown castigated bankers, depicting some of their practices as 'not only unacceptable, they are indefensible', and claiming, 'Some acted as though free markets could be value-free markets'.[65] Brown forgot that it was his FSA-led model which had failed to provide the necessary supervision and regulation necessary to encourage moral sentiments rather than immoral action.

Brown further promised a new system where 'Banks must act in the long-term interests of their shareholders and therefore of the economy as a whole, not in the short-term interests of bankers'. There must also be 'better governance of banks', and 'the reinvention of the traditional savings and mortgage bank in Britain, for loans to be made on prudent and careful terms'.[66] This statement ignored the fact that, for a decade as Chancellor, Brown had championed a light-touch approach to bank governance, and done nothing to stop the erosion of the traditional savings and mortgage bank, and its replacement by the originate-and-distribute model of mortgage-based risk-taking exemplified by Northern Rock. The FSA itself, and the tripartite system of regulation involving it, the Bank of England and the Treasury, had been established by Gordon Brown. The responsibility for any shortcomings in that system of regulation would have to lie on his shoulders.

Further embarrassment for the Brown Government came with the sudden resignation of Sir James Crosby, the deputy chairman of the FSA and former chief executive officer of HBOS. His resignation was prompted by accusations from Paul Moore, a former head of risk assessment at HBOS, whom Crosby had sacked. Moore alleged that Crosby and the HBOS board had ignored his warning that the bank's growth strategy was exposing it to excessive risks.[67] The market environment prompted the leading hedge fund manager Jim Rogers, who with George Soros had founded the Quantum Fund, to proclaim 'I don't think there is a sound UK bank now. The City of London is finished, the financial centre of the world is moving east. All the money is in Asia. You don't need London'.[68] The practice of Brown's light-touch, risk-based approach to bank supervision had enabled the City of London to prosper in the short term. In the longer term, the collapse in market liquidity and investor confidence threatened the future status of London as one of the world's major financial centres.

THE QUEST FOR A NEW MODEL OF POLITICAL ECONOMY

From the outset, Gordon Brown's explanation of the credit crunch was designed to absolve his British model of political economy, with its risk-based approach to financial regulation, from any responsibility for the growing financial crisis. Above all else, the credit crunch was to be understood as an externally generated product of globalisation, being both 'the first financial crisis of this global age' and 'the first problem of the new global age'.[69] In short, 'we have a global financial crisis that is caused by the failures of the banking system'.[70] This analysis failed to acknowledge that the historical subtleties of the causes of the credit crunch might be lost on those experiencing the very same consequences as previous recessions and depressions – unemployment and falling living standards. It also failed to recognise the degree to which the causes of the credit crunch were home-grown and intrinsic to the British model, rather than imported and extrinsic.

Brown had undertaken a very personal political and philosophical odyssey from his early advocacy of democratic socialism to his eventual messianic conversion to supply-side liberalism and a moral defence of the benefits of liberalised market capitalism. This journey had culminated in Brown's close adherence to the maxims of Alan Greenspan, who had served from 1987 until 2006 as the chairman of the United States' Federal Reserve Board. Greenspan had based his economic policy prescriptions on a belief in the invisible hand of the market, the freedom for individuals to pursue their own self-interest, and a hostility towards regulation.[71] For Greenspan, 'Since markets have become too complex for effective human intervention, the most promising anticrisis policies are those that maintain maximum market flexibility – freedom of action for key market participants such as hedge funds, private equity funds, and investment banks'. Moreover, 'Regulation, by its nature, inhibits freedom of market action, and that freedom to act expeditiously is what rebalances markets. Undermine this freedom and the whole market-balancing process is put at risk'.[72]

Greenspan's philosophy, with its debt to the classical economics and moral sentiments of Adam Smith beloved by Brown, had inspired the light-touch, risk-based approach to regulation of the British model of political economy. However, in an extraordinary ideological and policy-based U-turn, when giving testimony to a House of Representatives Committee hearing on the financial crisis and the role of Federal regulators, Greenspan confessed, 'I made a mistake in presuming that the self-interest of organizations, specifically banks and others, were such that they were best capable of protecting their own shareholders and their equity in the firms'.[73] In a further shocking admission, Greenspan indicated that he had found 'a flaw in the model that I perceived is the critical functioning structure that defines how the world works, so to speak'. Greenspan added, 'That's precisely the reason I was shocked, because I had been going for 40 years or more with very considerable evidence that it was working exceptionally well'.[74] At a stroke, the whole ideological edifice that had provided the justification for Brown's risk-based approach to regulation had been cast aside.

However, for Brown, the credit crunch had 'certainly started in the United States', because these were 'global problems, global action is required'. Other European countries would be invited by Brown to participate in a European-wide funding plan.[75] This was where Brown's Euroscepticism and reluctance to sign the Lisbon Treaty would cost him vital political capital. He could hardly expect European leaders to rally to his financial plan when he and Ed Balls had lectured them previously on the merits of their 'Global Europe' vision, and of the need for the continental European economies to converge towards the British model, rather than vice versa. Indeed, Peter Steinbrück, the Social Democratic German finance minister asserted that 'the Great Rescue Plan' for the European economies did not exist, and that the Brown Government's strategy of a temporary cut in Value Added Tax would simply 'raise Britain's debt to a level that will take a generation to work off'. Moreover, Steinbrück could not have been less impressed when 'the same people who would never touch deficit spending are now tossing around billions. The switch from decades of supply-side politics all the way to a crass Keynesianism is breathtaking'.[76]

For Brown, this unprecedented crisis would require unprecedented intervention and a new political economy, for 'these are extraordinary times, and they require extraordinary measures'.[77] In short, 'If we have learnt anything in these last tumultuous and unprecedented months, it is that this is not the time to become prisoners of old dogmas of the past. All over the world policy makers are leaving behind the old orthodoxies of the past'.[78] Moreover, Brown claimed that what was being witnessed was 'the redefining of the relationship between individual markets and state. I think that happened in the 1930s and 1940s, the '30s in America, '40s in Britain. I think it is happening now'.[79] But why had Brown himself remained a prisoner of the old orthodoxies for more than a decade, especially when he had advocated wholesale reform of the international financial system as long ago as December 1998?[80]

To redress the effects of the credit crunch would require the modernisation of the International Monetary Fund and World Bank, because Brown did not think 'you can deal with the problems of 2008 with the institutions of 1945'.[81] In short, 'we have institutions that were created in the 1940s that are not fit for the task of 2008'.[82] The world was now entering 'the era for global society' which would require the reform of the international institutions.[83] Brown described the November 2008 Washington summit of the Group of 20 (G20) leading industrialised economies as providing 'the road to the new Bretton Woods'.[84] What was now required was 'an early warning system for the world economy, you need a better surveillance of what is happening, you need as I said a better crisis prevention means'.[85]

Brown had maintained his faith in the capacity of technocratic expertise to forewarn of future financial crises. What he failed to acknowledge was that the IMF's existing surveillance and crisis prevention mechanisms had warned him repeatedly from 1999 onwards of the dangers facing the United Kingdom economy, because of the build-up of private and public debt, and the inflationary bubble in the housing market. He had chosen to ignore those warnings, and similar concerns expressed by the European Union and Organization for Economic Co-operation and Development. Fine-tuning or wholesale reorganisation of the international financial architecture would be futile if politicians continued to choose to ignore warnings, as he had done both as Chancellor of the Exchequer and as Chairman of the IMF's International Monetary and Financial Committee.

CONCLUSION

During the tenure of the Brown Government, each of the three core elements of the British model of political economy bequeathed from Brown's tenure as Chancellor of the Exchequer in the Blair Governments was undermined. The British model of monetary policy witnessed the end of macro-economic stability in the face of volatility and uncertainty on the financial markets, inflation and unemployment, and currency instability as the pound depreciated in value against the dollar, euro and yen. The British model of fiscal policy underwent transformation from having been a beacon of fiscal prudence to a tarnished symbol of public and private imprudence. The British model of competitiveness, with its risk-based approach to financial regulation, was blown away by successive nationalisations and taxpayer-funded bailouts of private, risk-taking financial institutions.

Above all else, the British model was based upon the central conceit that it would be able 'not only to support but positively enhance markets'. Indeed, Treasury officials stated their conviction that 'Markets are a powerful means of advancing the public interest'.[86]Where Old Labour governments had sought to manipulate nationalised industries, trades unions and the other institutions of the public domain provided by the British state, New Labour had promised to manipulate private institutions such as entrepreneurs and corporations to make liberalised markets serve the public good. For the Brown Government, the debacles of Northern Rock, Bradford and Bingley, and the recapitalisation of four other major United Kingdom banks were to demonstrate this was a fatal error for the British model of political economy.

The most remarkable aspect of the demise of the British model of political economy during the first eighteen months of the Brown Government was that Gordon Brown himself did not anticipate the global credit crunch. He had, after all, been uniquely privileged for almost a decade to identify the coming crisis. Brown had served as the Chairman of the International Monetary and Financial Committee from September 1999 – the IMF's most important advisory committee. Its role was to advise the IMF's Board of Governors on the supervision of the management of the international monetary system, and to 'deal with sudden disturbances that might threaten the stability of the system'.[87] Given the quality of advice and information provided to him, both by IMF officials and his own Treasury civil servants and special advisers, it was inexplicable why Brown did not act earlier to implement counter-cyclical measures to curb government borrowing, curtail private debt and deflate the asset bubble. This was especially puzzling given that a similar collapse of a speculative, 'bubble' economy had occurred in Japan in 1990, and Brown's own formative months as Chancellor had coincided with the onset of the Asian financial crisis. Brown's explanation was that he had advocated proposals for reform of the international financial system as early as December 1998 in a speech at Harvard University, but he had 'found it hard to persuade other countries that this was the time to adopt these changes'.[88] It was regrettable that he chose not to persist with that particular alternative agenda, but opted instead to evangelise his now failed British model of political economy.

While Brown cannot be held entirely responsible for the onset of the credit crunch, he did ignore repeated warnings, from the IMF, the Bank of England and other agencies, of the attendant dangers arising from public and private debt and imprudence. This resulted in the United Kingdom economy being particularly vulnerable, among the major industrialised economies, to the effects of the onset of domestic and global recession. As chairman for nearly eight years of the International Monetary and Financial Committee, the most powerful committee at the IMF with particular responsibility for monitoring liquidity in the world's financial markets, Brown did nothing to challenge the orthodoxy of neo-liberal globalisation. This inaction continued even when his own political philosophy and instincts had convinced him of the need for fundamental reform of the governance of global financial markets. Brown became a convert to the neo-liberal approach to globalisation, the political economy of Alan Greenspan, and a risk-based approach to financial regulation. It was this framework, which was fundamentally flawed, as Greenspan has admitted, which ultimately gave the freedom to bankers and markets to originate and distribute risk irresponsibly, in pursuit of short-term profit but without regard to the longer-term health of either their own institution or the wider economy. To this extent, Gordon Brown must be held responsible for the transition from boom to bust.

Chapter 9

Conclusion

INTRODUCTION

Gordon Brown has presided over both one of the most remarkable economic and political transitions, and one of the greatest policy U-turns in modern British political history. As Chancellor, his immediate legacy was the Brown Boom, delivered by his own British model of political economy, his nationalisation of policy design and resource allocation, and his British Way of citizenship and identity. His political economy was New Labour. Brown was the passionate advocate of a light-touch, risk-based approach to the regulation of financial markets. As Prime Minister, his immediate legacy is the Brown Bust, which has witnessed the dismantling of his British model of political economy, and the nationalisation and state-led recapitalisation of the United Kingdom's major banks. This political economy has owed more to Old Labour. Brown has become, albeit belatedly and after exposing the taxpayer to potential losses of tens of billions of pounds, the champion of old-fashioned, prudential banking practices.

In undertaking this transition from boom to bust, and in orchestrating the policy U-turns his government has implemented, Brown has engaged in one of the greatest acts of short-term political and economic amnesia. In portraying the credit crunch and deepening recession as an external product of globalisation, fermented in the sub-prime housing markets of the United States, Brown has forgotten the central role he played in championing a competitiveness policy based upon his own conversion to the neoliberal approach to globalization, and the Alan Greenspan-led approach to financial governance. This championed the City of London, and gave bankers and market traders the licence to engage in the irresponsible risk-taking which has left the present and future generations of taxpayers and consumers with a legacy of massive public and private debt. Brown did nothing to apply a brake to the unsustainable property-led and consumer-led boom before the speculative bubble inevitably burst. He also sanctioned irresponsible levels of government borrowing and spending at a time when the domestic economy was already expanding above its trend rate of growth.

BROWN'S POLITICAL LEGACY: THE NEW POLITICS?

Gordon Brown's central role in the Blair Governments ensured that when he became Labour Party leader on 24 June 2007, and Prime Minister on 27 June, he carried a major political legacy. Gordon Brown has undertaken a personal political odyssey, from parliamentary and supply-side socialism to the more recent sympathetic and supply-side liberalism of the New British Enlightenment, that has shaped the agenda of his Government. Brown has returned to the American liberalism of the 1930s New Deal and 1960s Great Society eras first taught to him by his father. His personal moral compass is calibrated against the liberalism of Adam Smith, fellow Scot and son of Kirkcaldy, ideas that are a significant departure from and are alien to the mainstream history and traditions of the Labour Party. Gordon Brown has become the third British Prime Minister, following Margaret Thatcher and Tony Blair, to base his modernisation programme on an ideology rooted in liberalism, implemented through a statecraft that entails further centralised state control.

As Prime Minister, Gordon Brown and his government have failed to deliver any of the five promises and commitments made on the day he entered Number Ten Downing Street. First, rather than 'a new government with new priorities', the Brown Government has offered essential continuity with, rather than departure from, the ideas, policies and priorities of the Blair Governments. Brown only departed from that agenda when forced to do so by the onset of recession. Brown's British Way attempted to renew New Labour and Blair's third way, but it failed to identify an alternative 'fourth way' programme for political, economic and social renewal. Brown even restored New Labour stalwarts and previous political enemies, notably

Peter Mandelson and Alan Milburn, to the ranks of his government and its advisers. Mandelson's return in particular, and his proposals for the part-privatisation of the Post Office, threatened to divide the Labour Party in the run-up to the next General Election. Only Tony Blair and Alistair Campbell remained to be recalled by Brown for a reunion of the architects of New Labour.

Second, Brown's character and judgement as Prime Minister proved to be insufficiently robust to, at all times, remain 'strong in purpose, steadfast in will' and resolute in action. He hesitated over critical decisions, not least whether to call an early General Election. During his tenure at the Treasury, Brown favoured an approach to decision-making in which he relied upon the technocratic expertise of eminent figures, largely drawn from the private sector and beyond the realms of democratic scrutiny or accountability, to undertake major reviews of policy before action was taken. Once cast as Prime Minister, Brown soon demonstrated an inability to deal with the very different demands of that office. In particular, Brown appeared to lack both the ability to set the agenda for a twenty-four-hour media, rather than always to be reacting to its interests, and the capability of concentrating, often at short notice, upon issues requiring immediate decision and action, rather than his previous Treasury-based careful reflection, which often bordered upon prevarication, with the promise of a five- or ten-year strategic plan.

Third, rather than fulfilling the potential and realising the talents of all British people, one of Brown's principal legacies would be the wasting of potential and talent in lengthening dole queues. Even during the 'nice' decade, the overwhelming majority of new jobs created by the Brown Boom had been taken by workers born outside the United Kingdom. Thus, by the fourth quarter of 2008, the official labour market survey calculated that there were 3,819,000 workers born outside the United Kingdom in the labour force, equivalent to thirteen per cent of the total. Of these, nearly seventy per cent were born outside the European Union. At the same time, 7,858,000 or 20.8 per cent of the workforce remained economically inactive.[1] Rather than providing sufficient avenues for the affordable retraining of indigenous workers, the British model of political economy's short-termist solution to skilled labour shortages had been to adopt a *laissez-faire* approach to migration, and to offer migrants a shorter route to British nationality. A notable legacy of this approach to skill shortages would be a rise in support for the British National Party, and the concern among senior police officers and the security services that rapidly rising unemployment might ignite a summer of discontent in England's multiracial communities.

Fourth, despite Brown's claim to have listened to and learnt from the British people, his government would continue to display a selective deafness. This would apply both to major issues attracting significant public support, notably the demands for a referendum on the European Union's Lisbon Treaty, and those issues of specific interest to Brown, notably *The Governance of Britain* agenda, for which there was no public demand whatsoever. Fifth, rather than leading a government 'beyond the old politics' and narrow party political interest, to mobilise all the talents, Brown as Prime Minister had shown little evidence that he could trust his own Cabinet colleagues to mobilise all of their talents, let alone those of the broader public and private sectors. Brown described Alistair Darling, his Chancellor of the Exchequer, as 'the man with the power'.[2] This might help explain why Brown appeared incapable of entrusting Darling with orchestrating the Brown Government's response to the credit crunch and recession.

BROWN'S ECONOMIC LEGACY: AN END TO BOOM AND BUST?

There is a very real danger for Brown that future historians of early twenty-first-century British politics will find a dual legacy for him. On the one hand, he will be known for being the Chancellor responsible for the Brown Boom, the 'nice' decade of non-inflationary consistently expansionary economic performance resulting in the 'Great Stability'[3] that propelled the Labour Party to consecutive General Election victories. On the other hand, he will be known as the architect of the Brown Bust, the onset of domestic recession and a new era of austerity, rendered worse by Brown's failure to curb the escalation in both public and private debt during his tenure at the Treasury. His former chief economic adviser and closest political confidant, Ed Balls, described the financial crisis as 'more extreme and more serious than that of the 1930s and we all remember how the politics of that era were shaped by the economy'. The implications of Balls's comments for Brown's political and economic legacy appeared grave. Balls further suggested that these were 'seismic events that are going to change the political landscape'. Indeed, he asserted: 'The economy is going to define our politics in this region and in Britain in the next year, the next five years, the next ten and even the next fifteen years'. Moreover, 'The reality is that this is becoming the most serious global recession for, I'm sure, over one hundred years'.[4]

In its 2009 Green Budget, the Institute for Fiscal Studies (IFS) identified the close parallels between the pattern of economic performance during the Thatcher and Major Governments on the one hand, and the Blair and Brown Governments on the other.[5] However, of even greater significance may be the parallels in the political and economic legacy between the Thatcher/Major and Blair/Brown era. First, both the Conservative and New Labour modernisation programmes helped engineer economic and social policy reforms which delivered General Election victories and terms of office. Second, both programmes made economic (particularly fiscal) and social policy choices that shaped the political agenda for at least the following decade. Third, the domestic recessions bequeathed by both programmes eventually rendered their party unelectable, confining a generation of politicians to opposition.

During evidence given to the House of Commons Treasury Committee on 18 July 2002, Gordon Brown had identified the eras in post-war British economic policy of the worst 'boom bust' or 'stop go', i.e. 'high levels of growth followed by quite deep recessions', as those between '1980–82 and 1990–92'. Brown further defined 'boom bust' as the running of 'a policy where you allow the economy to grow too fast and then it sinks further than it has in other countries, even where there is a world downturn, and that is what we mean in Britain by the history of "stop go"'. Brown had suggested 1980–1982 and 1990–1992 as appropriate periods when a recession, i.e. two consecutive quarters of negative growth, had been replaced by a 'bust', because 'GDP fell 1.5 per cent in 1981 and 1.4 per cent in 1991'.[6] Therefore, the benchmark for the United Kingdom's economic performance to be classified as a 'bust' had been set by Brown as Chancellor as a minimum contraction of 1.4 per cent of GDP.

With particular irony, a potential political and economic blow for Brown's legacy was delivered by an institution that he had served faithfully for almost eight years, and through which, as the chairman of one of its most important committees, he had studiously defended the actual liberalised financial markets whose turbulence had ushered in the age of irresponsibility. On 28 January 2009, the International Monetary Fund (IMF) forecast that not only would there be a global economic slump during which world growth was projected 'to fall to ½ per cent in 2009, its lowest rate since World War II', but also that the United Kingdom would experience a 2.8 per cent contraction in its output during 2009, the worst performance among the Group of Eight industrialised economies.[7] In Brown's own terms, the United Kingdom economy was being forecast by the IMF to enter a new era of 'boom bust' and 'stop go' during 2009.

BROWN'S FINANCIAL LEGACY: IMPRUDENT PUBLIC AND PRIVATE DEBT FOR A GENERATION

One of Brown's principal economic legacies, both as Chancellor and Prime Minister, is to have presided over a massive deterioration in both the public finances of the British state and the private finances of millions of consumers and property-owners. The Brown Government's greatest challenge is that it will have to cast a programme for further economic, social and political renewal against the backdrop of a new austerity for both the public and private sectors. For the private sector, the reluctance of the banks to extend credit while they rebuild their balance sheets has cast a huge shadow of doubt over the viability of its involvement in new building and infrastructure projects at the very juncture when the Government has been seeking to bring forward capital investment projects in order to provide a boost to employment, investment and output. For the public sector, the fiscal implications of the rescue of ailing British banks and manufacturing industries, allied to the impact of the recession, are severe in both the short, medium and long term. In the short term, the Brown Government has had to sanction additional expenditure and massive borrowing at the cost of suspending (to avoid breaking) its own fiscal rules, and limiting funding for frontline public services.

In the medium term, the Treasury has forecast in the 2008 Pre-Budget Report that the combination of planned cuts in public expenditure and future increases in taxation will by 2015–2016 generate additional revenue equivalent to 2.6 per cent of GDP or about £38 billion in today's money. However, the IFS has noted that if this revenue is not generated, through a failure to deliver the necessary spending cuts or tax increases, then 'debt and debt interest would be put on an unsustainable upward path by the long-term impact of the credit crunch'.[8] Indeed, by the IFS's own less optimistic forecasts for the growth of tax revenues, the Treasury would be likely to have to borrow an additional 1.5 per cent of GDP in 2015–2016, unless the next government was prepared to implement a further £20 billion of tax increases and spending cuts by the end of the next Parliament. In the longer term, the Institute for Fiscal Studies (IFS) has estimated that public sector net debt is unlikely to fall below forty per cent of GDP, and thereby satisfy Brown's (suspended) Sustainable Investment fiscal rule, before 'the early 2030s'.[9]

Despite these imprudent levels of government debt and borrowing, by the end of February 2009 the full impact of the Brown Government's nationalisation and recapitalisation of the United Kingdom's major banks had only just begun to materialise. In this regard, Goldman Sachs estimated that the eventual direct cost to the taxpayer could be as much as eight per cent of national income, or around £120 billion at current prices.[10] Irrespective of the outcome of the next General Election, Brown's imprudent fiscal legacy has been to usher in an age of austerity for the public sector, which will necessitate some very difficult political choices. Many projects, programmes and services will have to be cut back or rescheduled. Some will have to be cut out completely. Given that the reform of the public services has proven intractable during the 'nice' decade, it is likely to prove more difficult during the forthcoming age of austerity.

BROWN'S LEGACY FOR SOCIETY: LIMITED PROGRESS IN REDUCING INEQUALITY

In becoming a more affluent society during Brown's tenure as Chancellor, the United Kingdom also saw increases in inequalities in the distribution of income and wealth. The IFS noted that 'Income growth since 2004–05 has tended to be faster the higher are incomes', with incomes among the richest fifth of the United Kingdom rising by 1.5 per cent but incomes among the poorest fifth falling by 0.4 per cent.[11] In that respect, the Brown Boom continued the trend experienced under the Thatcher and Major Governments. During the latter half of the 1980s, the wealthiest one per cent of the population owned between seventeen and eighteen per cent of United Kingdom wealth; during Brown's tenure as Chancellor, that proportion increased to between twenty and twenty-four per cent of total wealth.[12]

The very rich prospered the most under Gordon Brown. This conclusion was confirmed by a major study from the Joseph Rowntree Foundation which found that between 2003 and 2005 'areas with the highest average incomes experienced the greatest increases, in both absolute and relative terms, while some areas with the lowest average incomes experienced declining incomes, increasing polarisation'.[13] Between 1999 and 2003, wealth rose most in areas in a band between fifty and a hundred miles from London but fell most in the cities of northern England and across Scotland.[14] The Brown Boom accentuated both the income gap between the very rich and very poor and the inequalities in wealth between the North and the South East.

For the Brown Government to meet the stated objective of halving child poverty (from its 1998–1999 level) by 2010–2011, an annual average of more than 200,000 children would have to be lifted out of poverty each year. This follows annual falls of fewer than 100,000 since 2000.[15] The IFS has estimated that the lowest cost route to achieving the 2010 child poverty target would be to increase the per-child element of the Child Tax Credit by around thirty per cent, on top of the already planned increases, at a cost of about £4.2 billion. To cut the child poverty rate by a further half to five per cent by 2020 would cost an estimated £37 billion a year, and involve 5.5 per cent annual real terms' increases in the per-child element of the Child Tax Credit. However, as a further sign of the growing austerity to come, the Brown Government announced in February 2009 that a child poverty rate of ten per cent might now be consistent with meeting its 2020 target of eradicating child poverty, since it had concluded that total eradication would be impossible.[16] But, as one influential report suggested, this conclusion was 'a matter of opinion and political judgement'.[17]

In overall terms, Gordon Brown's legacy for poverty is one of limited progress. On the one hand, 'Compared to the period before 1997, trends have improved in more policy areas than they have worsened in, but what has happened has varied between areas and over time'.[18] Consequently, there has been a reduction in both child and pensioner poverty, improved educational attainment for the poorest areas and schools, and 'a narrowing of economic and other divides between deprived and other areas'.[19] On the other hand, health inequalities have continued to grow, as have the inequalities in income between the very rich and the very poor. Where the Blair and Brown Governments have initiated policy, some limited progress has been made, notably in education, employment and neighbourhoods, and through tax-benefit reform. However, the effects of policies have often been 'small in relation to the scale of the problems, and were sometimes offset by external changes'.[20] Had these policies not been implemented, it was estimated that overall poverty rates in the United Kingdom would have been between six and seven percentage points higher than the actual outcome. Thus, 'Rather than falling, the child poverty rate would have risen by 6–9 points and the pensioner poverty rate by 7 points'.[21] The problem for Brown and his Government is that the onset of recession might see all of the previous gains eliminated by rising unemployment and lower incomes.

BROWN'S LEGACY FOR THE LABOUR PARTY: THE BROWN BACKLASH

In July 1995, when Tony Blair commemorated the fiftieth anniversary of the Labour Party's historic 1945 General Election landslide, his speech had identified three key lessons and prerequisites for New Labour. These were the need for 'a clear sense of national purpose'; the need 'to win the battle of ideas'; and the need 'to mobilise all people of progressive mind around a party always outward-looking, seeking new supporters and members'. In short, the task confronting New Labour was 'nothing less than national renewal', which would necessitate 'economic renewal, social renewal and political renewal'.[22] The stark truth confronting Gordon Brown was that during the first eighteen months of his premiership, he had failed to deliver a clear sense of national purpose to either his own party's members and supporters or people of the United Kingdom. He had equally failed to win the battle of ideas. Indeed, David Cameron had been able to portray the whole New Labour project as signifying 'the triumph of our ideas'.[23] Brown appeared snookered. On the one hand, if he acknowledged that triumph in order to blame the Thatcher Government's deregulation and liberalisation of financial markets in general and the mortgage and personal credit markets in particular for the onset of a deep domestic recession, he would admit that New Labour had indeed signified the Labour Party's embracing of the political economy of Thatcherism. On the other hand, to continue with an agenda for economic, social and political renewal now heavily discredited by recession, popular indifference at best, and open hostility at worst, would risk electoral oblivion.

By the time that Gordon Brown succeeded Tony Blair as Labour Party leader and Prime Minister, almost four million voters who had supported New Labour in May 1997 had deserted the party. For his party to win a fourth term of office, it was vital that Brown convince a sceptical electorate that he would deliver genuine change, refresh a tired and drifting government, and sustain the prosperity to which people had become accustomed during his decade as Chancellor. During the 'Brown Bounce', successive opinion polls suggested that Brown was convincing the electorate, but he failed to call an early General Election to secure a fresh democratic mandate.

Confronted by the worst recession since the 1930s, there was increasing evidence of a backlash among the general public against Brown's handling of the credit crunch. There was also an increasing tendency for the public to hold Brown responsible for soaring levels of public and private debt. The trend in opinion polls appeared to have turned decisively against Brown and his faltering government. For example, on 30 January 2009, a YouGov poll for *The Daily Telegraph* gave the Conservative Party (forty-three per cent) an eleven per cent lead over the Labour Party (thirty-two per cent). More worrying for Brown was the fact that sixty-two per cent of respondents disapproved of his government's record to date (only twenty-two per cent approved), while sixty-three per cent were dissatisfied with him as Prime Minister, and only twenty-seven per cent were satisfied. By contrast, more people (thirty-five per cent) thought David Cameron would make the best Prime Minister than Brown (twenty-seven per cent). Forty-six per cent of the Conservative Party thought that Cameron was proving to be a good leader (against thirty-four per cent who thought he was not), and forty-six per cent also preferred to see the election of a Cameron-led Conservative Government after the next General Election, compared to thirty-eight per cent preferring a Brown-led Labour Government. Most damagingly of all, sixty-four per cent thought there was nothing the Brown Government could have done to avoid a downturn, while fifty-three per cent thought Brown had handled the current financial crisis fairly badly or very badly. Despite only twenty-one per cent of those questioned thinking that Brown and his government should bear the largest responsibility for the problems facing Britain's economy, seventy-nine per cent thought Brown should bear much or at least some of the responsibility for allowing lending and borrowing to get out of hand in the first place. More people (thirty-five per cent) now trusted the Conservatives to get Britain out of the present financial crisis than Labour.[24] When the Major Government had fallen behind the Blair-led Labour Party in opinion polls on the issue of economic competence prior to the 1997 General Election, it had been regarded as a vital factor in the election of a New Labour Government in May 1997.

During the Brown Boom, Gordon Brown had been an electoral asset for the Labour Party. With the onset of the Brown Bust, the Prime Minister was in danger of becoming an electoral liability. For example, an Ipsos MORI poll conducted in mid-February 2009 identified that sixty-four per cent of respondents were dissatisfied with the way he was doing his job, and only twenty-six per cent were satisfied.[25] In a similar vein, a Guardian/ICM poll conducted in the same period found that sixty-three per cent of voters thought the Labour Party would do better with another leader, with only twenty-eight per cent of voters identifying Brown as the leader most likely to attract support to Labour on polling day. Most damagingly of all for Brown, while forty-five per cent of Labour voters regarded Brown as the best leader, forty-nine per cent thought the Labour Party would be better off with a different leader.[26] Following the transition from boom to bust, the prospects of a fourth consecutive General Election victory for the Labour Party were diminishing rapidly.

BROWN'S LEGACY FOR THE CONSERVATIVE PARTY: THE RETURN OF THATCHERISM

One major consequence of the transition from the Brown Boom to the Brown Bust is that it has helped create a political and economic scenario where the Conservative Party once more is capable of winning a General Election on the basis of a quintessentially Thatcherite agenda. Indeed, the onset of the deepest domestic recession since the 1930s has inspired a major change in the strategy pursued by David Cameron and the Conservative Party. An initial ideological and policy convergence between the two political parties has been replaced by a growing divergence.

During the early months of Brown's premiership, the key political and ideological contest between Gordon Brown and David Cameron was over who would be the truest advocate of liberalism in twenty-first-century British politics. The degree of agreement was striking both in their political philosophy and in their respective agendas for domestic and foreign policy.

The danger of Brown's sympathetic liberalism was that it had stranded him on the political and philosophical territory occupied by the Conservative Party from the mid-1970s onwards. Brown had occupied Keith Joseph's 'common ground', a political agenda embracing the moral and material benefits of the market order and a politics based on a descending hierarchy of 'values, aspiration, understanding, policies'. For Joseph, the common ground was the territory occupied by those politicians seeking to serve the values and the aspirations of the British people for prosperity, low inflation, private profit and investment, 'housing choice, decent education, less dependency, less crime' and 'freedom within the law to run our own lives'.[27]

David Cameron described the political philosophy that underpinned his domestic and foreign policy agendas as liberal conservatism.[28] Cameron's belief was that 'we need a new liberal Conservative consensus on our country'.[29] This philosophy purported to believe in individual freedom and social responsibility, rather than state control. It was a vision whose aims and values were based on the need for 'a responsibility revolution', embracing personal responsibility, professional responsibility, civic responsibility and corporate responsibility.[30]

With the prospect of an early General Election fuelled by the 'Brown Bounce' in the opinion polls, it appeared that the forthcoming battle of ideas for the common ground in British politics would be between Gordon Brown's sympathetic liberalism and David Cameron's liberal conservatism. It would be fought across an ideological and political territory defined by Margaret Thatcher and Sir Keith Joseph in the late 1970s. The ultimate victor in the battle of ideas might prove to be Thatcherism itself.[31]

The key electoral fight for the common ground at the next General Election would be in England, in particular the marginal constituencies in London, the Home Counties and the Midlands that were instrumental in the General Election victories of the Blair-led Labour Party and the Margaret Thatcher-led Conservative Party. David Cameron's strategy to win Middle England was clear: he had attempted to put the Conservative Party in a position to be the natural inheritor of Tony Blair's legacy. In defining modern conservatism, Cameron asserted that the Conservative Party had long since been victorious in the battle of ideas. Indeed, its principal problem 'arose from the triumph of our ideas' and not knowing how to deal with that victory.[32] Cameron's analysis was simple: Margaret Thatcher had defeated both Old Labour and the British Disease of economic decline and trades union unrest by identifying 'a means of transforming both the British economy and British society' and transformed Britain into 'a more middle-class country with a functioning market economy', based on 'monetary and fiscal control matched by supply-side reform'. For Cameron, 'the Thatcher revolution' had changed the Labour Party and brought about Tony Blair's New Labour project of social justice and economic efficiency. Blair had delivered 'neither economic efficiency, nor social justice', because of his preoccupation with spin and the short-term and with 'the quest for a legacy becoming an all-consuming mission'.[33] For Cameron, social justice and economic efficiency had become 'the common ground of British politics'.[34]

The challenge for the Conservative Party had been to come to terms with its victory in the battle of ideas. Before Brown became Prime Minister, Cameron's strategy was to place the Conservative Party as the natural successor to Tony Blair's reforms, because of their alleged philosophical and policy debt to and inheritance from Thatcherism. On the critical issue of public services, Cameron argued that Blair was right to seek investment in and reform of those services; his failure and legacy was that 'his reforms were faltering, half-hearted and ultimately thwarted'.[35] In his speeches, Cameron sought to portray those failures as a result of Gordon Brown's shortcomings. Brown had imposed reform of the public services 'through centralised command and control, with targets and inspections' and the investment had delivered a poor return because of the waste of 'billions of pounds on the bureaucratic apparatus needed to operate a command and control system' and the 111 new quangos established since 1997. Moreover, as the pre-election Warwick Agreement between the Labour Party and the unions had demonstrated, 'the trades unions act as a powerful brake on reform'. Consequently, Cameron concluded, 'the task for a modern Conservative Party is to deliver the radical reform that Labour are temperamentally and politically incapable of'.[36]

Initially, the Conservative Party portrayed Gordon Brown as 'a "road block" to further reform' of the public services. It portrayed itself as the natural inheritor of Blair's legacy of choice and competition and as drivers of higher standards in delivery of services, given what had been depicted as a 'growing consensus between the current Prime Minister [Blair at the time the speech was made] and the Conservative Party', which Brown was deemed not to share.[37] In practice, there was evidence of a growing convergence in ideas between Gordon Brown and David Cameron. For example, Gordon Brown had described Robert Kennedy as 'my moral beacon' and written an effusive essay praising Kennedy's moral courage and vision in identifying a 'genuinely original vision of empowerment', embracing 'not just freedom from but freedom to'.[38] For his part, and in articulating his perspective on civil society and the need for 'a revolution in responsibility', David Cameron cited Robert Kennedy's critique of Gross National Product for failing to 'allow for the health of our children's education, the quality of their education or the joy of their play'.[39]

There was also growing evidence of convergence between Brown and Cameron in economic policy. For example, Brown's 2007 Budget confirmed that the Spending Review covering 2008–2009 until 2010–2011 would see a growth in current public spending at an average of 1.9 per cent a year in real terms. This would be a slower rate of increase than Brown's forecast rates of GDP growth of 2.75 to 3.25 per cent in 2007 and a trend of between 2.5 and 3 per cent in the following years.[40] In this, Brown had moved towards the second of the Cameron-led Conservative Party's three Sound Money Tests: 'Sharing the Proceeds'. This test was that 'Over time, and only when the country can afford it, we will move in the direction of lower taxes. We will do this by sharing the proceeds of economic growth between lower taxes and well-funded public services'.[41] Both Cameron and Brown had also committed themselves to rebuilding trust in politics and expressed their commitment to maintaining the British Union.[42]

In terms of foreign policy, both Gordon Brown and David Cameron had indicated that theirs would be based on what they determined to be the British national interest. Cameron, in a lecture given on 11 September 2006, stated his policy would be founded on the principles of a strategy arising from more than the simple exercise of military force, an understanding that democracy cannot be imposed from the outside, a commitment to a new multilateralism and a policy based on moral authority.[43] The greatest convergence had been in relation to the European Union. The pro-European realism of Gordon Brown's vision of a 'Global Europe' had been matched by Cameron's vision of the '3G Europe'.[44] Neither wants further European integration through closer political union and neither wants a revival of the European Constitution.

Cameron's initial strategy of convergence with Brown's British Way and British model of political economy had been based upon the pragmatic political calculation that the Conservative Party could not claim plausibly that the economy was broken as long as the Brown Boom continued.[45] As an alternative, Cameron chose to develop the thesis of Britain as 'the broken society', contending that where Margaret Thatcher had 'mended the broken economy in the 1980s, so we want to mend Britain's broken society in the early decades of the twenty-first century'.[46]

From September 2007, with the onset of the Northern Rock nationalisation and the series of massive financial bailouts and recapitalisations of other failing British banks, the Conservative Party began to change significantly, in the face of mounting evidence that the British model of political economy was indeed broken.[47] From September 2007 until November 2008, Cameron and his Shadow Chancellor, George Osborne, led the development of a burgeoning critique of the United Kingdom's faltering economic performance which sought to vest personal responsibility for the onset of recession with the imprudence of Gordon Brown. As an alternative, Cameron and Osborne began to stress the importance of fiscal conservatism and 'living within our means'.[48]

In the week before Alistair Darling was due to deliver the 2008 Pre-Budget Report, Conservative Party policy sought to exploit the Brown Bust by launching a strategy of policy divergence from Brown's British model of political economy. Cameron announced that the Conservative Party had abandoned its pledge to match the Brown Government's planned public spending totals from 2010 to 2011. Although it would continue to match Labour's spending on health, education, defence and international development, the Conservative Party pledged to cut spending elsewhere by limiting the overall total to a one per cent real terms increase, including £5 billion of cuts during 2009–2010 that would pay for tax cuts for savers and businesses. From the fiscal year 2010–2011, if elected, a future Conservative Government would increase public spending well below the Brown Government's 'unsustainably high' planned totals. This would avoid a 'borrowing bombshell' being dropped on the United Kingdom.[49]

David Cameron had exploited the transition from boom to bust to position the Conservative Party as the true party of prudence for 'Britain's economic future', capable of redressing Brown's 'Debt Crisis' and transforming Britain 'from a spend, spend, spend society into a save, save, save society'. The Conservative Party would establish a 'culture of thrift at the heart of government, and a culture of savings at the heart of the economy'.[50]

Cameron could now fight British politics on similar terms to the strategy pursued by Margaret Thatcher and Sir Keith Joseph in the late 1970s. Then, a faltering Labour Government was portrayed as having left Britain 'over-governed, over-spent, over-taxed, over-borrowed'.[51] Now, Cameron could portray Brown and the Brown Government in a similar light, for 'The longer Labour are in, the worse it gets. The worse it gets for the economy – with Labour's Debt Crisis and extra borrowing making the recession longer and deeper'. It was 'Labour's Debt Crisis', contributing to 'Labour's Broken Britain'.[52]

The political and ideological common denominator between the late 1970s and the forthcoming General Election campaign would be Thatcherism. Cameron contended, 'You can trace very clearly the line between the Thatcher Conservative Party that was about transforming our economy and recognising the limitations of government in regard to the economy and what I'm saying, which is that we need a similar scale of trans-formation in terms of our society'.[53] The end of the Brown Boom and the onset of the Brown Bust had provided the political and economic context for Cameron to campaign for the widening, rather than abandonment, of the application of the Thatcherite principles of entrepreneur-led growth and market-led initiative and innovation from the economy to society. Cameron was convinced that 'The centre right have still got some of the best arguments about how we change society, how we improve the economy, how we get people back to work, how we get better results from schools, and a modern generation of Conservatives can make those arguments free of the baggage of the past'.[54] With a consistent lead in the opinion polls during January and February 2009 of between ten and fifteen percentage points, the Conservative Party was well placed to win the next General Election.[55]

BROWN'S HISTORICAL LEGACY?

When future historians of British politics write their political biographies of Gordon Brown, they may be tempted to conclude that Brown's British Way of state-led modernisation, the fourth great British modernisation pro-gramme of post-1945 politics (following the First Way of Beveridge, Keynes and Old Labour; the Second Way of Thatcher, Joseph and the New Right; and the Third Way of Blair and New Labour), was politically, democratically, ideologically and electorally flawed. It was politically flawed because it relied upon a statecraft that (for the governance of England in particular) was overly centralised and too reliant on unaccountable technocrats. It was democratically flawed because it championed devolution to Scotland, Wales and Northern Ireland, but denied that same enhancement of democratic citizenship and accountability to the people of England. It celebrated Britain and Britishness at every opportunity, but at the expense of the repeated denial of England and Englishness. It was ideologically flawed because it mistakenly regarded and treated market actors as if they were institutions in the public domain, wrongly believing them to be capable of moral sentiments like responsibility, duty and fairness. It turned out that their pursuit of profit, opportunity and risk wasn't capable of being improved upon and harnessed for the public interest. Ultimately, Brown's British Way was electorally flawed because it alienated the very middle-class, middle-income professional people in middle England who once voted for Tony Blair and New Labour.

Endnotes

PREFACE

1. G. Brown, 'The special relationship is going global', *The Sunday Times*, 1 March 2009.
2. M. King, speech given to an East Midlands Development Agency/Bank of England dinner, Leicester, 14 October 2003; Sir J. Gieve, 'Seven lessons from the last three years', speech given at the London School of Economics, London, 19 February 2009.
3. Council of Mortgage Lenders, *Gross Lending Table: December 2008* (London: Council of Mortgage Lenders, 2009).
4. Society of Motor Manufacturers and Traders, *Vehicle Production Figures: Press Release 4629, 20 February 2009* (London: Society of Motor Manufacturers and Traders, 2009), p. 1.
5. H. M. Treasury, *Facing Global Challenges: Supporting People through Difficult Times. Pre-Budget Report*, Cm.7484 (London: The Stationery Office, 2008), p. 198; H. M. Treasury, *Budget 2007. Building Britain's Long-Term Future: Prosperity and fairness for families. Economic and fiscal strategy report and financial and budget report*, HC. 342 (London: The Stationery Office, 2007), p. 278.
6. Credit Action, *Debt Statistics February 2009* (London: Credit Action).
7. E. Balls, speech to Labour Party activists, Sheffield, 14 February 2009.
8. Ipsos MORI, *Political Monitor: Satisfaction Ratings, February 2009* (London: Ipsos MORI, 2009).
9. Ipsos MORI, *Political Monitor: State of the Economy – Economy Optimism Index, February 2009* (London: Ipsos MORI, 2009).
10. G. Brown, speech to a Labour Party special conference, Manchester, 24 June 2007.

11. Ibid.

12. G. Brown, Pre-Budget Report Statement, 25 November 2007.

13. G. Brown, Budget Statement, 21 March 2007.

14. G. Brown, speech at the Lord Mayor's Banquet, Mansion House, London, 21 June 2007.

15. G. Brown, transcript of an interview with Andrew Marr for the BBC Andrew Marr Show, 7 October 2007.

16. K. Joseph, *Stranded on the Middle Ground* (London: Centre for Policy Studies, 1976), p. 19.

INTRODUCTION

1. G. Brown, speech outside Number Ten Downing Street, 27 June 2007.

2. Ibid.

3. B. Obama, Inaugural Address, Washington DC, 20 January 2009.

4. Ibid.

5. H. M. Treasury, *Budget 2007. Building Britain's long-term future: Prosperity and fairness for families. Economic and Fiscal Strategy report and Financial Statement and Budget Report.* HC. 342 (London: The Stationery Office, 2007), p. 3.

6. H. M. Treasury, *Pre-Budget Report. Investing in Britain's Potential: Building our long-term future,* Cm. 6984 (London: The Stationery Office, 2006), p. 14.

7. Ibid.

8. YouGov, *YouGov/Daily Telegraph Survey, March 21–22 2007* (London: YouGov, 2007).

9. Electoral Calculus, *Recent Opinion Polls* (London: Electoral Calculus, 2007), available online at http://www.electoralcalculus.co.uk (accessed 26 March 2007).

10. YouGov, *Budget Polls for Daily Telegraph – Trends* (London: YouGov, 2007).

11. Ipsos MORI, *Ipsos MORI February Political Monitor: 13–15 February 2009* (London: Ipsos MORI, 2009).

12. J. Glover, 'Brown affecting Labour's chances as Guardian poll shows Lib Dem gain', *The Guardian,* 23 February 2009.

13. G. Brown, '"I'll leave when I finish my job": interview with Gloria De Piero', *New Statesman,* 10 July 2008.

14. G. Owen, 'I am like Titian, Gordon Brown tells baffled world leaders', *The Daily Telegraph,* 31 January 2009.

15. V. Cable, 'Questions to the Prime Minister', *Hansard,* 28 November 2007, c. 275.

16. A. Thomson and R. Sylvester, 'Clarke on Brown: he lacks courage and vision, he's delusional and a control freak', *The Daily Telegraph*, 10 September 2006.

17. N. Timmins, '"Stalinist" Brown, by ex-cabinet secretary', *Financial Times*, 20 March 2007.

18. Ibid.

19. A. Rawnsley, *Servants of the People: The Inside Story of New Labour* (London: Penguin, 2000), p. 150.

20. Press Association, 'Blair denies calling Brown "psychologically flawed"', *The Guardian*, 17 January 2007.

21. G. Brown, remarks at the launch of the *Road to the London Summit* document, Downing Street, London, 18 February 2009.

22. G. Brown, speech to the Scottish Labour Party, Dundee, 5 March 2009.

23. A. Darling cited in M. Riddell, 'Chancellor Alistair Darling speaks to Mary Riddell and admits economic mistakes', *The Daily Telegraph*, 3 March 2009; E. Balls, interview, *Channel Four News*, 3 March 2009, cited in Press Association, 'Alistair Darling: We must show humility over financial crisis', 3 March 2009.

24. P. Routledge, *Gordon Brown: The Biography* (London: Simon and Schuster, 1988); W. Keegan, *The Prudence of Mr Gordon Brown* (Chichester: John Wiley & Sons, 2003); and T. Bower, *Gordon Brown* (London: HarperCollins, 2004).

25. G. Brown, speech to the United States Congress, Washington DC, 4 March 2009.

CHAPTER 1

1. M. Thatcher, *Let Our Children Grow Tall: Selected speeches 1975–77* (London: Centre for Policy Studies, 1977), p. 51.

2. For Joseph, the middle ground was nothing more than 'a compromise between politicians, unrelated to the aspirations of the people,' 'a slippery slope to socialism and state control' and a guarantor of 'the left-wing ratchet.' Sir K. Joseph, *Stranded on the Middle Ground? Reflections on Circumstances and Policies* (London: Centre for Policy Studies, 1976), pp. 19, 21.

3. Ibid., pp. 21, 25.

4. Sir K. Joseph, *Hansard*, 21 May 1979, c. 706.

5. T. Blair, *Change and National Renewal* (London: The Labour Party, 1994).

6. T. Blair, *New Britain: My vision of a young country* (London: Fourth Estate, 1996), p. 56.

7. Ibid., p. 13.

8. Ibid., p. 20.

9. The Labour Party, *New Labour: Because Britain deserves better* (London: The Labour Party, 1997), pp. 3–4.

10. The Conservative Party, *The Conservative Party 1979 General Election Manifesto* (London: Conservative Central Office, 1979). The manifesto referred only to a commitment 'to sell back to private ownership the recently nationalised aerospace and shipbuilding concerns' and the aim 'to sell shares in the National Freight Corporation to the general public,' p. 15.

11. The term 'Thatcherism' was popularised first in a series of articles in *Marxism Today*. These articles are reproduced in S. Hall and M. Jacques (ed.), *The Politics of Thatcherism* (London: Lawrence and Wishart, 1983).

12. T. Blair, *The Third Way: New politics for the new century* (London: The Fabian Society, 1998); A. Giddens, *The Third Way: The renewal of social democracy* (Cambridge: Polity Press, 1988).

13. W. Clinton, *State of the Union*, The White House, Washington DC, 27 January 1998. The peripheral importance of the Third Way to Clinton's politics was demonstrated by the devotion of only one per cent of the 957 pages of his biography to this subject. See W. Clinton, *My Life* (London: Hutchinson, 2004), pp. 381–382, 813, 854, 878–879, 907–908 and 934.

14. These speeches can be viewed on the website of the Margaret Thatcher Foundation, www.margaretthatcher.org.

15. G. Brown, *Moving Britain Forward: Selected speeches 1997–2006* (edited by W. Stevenson) (London: Bloomsbury, 2006). A more comprehensive collection of Brown's speeches was published simultaneously in G. Brown, *Speeches, 1997–2006* (London: Bloomsbury, 2006).

16. G. Brown, 'Securing Our Future,' speech at the Royal United Services Institute, London, 13 February 2006.

17. G. Brown, 'We Will Always Strive to be on Your Side,' speech to the Labour Party Conference, Manchester, 25 September 2006.

18. G. Brown, 'Meeting the Terrorist Challenge,' speech given to Chatham House, London, 10 October 2006.

19. G. Brown, 'We Will Always Strive to be on Your Side,' speech to the Labour Party Conference, Manchester, 25 September 2006.

20. For an insider's perspective on Blair's commitment, see P. Ashdown, *The Ashdown Diaries: Volume two 1997–1999* (London: Penguin, 2002).

21. D. Marquand, *The Progressive Dilemma: From Lloyd George to Kinnock* (London: Heinemann, 1991).

22. T. Blair, *The Third Way: New politics for the new century* (London: The Fabian Society, 1998), p. 1. For a detailed analysis of the Third Way, see S. Lee, *Blair's Third Way* (London: Palgrave Macmillan, 2008).

23. Home Office, *The Report of the Independent Commission on the Voting System*, Cm. 4090-I (London: The Stationery Office, 1998).

24. The Labour Party, *New Labour Because Britain Deserves Better: The 1997 general election manifesto* (London: The Labour Party).

25. Among its principal recommendations, the Jenkins Commission advocated 'a two-vote mixed system, which can be described as either limited AMS or AV Top-up', be introduced throughout the United Kingdom, as 'the best alternative to First Past the Post.' Under the AMS (Additional Member System) or AV (Alternative Vote) Top-up system, 'voters cast two distinct votes – the first for a constituency MP and the second a party vote,' Home Office, *The Report of the Independent Commission on the Voting System*, Cm. 4090-I (London: The Stationery Office, 1998), Chapter 9, Glossary.

26. B. Crick, 'Still Missing: A public philosophy,' *Political Quarterly*, 68, 4, 1997, pp. 344–351; B. Pimlott, 'New Labour, New Era,' *Political Quarterly*, 68, 4, 1997, pp. 325–334; and C. Crouch, 'The Terms of the Neo-Liberal Consensus,' *Political Quarterly*, 68, 4, 1997, pp. 352–371.

27. B. Gould, 'The Long Retreat from Principle,' *New Statesman*, 29 January 1999.

28. D. Marquand, 'After Euphoria: The dilemma of New Labour,' *Political Quarterly*, 68, 4, 1997, pp. 335–343.

29. G. Brown, speech to the Labour Party Conference, Brighton, 27 September 2004.

30. W. H. Greenleaf, *The British Political Tradition. Volume Two: The ideological heritage* (London: Methuen, 1983), p. 359.

31. S. Webb, *The Basis & Policy of Socialism* (London: Fabian Socialist Series No.4, 1908), p. 71.

32. Recent examples of technocratic reports commissioned by Brown have included H. M. Treasury, *Prosperity for All in the Global Economy: World class skills* (The Leitch Review of Skills) (London: H. M. Treasury, 2006); H. M. Treasury, *Barker Review of Land Use Planning: Final Report – Recommendations* (London: H. M. Treasury, 2006); H. M. Treasury, *Stern Review: The Economics of Climate Change* (London: H. M. Treasury, 2006).

33. N. Dennis and A. H. Halsey, *English Ethical Socialism: Thomas More to R. H. Tawney* (Oxford: Clarendon Press, 1988), p. 1.

34. Ibid., pp. 4–5.

35. M. Carter, *T. H. Green and the Development of Ethical Socialism* (Exeter: Imprint Academic, 2003), p. 172.

36. N. Dennis and A. H. Halsey, *English Ethical Socialism: Thomas More to R. H. Tawney* (Oxford: Clarendon Press, 1988), p. 150.

37. G. Brown, 'Interview with Lynn Barber,' *The Daily Telegraph*, 10 July 1995, cited in P. Routledge, *Gordon Brown: The biography* (London: Pocket Books, 1998), p. 25.

38. Ibid., p. 25.
39. G. Brown, 'We Will Always Strive to be on Your Side,' speech to the Labour Party Conference, Manchester, 25 September 2006.
40. Ibid.
41. This thesis was most clearly developed in G. Brown, British Council Annual Lecture, 7 July 2004.
42. A prime example is provided by G. Brown, The Hugo Young Memorial Lecture, 13 December 2005.
43. G. Brown, 'We Will Always Strive to be on Your Side,' speech to the Labour Party Conference, Manchester, 25 September 2006.
44. G. Brown, 'Interview with Paul Routledge,' 20 April 1997, cited in P. Routledge, *Gordon Brown: The biography* (London: Pocket Books, 1998), p. 27.
45. *Student,* 9 November 1972, cited in P. Routledge, *Gordon Brown: The biography* (London: Pocket Books, 1998), p. 56.
46. J. Allison, *Guilty by Suspicion* (Glendaruel: Argyll Publishing, 1995), p. 119, cited in P. Routledge, *Gordon Brown: The biography* (London: Pocket Books, 1998), p. 96.
47. The first Red Paper, B. Cuddihy (ed.), *The Red Paper on Education* (Edinburgh: Edinburgh University Student Press, 1970), had been published in 1970 as a forum for the Left to express an alternative to C. B. Cox and A. E. Dyson (ed.), *The Black Papers on Education* (London: Davis-Poynter, 1971).
48. G. Brown, 'Introduction: The socialist challenge,' to G. Brown (ed.), *The Red Paper on Scotland* (Edinburgh: Edinburgh University Student Press, 1975), p. 7.
49. Ibid., pp. 7–8
50. Ibid., p. 8.
51. Ibid., p. 8.
52. Ibid., p. 8.
53. Ibid., p. 9.
54. Ibid., p. 10.
55. Ibid., p. 11.
56. Ibid., p. 13.
57. Ibid., p. 14.
58. Ibid., p. 17.
59. Ibid., p. 18.
60. Despite his scepticism about the benefits of devolution, Brown was later chosen to chair the Scottish Labour Party's Devolution Committee, at the tender age of twenty-seven. However, other prominent figures within the Scottish Labour Party retained Brown's scepticism. For example, devolution was

dismissed by Robin Cook, a fellow graduate of Edinburgh University, as 'irrelevant to the real problems we face. Given the present economic situation, to go ahead with devolution seems to be like fiddling while Rome Burns.' R. Cook, cited in P. Routledge, *Gordon Brown: The biography* (London: Pocket Books, 1998), p. 81.

61. Ibid., p. 19.
62. G. Brown, *The Labour Party and Political Change in Scotland, 1918–1929* (Edinburgh University: Edinburgh University PhD thesis, 1981).
63. F. W. Jowett, *Socialism in Our Time* (London: Independent Labour Party, 1926), p. 4.
64. J. Maxton, *New Leader*, 9 January 1928, cited in G. Brown, *Maxton* (Edinburgh: Mainstream Publishing, 1986), p. 182.
65. G. Brown, *Maxton* (Edinburgh: Mainstream Publishing, 1986), p. 294.
66. G. Brown, 'Social Security,' *Hansard*, 27 July 1983, cc. 1239–1244.
67. Ibid., c. 1240.
68. Ibid., c. 1243.
69. Ibid., c. 1244.
70. G. Brown, 'Introduction' to G. Brown and R. Cook (ed.), *Scotland: The Real Divide. Poverty and Deprivation in Scotland* (Edinburgh: Mainstream, 1983), p. 9.
71. Ibid., pp. 16, 19.
72. Ibid., pp. 21–22.
73. The Labour Party, *Report of the Annual Conference of the Labour Party 1985* (London: The Labour Party, 1986), p. 114.
74. N. Kinnock, *Making Our Way: Investing in Britain's future* (Oxford: Basil Blackwell, 1986), p. vi.
75. Labour Party, *Social Justice & Economic Efficiency: First report of Labour's policy review for the 1990s* (London: The Labour Party, 1988), pp. 3, 4.
76. Labour Party, *Meet the Challenge, Make the Change: A new agenda for Britain* (London: The Labour Party, 1989), p. 6.
77. Labour Party, *Looking to the Future* (London: The Labour Party, 1990), pp. 5, 7.
78. Labour Party, *Opportunity Britain: Labour's better way for the 1990s* (London: The Labour Party, 1991), pp. ii, 5.
79. Labour Party, *It's Time to Get Britain Working Again: Labour's election manifesto* (London: The Labour Party, 1992), pp. 12–13.
80. For a concise analysis of the British tradition of state-led industrial modernisation programmes, see S. Lee, 'Manufacturing,' in D. Coates (ed.), *Industrial Policy in Britain* (London: Macmillan, 1996).
81. G. Brown, *Where There is Greed: Margaret Thatcher and the betrayal of Britain* (Edinburgh: Mainstream Publishing, 1989), pp. 3, 6.
82. Ibid., p. 10.

83. Ibid., p. 23.

84. Ibid., p. 61.

85. The developmental state has been defined by academics as one 'whose politics have concentrated sufficient power, autonomy and capacity at the centre to shape, pursue and encourage the achievements of explicit developmental objectives, whether by establishing and promoting the conditions and direction of economic growth or by organising it directly or a varying combination of both,' A. Leftwich, 'Bringing Politics Back in: Towards a model of the developmental state,' *Journal of Development Studies*, 31, 3, 1995, pp. 400–427. For an explanation of the concept of the developmental state, see S. Lee 'Developmental State,' in R. Barry Jones (ed.), *The Routledge Encyclopaedia of International Political Economy*, Volume 1 (London: Routledge, 2001), pp. 343–346.

86. F. List, *The National System of Political Economy* (London: Longmans, Green and Company, 1928). List's agenda for industrialising economies is summarised in M. Shafaeddin, *What Did Frederick List Actually Say? Some Clarifications on the Infant Industry Argument* (Geneva: United Nations Conference on Trade and Development, Discussion Paper No.149, 2000).

87. F. List, *The National System of Political Economy* (London: Longmans, Green and Company, 1928), pp. 116, 150.

88. Labour Party, *Made in Britain* (London: The Labour Party, 1992).

89. P. Anderson, 'Stable Climate for Business Planned,' *Tribune*, 10 January 1992.

90. C. Hughes and P. Wintour, *Labour Rebuilt: The New Model Party* (London: Fourth Estate, 1990), p. 135.

91. T. Blair, *Change and National Renewal* (London: The Labour Party, 1994).

92. P. Anderson, 'The Tribune Interview: Gordon Brown,' *Tribune*, 1 January 1993.

93. Ibid.

94. Ibid.

95. Ibid.

96. N. Kinnock, 'Introduction' to Labour Party, *Opportunity Britain: Labour's better way for the 1990s* (London: The Labour Party, 1991), p. iii.

97. G. Brown, *Fair Is Efficient: A socialist agenda for fairness* (London: The Fabian Society, 1994), p. 1.

98. Ibid., p. 2.

99. Ibid., p. 3.

100. Ibid., p. 3.

101. Ibid., p. 3.

102. R. H. Tawney, *Equality* (London: Unwin Books, 1931), p. 268, cited in G. Brown, *Fair Is Efficient: A socialist agenda for fairness* (London: The Fabian Society, 1994), p. 3.

103. A. Bevan, *In Place of Fear* (London: William Heinemann, 1952), p. 170, cited

in G. Brown, *Fair Is Efficient: A socialist agenda for fairness* (London: The Fabian Society, 1994), p. 3.

104. G. Brown, *Fair Is Efficient: A socialist agenda for fairness* (London: The Fabian Society, 1994), p. 3.

105. D. Miliband, 'Introduction' to D. Miliband (ed.), *Reinventing the Left* (Cambridge: Polity Press, 1994), pp. 5–8.

106. G. Brown, 'The Politics of Potential: A new agenda for Labour,' in D. Miliband (ed.), *Reinventing the Left* (Cambridge: Polity, 1994), p. 114.

107. Ibid., p. 115.

108. Ibid., p. 115.

109. Ibid., p. 119.

110. Ibid., p. 119.

111. A. Phillips, 'Comment: Whose community? Which individuals?' in D. Miliband (ed.), *Reinventing the Left* (Cambridge: Polity, Press), p. 124.

112. J. Smith, 'Reclaiming the Ground,' The R. H. Tawney Memorial Lecture, 20 March 1993, cited in G. Brown, 'John Smith's Socialism: His writings and speeches,' in G. Brown and J. Naughtie (ed.), *John Smith: Life and soul of the party* (Edinburgh: Mainstream Publishing, 1994), p. 67.

113. G. Brown and T. Wright, 'Introduction' to G. Brown and T. Wright (ed.), *Values, Visions and Voices: An anthology of socialism* (Edinburgh: Mainstream, 1995), p. 14.

114. Ibid., p. 16.

115. Ibid., pp. 16–17.

116. Ibid., p. 17.

117. Ibid., pp. 18–19.

118. Ibid., p. 19.

119. G. Brown and T. Wright, 'Introduction' to G. Brown and T. Wright (ed.), *Values, Visions and Voices: An anthology of socialism* (Edinburgh: Mainstream, 1995), pp. 25–26.

120. T. Blair, speech to business leaders, Singapore, 7 January 1996.

121. W. Hutton, 'Fool's Gold in a Fool's Paradise,' *The Observer*, 2 June 1996.

122. Ibid.

123. Labour Party, *New Labour, New Life for Britain* (London: The Labour Party, 1996).

124. For a detailed analysis of the evolution of Labour Party policy on economy and society during this period, see S. Lee, 'Finance for Industry,' in J. Michie and J. Grieve Smith (ed.), *Creating Industrial Capacity: Towards full employment* (Oxford: Oxford University Press, 1996); and S. Lee, 'Competitiveness and the Welfare State in Britain,' in M. Mullard and S. Lee (ed.), *Social Policy in Europe* (Cheltenham: Edward Elgar 1997).

125. T. Blair, speech at a Fabian Society Commemoration of the Fiftieth Anniversary of the 1945 General Election, 5 July 1995, in T. Blair, *New Britain: My vision of a young country* (London: Fourth Estate, 1996), p. 13.

126. Ibid., p. 20.

127. Ibid., p. 16.

128. T. Blair, 'Why I am a Christian,' *The Sunday Telegraph*, 7 April 1996, in T. Blair, *New Britain: My vision of a young country* (London: Fourth Estate, 1996), pp. 59–60.

129. T. Blair, 'The Young Country,' speech to the Labour Party Conference, Brighton, 3 October 1995, in T. Blair, *New Britain: My vision of a young country* (London: Fourth Estate, 1996), p. 62.

130. T. Happold and K. Maguire, 'Revealed: Brown and Blair's pact,' *The Guardian*, 6 June 2003.

131. M. Kettle, 'The Granita Guarantee Decoded,' *The Guardian*, 6 June 2003.

132. Labour Party, *A New Economic Future for Britain: Economic and employment opportunities for all* (London: The Labour Party, 1995), p. 4.

133. Labour Party, *New Labour: Because Britain deserves better* (London: The Labour Party, 1997), pp. 3–4.

134. Labour Party, *A New Economic Future for Britain: Economic and employment opportunities for all* (London: The Labour Party, 1995), p. 28.

135. Department of Trade and Industry, *DTI – Department for Enterprise* (London: Her Majesty's Stationery Office, 1988), p. ii.

CHAPTER 2

1. G. Brown, The 1997 Allied Dunbar/Spectator Lecture, reprinted as G. Brown, 'Outward Bound,' *The Spectator*, 8 November 1997, pp. 15–16.

2. G. Brown, 'Modernising the British Economy: The new mission for the Treasury,' 30th Anniversary Lecture to the Institute of Fiscal Studies, London, 27 May 1999.

3. G. Brown, speech at the Smith Institute, London, 15 April 1999.

4. Ibid.

5. G. Brown, 'Civic Society in Modern Britain,' The 17th Arnold Goodman Lecture, Merchant Taylor's Hall, London, 20 July 2000.

6. A. Seldon and S. Ball (ed.), *The Conservative Century* (London, Macmillan, 1994).

7. I. McLean and G. Lodge, *The Progressive Consensus in Perspective* (London: Institute for Public Policy Research, 2007), p. 3.

8. J. M. Keynes, *The Economic Consequences of the Peace* (London: Macmillan,

1920); J. M. Keynes, *The End of* Laissez-Faire (London: L and V. Woolf at the Hogarth Press, 1926); J. M. Keynes, *The General Theory of Employment, Interest and Money* (London: Macmillan and Co., 1936); J. M. Keynes, *How to Pay for the War: A radical plan for the Chancellor of the Exchequer* (London: Macmillan, 1940). For an analysis of Keynes' liberalism on the development of economic policy in the interwar period, see A. Booth, *British Economic Policy 1931–49: Was there a Keynesian revolution?* (London: Harvester Wheatsheaf, 1989).

9. The ideas and policies for full employment were identified by the wartime Minister of Reconstruction in the White Paper, *Employment Policy*, Cmnd. 6527 (London: His Majesty's Stationery Office, 1944).

10. Lord W. Beveridge, *Social Insurance and Allied Services* (London: Her Majesty's Stationery Office, 1942); Lord W. Beveridge, *Full Employment in a Free Society* (London: George Allen & Unwin, 1944).

11. In her speeches, Thatcher paid tribute frequently to the work of Adam Smith and Friedrich Hayek. For example, in a single speech Thatcher once paid tribute to the importance of moral philosophy for both the American Declaration of Independence and contemporary political economy and the contribution played by Hayek in demonstrating that Keynes would have opposed the inflationary post-war policies of Keynesians (M. Thatcher, Walter Heller International Finance Lecture, Roosevelt University, Chicago, 22 September 1975, reproduced in The Thatcher Archive, CCOPR 789/75, available online from the Thatcher Foundation at www.margaretthatcher.org/speeches/displaydocument.asp?docid=102465 (accessed 30 March 2007).

12. For an analysis of Sir Keith Joseph's political philosophy, including his debt to liberalism, see K. Bosanquet, 'Sir Keith's Reading List,' *Political Quarterly*, 52, 3, 1981, pp. 324–341.

13. N. Lawson, 'The New Conservatism,' Lecture to the Bow Group, 4 August 1980, reproduced as Annexe I of N. Lawson, *The View from No.11: Memoirs of a Tory radical* (London: Bantam Press, 1992), p. 1041.

14. T. Blair, speech to the Annual Conference of the Confederation of British Industry, 13 November 1995, in T. Blair, *New Britain: My vision of a young country* (London: Fourth Estate, 1996), p. 110.

15. G. Brown, CAFOD Pope Paul VI Memorial Lecture, London, 8 December 2004.

16. Ibid.

17. See for example, G. Brown, 'Foreword' to I. McLean, *Adam Smith, Radical and Egalitarian: An interpretation for the twenty-first century* (Edinburgh: Edinburgh University Press, 2006), pp. viii–ix.

18. G. Brown, CAFOD Pope Paul VI Memorial Lecture, London, 8 December 2004.

19. A. Smith, *The Theory of Moral Sentiments* (London: A Millar, 1759; Indianapolis: LibertyClassics edition, 1982), p. 1.

20. 'This can only happen if we build from solid foundations of prudent economic management,' G. Brown, 'Statement from the Chancellor of the Exchequer: Central economic objectives of the new Government,' *H. M. Treasury Press Release*, 6 May 1997 (London: H. M. Treasury, 1997).

21. A. Smith, *The Theory of Moral Sentiments* (London: A Millar, 1759; Indianapolis: LibertyClassics edition, 1982), p. 216.

22. Ibid., p. 215.

23. Ibid., p. 217.

24. I. McLean, *Adam Smith, Radical and Egalitarian: An interpretation for the twenty-first century* (Edinburgh: Edinburgh University Press, 2007), p. xix

25. Ibid., pp. 142–143.

26. Ibid., p. 145.

27. Ibid., p. 120.

28. Ibid., p. 138.

29. A. Smith, *An Inquiry into the Nature and Causes of the Wealth of Nations, Book II* (Glasgow, 1759), V.ii.b., cited in I. McLean, *Radical and Egalitarian: An interpretation for the twenty-first century* (Edinburgh: Edinburgh University Press, 2006), p. 76.

30. A. Smith, *The Theory of Moral Sentiments* (London: A Millar, 1759; Indianapolis: LibertyClassics edition, 1982), p. 55.

31. G. Brown, 'Introduction' to the 'Can Both the Left and Right Claim Adam Smith?' Enlightenment Lecture, Playfair Library Hall, Old College, Edinburgh University, 25 April 2002.

32. G. Brown, First Donald Dewar Memorial Lecture, Glasgow University, 12 October 2006.

33. Ibid.

34. J. Sacks, *The Politics of Hope* (London: Vintage, 2000), pp. 1–4, 112–120.

35. A. Smith, *The Wealth of Nations: Books I – III* (Harmondsworth: Penguin, 1983), p. 512, partially cited in G. Brown, First Donald Dewar Memorial Lecture, Glasgow University, 12 October 2006.

36. G. Brown, First Donald Dewar Memorial Lecture, Glasgow University, 12 October 2006.

37. A. Greenspan, The Adam Smith Memorial Lecture, Kirkcaldy, 6 February 2005.

38. M. King, 'Trusting in Money: From Kirkcaldy to the MPC,' The Adam Smith Memorial Lecture, Kirkcaldy, 29 October 2006.

39. J. Sacks, *The Politics of Hope* (London: Vintage, 2000); J. Sacks, *The Dignity of Difference: How to avoid the clash of civilisations* (London: Continuum, 2006).

40. J. Sacks, *The Politics of Hope* (London: Vintage, 2000), p. 2.

41. Ibid., pp. 3–4, 47.

42. Ibid., p. 64.

43. J. Sacks, *The Dignity of Difference: How to avoid the clash of civilisations* (London: Continuum, 2006), p. 3.

44. Sacks has argued that a covenant occurs 'when two individuals or groups, differing perhaps in power but each acknowledging the integrity and sovereignty of the other, pledge themselves in mutual loyalty to achieve together what neither can achieve alone.' Ibid., p. 202.

45. Ibid., pp. 14, 35.

46. Ibid., p. 17.

47. Ibid., p. 78.

48. Ibid., p. 87.

49. Ibid., pp. 88–89.

50. Ibid., p. 98.

51. Advocates of comparative advantage, such as Adam Smith and David Ricardo, argued that 'by specialising in producing and trading those goods for which they have greater cost advantage, nations and their populations maximise their access to wealth and welfare.' R. Korzeniewicz, 'Comparative Advantage and Unequal Exchange,' in P. O'Hara (ed.), *Encyclopedia of Political Economy, Volume I* (London: Routledge, 1999), p. 127.

52. Sacks, *The Dignity of Difference*, p. 101.

53. Ibid., p. 103.

54. Ibid., p. 202.

55. Ibid., p. 205.

56. G. Brown, CAFOD Pope Paul VI Memorial Lecture, 8 December 2004.

57. G. Brown, The Hugo Young Memorial Lecture, Chatham House, London, 13 December 2005.

58. Ibid.

59. G. Brown, speech to the National Council of Voluntary Organisations' Annual Conference, London, 9 February 2000.

60. Ibid.

61. G. Brown, 'Civic Society in Modern Britain,' 17th Arnold Goodman Lecture, Merchant Taylor's Hall, London, 20 July 2000.

62. G. Brown, speech to the National Council of Voluntary Organisations' Annual Conference, London, 9 February 2000.

63. G. Brown, 'Civic Society in Modern Britain,' 17th Arnold Goodman Lecture, Merchant Taylor's Hall, London, 20 July 2000.

64. Ibid.

65. Ibid.

66. G. Brown, speech to the Volunteering Conference, London, 31 January 2005.

67. M. Sandel, 'What Money Can't Buy: The moral limits of markets.' The Tanner Lectures on Human Values, delivered at Brasenose College, Oxford, 11 and 12 May 1998, cited in G. Brown, 'A Modern Agenda for Prosperity and Social Reform,' speech to the Social Market Foundation, Cass Business School, London, 3 February 2003.

68. M. Sandel, 'What Money Can't Buy: The moral limits of markets.' The Tanner Lectures on Human Values, delivered at Brasenose College, Oxford, 11 and 12 May 1998.

69. Ibid.

70. G. Brown, speech at the Smith Institute, London, 15 April 1999.

71. M. Walzer, *Spheres of Justice: A defense of pluralism and equality* (New York: Basic Books, 1983), p. 100, cited in G. Brown, 'State and Market: Towards a public interest test,' *Political Quarterly*, 73, 2003, pp. 268–284, cf p. 269.

72. A. Okun, *Equality and Efficiency: The big tradeoff* (Washington DC: The Brookings Institution, 1975), p. 119, cited in G. Brown, 'State and Market: Towards a public interest test,' *Political Quarterly*, 73, 2003, pp. 268–284, cf p. 269.

73. J. Pechman (ed.), *Economics for Policymaking: Selected essays of Arthur M. Okun* (Cambridge, Massachusetts: The MIT Press, 1983), pp. 634–635.

74. G. Brown, Keynote speech at the 2004 National Council for Voluntary Organisations' Annual Conference, London, 18 February 2004.

75. G. Brown, speech to the Volunteering Conference, London, 31 January 2005.

76. Ibid.

77. D. Brooks, 'Questions of Culture,' *New York Times*, 19 February 2006, cited in G. Brown, First Donald Dewar Memorial Lecture, Glasgow University, 12 October 2006.

78. M. Yoe, 'Everybody's a critic,' *The University of Chicago Magazine*, February 2004.

79. J. Q. Wilson, *The Moral Sense* (New York: The Free Press, 1993), p. xiv.

80. Ibid., p. xiii.

81. G. Brown, 'Politics as a moral duty,' speech to the Labour Party Annual Conference, Brighton, 26 September 2005.

82. J. Q. Wilson, *The Moral Sense* (New York: The Free Press, 1993), p. xiii.

83. N. Temko, 'Brown: my mother's pain shaped my life,' *The Observer*, 8 October 2006.

84. J. Q. Wilson, *The Moral Sense* (New York: The Free Press, 1993), p. 251, cited in G. Brown, CAFOD Pope Paul VI Memorial Lecture, 8 December 2004.

85. J. Q. Wilson, *The Moral Sense* (New York: The Free Press, 1993), p. 244.

86. The White House, 'President Honours 2003 Presidential Medal of Freedom Recipients,' *White House Press Release*, 23 July 2003.

87. J. Q. Wilson, *The Moral Sense* (New York: The Free Press, 1993), p. vii.

88. Elsewhere, Wilson has defined moral sense as 'a directly felt impression of some standards by which we ought to judge voluntary action. The standards are usually general and imprecise.' J. Q. Wilson, *On Character* (Washington DC: The AEI Press, 1995), p. 192.

89. J. Q. Wilson, *The Moral Sense* (New York: The Free Press, 1993) pp. xi–xii.

90. Ibid., p. 250.

91. Ibid., p. 231.

92. Ibid., p. 234.

93. J. Q. Wilson, *On Character* (Washington DC: The AEI Press, 1995), pp. 198, 202.

94. Ibid., p. 205.

95. Wilson, *The Moral Sense* p. 240

96. J. Campbell, *The Power of Myth* (New York: Broadway Books, 1988), p. 123. This quotation was cited by Gordon Brown in his CAFOD Pope Paul VI Memorial Lecture, London, 8 December 2004, and in his speech at the Muslim News Awards for Excellence, 23 March 2005.

97. J. Campbell, *The Power of Myth* (New York: Broadway Books, 1988), p. 5.

98. Ibid., p. 13.

99. Ibid., pp. 9, 24.

100. Ibid., p. 28.

101. Ibid., p. 31.

102. G. Brown, *Courage: Eight portraits* (London: Bloomsbury, 2007), p. 1.

103. G. Himmelfarb, *The Roads to Modernity: The British, French and American Enlightenments* (New York: Alfred A. Knopf, 2004).

104. See for example, G. Himmerlfarb, *The De-Moralisation of Society: from Victorian virtues to modern values* (London: Institute for Economic Affairs Health and Welfare Unit, 1995).

105. See for example, I. Kristol, *Neoconservatism: The autobiography of an idea* (New York: The Free Press, 1995). Kristol has impeccable right-wing credentials, being a longstanding Senior Fellow at the free market American Enterprise Institute and the founder of the journals *The Public Interest* and *The National Interest*. In recent years the latter journal has seen an embittered debate between the neo-conservatives Francis Fukuyama and Charles Krauthammer about the efficacy of the Bush Administration's 'War on Terror.' In July 2002, Kristol was awarded the Presidential Medal of Freedom by George W. Bush.

106. G. Himmelfarb, *The Roads to Modernity: The British, French and American Enlightenments* (New York: Alfred A. Knopf, 2004), p. 5.

107. Ibid., p. 150.

108. Ibid., pp. 19–20.
109. Ibid., p. 13.
110. Himmelfarb later describes Adam Smith as 'one of England's most eminent philosophers,' Ibid., p. 69.
111. Ibid., pp. 66–67.
112. Ibid., p. 233.
113. Ibid., p. 231.

CHAPTER 3

1. G. Brown, speech to the Labour Party Conference, Manchester, 23 September 2008.
2. Indeed, Cowley has noted that 'in December 1993 the Gallup 9000 poll – an aggregate of all the polls Gallup conducted that month – showed that just under nineteen per cent of the public thought the Conservatives could better handle the economy compared with fifty-one per cent who chose Labour, a gap of thirty-two percentage points. Throughout 1994 and 1995 the gap averaged at least twenty-five percentage points,' P. Cowley, 'The Conservative Party: Decline and fall,' in A. Geddes and J. Tonge (ed.), *Labour's Landslide* (Manchester: Manchester University Press, 1997), p. 40.
3. E. Balls, 'Delivering Economic Stability,' Oxford Business Alumni Annual Lecture, Merchant Taylors' Hall, London, 12 June 2001.
4. International Monetary Fund, 'IMF Executive Board Concludes 2005 Article IV Consultation with the United Kingdom,' *Public Information Notice No.06/24*, 3 March 2006 (Washington, DC: International Monetary Fund). Available online: http://www.imf.org/external/np/sec/pn/2006/pn0624.htm (accessed 1 March 2007), p. 1; International Monetary Fund, *United Kingdom: 2006 article IV consultation – staff report, March 2007* (Washington DC: International Monetary Fund, 2007), p. 3.
5. H. M. Treasury, *Pre-Budget Report. Investing in Britain's Potential: Building our long-term future*, Cm. 6984 (London: H. M. Treasury, 2006), p. 14.
6. G. Brown, Budget Statement, 17 March 2004; G. Brown, Budget Statement, 16 March 2005.
7. G. Brown, 'Modernising the British Economy: The new mission for the Treasury,' *Treasury Press Release 86/99*, 27 May 1999.
8. International Monetary Fund, *United Kingdom: 2006 article IV consultation – staff report, March 2007* (Washington DC: International Monetary Fund, 2007), p. 22.
9. For the thesis of the Treasury's 'contempt for production,' see S. Pollard, *The*

Wasting of the British Economy: British economic policy 1945 to the present (London: Croom Helm, 1982), p. 73. For the thesis of the 'core institutional nexus,' composed of the Bank of England, City of London and Treasury, see G. Ingham, *Capitalism Divided? The City and Industry in British Social Development* (London: Macmillan, 1984). For the thesis of the frustration of successive state-led modernisation programmes, see S. Newton and D. Porter, *Modernisation Frustrated: The politics of industrial decline in Britain since 1900* (London: Unwin Hyman, 1988).

10. G. Brown, 'Modernising the British Economy: The new mission for the Treasury,' *Treasury Press Release 86/99*, 27 May 1999.

11. G. Brown, *In My Way* (Harmondsworth: Penguin, 1971), pp. 104–105.

12. C. Johnson, *MITI and the Japanese Miracle: The growth of industrial policy, 1925–1975* (Stanford University Press, 1982), p. 323.

13. E. Balls, J. Grice and G. O'Donnell (ed.), *Microeconomic Reform in Britain: Delivering opportunities for all* (London: Palgrave Macmillan, 2004), pp. 6, 8.

14. It is this continuity of ideology and policy that has led one influential commentator on British politics to see the transition from Thatcher to Major, Major to Blair, and from Blair to Brown, as a political and economic revolution in three acts, S. Jenkins, *Thatcher & Sons: A revolution in three acts* (London: Allen Lane, 2006).

15. W. Keegan, *The Prudence of Mr Gordon Brown* (Chichester: John Wiley, 2003), p. 130.

16. E. Balls, *Euro-Monetarism: Why Britain was ensnared and how it should escape* (London: Fabian Society, 1992), p. 3.

17. Ibid., pp. 10–11, 14.

18. Ibid., p. 15.

19. Ibid., pp. 18, 23.

20. Ibid., p. 16.

21. Ibid., pp. 17–18.

22. E. Balls, 'Delivering Economic Stability,' Inaugural Oxford Business Alumni Lecture, Merchant Taylors' Hall, London, 12 June 2001.

23. E. Balls, 'Stability, Growth and UK Fiscal Policy,' Inaugural Ken Dixon Lecture, Department of Economics, University of York, 23 January 2004. Monetarism is the belief among certain economists that the money supply is the most important factor affecting economic performance in general and the rate of inflation in particular. The belief that economic stability and low inflation could be best achieved by governmental control of the money supply was popularised by the American economist Milton Friedman during the late 1960s and given effect by the policies of the Thatcher Governments and

Reagan Administration during the 1980s. The Brown/Balls model was 'post-monetarist' because it had moved on from this economic policy agenda.

24. M. Friedman, 'The Role of Monetary Policy,' *The American Economic Review*, 58, 1, 1968, pp. 1–17. Friedman's work was cited in G. Brown, 'The Conditions For Full Employment: The Mais Lecture,' City University, London, 19 October 1999 and E. Balls, 'Open Macroeconomics in an Open Economy,' *Scottish Journal of Political Economy*, 45, 2, 1998, pp. 113–132, cf. 118.

25. E. Balls, 'Stability, Growth and UK Fiscal Policy,' Inaugural Ken Dixon Lecture, Department of Economics, University of York, 23 January 2004.

26. Ibid.

27. G. Brown, 'Statement from the Chancellor on the Central Economic Objectives of the New Government,' *H. M. Treasury Press Release*, 6 May 1997 (London: H. M. Treasury, 1997).

28. Minister of Reconstruction, *Employment Policy*, Cmnd. 6527 (London: His Majesty's Stationery Office, 1944), p. 3.

29. In economic policy-making, monetary policy refers to the policies adopted by monetary authorities, in this case the Treasury and the Bank of England, in pursuit of stable prices, low inflation and confidence in the currency. Fiscal policy refers to government policy towards government income (i.e. through taxation and revenue collection) and expenditure.

30. G. Brown, 'Statement from the Chancellor on the Central Economic Objectives of the New Government,' *H. M. Treasury Press Release*, 6 May 1997 (London: H. M. Treasury, 1997).

31. G. Brown, speech to the Royal Institute for International Affairs, Chatham House, London, 17 July 1997.

32. E. Balls, J. Grice and G. O'Donnell (ed.), *Microeconomic Reform in Britain: Delivering opportunities for all* (London: Palgrave Macmillan, 2004), p. 381.

33. E. Balls, 'Stability, Growth and UK Fiscal Policy,' Inaugural Ken Dixon Lecture, Department of Economics, University of York, 23 January 2004.

34. E. Balls, 'Open Macroeconomics in an Open Economy,' *Scottish Journal of Political Economy*, 45, 2, 1998, p. 121.

35. E. Balls, J. Grice and G. O'Donnell (ed.), *Microeconomic Reform in Britain: Delivering opportunities for all* (London: Palgrave Macmillan, 2004), p. 381.

36. E. Balls, 'Open Macroeconomics in an Open Economy,' *Scottish Journal of Political Economy*, 45, 2, 1998, pp. 113–132, cf. p. 120.

37. M. King, 'Credibility and Monetary Policy: Theory and evidence,' *Scottish Journal of Political Economy*, 42, 1, 1995, pp. 1–19, cf.17–18.

38. E. Balls, 'Open Macroeconomics in an Open Economy,' *Scottish Journal of Political Economy*, 45, 2, 1998, p. 122.

39. G. Brown, 'Foreword' to E. Balls, J. Grice and G. O'Donnell (ed.), *Microeconomic Reform in Britain: Delivering opportunities for all* (London: Palgrave Macmillan, 2004), p. xiii.

40. E. Balls and G. O'Donnell (ed.), *Reforming Britain's Economic and Financial Policy: Towards greater economic stability* (Houndmills: Palgrave Macmillan, 2002), pp. 5–8.

41. Ibid., pp. 17–18.

42. Labour Party, *New Labour: Because Britain deserves better* (London: The Labour Party, 1997), p. 13.

43. H. M. Treasury, 'Remit for the Monetary Policy Committee,' *H. M. Treasury Press Release 64/97*, 12 June 1997

44. E. Balls, 'Stability, Growth and UK Fiscal Policy,' Inaugural Ken Dixon Lecture, Department of Economics, University of York, 23 January 2004.

45. H. M. Treasury, *The Strength to Take the Long-Term Decisions for Britain: Seizing the opportunities of the global recovery. Pre-budget report 2003*, Cm. 6042 (London: The Stationery Office, 2003), p. 3.

46. H. M. Treasury, *Budget 2007. Building Britain's Long-Term Future: Prosperity and fairness for families. Economic and fiscal strategy report and financial statement and budget report*, HC. 342 (London: The Stationery Office, 2007), pp. 20–21.

47. Office for National Statistics, *Consumer Price Indices: June 2007* (London: Office for National Statistics, 2007), p. 1.

48. Ibid., p. 20.

49. A. Dilnot and P. Johnson (ed.), *Election Briefing 1997* (London: Institute for Fiscal Studies, 1997), p. i.

50. E. Balls and G. O'Donnell (ed.), *Reforming Britain's Economic and Financial Policy: Towards greater economic stability* (Houndmills: Palgrave Macmillan, 2002), p. 19.

51. A. Dilnot and P. Johnson (ed.), *Election Briefing 1997* (London: Institute for Fiscal Studies, 1997), p. i.

52. Ibid., pp. 14–16.

53. H. M. Treasury, *Fiscal Policy: Lessons from the last economic cycle* (London: H. M. Treasury, 1997), p. 1.

54. G. Brown, speech at the Lord Mayor's Dinner, Mansion House, London, 12 June 1997.

55. E. Balls, 'Stability, Growth and UK Fiscal Policy,' Inaugural Ken Dixon Lecture, Department of Economics, University of York, 23 January 2004.

56. Institute for Fiscal Studies, *The IFS Green Budget: January 2006* (London: Institute for Fiscal Studies, 2006), p. 45.

57. Ibid., p. 37.

58. Ibid., pp. 26, 32.

59. Ibid., pp. 38–40.
60. E. Balls, 'Stability, Growth and UK Fiscal Policy,' Inaugural Ken Dixon Lecture, Department of Economics, University of York, 23 January 2004.
61. Ibid.
62. G. Brown, *G8 and other International Issues.* Evidence given to the House of Commons Treasury Select Committee, 19 July 2005, Session 2005–2006, HC. 399-I (London: The Stationery Office, 2005), Q7.
63. H. M. Treasury, *Britain Meeting the Global Challenge: Enterprise, fairness and responsibility. Pre-budget report December 2005*, Cm. 6701 (London: H. M. Treasury), p. 208.
64. H. M. Treasury, *Investing in Britain's Potential: Building our long-term future. Pre-budget report 2006*, Cm. 6984 (London: The Stationery Office, 2006), p. 218.
65. Institute for Fiscal Studies, *Public Finance Bulletin*, 20 March 2007 (London: Institute for Fiscal Studies, 2007), p. 2.
66. H. M. Treasury, *Budget 2007. Building Britain's Long-Term Future: Prosperity and fairness for families. Economic and fiscal strategy report and financial statement and budget report*, HC. 342 (London: The Stationery Office, 2007).
67. R. Chote and C. Emmerson, *The Public Finances: Election briefing 2005* (London: Institute for Fiscal Studies, 2005), p. 4.
68. Office for National Statistics, *Public Sector Finances June 2007* (London: Office for National Statistics, 2007), p. 1
69. C. Frayne, 'Public Finances,' presentation at the Institute for Fiscal Studies' Post-Budget Briefing, 23 March 2007.
70. House of Commons Treasury Committee, *The 2006 Pre-Budget Report, Second Report of Session 2006–07*, HC. 115 (London: The Stationery Office, 2007), p. 20.
71. G. Brown, 'Foreword' to E. Balls, J. Grice and G. O'Donnell, *Microeconomic Reform in Britain: Delivering opportunities for all* (London: Palgrave Macmillan, 2004), p. xii.
72. E. Balls, *Euro-Monetarism: Why Britain was ensnared and how it should escape* (London: Fabian Society, 1992), p. 18.
73. Ibid., p. 21.
74. Ibid., pp. 22–23.
75. Ibid., p. 23.
76. Ibid., p. 23.
77. Ibid., p. 23.
78. G. Brown, speech at the Lord Mayor's Banquet, Mansion House, London, 21 June 2006.
79. Ibid.
80. Business Guardian, 'Banking Bonanza – How the Profits Stack Up,' *Guardian Unlimited*, 15 April 2007.

81. Ibid.

82. E. Balls, 'The City as the Global Finance Centre: Risks and opportunities,' speech at Bloomberg, City of London, 14 June 2006.

83. H. M. Treasury, 'Economic Secretary Leads Discussion on City Competitiveness,' *H. M. Treasury Press Release 102/06* (London: H. M. Treasury, 2006).

84. House of Lords, *Overseas Trade. Report of the House of Lords Select Committee, 1984–85 Session*, HL.41-I (London: Her Majesty's Stationery Office, 1985), p. 6.

85. E. Balls, 'Britain's Next Decade,' The Fabian Lecture, 1 November 2006.

86. Institute for Fiscal Studies, *The IFS Green Budget: January 2006*, p. 61.

87. Office for National Statistics, *Business Investment: Revised results – 4th quarter 2006* (London: The Stationery Office, 2007), p. 1.

88. House of Commons Treasury Committee, *The 2006 Pre-Budget Report. Second Report of Session 2006–07*, HC. 115 (London: The Stationery Office, 2007), pp. 7–8.

89. Office for National Statistics, *International Comparisons of Productivity, 21 February 2007* (London: The Stationery Office, 2007), p. 10.

90. G. Brown, 'Exploiting the British Genius – The Key to Long-Term Economic Success,' speech to the Confederation of British Industry, 20 May 1997.

91. G. Brown, speech at the Confederation of British Industry President's Dinner, London, 22 April 1998.

92. P. Aldrick and E. Conway, 'Brown's Pension Grab Secret is Revealed,' *The Daily Telegraph*, 31 March 2007.

93. Office for National Statistics, *United Kingdom Balance of Payments: The Pink Book* (Newport: Office for National Statistics, 2008), p. 24.

94. Ibid.

95. Office for National Statistics, *Balance of Payments 1st Quarter 2007* (London: Office for National Statistics, 2007), p. 10.

96. Institute for Fiscal Studies, *The IFS Green Budget: January 2006* (London: Institute for Fiscal Studies, 2006) p. 58.

97. Office for National Statistics, *United Kingdom Balance of Payments: The Pink Book* (Newport: Office for National Statistics, 2008), pp. 26, 106.

98. Office for National Statistics, *The Pink Book: 2006 edition* (London: The Stationery Office, 2006), p. 96.

99. Ibid., p. 78.

100. Office for National Statistics, *Balance of Payments 4th Quarter and Annual 2006* (London: The Stationery Office, 2007), p. 8.

101. Stephen Nickell, *The UK Current Account Deficit and All That* (London: Bank of England, 2006), p. 2.

102. Association of Payment Clearing Systems (APACS), 'Record number of trans-actions on plastic cards over festive season,' *APACS Press Release*, 2 January (London: Association of Payment Clearing Systems, 2007).

103. Credit Action, *Debt Facts and Figures: Compiled 1 February 2007* (Lincoln: Credit Action, 2007). Available online: http://www.creditaction.org.uk/ debtstats.htm (accessed 1 March 2007).

104. Citizens Advice, '2007 starts with fifteen per cent more debt problems than 2006,' *Citizens Advice Press Release*, 16 February (London: Citizens Advice, 2007). Available online: http://www.citizensadvice.org.uk/press_041006 (accessed 1 March 2007).

105. Credit Action, *Debt Facts and Figures: Compiled 1 February 2007* (Lincoln: Credit Action, 2007). Available online: http://www.creditaction.org.uk/ debtstats.htm (accessed 1 March 2007).

106. N. Lawson, *The View from No.11: Memoirs of a tory radical* (London, Bantam Press, 1992), pp. 366–367, 631.

107. Halifax, *Halifax House Price Index: January 2007* (Halifax: Halifax plc, 2007).

108. Ibid.

109. Credit Action, *Debt Facts and Figures: Compiled 1 February 2007* (Lincoln: Credit Action, 2007). Available online: http://www.creditaction.org.uk/ debtstats.htm (accessed 1 March 2007).

110. The Guardian/Reward Technology Forum (RTF) Directors' Pay Survey, *The Guardian*, 2 October 2006.

111. N. Isles, *The Risk Myth: CEOS and labour market risk* (London: The Work Foundation, 2006).

112. G. Brown, 'Exploiting the British Genius – The Key to Long-Term Economic Success,' speech to the Confederation of British Industry, 20 May 1997.

113. Commission on Public Policy and British Business, *Promoting Prosperity: A business agenda for Britain* (London: Vintage, 1997).

114. Gordon Brown, *Pre-Budget Report statement to the House of Commons, 6 December 2006* (London: H. M. Treasury, 2006). Available online: http://www. hm_treasury.gov.uk/pre_budget_report/prebud_pbr06/prebud_pbr06_speech. cfm (accessed 27 February 2007).

115. Institute for Fiscal Studies, *The IFS Green Budget: January 2009* (London: Institute for Fiscal Studies, 2009), p. 1.

116. Ibid., p. 15.

117. Ibid., pp. 17–18.

118. Ibid., p. 19.

119. Ibid., p. 11.

120. Ibid., p. 13.

121. Ibid., p. 86.

122. Ibid., p. 1.
123. Ibid., p. 28.

CHAPTER 4

1. Labour Party, *New Labour: Because Britain deserves better* (London: The Labour Party, 1997), p. 5.
2. Ibid., p. 20.
3. Ibid., p. 13.
4. Ibid., p. 21.
5. A. Goodman and L. Sibieta, *Public Spending on Education in the UK*. Prepared for the Education and Skills Select Committee (London: Institute for Fiscal Studies, 2006), pp. 9–10.
6. Department of Health, *Department of Health Departmental Report 2007* (London: Department of Health, 2007), pp. 128–129.
7. Ipsos MORI, *Ipsos MORI Delivery Index*, 16 May 2007 (London: Ipsos MORI, 2007).
8. V. Garrow and E. Sterling, *The Management Agenda 2007: Overview of findings* (Horsham: Roffey Park Institute, 2007), p. 2.
9. British Medical Association, speech by Dr Jonathan Fielden, Chairman of the Central Consultants and Specialists' Committee, Westminster Conference Centre, London, 6 June 2007.
10. Cabinet Office, *Ministerial Committees of the Cabinet and Policy Review Working Groups: Composition and terms of reference* (London: Cabinet Office, 2006), p. 35.
11. Department of Health, *The NHS Plan: A plan for investment, a plan for reform*, Cm. 4818 (London: The Stationery Office, 2000), p. 11.
12. E. Balls, J. Grice and G. O'Donnell (ed.), *Microeconomic Reform in Britain: Delivering opportunities for all* (Houndmills: Palgrave Macmillan, 2004), p. 18.
13. Office of Public Services Reform, *Reforming Our Public Services: Principles into practice* (London: The Prime Minister's Office of Public Services Reform, 2002), p. 17.
14. Ibid., pp. 2–3, 28.
15. E. Balls, J. Grice and G. O'Donnell (ed.), *Microeconomic Reform in Britain: Delivering opportunities for all* (Houndmills: Palgrave Macmillan, 2004), p. 9.
16. T. Blair, interview with *Breakfast With Frost*, BBC 1, 16 January 2000, cited in A. Rawnsley, *Servants of the People: The inside story of New Labour* (London: Penguin, 2001), p. 337.
17. Brown was reported to have told Blair, 'you have stolen my fucking Budget,'

cited in A. Rawnsley, *Servants of the People: The inside story of New Labour* (London: Penguin, 2001), p. 338.

18. D. Wanless, *Securing our Future Health: Taking a long-term view* (London: H. M. Treasury, 2002).

19. This was published as Prime Minister's Strategy Unit, *Health Strategy Review: Analytical report* (London: Prime Minister's Strategy Unit, 2002).

20. H. M. Treasury, *Opportunity and Security For All: Investing in an enterprising, fairer Britain. New Public Spending Plans 2003–2006*, Cm. 5570 (London: The Stationery Office, 2002), p. 2; D. Wanless, *Securing our Future Health: Taking a long-term view* (London: H. M. Treasury, 2002), p. 75.

21. D. Osborne and T. Gabeler, *Reinventing Government: How the entrepreneurial spirit is transforming the public sector* (Reading, Massachusetts: Addison-Wesley, 1992), p. xix.

22. Ibid., pp. 19–20.

23. Ibid., p. xxi.

24. Ibid., pp. 23–24.

25. Ibid., p. 35.

26. Ibid., p. 40.

27. Ibid., p. 45.

28. C. Thain and M. Wright, *The Treasury and Whitehall: The planning and control of public expenditure, 1976–1993* (Oxford: Clarendon Press, 1995), p. 537.

29. For a concise analysis of this approach, see S. Lee and R. Woodward, 'Implementing the Third Way: The delivery of public services under the Blair Government,' *Public Money and Management*, October–December 2002, pp. 1–8.

30. H. M. Treasury, *Modern Public Services: Investing in reform. Comprehensive Spending Review: New public spending plans 1999–2000*, Cm. 4011 (London: The Stationery Office, 1998), p. 6.

31. R. Chote, C. Emmerson and C. Frayne, *The Public Finances: Election briefing 2005* (London: Institute for Fiscal Studies, 2005), p. 7; C. Emmerson and C. Frayne, *Public Spending: Election briefing 2005* (London: Institute for Fiscal Studies, 2005), p. 2.

32. R. Chote, C. Emmerson and C. Frayne, 'Public Spending Pressures,' in R. Chote, C. Emmerson, R. Harrison and D. Miles (ed.), *The IFS Green Budget: January 2006* (London: Institute for Fiscal Studies, 2006), pp. 74, 76.

33. H. M. Treasury, *Building Opportunity and Security for All: 2000 spending review. New public spending plans 2001–2004* (London: H. M. Treasury, 2000), pp. 1–2.

34. H. M. Treasury, *Opportunity and security for all: Investing in an enterprising, fairer Britain. 2002 Spending Review: New Public Spending Plans 2003–2006*, Cm. 5570 (London: The Stationery Office, 2002), pp. 2–3.

35. H. M. Treasury, *Stability, Security and Opportunity for All: Investing for Britain's long-term future. 2004 Spending Review: New Public Spending Plans 2005–2008*, Cm. 6237 (London: The Stationery Office, 2004), pp. 85, 93.

36. E. Balls, J. Grice and G. O'Donnell (ed.), *Microeconomic Reform in Britain: Delivering opportunities for all* (Houndmills: Palgrave Macmillan, 2004), p. 346.

37. H. M. Treasury, *Modern Public Services for Britain: Investing in reform. Comprehensive Spending Review: new public spending plans 1999–2002*, Cm. 4011 (London: The Stationery Office, 1998), p. 13.

38. H. M. Treasury, *Service Delivery Agreements and Technical Notes*, Available online: http://www.hm-treasury.gov.uk./Spending_Review/Spending_Review_2000/Service_Delivery_Agreements/spend_sr00_sda_index.cfm (accessed 10 June 2007).

39. Treasury Select Committee, *H. M. Treasury. Third Report from the House of Commons' Treasury Select Committee, Session 2000–2001*, HC. 73-I (London: The Stationery Office, 2001), paras 19–21.

40. Ibid., paras 31–32.

41. Ibid., para 48.

42. H. M. Treasury/Cabinet Office, *Delivering Decision Making: 1-Delivering better public services: refining targets and performance management* (London: H. M. Treasury, 2004); H. M. Treasury/Office of the Deputy Prime Minister/Department of Trade and Industry, *Devolving Decision Making: 2-Meeting the regional economic challenge: Increasing regional and local flexibility* (London: H. M. Treasury, 2004).

43. H. M. Treasury, *Budget 2007: Building Britain's long-term future: prosperity and fairness for families. Economic and Financial Statement and Budget Report*, HC. 342 (London: The Stationery Office, 2006), p. 153.

44. Department for Communities and Local Government, *Strong and Prosperous Communities: The Local Government White Paper*, Cm. 6939-II (London: The Stationery Office, 2006), pp. 4–5, 122. For a more detailed analysis of the impact of constrained discretion on the English regions, see S. Lee, 'Constrained Discretion and English Regional Governance: The case of Yorkshire and the Humber,' in J. Bradbury (ed.), *Devolution, Regionalism and Regional Development in the UK* (London: Taylor & Francis, 2007).

45. E. Balls, G. O'Donnell and J. Grice (ed.), *Microeconomic Reform in Britain: Delivering opportunities for all* (London: Palgrave Macmillan, 2004), pp. 6, 8.

46. Ibid., p. 380.

47. Ibid., p. 17.

48. Ibid., p. 17.

49. G. Brown, 'State and Market: Towards a public interest test,' *The Political Quarterly*, 74, 3, 2003, p. 267.

50. Ibid., p. 267.
51. Ibid., p. 268.
52. M. Sandel, *What Money Can't Buy: The moral limits of markets*. The Tanner Lectures on Human Values, delivered at Brasenose College, Oxford, 11 and 12 May 1998, cited in G. Brown, 'A Modern Agenda for Prosperity and Social Reform,' speech to the Social Market Foundation, Cass Business School, London, 3 January 2003.
53. Ibid., p. 270.
54. Ibid., pp. 271–272.
55. Ibid., pp. 277–278.
56. Ibid., pp. 279–280.
57. H. M. Treasury, *Investing in Britain's Potential: Building our long-term future. Pre-budget report*, Cm. 6984 (London: The Stationery Office, 2006), p. 246.
58. Ibid., p. 246.
59. See for example, A. Pollock, *NHS plc: The privatisation of our health care* (London: Verso, 2005).
60. The role of consultants in inflating PFI projects has been documented extensively in D. Craig and R. Brooks, *Plundering the Public Sector* (London: Constable, 2006).
61. P. Gosling, *PFI: Against the public interest* (London: UNISON, 2005).
62. UNISON, *Private Finance Initiative (PFI): The case against PFI* (London: UNISON, 2007). Available online: http://www.unison.org.uk/pfi/caseagainst.asp (accessed 10 June 2007).
63. A. Pollock and D. Price, *Public Risk for Private Gain? The public audit implications of risk transfer and private finance* (London: UNISON, 2004), p. 3.
64. A. Pollock, D. Price and S. Player, *The Private Finance Initiative: A policy built on sand* (London: UNISON, 2005).
65. Ibid., p. 3.
66. H. M. Treasury, *PFI: Meeting the investment challenge* (London: H. M. Treasury, 2003).
67. A. Pollock, D. Price and S. Player, *The Private Finance Initiative: A policy built on sand* (London: UNISON, 2005), p. 3.
68. House of Commons Committee of Public Accounts, *Update on PFI Debt Refinancing and the PFI Equity Market. Twenty-fifth Report on Session 2006–07*, HC. 158 (London: The Stationery Office, 2007), p. 7.
69. G. Brown, 'State and Market: Towards a public interest test,' *The Political Quarterly*, 74, 3, 2003, pp. 281–282.
70. Ibid., p. 282.
71. Ibid., p. 283.
72. Ibid., p. 277.

73. H. M. Treasury, *Public Expenditure Statistical Analyses 2007*, Cm. 7091 (London: The Stationery Office, 2007), pp. 131–132.

74. D. Wilkes, 'Postcode Lottery for Cancer Wonder Drug,' *The Daily Mail*, 10 April 2006.

75. House of Commons Committee of Public Accounts, *The NHS Cancer Plan: A progress report, HC. 791* (London: The Stationery Office, 2005).

76. The Northern Way was established in 2004 by bringing together the RDAs in the North East, North West and Yorkshire and the Humber. It was intended to create 'a new system of regional government for the North' that would permit 'the regions to plan more strategically, establish priorities and take key decisions on a region-wide basis,' Office of the Deputy Prime Minister, *Draft Regional Assemblies Bill: Policy statement* (London: Office of the Deputy Prime Minister, 2004), pp. 3–4.

77. E. Balls, G. O'Donnell and J. Grice (ed.), *Microeconomic Reform in Britain: Delivering opportunities for all* (London: Palgrave Macmillan, 2004), pp. 17, 346.

78. G. Brown, 'Introduction' to E. Balls, G. O'Donnell and J. Grice (ed.), *Microeconomic Reform in Britain: Delivering opportunities for all* (London: Palgrave Macmillan, 2004), p. xiii.

79. G. Brown, speech to the Labour Party Conference, 26 September 2005.

80. Ibid.

81. H. M. Treasury, *Budget 2007: Building Britain's long-term future: Prosperity and fairness for families. Economic and financial statement and budget report*, HC. 342 (London: The Stationery Office, 2006), p. 148.

82. ICM Research, *March 2007 Poll* (London: ICM Research, 2007), p. 4.

83. Ipsos MORI, *Public Expectations About The NHS-Government Delivery Index* (London: Ipsos MORI, 2007), pp. 1–2.

84. Ipsos MORI, *10 Years of Blair: How did he do?* Poll, 10 May 2007 (London: Ipsos MORI, 2007).

85. ICM Research, *Political Trust.* A poll prepared on behalf of the *Sunday Telegraph*, 30–31 May 2007 (London: ICM Research).

86. A. Johnson, 'NHS Next State Review,' *Hansard*, 4 July 2007, cc. 961–962.

87. Department of Health, 'Shaping Health Care for the Next Decade,' 4 July 2007, p. 1.

88. Department for Children, Schools and Families, 'Ed Balls Appointed Secretary of State for Children, Schools and Families,' 28 June 2007, p. 2.

89. G. Brown, presentation at the Public Service Reform Conference: Twenty-first century public services – learning from the front line,' London, 27 March 2007.

90. G. Brown, remarks at the Twenty-first Century Public Services: Putting

People First Conference, Queen Elizabeth II Conference Hall, London, 6 June 2006.

91. G. Brown, presentation at the Public Service Reform Conference: Twenty-first century public services – learning from the front line,' London, 27 March 2007.

92. Ibid.

93. Ibid.

94. G. Brown, remarks at the Twenty-first Century Public Services: Putting People First Conference, Queen Elizabeth II Conference Hall, London, 6 June 2006.

95. H. M. Treasury, *Budget 2007: Building Britain's long-term future: Prosperity and fairness for families. Economic and financial statement and budget report*, HC. 342 (London: The Stationery Office, 2007), p. 139.

96. H. M. Treasury, *Stability, Security and Opportunity for All: Investing for Britain's long-term future. 2004 spending review: New public spending plans 2005–2008*, Cm. 6237 (London: The Stationery Office, 2004), p. 85; H. M. Treasury, *Opportunity and Security For All: Investing in an enterprising, fairer Britain. New public spending plans 2003–2006*, Cm. 5570 (London: The Stationery Office, 2002), p. 59; H. M. Treasury, *Prudent for a Purpose: Building opportunity and security for all. New public spending plans for 2001–2004* (London: The Stationery Office, 2000), section 7.19.

97. H. M. Treasury, *Releasing resources to the front line: Independent Review of Public Sector Efficiency by Sir Peter Gershon* (London: H. M. Treasury, 2004), p. 35.

98. H. M. Treasury, *Long-term Opportunities and Challenges for the UK: Analysis for the 2007 Comprehensive Spending Review* (London: H. M. Treasury, 2006), p. 24.

99. D. Coats, *Efficiency, efficiency, efficiency. The Gershon Review: Public service efficiency and the management of change* (London: The Work Foundation, 2004), p. 4.

100. Healthcare Commission, *Briefing note: NHS trust declarations on standards for 2006/2007* (London: Healthcare Commission, 2007), p. 8.

101. Ibid., p. 4.

102. H. M. Treasury, *Budget 2007: Building Britain's long-term future: Prosperity and fairness for families. Economic and financial statement and budget report*, HC. 342 (London: The Stationery Office, 2006), p. 148.

103. Department of Health, *NHS Financial Performance Quarter Four 2007–7* (London: Department of Health, 2007), p. 1.

104. UNISON/Compass, *Voices for Real Reform: A public service discussion paper based on a joint Compass and UNISON Summit January 2007* (London: Compass and UNISON, 2007), pp. 2–3.

105. Ibid., p. 4.
106. T. Blair, speech to the Venture Capitalists' Association Conference, London, 6 July 1999.
107. T. Blair, speech to the Labour Party Conference, Bournemouth, 28 September 1999; BBC, 'Blair's Stern Lesson for Teachers,' BBC News, 21 October 1999.
108. A. Goodman and L. Sibieta, *Public spending on education in the UK*. Prepared for the Education and Skills Select Committee (London: Institute for Fiscal Studies, 2006), pp. 1, 7.
109. G. Brown, transcript of interview with Andrew Marr for the Sunday AM programme, 7 January 2007. Available online: http://www.bbc.co.uk/1/hi/uk_politics/6241819.stm (accessed 8 January 2007).
110. Ibid.
111. Ibid.
112. P. Wintour, 'Brown Backs City Academies with Words and Cash,' *The Guardian*, 20 March 2007.
113. G. Brown, 'Financial Statement,' 22 March 2006, c. 287–302.
114. '£34 Billion Schools Bonanza,' *The Daily Mirror*, 23 March 2006, cited in A. Goodman and L. Sibieta, *Public Spending on Education in the UK*. Prepared for the Education and Skills Select Committee (London: Institute for Fiscal Studies, 2006), p. 2.
115. A. Goodman and L. Sibieta, *Public Spending on Education in the UK*. Prepared for the Education and Skills Select Committee (London: Institute for Fiscal Studies, 2006), p. 2.
116. H. M. Treasury, 'Modern Public Services: Investing in Reform,' *Her Majesty's Treasury Press Release HMT 1*, 14 July 1998. Brown was criticised for a lack of transparency by a parliamentary select committee, which recommended that this confusing practice should be ended. House of Commons Treasury Committee, *The New Fiscal Framework and the Comprehensive Spending Review. Eighth Report of Session 1997–98*, HC. 960-I (London: The Stationery Office, 1998), para 33.
117. Ibid., p. 7.
118. G. Brown, transcript of interview with Andrew Marr for the Sunday AM programme, 7 January 2007. Available online: http://www.bbc.co.uk/1/hi/uk_politics/6241819.stm (accessed 8 January 2007).
119. G. Brown, speech to the special Labour Party Conference, Manchester, 24 June 2007.
120. G. Brown, speech to the Labour Party Conference, Bournemouth, 24 September 2007.
121. G. Brown, statement on the Draft Legislative Programme, *Hansard*, 11 July 2007, c. 50; Office of the Leader of the House of Commons, *The Governance of*

Britain: The Government's Draft Legislative Programme, Cm. 7175 (London: The Stationery Office, 2007), p. 14.

122. G. Brown, statement on the Draft Legislative Programme, *Hansard*, 14 May 2008, c. 1386.

123. Office of the Leader of the House of Commons, *Preparing Britain for the Future: The Government's Draft Legislative Programme 2008/09*, Cm. 7372 (London: The Stationery Office, 2008), pp. 14, 22.

124. G. Brown, speech to the Labour Party Conference, Manchester, 23 September 2008.

125. House of Commons Children, Schools and Families Committee, *Public Expenditure*, First Report of Session 2008–09, HC. 46 (London: The Stationery Office, 2009), p. 10.

126. P. Curtis, 'Where now after damning indictment of education?', *The Guardian*, 20 February 2009.

127. House of Commons Public Accounts Committee, *Skills for Life: Progress in Improving Adult Literacy and Numeracy*. Third Report of Session 2008–09, HC. 154 (London: The Stationery Office, 2009), pp. 5–7.

128. House of Commons Public Accounts Committee, *The National Programme for IT in the NHS: Progress since 2006*, Second Report of Session 2008–09, HC. 153 (London: The Stationery Office, 2009), p. 3.

129. The Press Association, 'Hospital boss says £12bn IT system means fewer patients can be seen', *The Guardian*, 13 February 2009.

130. House of Commons Public Accounts Committee, *NHS Pay Modernisation: New Contracts for General Practice Services in England*, Forty-First Report of Session 2007–08, HC. 463 (London: The Stationery Office, 2008), pp. 5–6.

131. Cabinet Office, 'Prime Minister sets out his vision for world-class public services', *Cabinet Office Press Release CAB/074/08*, 27 June 2008.

132. G. Brown, 'Foreword', to Cabinet Office, *Excellence and Fairness: Achieving World Class Public Services* (London: The Cabinet Office, 2008), p. 6.

133. H. M. Treasury, *Pre-Budget Report: Facing Global Challenges: Supporting People through Difficult Times*, Cm. 7484 (London: The Stationery Office, 2008), p. 3.

134. Institute for Fiscal Studies, *The IFS Green Budget: January 2009* (London: Institute for Fiscal Studies, 2009), p. 167.

135. Ibid., p. 167.

136. H. M. Treasury, *Pre-Budget Report: Facing Global Challenges: Supporting People through Difficult Times*, Cm. 7484 (London: The Stationery Office, 2008), p. 3.

137. Institute for Fiscal Studies, *The IFS Green Budget: January 2009* (London: Institute for Fiscal Studies, 2009), p. 19.

138. H. M. Treasury, *Budget 2007: Building Britain's long-term future: Prosperity*

     and fairness for families. Economic and financial statement and budget report,
     HC. 342 (London: The Stationery Office, 2006), p. 140.

139. House of Commons Committee of Public Accounts, *Financial Management in the NHS. Seventeenth Report of Session 2006–07*, HC. 361 (London: The Stationery Office, 2007), p. 5.

140. P. Hewitt, speech at the London School of Economics, 14 June 2007.

141. House of Commons Office of the Deputy Prime Minister: Housing, Planning, Local Government and the Regions Committee, *The Draft Assemblies Bill. First Report of Session 2004–05*, H. C. 61-I (London: The Stationery Office, 2004), p. 6.

142. The Cabinet Office, *Building on Progress: Public services* (London: Prime Minister's Strategy Unit, The Cabinet Office, 2007), p. 7.

143. Ibid., p. 15.

144. Ibid., p. 39.

145. H. M. Treasury/Cabinet Office, *The Future Role of the Third Sector in Social and Economic Regeneration: Interim report* (London: H. M. Treasury, 2006).

146. This thesis has been developed brilliantly in D. Marquand, *Decline of the Public* (Cambridge: Polity, 2004).

147. Ipsos MORI, *Ipsos MORI Delivery Index*, 16 May 2007 (London: Ipsos MORI, 2007).

148. YouGov, *YouGov/Daily Telegraph Survey Results*, 21–23 May 2007 (London: YouGov, 2007), pp. 4–5.

149. ICM, *ICM Guardian Poll: February 20–22 2009* (London: ICM Research, 2009), pp. 7, 8, 14.

150. Ipsos MORI, *Best Party on Key Issues: Health Care:18 February 2009* (London: Ipsos MORI, 2009); Ipsos MORI, *Best Party on Key Issues: Education: 18 February 2009* (London: Ipsos MORI, 2009).

151. G. Brown, speech to the NESTA conference, London, 10 March 2009.

CHAPTER 5

1. G. Brown, Annual British Council Lecture, London, 7 July 2004; G. Brown, 'The Future of Britishness,' speech to the Fabian Society 'Future of Britishness' conference, London, 14 January 2006; G. Brown, 'Securing Our Future,' lecture at the Royal Institute of International Affairs, Chatham House, London, 13 February 2006; 'Brown's Language Call to Migrants,' *BBC News*, 6 June 2006.

2. G. Brown, 'Britain Leading in Europe,' speech by the Chancellor of the Exchequer to the Royal Institute of International Affairs, London, 7 July 1997.

3. House of Commons, Higher Education Bill in Standing Committee H, 4 March 2004, c. 504.

4. G. Himmelfarb, *The Roads to Modernity: The British, French and American Enlightenment* (New York: Alfred A. Knight, 2004).

5. J. Q. Wilson, *The Moral Sense* (New York: The Free Press, 1993), cited in G. Brown, CAFOD Pope Paul VI Memorial Lecture, 8 December 2004.

6. N. Dennis and A. H. Halsey, *English Ethical Socialism: Thomas More to R. H. Tawney* (Oxford: Clarendon Press, 1988), p. 4.

7. A rare example was when Brown noted 'Crosland's study of the values of British democratic socialism is a compelling case to focus on what a great influence on him, R. H. Tawney, called the extraordinary potential of ordinary people,' G. Brown, 'Foreword' to A. Crosland, *The Future of Socialism* (London: Constable, 2006 edition), p. x.

8. G. Brown, 'Outward Bound,' *The Spectator*, 8 November 1997, pp. 15–16.

9. G. Brown, speech at the Smith Institute, London, 15 April 1999.

10. G. Brown, British Council Annual Lecture, London, 7 July 2004.

11. Ibid.

12. For example, '...only English and Welsh MPs will be entitled to vote on Government Bills relating to England and Wales. And English MPs alone will vote on the remaining laws which apply exclusively to England,' Conservative Party, *Time For Common Sense: 2001 Conservative Party General Election Manifesto* (London: The Conservative Party, 2001), p. 11 ; 'We will act to ensure that English laws are decided by English votes,' Conservative Party, *Are You Thinking What We're Thinking. It's Time For Action* (London: Conservative Party, 2005), p. 22.

13. D. Cameron, 'Modernisation with a purpose,' 6 February 2006.

14. Conservative Party, 'Ken Clarke's Democracy Taskforce Restoring Trust in Politics,' *Conservatives.com*. Available online: http://www.conservatives.com/tile.do?def=democracy.taskforce.page (accessed 25 May 2007).

15. 'English voters "oppose Scots PM",' *BBC News*, 14 May 2006.

16. 'England' in the Encyclopaedia Britannica, *The New Encyclopaedia Britannica*, (Chicago: Encyclopaedia Britannica, 2002), pp. 496–497.

17. Royal Commission on the Constitution 1969–1973, *Volume I: Report*, Cmnd. 5460 (London: Her Majesty's Stationery Office, 1973), p. 159.

18. Royal Commission on the Constitution 1969–1973, *Volume II: Memorandum of Dissent*, Cmnd. 5460-I (London: Her Majesty's Stationery Office, 1973), p. viii.

19. G. Brown, 'We Have Renewed Britain; Now We Must Champion It,' *The Guardian*, 27 February 2006.

20. Ibid.

21. G. Brown, speech at the University of Manchester Institute of Science and Technology, 26 January 2001.

22. G. Brown, speech to the Sustainable Communities Summit, Manchester, 2 February 2005.

23. G. Brown, 'Prosperity and Justice for All,' speech to the Labour Party Annual Conference, Brighton, 27 September 2004.

24. T. Dalyell, *Devolution: The End of Britain?* (London: Jonathan Cape, 1977), p. 247.

25. Prime Minister's Office of Public Services Reform, *Reforming Our Public Services: Principles into practice* (London: Prime Minister's Office of Public Services Reform, 2002), pp. 12, 28.

26. E. Balls, J. Grice and G. O'Donnell, *Microeconomic Reform in Britain: Delivering opportunities for all* (London: Palgrave Macmillan, 2004).

27. T. Shifrin, 'Scotland Launches Youth Volunteering Programme,' *The Guardian*, 11 May 2004.

28. Scottish Executive, 'Programme for Young Volunteers,' *Scottish Executive News Release*, 11 May 2004. Available online: http://www.scotland.gov.uk/News/Releases/2004/05/5496 (accessed 15 May 2007).

29. Russell Commission, *A National Framework for Youth Action and Engagement: The Report of the Russell Commission* (London, The Stationery Office, 2005), pp. 169–170.

30. Russell Commission, *The Russell Commission-Frequently Asked Questions.* Available online: http://www.russellcommission.org/faq/index.html (accessed 11 May 2006).

31. G. Brown, speech at the Smith Institute, London, 15 April 1999

32. Ibid.

33. Cited in D. Blair, 'Mbeki Lambasts Brown for "Imperial Nostalgia",' *Daily Telegraph*, 30 May 2005.

34. Cited in M. Kearney, 'Brown Seeks Out "British Values",' *BBC News*, 14 March 2005.

35. Cited in '"No UK Apology" for Colonial Past,' *BBC News*, 15 Jan 2005.

36. S. Milne, 'Britain: Imperial Nostalgia,' *Le Monde Diplomatique*, May 2005, cited in T. Mbeki, 'Lies Have Short Legs!' *ANC Today*, Vol.5, No.21, 27 May 2005.

37. J. A. Hobson, *Imperialism: A Study* (London: George Allen and Unwin, 1902).

38. G. Brown, 'The Future of Britishness,' speech to the Fabian Society 'Future of Britishness' conference, London, 14 January 2006.

39. Cited in M. Mendle, 'Putney's Pronouns: Identity and Indemnity in the Great Debate' in M. Mendle (ed.), *The Putney Debates of 1647: The Army, the Levellers and the English State* (Cambridge: Cambridge University Press, 2001), pp. 136–137.

40. G. Brown, 'The Future of Britishness,' speech to the Fabian Society 'Future of Britishness' conference, London, 14 January 2006.

41. F. de Voltaire, *Letters Concerning the English Nation* (London: C. Davis and A. Lyon, 1733), p. 34.

42. G. Brown, The Hugo Young Memorial Lecture, Chatham House, London, 13 December 2005.

43. C.-L. de Montesquieu, '*Notes on England,* with commentary, translation and annotations by Iain Stewart,' *Oxford University Comparative Law Forum,* 6. Available online: http://www.ouclf.iuscomp.org (accessed 23 December 2006).

44. N. Cronk, 'Introduction' to N. Cronk (ed.), *Letters Concerning the English Nation* (Oxford: Oxford University Press, 1994), p. xvii.

45. T. Pangle, *Montesquieu's Philosophy of Liberalism: A commentary on 'The Spirit of the Laws'* (Chicago:University of Chicago Press, 1973), p. 228.

46. E. Burke, *Reflections on the Revolution in France,* (first published in 1790; Buffalo, New York: Prometheus Books, 1987), p. 51.

47. Ibid., pp. 93, 133.

48. T. Furniss, 'Cementing the Nation: Burke's *Reflections* on nationalism and national identity,' in J. Whale (ed.), *Edmund Burke's 'Reflections on the Revolution in France: New interdisciplinary essays* (Manchester, Manchester University Press, 2000), pp. 123, 125.

49. C. Connolly, '*Reflections* on the Act of Union,' in J. Whale (ed.), *Edmund Burke's Reflections on the Revolution in France: New interdisciplinary essays* (Manchester: Manchester University Press, 2000), pp. 185–186.

50. T. Gray, 'Elegy Written in a Country Churchyard,' in A. Quiller-Couch (ed.), *The Oxford Book of English Verse: 1250–1900* (Oxford: Oxford University Press, 1919), p. 533, cited in G. Brown, The Hugo Young Memorial Lecture, Chatham House, London, 13 December 2005.

51. W. Wordsworth, 'England, 1802,' in A. Quiller-Couch (ed.), *The Oxford Book of English Verse: 1250–1900* (Oxford: Oxford University Press, 1919), p. 618.

52. W. Hazlitt, *Political Essays with Sketches of Public Characters* (London: William Hone, 1819), p. viii, cited in G. Brown, 'The Future of Britishness,' speech to the Fabian Society 'Future of Britishness' conference, London, 14 January 2006.

53. W. Hazlitt, *Political Essays with Sketches of Public Characters* (London: William Hone, 1819), p. viii

54. G. Brown, 'The Future of Britishness,' speech to the Fabian Society 'Future of Britishness' conference, London, 14 January 2006.

55. S. Gwynn, *Henry Grattan and His Times* (Dublin: Browne and Nolan, 1939), p. 129.

56. Ibid., pp. 236–238.

57. R. McDowell, *Ireland in the Age of Imperialism and Revolution 1760–1801* (Oxford: Clarendon Press, 1979), p. 249.

58. G. Brown, The Hugo Young Memorial Lecture, Chatham House, London, 13 December 2005.

59. A. de Tocqueville, *Democracy in America* (originally published in 1835; specially edited and abridged by Richard Heffner: New York: Mentor, 1956), p. 97.

60. Ibid., p. 205.

61. Ibid., p. 64.

62. G. Orwell, *The Lion and the Unicorn: Socialism and the English genius* (first published in 1941; London: Secker and Warburg, 1962), pp. 19–20, cited in G. Brown, The Hugo Young Memorial Lecture, Chatham House, London, 13 December 2005.

63. G. Brown, speech at the Smith Institute, London, 15 April 1999.

64. G. Orwell, *The Lion and the Unicorn: Socialism and the English genius* (London: Secker and Warburg, 1962), p. 96.

65. G. Brown, The Hugo Young Memorial Lecture, Chatham House, London, 13 December 2005.

66. W. Churchill, 'Motion on the Statement on Defence, 1955, Command Paper No.9391,' *Official Record,* 1 March 1955, c. 1906.

67. Churchill was cited by a Scot, James Gray MP, representing an English constituency (North Wiltshire), during a parliamentary debate Gray had introduced on the topic of 'Constitutional Reform (England).' Having introduced himself as 'an honorary Englishman' and after citing Churchill, Gray concluded his speech, 'Now is the time for the House to speak for England,' *Hansard,* 9 June 1999, cc. 581, 586.

68. H. M. Treasury, *Hosting the World Cup: A feasibility study* (London: H. M. Treasury, 2007), p. 5.

69. Ibid., p. 3.

70. Ibid., p. 35.

71. Ibid., p. 4.

72. BBC, 'World Cup Own Goal for Chancellor,' *BBC News,* 19 January 2007. Available online: http://news.bbc.co.uk/1/hi/scotland/6280663.stm (accessed 21 May 2007).

73. Ibid.

74. E. Harrell, 'Brown's Fond Memories of Gazza's Goal Against Scots,' *The Scotsman,* 22 May 2006. Available online: http://www.news.scotsman.com/politics.cfm?id=757742006 (accessed 21 May 2007).

75. Ibid.

76. G. Brown, 'Why Scotland Means the World to Me,' in D. Bull and A. Campbell (ed.), *Football and the Commons People* (Sheffield: Juma, 1994), p. 142.

77. Ibid., p. 145.

78. BBC, 'Government Rejects "Britain FC" Plans,' *BBC News*, 29 November 2000.

79. J. Naughtie, 'A British Football Team? No Chance,' *The Guardian*, 30 November 2000.

80. BBC, 'No Scots for GB Olympic Football,' *BBC News*, 11 November 2005.

81. Football Supporters' Federation, *Football – Our Game! The fans' blueprint for the future of the beautiful game* (Kingston On Thames: Football Supporters' Federation, 2006).

82. Football Supporters' Federation, 'FSF Poll Results: "Do you support a combined Home Nations team for the 2012 London Olympics?"' (Kingston On Thames, Football Supporters' Federation 2007). Available online: http:// www.fsf.org.uk/site-pages/poll_olympic.html (accessed 25 May 2007).

83. Reflecting the devolved nature of sport, the arts and culture in Scotland, the Scottish Executive had published its first National Cultural Strategy as early as August 2000, *Creating Our Future, Minding Our Past* (Edinburgh: Scottish Executive, 2000).

84. National Sports Foundation, 'About the Foundation' (London: National Sports Foundation, 2007). Available online: http://www.nationalsports foundation.org/about_foundation.html (accessed 25 May 2007).

85. Office for National Statistics, *Social Trends 36* (London: Palgrave Macmillan, 2006), p. 3.

86. G. Brown, 'Securing our Future,' speech at the Royal United Services Institute, London, 13 February 2006.

87. YouGov, *YouGov/Sunday Times Survey Results* (London: YouGov, 2007), pp. 4–5.

88. J. Straw, 'We Need a British Story: Nationality should not require individuals to give up distinctive cultural attributes,' *The Sunday Times*, 29 April 2007.

89. Ibid.

90. Office of the Deputy Prime Minister, *State of the English Cities* (London: Office of the Deputy Prime Minister, 2006).

91. These arguments are developed further in S. Lee, *Blair's Third Way* (London: Palgrave Macmillan, 2008); S. Lee, 'Constrained Discretion and English Regional Governance: The case of Yorkshire and the Humber' in J. Bradbury (ed.), *Devolution, Regionalism and Regional Development in the UK* (London: Taylor Francis, 2007), pp. 240–272; and S. Lee, 'The Competitive

Disadvantage of England,' in K. Cowling (ed.), *Industrial Policy in Europe: Theoretical perspectives and practical proposals* (London: Routledge, 1999), pp. 88–117.

92. J. Straw, 'Reclaiming the Flag: It's time the left redefined its patriotism,' *New Statesman and Society*, 24 February 1995, p. 24.

93. Jonathan Freedland has conflated English ideas into British ideas about liberty and democracy to make the case for a British republic, which might equally and more appropriately (given their particular intellectual and political lineage) be applied to the constitutional future of England. J. Freedland, *Bring Home the Revolution: The case for a British Republic* (London: Fourth Estate, 1998).

94. J. A. Hobson, *The Crisis of Liberalism: New issues of democracy* (London: P. S. King and Son, 1909).

95. The possibility of an English Way, in accordance with these principles, is outlined in S. Lee, *Blair's Third Way* (London: Palgrave Macmillan, 2008).

96. Ministry of Justice, *The Governance of Britain – The Government's Draft Legislative Programme*, Cm. 7175 (London: The Stationery Office, 2007); Ministry of Justice, *The Governance of Britain*, Cm. 7170 (London: The Stationery Office, 2007).

97. Ministry of Justice, *The Governance of Britain*, Cm. 7170 (London: The Stationery Office, 2007).

98. See Labour Party, *The Labour Party Manifesto 2005* (London: The Labour Party, 2005), chapters 4, 8 and 9.

99. Ministry of Justice, *The Governance of Britain*, Cm. 7170 (London: The Stationery Office, 2007), pp. 38–9.

100. D. Dewar, 'Foreword' to The Scottish Office, *Scotland's Parliament*, Cm. 3658 (Edinburgh: The Scottish Office, 1997).

101. Ministry of Justice, *The Governance of Britain*, Cm. 7170 (London: The Stationery Office, 2007), p. 8.

102. Department for Communities and Local Government, *Communities in Control: Real People, Real Power*, Cm.7427 (London: The Stationery Office, 2008), pp. 17, 23.

103. Ibid., p. 20.

104. S. Weir, 'A super-quango is born', *Open Democracy News Analysis* (London: Open Democracy, 2008). Available online: http://www.opendemocracy.net/blog/ourkingdom-theme/stuat-weir/2008/07/28/a-super-quango-is-born (accessed 28 July 2008).

105. Ibid.

106. D. Beetham, A. Blick, H. Margetts and S. Weir, *Power and Participation in Modern Britain* (Colchester: Democratic Audit, 2008), p. 12.

CHAPTER 6

1. H. M. Treasury, *Tackling Poverty: A global new deal. A modern Marshall Plan for the developing world* (London: H. M. Treasury, 2002). Although this document was published as a Treasury strategy, it was actually based on two speeches given by Gordon Brown in the immediate wake of 9/11, namely G. Brown, speech to the Federal Reserve, New York, 16 November 2001; and G. Brown, speech at the Press Club, Washington DC, 17 December 2001. These speeches were also adapted into G. Brown, 'Governments and Supranational Agencies: A new consensus?' in J. Dunning (ed.), *Making Globalisation Good: The moral challenges of global capitalism* (Oxford: Oxford University Press, 2004), pp. 320–332.

2. G. Brown, 'Governments and Supranational Agencies: A new consensus?' in J. Dunning (ed.), *Making Globalisation Good: The moral challenges of global capitalism* (Oxford: Oxford University Press, 2004), p. 320.

3. For an analysis of Blair's foreign policy and its close alignment with the neo-conservatism of George W. Bush, see S. Lee 'The Politics of Globalisation and the War on Terror,' in M. Mullard and B. Cole (ed.), *Globalisation, Citizenship and the War on Terror* (Cheltenham: Edward Elgar, 2007).

4. G. Brown, 'Governments and Supranational Agencies: A new consensus?' in J. Dunning (ed.), *Making Globalisation Good: The moral challenges of global capitalism* (Oxford: Oxford University Press, 2004), p. 320.

5. H. M. Treasury, *Tackling Poverty: A global new deal. A modern Marshall Plan for the developing world* (London: H. M. Treasury, 2002), p. 2.

6. G. Brown, 'Governments and Supranational Agencies: A new consensus?' in J. Dunning (ed.), *Making Globalisation Good: The moral challenges of global capitalism* (Oxford: Oxford University Press, 2004), p. 322.

7. Department for International Development, *Eliminating World Poverty: A challenge for the 21st century*, Cm. 3789 (London: The Stationery Office, 1997); Department for International Development, *Eliminating World Poverty: Making globalisation work for the poor*, Cm. 5006 (London: The Stationery Office, 2000); and Department for International Development, *Eliminating World Poverty: Making governance work for the poor*, Cm. 6876 (London: The Stationery Office, 2006).

8. Cabinet Office, *Ministerial Committees of the Cabinet and Policy Review Working Groups: Composition and terms of reference* (London: Cabinet Office, 2006), p. 35.

9. Ibid., pp. 54–55; and Commission for Africa, *Our Common Interest: Report of the Commission for Africa* (London: Commission for Africa, 2005).

10. N. Stern, *The Economics of Climate Change: The Stern Review* (London: H. M. Treasury and Cabinet Office, 2006). Stern had served as the Chief Economist

at the World Bank between 2000 and 2003 before becoming Second Permanent Secretary at the Treasury and Director of Policy and Research for the Commission for Africa.

11. International Monetary Fund, 'Interim Committee Selects UK's Brown as New Chairman,' *International Monetary Fund Press Release No.99/41*, 10 September 1999 (Washington DC: International Monetary Fund, 1999), p. 1.

12. International Monetary Fund, 'IMF Board of Governors Approves Transformation of Interim Committee,' *International Monetary Fund Press Release No.99/47*, 30 September 1999 (Washington DC: International Monetary Fund, 1999), p. 1.

13. United Nations, *Delivering as One: Report of the Secretary-General's high-level panel on UN system-wide coherence in the areas of development, humanitarian assistance and the environment* (New York: United Nations, 2006), p. 1.

14. Group of Eight (G8), *The Gleneagles Communiqué* (London: Group of Eight, 2005), pp. 15–28.

15. For a detailed analysis, critique and alternative to the 'Washington Consensus,' see S. Lee and S. McBride, 'Introduction: Neo-liberalism, state power and global governance in the twenty-first century,' and S. Lee and S. McBride, 'Conclusion: The need to rebuild the public domain,' in S. Lee and S. McBride (ed.), *Neo-Liberalism, State Power and Global Governance* (London: Springer-Verlag, 2007).

16. Group of Eight (G8), *The Birmingham Summit 15–17 May 1998 Communiqué* (Toronto: G8 Information Centre, 1998), p. 1.

17. H. M. Treasury, 'G7 Report on Strengthening the Architecture of the Global Financial System,' *H. M. Treasury Press Release 79/98*, 15 May 1998; H. M. Treasury, 'Seven Principles for Jobs: G8 agrees new agenda,' *H. M. Treasury Press Release 25/98*, 22 February 1998.

18. President John F. Kennedy, Inaugural Address to the American people, Capitol Building, Washington DC, 20 January 1961; M. Luther King, Jr., 'Remaining Awake Through a Great Revolution,' sermon delivered at the National Cathedral, Washington DC, 31 March 1968.

19. The poem appears in J. Stockinger, 'Locke and Rousseau: Human nature, human citizenship and human work,' unpublished PhD dissertation, Department of Sociology, University of California, Berkeley, 1990, cited in R. Bellah, R. Marsden, W. Sullivan, A. Swidler and S. Tipton, *The Good Society* (New York: Vintage Books, 1992), p. 104.

20. G. Brown, Gilbert Murray Memorial Lecture, Oxford, 11 January 2000.

21. Ibid.

22. This commitment had been embodied in World Bank, *The State in a Changing*

World: The 1997 World Development Report (New York: Oxford University Press, 1997).

23. World Commission on Environment and Development, *Our Common Future* (Oxford: Oxford University Press, 1987), p. 89.

24. United Nations, *Programme for the Further Implementation of Agenda 21: Adopted by the Special Session of the General Assembly,* 23–27 June 1997, published as Annex 4 of D. Osborn and T. Bigg, *Earth Summit II: Outcomes and analysis* (London: Earthscan, 1998), p. 144.

25. United Nations, *Report of the UN Secretary-General: Overall progress achieved since the United Nations Conference on Environment and Development,* E/CN.17/1997/Z, 31 January 1997, published as Annex 3 of D. Osborn and T. Bigg, *Earth Summit II: Outcomes and analysis* (London: Earthscan, 1998), p. 95.

26. For a critical perspective on the role of the Marshall Plan in fostering the Pax Americana, see C. Mee, *The Marshall Plan* (New York: Simon and Schuster, 1984). For an analysis of New Deal liberalism and its role in fostering both the inter-war New Deal and post-war international reconstruction, see A. Brinkley, *The End of Reform: New deal liberalism in recession and war* (New York: Vintage Books, 1996).

27. George C. Marshall, speech at Harvard University, Cambridge, Massachusetts, 5 June 1947.

28. For an analysis of the impact of the Marshall Plan on Britain during the Attlee Government, see H. Pelling, *Britain and the Marshall Plan* (London: Macmillan, 1988).

29. H. M. Treasury, *Tackling Poverty: A global new deal. A modern Marshall Plan for the developing world* (London: H. M. Treasury, 2002), pp. 1–2. This pamphlet was based on G. Brown, speech at the Federal Reserve, New York, 16 November 2001; and G. Brown, speech at the Press Club, Washington DC, 17 December 2001.

30. Ibid., p. 3.

31. Ibid., pp. 7–8.

32. United Nations Conference on Trade and Development, *World Investment Report 2001: Promoting linkages* (New York: United Nations, 2001), p. xiii.

33. United Nations Conference on Trade and Development, *World Investment Report 2006: FDI from developing and transition economies; implications for development* (New York: United Nations, 2006), p. xvii.

34. A detailed analysis of the demise of the Doha 'Development' Round of trade negotiations has been provided by The World Development Movement, *The Death of the Doha "Development" Round* (London: World Development Movement, 2006) and W. Bello, 'Why Today's Collapse of the Doha Round

Negotiations is the Best Outcome for Developing Countries,' *Focus on the Global South*, 25 July 2006, p. 1. The absence of a global consensus between Gordon Brown's advocacy of market liberalisation and Trade Justice campaigners' demands for an alternative approach to WTO negotiations can be gauged from the World Development Movement's Trade campaign briefings (available at http://www.wdm.org.uk/resources/briefings/trade/ index.htm).

35. International Monetary Fund, 'Interim Committee Selects UK's Brown as New Chairman,' *International Monetary Fund Press Release No.99/41*, 10 September 1999 (Washington DC: International Monetary Fund, 1999), p. 1.

36. International Monetary Fund, 'IMF Board of Governors Approves Transformation of Interim Committee,' *International Monetary Fund Press Release No.99/47*, 30 September 1999 (Washington DC: International Monetary Fund, 1999), p. 1.

37. International Monetary Fund, *Communiqué of the International Monetary and Financial Committee of the Board of Governors of the International Monetary Fund*, 16 April 2000 (Washington DC: International Monetary Fund, 2000), pp. 1, 6.

38. US Treasury, *Report on Implementation of Recommendations made by the International Financial Institutions Advisory Commission* (Washington DC: Office of Public Affairs, 2001), p. 2.

39. International Monetary Fund, *Articles of Agreement of the International Monetary Fund: Article I-purposes* (Washington DC: International Monetary Fund, 2007), p. 1.

40. For a detailed analysis of the economic dimension of the 'war on terror' and the Bush Administration's agenda for the World Bank and IMF, see S. Lee, 'Building Institutions for Freedom: The economic dimension of the "war on terror",' in M. Mullard and B. Cole (ed.), *Globalisation, Citizenship and the War on Terror* (Cheltenham: Edward Elgar, 2007).

41. International Monetary Fund, *Communiqué of the International Monetary and Financial Committee of the Board of Governors of the International Monetary Fund*, 29 April 2001 (Washington DC: International Monetary Fund, 2001), p. 2.

42. For a critical overview of the role of the IMF, see S. Lee, 'The International Monetary Fund,' *New Political Economy*, 7, 2, 2002, pp. 283–298.

43. Independent Evaluation Office, *Evaluation of Prolonged Use of IMF Resources* (Washington DC: International Monetary Fund, 2002).

44. Independent Evaluation Office, *Report on the Evaluation of the Role of the IMF in Argentina, 1991–2001* (Washington DC: International Monetary Fund, 2004), p. 6.

45. International Monetary Fund, *Communiqué of the International Monetary*

and Financial Committee of the Board of Governors of the International Monetary Fund, 16 April 2005 (Washington DC: International Monetary Fund, 2005), p. 3.

46. For a detailed and critical analysis of the role of the IMF in the governance of global financial markets, see S. Lee, 'Global Governance and the International Monetary Fund,' in G. Hook and H. Dobson (ed.), *Global Governance and Japan: The institutional architecture* (London: Routledge, 2007), pp. 126–142.

47. H. M. Treasury, *Tackling Poverty: A global new deal. A modern Marshall Plan for the developing world* (London: H. M. Treasury, 2002), p. 8.

48. Ibid., p. 34.

49. H. M. Treasury/Department for International Development, *International Finance Facility* (London: H. M. Treasury/Department for International Development, 2003), pp. 4–5.

50. G. Brown, speech to the Royal Institute for International Affairs/Chatham House Conference on 'Financing Sustainable Development, Poverty Reduction and the Private Sector: Financing common ground on the ground,' Chatham House, London, 22 January 2003.

51. H. M. Treasury/Department for International Development, *The International Finance Facility* (London H. M. Treasury/Department for International Development, 2005), p. 1.

52. Ibid., p. 14.

53. Ibid., p. 17.

54. For an explanation of why the Bush Administration has refused to back the IFF, see S. Lee, 'Building Institutions for Freedom: The economic dimension of the "war on terror",' in M. Mullard and B. Cole (ed.), *Globalisation, Citizenship and the War on Terror* (Cheltenham: Edward Elgar, 2007).

55. World Development Movement, *The International Finance Facility: Boon or burden for the poor?* (London: World Development Movement, 2005), pp. 5–6.

56. T. Moss, *Ten Myths of the International Finance Facility* (Washington DC: Centre for Global Development, 2005), p. 6.

57. Ibid., pp. 9–10.

58. The five formal objectives of the Commission are listed at Commission for Africa, 'Objectives of the Commission' (London: Commission for Africa, 2004). Available online: http://www.commissionforafrica.org/english/about/objectives.html (accessed 1 May 2007).

59. House of Commons International Development Committee, *The Commission for Africa and Policy Coherence for Development: First do no harm.* First Report of Session 2004–05, HC. 123 (London: The Stationery Office, 2005), p. 30.

60. ActionAid, 'ActionAid Turns Tables with an African Commission for Britain,' 23 February 2005. Available online: http://www.actionaid.org/pages.aspx? PageID=35&ItemID=53 (accessed 1 May 2007).

61. The Africa Commission for Britain identified ten actions that Britain must take to support Africa's development, including the cessation of export dumping and African countries being forced to open their markets; the cancellation of un-payable debts; the reduction of carbon emissions; the untying of economic policy conditions to aid; and ensuring access to free and comprehensive treatment for all people living with HIV and AIDS. The African Commission for Britain, *Ten Actions Britain Must Take to Support Africa's Development* (London: ActionAid International, 2005), p. 3.

62. Commission for Africa, *Our Common Interest: Report of the Commission for Africa* (London: Commission for Africa, 2005), pp. 60–79.

63. War on Want, 'Africa Commission Issues "Damning Indictment" of UK Policy,' 11 March 2005 (London: War on Want, 2005), p. 1.

64. Ibid., p. 285.

65. Department of Trade and Industry, *Making Globalisation a Force for Good*, Cm. 6278 (London: The Stationery Office, 2004).

66. World Development Movement, *Commission for Africa: WDM analysis of the final report* (London: World Development Movement, 2005), pp. 1–2.

67. Ibid., pp. 5–7. See Brandt Commission, *North-South: A programme for survival. Report of the Independent Commission on International Development Issues* (London: Pan Books, 1980); Brandt Commission, *Common Crisis. North-South: Co-operation for world recovery* (London: Pan Books, 1983).

68. Full details of the United Kingdom's priorities for its Presidency of the G8 and European Union are available from http://www.g8.co.uk and http://www.eu2005.gov.uk.

69. The Foreign Office, *The Gleneagles Communiqué* (London: The Foreign Office, 2005).

70. Organisation for Economic Co-operation and Development, 'Development Aid from OECD Countries Fell 5.1 per cent in 2006,' *OECD News Release*, 3 April 2007 (Paris: Organisation for Economic Co-operation and Development, 2007), pp. 1–2.

71. G. Brown, 'Our 2p Pledge to All Children,' *The Guardian*, 4 January 2007.

72. Africa Progress Panel, *Africa Progress Panel Communiqué* (London: Africa Progress Panel, 2007), pp. 1–6.

73. The World Can't Wait, *The World Can't Wait – For What?* (London: The World Can't Wait, 2007). Available online: http://www.yourvoiceagainstpoverty. org.uk/about-us/ (accessed 15 May 2007).

74. Christian Aid, *The Economics of Failure: The real cost of "free" trade for poor countries* (London: Christian Aid, 2005), p. 1.

75. World Development Movement, *Climate Calendar: The UK's unjust contribution to global climate change* (London: World Development Movement, 2007); P. Watt and T. Sharman, *The G8 summit in 2006* (London: ActionAid, 2006); ActionAid, *Delivering the 2010 Target: Financing universal access to HIV and AIDS treatment* (London: ActionAid, 2007), p. 1.

76. The World Bank, *Global Monitoring Report 2006* (Washington DC: The World Bank, 2006), p. xvii–xviii.

77. World Economic Forum, *Global Governance Initiative: Annual Report 2006* (Geneva: World Economic Forum, in partnership with The Centre for International Governance Innovation, 2006), pp. 5–6.

78. The World Bank, *Economic Growth in the 1990s: Learning from a decade of reform* (Washington DC: The World Bank, 2006), p. xii.

79. G. Brown, 'Foreword' to H. M. Treasury, *Meeting the Challenges of Globalisation for All: The UK and the IMF 2005* (London: H. M. Treasury, 2006), p. 3.

80. G. Brown, 'Foreword' to H. M. Treasury, *The UK and the IMF Report 2006: Reform to deliver prosperity for all* (London: H. M. Treasury, 2007), p. 1.

81. G. Brown, oral evidence, 11 May 2006, to the House of Commons Treasury Committee, *Globalisation: The role of the IMF. Ninth Report of Session 2005–06*, HC. 875 (London: The Stationery Office, 2006) Ev.37, answer to Q.164.

82. See, for example, the written and oral evidence given to the House of Commons Treasury Committee, *Globalisation: The role of the IMF. Ninth Report of Session 2005–06*, HC. 875 (London: The Stationery Office, 2006). For an analysis of the critique of the IMF's role, see S. Lee, 'Global Governance and the International Monetary Fund,' in G. Hook and H. Dobson (ed.), *Global Governance and Japan: The institutional architecture* (London: Routledge, 2007), pp. 126–142.

83. G. Brown, 'Foreword' to H. M. Treasury, *The UK and the IMF Report 2006: Reform to deliver prosperity for all* (London: H. M. Treasury, 2007), p. 1.

84. J. F. Kennedy, remarks in Naples at NATO Headquarters, 2 July 1963, in *John F. Kennedy: Public papers of the Presidents of the United States* (Washington DC: United States Government Printing Office, 1963), p. 552.

85. Ibid., pp. 550–551.

86. Debate on Iraq, *Hansard*, 18 March 2003, c. 911.

87. BBC, 'Brown Makes First Visit to Iraq,' *BBC News*, 18 November 2006.

88. Mark Oliver, 'Brown Surprises Troops in Afghanistan,' *The Guardian*, 30 March 2007.

89. H. M. Treasury, *Modern Public Services for Britain: Investing in reform. Comprehensive spending review: New public spending plans 1999–2002*, Cm. 4011 (London: The Stationery Office, 1998), paras 14.3–14.5.

90. H. M. Treasury, *Prudent for a Purpose: Building opportunity and security for all. New public spending plans for 2001–2004* (London: The Stationery Office, 2000), p. 1.

91. G. Brown, 'Statement by the Chancellor of the Exchequer on the 2002 Spending Review,' *Hansard*, 15 July 2002, cc. 21–30.

92. Ibid.

93. H. M. Treasury, *Steering a Steady Course: Delivering stability, enterprise and fairness in an uncertain world. Pre-budget report 2002* (London: The Stationery Office, 2002), p. 1.

94. 'Soft power' is the term coined by the American political scientist, Joseph Nye, to denote 'the ability to get what you want through attraction rather than coercion or payments.' Nye has argued that the soft power of a country rests primarily on its culture, its political values and its foreign policies. Hard power, by contrast, refers to military and economic might. See J. Nye, *Soft Power: The means to success in world politics* (New York: Public Affairs, 2004), pp. x, 11.

95. G. Brown, 'Budget Statement,' *Hansard*, 9 April 2003; G. Brown, 'Pre-Budget Report Statement,' *Hansard*, 10 December 2003, cc. 1061–1086.

96. H. M. Treasury, 'Further boost for Britain's armed forces,' *H. M. Treasury Press Notice A7*, 12 July 2004.

97. G. Brown, 'Securing Our Future,' speech at the Royal United Services Institute, London, 13 February 2006.

98. H. M. Treasury, *Long-Term Opportunities and Challenges for the UK: Analysis for the 2007 Comprehensive Spending Review* (London: The Stationery Office, 2006), pp. 105–107.

99. G. Brown, 'Securing Our Future,' speech at the Royal United Services Institute, London, 13 February 2006.

100. G. Brown, 'Meeting the Terrorist Challenge,' speech at Chatham House, London, 10 October 2006.

101. Ibid.

102. G. Brown, 'Meeting the Terrorist Challenge,' speech at Chatham House, London, 10 October 2006.

103. D. Acheson, speech at the Military Academy, West Point, 5 December 1962.

104. BBC, 'Trident Plan Wins Commons Support,' *BBC News*, 18 May 2005.

105. Labour Party, 'Gordon Brown is the Candidate for Leader of the Labour Party,' 18 May 2007. Available online: http://www.labour.org.uk/leadership/Gordon_brown123 (accessed 18 May 2007).

106. G. Brown, transcript of interview with Andrew Marr for the Sunday AM pro-
     gramme, 7 January 2007. Available online: http://www.bbc.co.uk/go/pr/fr/-
     /1/hi/uk_politics/6241819.stm (accessed 8 January 2007).

107. G. Brown, answer given at the Fabian Society Leadership Hustings, Institute
     of Education, London, 13 May 2007.

108. Office of the Prime Minister, 'UK forces to leave Iraq in 2009 – PM', 17
     December 2008.

109. G. Brown, transcript of interview with Andrew Marr for the Sunday AM pro-
     gramme, 7 January 2007. Available online: http://www.bbc.co.uk/go/pr/fr/-
     /1/hi/uk_politics/6241819.stm (accessed 8 January 2007).

110. D. Cameron, 'A new approach to foreign affairs: liberal conservatism', Annual
     J. P. Morgan Lecture at the British American Project, 11 September 2006.

111. Greenspan had served as Chairman of the Federal Reserve Board and was
     invited by Brown to Kirkcaldy in 2006 to deliver the annual Adam Smith
     Lecture. Robert Rubin and Larry Summers had served the Clinton
     Administration, Rubin between January 1993 and July 1999 as Director of the
     National Economic Council and Treasury Secretary (from January 1995) and
     Summers as Rubin's successor as Treasury Secretary until 2001.

112. D. Miliband, interview, *The Financial Times*, 9 July 2007.

113. D. Miliband, 'New diplomacy: challenges for foreign policy', speech at the Royal
     Institute of International Affairs, Chatham House, London, 19 July 2007.

114. Ibid.

115. For an analysis of Robin Cook's 'ethical dimension' and Tony Blair's 'doctrine
     of international community', see S. Lee, 'The politics of globalisation and the
     war on terrror', in M. Mullard and B. Cole (eds), *Globalisation, Citizenship
     and the War on Terror* (Cheltenham: Edward Elgar, 2007).

116. D. Miliband, 'New diplomacy: challenges for foreign policy', speech at the
     Royal Institute of International Affairs, Chatham House, London, 19 July
     2007.

117. M. Malloch Brown, United Nations Deputy Secretary-General, 'Power and
     super-power: global leadership in the twenty-first century', address to the
     Century Foundation and Centre for American Progress, New York, 7 June
     2006.

118. United States Department of State, 'UN official's remarks a "grave mistake",
     US's Bolton Says', 7 June 2006 (Washington DC: United States Department of
     State, 2006).

119. R. Sylvester and A. Thomson, 'Mark Malloch Brown: "Let's not just rely on
     US', *The Daily Telegraph*, 14 July 2007.

120. D. Alexander, speech delivered at the Council on Foreign Relations,
     Washington DC, 12 July 2007.

121. D. Browne, statement on CSR and Aircraft Carriers, *Hansard*, 25 July 2007, cc. 865–867. The 'warfare state' is frequently deployed as a convenient shorthand for that part of the institutional architecture of the British state that is devoted to the management of the armed forces, military strategy and procurement and defence industrial policy. For a detailed analysis of the role of the warfare state in British grand strategy during the twentieth century, see D. Edgerton, *Warfare State. Britain, 1920–1970* (Cambridge: Cambridge University Press, 2006).

122. D. Browne, statement on Ballistic Missile Defence, *Hansard*, 25 July 2007, cc. 72–73.

123. G. Brown, Kennedy Memorial Lecture, John F. Kennedy Presidential Library and Museum, Boston, Massachusetts, 18 April 2008.

124. G. Brown, speech at the Lord Mayor's Banquet, London, 12 November 2007.

125. Ibid.

126. G. Brown, Kennedy Memorial Lecture, John F. Kennedy Presidential Library and Museum, Boston, Massachusetts, 18 April 2008.

127. Ibid.

128. B. Obama, *The Audacity of Hope: Thoughts on Reclaiming the American Dream* (New York: Crown Publications, 2006), p. 320.

129. For an analysis of Blair's foreign policy and why he has so closely aligned himself with the neo-conservatism of George W. Bush, see S. Lee 'The Politics of Globalisation and the War on Terror,' in M. Mullard and B. Cole (ed.), *Globalisation, Citizenship and the War on Terror* (Cheltenham: Edward Elgar, 2007).

130. G. Brown, speech at the Confederation of Indian Industry, Bangalore, 17 January 2007.

131. Ibid.

132. Ibid.

CHAPTER 7

1. European Commission, *Communication from the Commission to the Council, the European Parliament, the European Economic and Social Committee and the Committee of the Regions: The Commission's contribution to the period of reflection and beyond: Plan-D for Democracy, Dialogue and Debate,* COM (2005) 494 final (Brussels: Commission of the European Communities, 2005), p. 2.

2. G. Brown, 'Global Britain, Global Europe: A Presidency founded on pro-European realism,' speech at the Mansion House, London, 22 June 2005.

3. A. Rawnsley, 'In France it's Under Constitution Blairiste,' *The Observer*, 31 October 2004.

4. 'Whether Paid in Sterling or Euro, Honda is Here to Stay,' *Financial Times*, 23 May 2007.

5. European Commission, *Communication from the Commission to the European Council: A citizens' agenda. Delivering results for Europe*, COM (2006) 211 final (Brussels: Commission of the European Communities, 2006), p. 2.

6. European Commission, *Communication from the Commission to the Council, the European Parliament, the European Economic and Social Committee and the Committee of The Regions: The Commission's contribution to the period of reflection and beyond: Plan-D for Democracy, Dialogue and Debate*, COM (2005) 494 final (Brussels: Commission of the European Communities, 2005), p. 3; European Commission, *Communication from the Commission to the European Council: A citizens' agenda. Delivering results for Europe*, COM (2006) 211 final (Brussels: Commission of the European Communities, 2006), p. 2.

7. H. Young, *This Blessed Plot: Britain and Europe from Churchill to Blair* (London: Macmillan, 1998), p. 1.

8. A. Gamble, *Between Europe and America: The future of British politics* (Houndmills: Palgrave Macmillan, 2003), p. 1.

9. Ibid., p. 230.

10. W. Hutton, *The World We're in* (London: Little Brown, 2002), p. 2.

11. J. Delors, speech to the Trades Union Congress, Brighton, 8 September 1988.

12. Labour Party, *It's Time to Get Britain Working Again: Labour's election manifesto* (London: The Labour Party, 1992, p. 27.

13. For a more detailed analysis of the events of 'Black Wednesday,' see P. Stephens, *Politics and the Pound: The Conservatives' struggle with Sterling* (London: Macmillan, 1996).

14. G. Brown, 'Europe Still the Answer,' *Tribune*, 25 September 1992, p. 8.

15. P. Anderson, 'New Economics. The Tribune Interview: Gordon Brown,' *Tribune*, 1 January 1993, p. 5.

16. E. Balls, *Euro-Monetarism: Why Britain was ensnared and how it should escape* (London: The Fabian Society, 1992), p. 10.

17. Ibid., p. 23.

18. P. Anderson, 'New Economics. The Tribune Interview: Gordon Brown,' *Tribune*, 1 January 1993, p. 5.

19. Labour Party, *A New Economic Future for Britain: Economic and employment opportunities for all* (London: The Labour Party, 1995), pp. 4–5.

20. Labour Party, *Economic Renewal in the European Union: The UK Labour party*

and the Delors white paper on growth, competitiveness and employment (London: The Labour Party, 1994), p. 1.

21. Labour Party, *New Labour: Because Britain deserves better* (London: The Labour Party, 1997), p. 37.

22. Ibid., pp. 37–38.

23. The Labour Party's agenda for the UK Presidency of the EU during the first half of 1998 were: rapid completion of the single market; EU enlargement with the requisite institutional reforms; urgent reform of the Common Agricultural Policy; greater openness and democracy in EU institutions; retention of the national veto over key matters of national interest such as taxation and budgetary matters, immigration, defence and security; and a British signature on the Social Chapter, Ibid., p. 37.

24. G. Brown, 'Britain Leading in Europe,' speech to the Royal Institute for International Affairs, Chatham House, London, 17 July 1997.

25. Ibid.

26. Ibid.

27. MORI, *Attitudes to Europe in Great Britain, 13–14 November* (London: Market Opinion Research International, 1997).

28. Ibid.

29. G. Brown, 'Statement on European Monetary Union,' 27 October 1997, cc. 583–588.

30. H. M. Treasury, *UK Membership of the Single Currency: An assessment of the Five Economic Tests* (London: H. M. Treasury, 1997), pp. 5–6.

31. G. Brown, 'Statement on European Monetary Union,' 27 October 1997, cc. 583–588.

32. Ibid.

33. T. Blair, *New Britain: My vision of a young country* (London: Fourth Estate, 1996), p. 283.

34. D. Scott, *Off Whitehall: A view from Downing Street by Tony Blair's adviser* (London: I. B. Taurus, 2004), p. 23.

35. *The Times*, 17 October 1997; *The Sun*, 17 October 1997.

36. A. Rawnsley, *Servants of the People: The inside story of New Labour* (London: Penguin Books, 2001), p. 83.

37. A. Rawnsley, 'What Blair Really Thinks of Brown,' *The Observer*, 18 January 1998.

38. H. M. Treasury, 'Getting Europe to Work: Building a strong European economy. Chancellor launches UK Action Plan to create lasting jobs in Europe,' 4 June 1997; H. M. Treasury, 'Chancellor Publishes Business Guide to Single Currency,' 24 July 1997.

39. A. Rawnsley, *Servants of the People: The inside story of New Labour* (London: Penguin Books, 2001), pp. 235–236.

40. For a more detailed account of the political machinations between Brown and Blair over EMU, see R. Peston, *Brown's Britain* (London: Short Books, 2005), pp. 178–245, and T. Bower, *Gordon Brown* (London: HarperCollins, 2004), pp. 247–252, 313–317.

41. Labour Party, *Ambitions for Britain: Labour's manifesto 2001* (London: The Labour Party, 2001), p. 13.

42. T. Blair, *Hansard*, 7 February 2001, c. 918.

43. The eighteen EMU studies that comprise the Treasury's assessment of United Kingdom membership of the single currency are available online: http://www. hm-treasury.gov.uk/documents/international_issues/the_euro/assessment/ report/euro_assess03_repindex.cfm (accessed 21 May 2007).

44. G. Brown, speech at the Mansion House, City of London, 20 June 2001.

45. E. Balls, 'Why The Five Economic Tests?,' The 2002 Alec Cairncross Lecture, Oxford, 4 December 2002.

46. H. M. Treasury, *UK Membership of the Single Currency: An assessment of the Five Economic Tests*, Cm. 5776 (London: The Stationery Office, 2003), p. 6.

47. G. Brown, 'Statement on Economic and Monetary Union,' 9 June 2003, cc. 407–415.

48. Ibid.

49. E. Balls, 'Stability, Growth and UK Fiscal Policy,' The Inaugural Ken Dixon Lecture, Department of Economics, University of York, 23 January 2004.

50. Ibid.

51. Ibid.

52. H. M. Treasury, *Fiscal Stabilisation and EMU: A discussion paper* (London: H. M. Treasury, 2003).

53. E. Balls, 'Stability, Growth and UK Fiscal Policy,' The Inaugural Ken Dixon Lecture, Department of Economics, University of York, 23 January 2004.

54. Ibid.

55. Ibid.

56. Ibid.

57. European Council, 'Presidency Conclusions, Lisbon European Council, 23–24 March,' *Press Release* (Brussels: Commission of the European Communities, 2000), p. 1.

58. Ibid., p. 1.

59. Ibid., p. 2.

60. Ibid., p. 2.

61. Ibid., pp. 5, 7, 9, 11.

62. This trend was deepened by the publication of the updated version of the EU's post-Lisbon agenda for innovation policy which noted the importance for long-term growth of increasing investment in R&D towards three per cent of

GDP, *European Commission, Fostering Structural Change: An industrial policy for an enlarged Europe*, COM (2004) 274 final (Brussels: Commission of the European Communities, 2004), p. 4. This closely paralleled the trajectory of Treasury policy under Gordon Brown who had identified similar targets for the United Kingdom.

63. European Commission, *Towards Enterprise Europe: Work programme for enterprise policy 2000–2005*, SEC (2000) 771 (Brussels: Commission of European Communities, 2000), pp. 2–3.

64. European Commission, *Challenges for Enterprise Policy in the Knowledge-Driven Economy: Proposal for a Council decision on a multinational programme for enterprise and entrepreneurship (2001–2005)*, COM (2000) 256 final/2 (Brussels: Commission of the European Communities, 2000), p. 4.

65. European Commission, *Action Plan: The European agenda for entrepreneurship*, COM (2004) 70 final (Brussels: Commission of the European Communities, 2004), p. 4.

66. H. M. Treasury, *European Economic Reform: Meeting the challenge* (London: H. M. Treasury, 2001); H. M. Treasury, *Realising Europe's Potential: Economic reform in Europe* (London: H. M. Treasury, 2002); H. M. Treasury, *Meeting the Challenge: Economic reform in Europe* (London: H. M. Treasury, 2003); H. M. Treasury, *Advancing Long-Term Prosperity: Economic reform in an enlarged Europe* (London: H. M. Treasury, 2004); H. M. Treasury, *Growth and Opportunity: Prioritising economic reform in Europe* (London: H. M. Treasury, 2005).

67. G. Brown, speech at the Confederation of British Industry Conference on 'Competitiveness in Europe-Post Enlargement,' 12 May 2004.

68. Ibid.

69. Ibid.

70. Ibid.

71. Ibid.

72. Ibid.

73. G. Brown, *Global Europe: Full-employment Europe* (London: H. M. Treasury, 2005), p. 1.

74. Ibid., pp. 1–2.

75. Ibid., pp. 7–8.

76. Ibid., pp. 8–9.

77. Ibid., p. 10.

78. Ibid., p. 10.

79. Ibid., p. 11.

80. Ibid., p. 12.

81. Ibid., p. 12.

82. Ibid., p. 13.
83. Ibid., pp. 13–14.
84. Ibid., p. 15.
85. Ibid., p. 3.
86. G. Brown, 'Global Britain, Global Europe: A Presidency founded on pro-European realism,' speech at the Mansion House, London, 22 June 2005.
87. Ibid.
88. Cabinet Office, *Ministerial Committees of the Cabinet and Policy Review Working Groups: Composition and terms of reference* (London: Cabinet Office, 2006), pp. 27–28.
89. See for example, H. M. Treasury, *The Case for Open Markets: How increased competition can equip Europe for global change* (London: H. M. Treasury, 2006).
90. H. M. Treasury/Department of Trade and Industry, *The Single Market: A vision for the 21st century* (London: The Stationery Office, 2007), p. 3.
91. Ibid., p. 3.
92. Ibid., p. 4.
93. Ibid., p. 12.
94. Ibid., p. 19.
95. Ibid., p. 23.
96. Ibid., p. 39.
97. E. Balls, *Britain and Europe: A City minister's perspective* (London: Centre for European Reform, 2007), p. 3.
98. Ibid., p. 4.
99. Ibid., pp. 21, 39.
100. D. Miliband, 'New Diplomacy: Challenges for Foreign Policy,' speech at the Royal Institute of International Affairs, Chatham House, London, 19 July 2007.
101. G. Brown, 'Foreword' to Foreign and Commonwealth Office, *The Reform Treaty: The British approach to the European Union Intergovernmental Conference,* July 2007, Cm. 7174 (London: The Stationery Office, 2007), p. 1.
102. Ibid., p. 1.
103. G. Brown, statement to Parliament on European Council, 22 October 2007; G. Brown, EU Council media briefing, London, 18 October 2007.
104. Office of the Prime Minister, '"Red lines secured" – PM', London, 19 October 2007.
105. G. Brown, statement prior to signing of EU Treaty, 13 December 2007.
106. D. Cameron, 'The EU – A New Agenda for the 21st Century,' speech at the Movement for European Reform conference, Brussels, 6 March 2007.
107. M. Thatcher, speech to the College of Europe, Bruges, 20 September 1988.

CHAPTER 8

1. G. Brown, Pre-Budget Report Statement, 25 November 1997.
2. The claim that there would no longer be 'boom and bust' was made, for example, in G. Brown, speech to the Labour Party Conference, Brighton, 27 September 2004; speech to the Labour Party Conference, Brighton, 26 September 2005; and G. Brown, Budget Statement, 22 March 2006.
3. G. Brown, speech at the Lord Mayor's Banquet, Mansion House, London, 21 June 2006.
4. G. Brown, speech at the Lord Mayor's Banquet, Mansion House, London, 20 June 2007.
5. Office for National Statistics, *Gross Domestic Product: Preliminary Estimate – 4th Quarter 2008* (Newport: Office for National Statistics, 2009), p. 1.
6. Office for National Statistics, *Public Sector Finances: December 2008* (Newport: Office for National Statistics, 2009), pp. 1–4.
7. Institute for Fiscal Studies, *The IFS Green Budget January 2009* (London: Institute for Fiscal Studies, 2009), p. 2.
8. Office for National Statistics, *Gross Domestic Product: Preliminary Estimate – 4th Quarter 2008* (Newport: Office for National Statistics, 2009), p. 1.
9. Office for National Statistics, *Labour Market Statistics: January 2009* (Newport: Office for National Statistics, 2009), p. 1.
10. Office for National Statistics, *Consumer Price Indices: December 2008* (Newport: Office for National Statistics, 2009), p. 1.
11. Council of Mortgage Lenders, 'Gross mortgage lending declines in December', 21 January (London: Council of Mortgage Lenders, 2009); Nationwide, 'New Year sees little change to recent house price trend', *Nationwide House Prices*, 29 January (London: Nationwide, 2009).
12. International Monetary Fund, 'IMF Executive Board Concludes 2005 Article IV Consultation with the United Kingdom', *Public Information Notice No. 06/24, 3 March* (Washington DC: International Monetary Fund, 2006).
13. International Monetary Fund, *World Economic Outlook: January 28 2009* (Washington DC: International Monetary Fund, 2009), p. 6.
14. YouGov, *YouGov Sunday Times Survey Results, 9–10 August 2007* (London: YouGov, 2007).
15. Ipsos MORI, *Voting Intention, 26 September 2007: Poll for The Observer* (London: Ipsos MORI, 2007); YouGov, *Telegraph YouGov poll: Labour Lead Conservatives, 26–28 September 2007, The Daily Telegraph*, 1 October 2007; YouGov, *YouGov Survey Results, 24–26 September 2007* (London: YouGov, 2007); and Populus, *Voting Intention, 26–27 September 2007: Poll published by The Times* (London: Populus, 2007).

16. For a detailed analysis of developments at Northern Rock, see House of Commons Treasury Committee, *The Run on the Rock. Fifth Report of Session 2007-08, Volume 1, HC. 56-I* (London: The Stationery Office, 2007).

17. G. Osborne, 'It's time for aspiration', speech to the Conservative Party Conference, Blackpool, 1 October 2007.

18. During an appearance on the BBC's Andrew Marr Show, Brown stated 'I'll not be calling an election. I have a vision for change in Britain and I want to show people how in government we're implementing it'. G. Brown, transcript of an interview with Andrew Marr for the Andrew Marr Show, 7 October 2007.

19. G. Brown, *Downing Street Press Conference – 8 October 2007*. Available online: http://www.number10.gov.uk/Page13457 (accessed 30 January 2009).

20. G. Brown, speech to the Labour Party Conference, Manchester, 23 September 2008.

21. G. Brown, speech to the Labour Party Conference, Bournemouth, 23 September 2007.

22. V. Cable, 'Questions to the Prime Minister', *Hansard*, 28 November 2007, c. 275.

23. G. Brown, Budget Statement, 21 March 2007.

24. S. Adam, M. Brewer and R. Chote, *The 10% Tax Rate: Where Next?* (London: Institute for Fiscal Studies, 2008), p. 12.

25. D. Miliband, 'We can win the election', *New Statesman*, 22 September 2008.

26. A. Darling, Budget Statement, 12 March 2008.

27. H. M. Treasury, *Budget 2007. Building Britain's Long-Term Future: Prosperity and fairness for families*. Economic and Fiscal Strategy Report and Financial Statement and Budget Report, HC. 342 (London: The Stationery Office, 2007), pp. 20–21.

28. A. Darling, 2007 Pre-Budget Report and Comprehensive Spending Review Statement, 9 October 2007.

29. A. Darling, Budget Statement, 12 March 2008.

30. S. Adam, M. Brewer and R. Chote, *The 10% Tax Rate: Where Next?* (London: Institute for Fiscal Studies, 2008), p. 1.

31. Office for National Statistics, *Public sector finances: September 2008* (Newport: Office for National Statistics, 2008), p. 1.

32. Institute for Fiscal Studies, *Public Finance Bulletin: October 2008* (London: Institute for Fiscal Studies, 2008), p. 2.

33. Office for National Statistics, *Public Sector Finances: January 2009* (Newport: Office for National Statistics, 2009), p. 4.

34. Institute for Fiscal Studies, *Public Finance Bulletin: October 2008* (London: Institute for Fiscal Studies, 2008), p. 3.

35. Ibid.

36. International Monetary Fund, *United Kingdom – 1999 Article IV Consultation* (Washington DC: International Monetary Fund, 1999), p. 2.

37. International Monetary Fund, *IMF Concludes Consultation with the United Kingdom: Public Information Notice No. 00/17* (Washington DC: International Monetary Fund, 2000), p. 4.

38. International Monetary Fund, *United Kingdom: 2000 Article IV Consultation: IMF Country Report No. 01/42* (Washington DC: International Monetary Fund, 2001), pp. 13, 23.

39. International Monetary Fund, *IMF Concludes 2002 Article IV Consultation with the United Kingdom: Public Information Notice No. 03/22* (Washington DC: International Monetary Fund), p. 2.

40. International Monetary Fund, *United Kingdom: 2006 Article IV Consultation: IMF Country Report No.07/91* (Washington DC: International Monetary Fund, 2007), p. 14.

41. See G. Brown, *Global Europe: Full-Employment Europe* (London: Her Majesty's Treasury, 2005); G. Brown, speech at the Lord Mayor's Banquet, Mansion House, London, 20 June 2007; E. Balls, *Britain and Europe: A City Minister's Perspective* (London: Centre for European Reform, 2007); and E. Balls, speech at the FSA Principles-Based Regulation Conference, London, 23 April 2007.

42. E. Balls, 'The City as the global finance centre: risk and opportunities', speech at Bloomberg, City of London, 14 June 2006.

43. G. Brown, Pre-Budget Report Statement, 6 December 2006.

44. International Monetary Fund, *Staff Report for the 2008 Article IV Consultation: IMF Country Report No. 08/271* (Washington DC: International Monetary Fund 2008), p. 52.

45. Ibid., p. 53.

46. G. Brown, transcript of press conference with the Chancellor of the Exchequer, 8 October (London: Prime Minister's Office, 2008).

47. Ibid.

48. A. Darling, Pre-Budget Report Statement, 24 November 2008.

49. G. Brown and A. Darling, transcript of press conference given by the Prime Minister and the Chancellor of the Exchequer, London, 8 October 2008.

50. H. M. Government, *The Road to the London Summit: The Plan for Recovery* (London: Her Majesty's Government, 2009).

51. A. Darling, statement on financial intervention to support lending in the economy, 19 January 2009.

52. Ibid.

53. A. Darling, statement on the Asset Protection Scheme, 20 February 2009.

54. Office for National Statistics, *Classification of Royal Bank of Scotland Group plc*

and Lloyds Banking Group plc (Newport: Office for National Statistics, 2009), p. 1.

55. H. Power, 'Lloyd's locked in Treasury row over debt deal', *The Times*, 27 February 2009.

56. G. Osborne, Banking (Asset Protection Scheme), *Hansard*, 26 February 2009, c. 370.

57. V. Cable, Banking (Asset Protection Scheme), *Hansard*, 26 February 2009, cc. 373–374.

58. G. Brown, transcript of interview by the Prime Minister with the BBC *Politics Show*, 23 November 2008.

59. G. Brown and A. Darling, transcript of press conference given by the Prime Minister and the Chancellor of the Exchequer, London, 8 October 2008.

60. G. Brown and A. Darling, transcript of press conference given by the Prime Minister and the Chancellor of the Exchequer, London, 8 October 2008.

61. A. Darling, 'The era of risk is over; what we now demand of banks is responsibility', *The Daily Telegraph*, 7 February 2009.

62. A. Darling, 'We won't pay for bankers' one-way bets', *The Times*, 18 February 2009.

63. Ibid.

64. G. Brown, speech to Labour Party National Policy Forum, Bristol, 28 February 2009.

65. Ibid.

66. G. Brown, 'We will put people first, not bankers', *The Observer*, 22 February 2009.

67. BBC, 'Sir James Crosby resigns from FSA', *BBC News*, 22 February 2009.

68. L. Elliott and J. Treanor, 'Darling kept in dark as FSA lifted ban on short-selling', *The Guardian*, 22 January 2009.

69. G. Brown, transcript of press conference given by the Prime Minister and Chancellor of the Exchequer, Washington DC, 15 November 2008; G. Brown, speech to the Council of Foreign Relations, New York, 14 November 2008.

70. G. Brown, speech given by the Prime Minister at the Employment Summit, London, 12 January 2009.

71. A. Greenspan, Adam Smith Memorial Lecture, Kirkcaldy, 6 February 2005.

72. A. Greenspan, *The Age of Turbulence: Adventures in a New World* (London: Allen Lane, 2007), pp. 489–490.

73. A. Greenspan, testimony on 'The Financial Crisis and The Role of Federal Regulators', before the House of Representatives, Committee on Oversight and Government Reform, Washington DC, 23 October 2008, cc. 768–772.

74. Ibid., cc. 854–856, 860–863.

75. G. Brown and A. Darling, transcript of press conference given by the Prime Minister and the Chancellor of the Exchequer, London, 8 October 2008.

76. S. Theli, '"It Doesn't Exist!" Germany's outspoken finance minister on the hopeless search for "The Great Rescue Plan"', *Newsweek*, 15 December 2008.

77. G. Brown, transcript of press conference given by the Prime Minister and the Chancellor of the Exchequer, Washington DC, 15 November 2008.

78. G. Brown, speech to the Confederation of British Industry annual conference, London, 24 November 2008.

79. G. Brown, speech to the Council of Foreign Relations, New York, 14 November 2008.

80. G. Brown, 'Rediscovering Public Purpose in the Global Economy', Kennedy School, Harvard University, 15 December 1998.

81. G. Brown, transcript of press conference given by the Prime Minister at the Financial Reform Summit, Brussels, 7 November 2008.

82. G. Brown, transcript of press conference given by the Prime Minister, London, 19 December 2008.

83. Ibid.

84. G. Brown, transcript of press conference given by the Prime Minister and the Chancellor of the Exchequer, Washington DC, 15 November 2008.

85. G. Brown, transcript of a press conference given by the Prime Minister at the Financial Reform Summit, Brussels, 7 November 2008.

86. E. Balls, J. Grice and G. O'Donnell (eds), *Microeconomic Reform in Britain: Delivering Opportunities for All* (London: Palgrave Macmillan, 2004), pp. 6, 8.

87. International Monetary Fund, *Interim Committee Selects UK's Brown as New Chairman: Press Release No. 99/41*, 10 September (Washington DC: International Monetary Fund, 1999).

88. G. Brown, speech on the global economy, Reuters Building, London, 13 October 2008.

CHAPTER 9

1. Office for National Statistics, *Labour Market Statistics: February 2009* (Newport: Office for National Statistics, 2009), p. 1.

2. G. Brown, speech to the Confederation of British Industry annual conference, 24 November 2008.

3. M. King, speech given to an East Midlands Development Agency/Bank of England dinner, Leicester, 14 October 2003; Sir J. Gieve, 'Seven lessons from the last three years', speech given at the London School of Economics, London, 19 February 2009.

4. E. Balls, speech to Labour Party activists, Sheffield, 14 February 2009.

5. Institute for Fiscal Studies, *The IFS Green Budget January 2009* (London: Institute for Fiscal Studies, 2009).

6. House of Commons Treasury Committee, *Minutes of Evidence for Thursday 18 July 2002: Rt. Hon Gordon Brown MP, Mr Ed Balls, Mr Nicholas Macpherson and Mr Adam Sharples (HM Treasury)*, HC. 1092-ii, Session 2001–2002 (London: The Stationery Office, 2002), cc. 236–237.

7. International Monetary Fund, *World Economic Outlook: January 28 2009* (Washington DC: International Monetary Fund, 2009), pp. 1, 6.

8. R. Chote, 'Debt burden could remain until 2030s', *The Independent*, 29 January 2009.

9. Ibid.

10. Institute for Fiscal Studies, 'IFS analysis of today's public finance figures', *IFS Press Release*, 19 February 2009.

11. M. Brewer, A. Goodman, A. Muriel and L. Sibieta, *Poverty and Inequality in the UK: 2007* (London: Institute for Fiscal Studies, 2007), p. 1.

12. Office for National Statistics, *Social Trends No. 37: 2007 Edition* (London: Office for National Statistics, 2007), p. 70.

13. D. Dorling, J. Rigby, B. Wheeler, D. Ballas, B. Thomas, E. Fahmy, D. Gordon and R. Lupton, *Poverty, Wealth and Place in Britain, 1968 to 2005* (York: Joseph Rowntree Foundation, 2007), p. xiii.

14. Ibid., p. xiii.

15. Ibid., p. 2.

16. Institute for Fiscal Studies, *Micro-Simulating Child Poverty in 2010 and 2020* (London: Institute for Fiscal Studies, 2009), p. 1.

17. Ibid., p. 6.

18. Joseph Rowntree Foundation, *Poverty, Inequality and Policy since 1997* (York: Joseph Rowntree Foundation, 2009), p. 1.

19. Ibid., p. 1.

20. Ibid., p. 1.

21. Ibid., p. 2.

22. T. Blair, *Let Us Face the Future: The 1945 Anniversary Lecture* (London: The Fabian Society, 1995), pp. 13, 20.

23. D. Cameron, 'Modern Conservatism', speech at Demos, London, 30 January 2006.

24. YouGov, *YouGov/Daily Telegraph Survey Results, 27–28 January 2009* (London: YouGov, 2009).

25. Ipsos MORI, *Ipsos MORI February Political Monitor: 13–15 February 2009* (London: Ipsos MORI, 2009).

26. J. Glover, 'Brown affecting Labour's chances as Guardian poll shows Lib Dem gain', *The Guardian*, 23 February 2009.

27. Sir K. Joseph, *Stranded on the Middle Ground: Reflections on Circumstances and Policies* (London: Centre for Policy Studies, 1976), pp. 27–33.

28. D. Cameron, 'A liberal Conservative consensus to restore trust in politics', speech, Bath, 22 March 2007; D. Cameron, 'A new approach to foreign affairs: liberal conservatism', annual J. P. Morgan Lecture at the British American Project, 11 September 2006.

29. D. Cameron, 'A liberal Conservative consensus to restore trust in politics', speech, Bath, 22 March 2007.

30. D. Cameron, 'Foreword' to Conservative Party, *Built to Last: The Aims and Values of the Conservative Party* (London: Conservative Party, 2006), p. 3.

31. This thesis has been developed by S. Jenkins, *Thatcher and Sons: A Revolution in Three Acts* (London: Allen Lane, 2006).

32. D. Cameron, 'Modern Conservatism', speech at Demos, London, 30 January 2006.

33. Ibid.

34. Ibid.

35. D. Cameron, 'The need for public service reform', speech at Portsmouth, 9 September 2005.

36. Ibid.

37. G. Osborne, 'Only Conservatives can maintain public service reform', speech to Policy Exchange, London, 30 May 2007.

38. G. Brown, 'My moral beacon', *New Statesman and Society*, 30 April 2007; G. Brown, 'Robert Kennedy', in G. Brown, *Courage: Eight Portraits* (London: Bloomsbury, 2007), p. 115.

39. R. F. Kennedy, 'What do we stand for? The liberation of the human spirit', speech to the Commonwealth Club of California, San Francisco, 4 January 1968, cited in D. Cameron, 'Civility and civil progress', speech at the Royal Society, London, 23 April 2007.

40. H. M. Treasury, *Budget 2007.Building Britain's Long-Term Future: Prosperity and fairness for families*. Economic and Fiscal Strategy Report and Financial Statement and Budget Report, HC. 342 (London: The Stationery Office, 2007), pp. 3, 5.

41. G. Osborne, speech to the Confederation of British Industry, London, 7 March 2007. The Conservative Party's other two Sound Money Tests are the 'Stability Test', which dictates that 'Economic stability will always be our priority. We will not cut taxes if that puts at risk the low interest rates and low inflation that families and businesses depend on. We will not be making up front promises of overall tax cuts at the election – promises we couldn't be sure I could keep'; and the 'Manifesto Test', which states that 'No policy proposals with implications for public spending are Conservative Party policy

until they have been approved by me and David Cameron, passed by the Shadow Cabinet and appear in our draft manifesto'. Ibid.

42. The convergence between Brown and Cameron on the future of the British Union is shown by G. Brown, 'Stronger together weaker apart', speech, Edinburgh, 8 September 2006; D. Cameron, 'I support the Union for what it can achieve in the future', speech, Gretna Green, 19 April 2007.

43. D. Cameron, 'A new approach to foreign affairs: liberal conservatism', annual J. P. Morgan Lecture at the British American Project, 11 September 2006.

44. D. Cameron, 'The EU – a new agenda for the 21st century', speech to the Movement for European Reform Conference, Brussels, 6 March 2007.

45. The nature of Conservative Party policy development under David Cameron is explored in S. Lee, 'David Cameron and the renewal of policy', in S. Lee and M. Beech (eds), *The Conservatives under David Cameron: Built to Last?* (London: Palgrave Macmillan, 2009).

46. D. Cameron cited in D. Jones, *Cameron on Cameron: Conversations with Dylan Jones* (London: Fourth Estate, 2008), pp. 308–309.

47. For a more detailed analysis of this change in strategy, see S. Lee, 'Convergence, critique and divergence: the development of economic policy under David Cameron', in S. Lee and M. Beech (eds), *The Conservatives under David Cameron: Built to Last?* (London: Palgrave Macmillan, 2009).

48. Conservative Party, *Reconstruction: A Plan for a Strong Economy* (London: Conservative Party, 2008).

49. D. Cameron, 'The choice on borrowing', speech, London, 18 November 2008.

50. D. Cameron, 'Britain's economic future', speech, London, 5 January 2009.

51. K. Joseph, *Monetarism Is Not Enough* (London: Rose, 1976), p. 19.

52. D. Cameron, 'Britain's economic future', speech, London, 5 January 2009.

53. D. Cameron cited in D. Jones, *Cameron on Cameron: Conversations with Dylan Jones* (London: Fourth Estate, 2008), p. 309.

54. Ibid., p. 177.

55. For example, an Ipsos MORI poll conducted between 13 and 15 February 2009 placed the Conservative Party on forty-four per cent, and the Labour Party on twenty-eight per cent. See Ipsos MORI, *Ipsos MORI February Political Monitor: 13–15 February 2009* (London: Ipsos MORI, 2009).

Index